J. M. W. Turner, *Rotterdam Ferry Boat*, 1833

BURDENS OF FREEDOM

BURDENS OF FREEDOM

CULTURAL DIFFERENCE AND AMERICAN POWER

Lawrence M. Mead

Encounter
BOOKS

New York • London

First American edition published in 2019 by Encounter Books,
an activity of Encounter for Culture and Education, Inc.,
a nonprofit, tax exempt corporation.
Encounter Books website address: www.encounterbooks.com

Manufactured in the United States and printed on
acid-free paper. The paper used in this publication meets
the minimum requirements of ANSI/NISO Z39.48-1992
(R 1997) (*Permanence of Paper*).

FIRST AMERICAN EDITION

LIBRARY OF CONGRESS CATALOGING-IN-PUBLICATION DATA
Names: Mead, Lawrence M., author.
Title: Burdens of freedom : cultural difference and American power /
by Lawrence M. Mead.
Description: New York : Encounter Books, [2019] |
Includes bibliographical references and index.
Identifiers: LCCN 2018043848 (print) | LCCN 2018055843 (ebook) |
ISBN 9781641770415 (ebook) | ISBN 9781641770408 (hardcover : alk. paper)
Subjects: LCSH: Individualism—Political aspects—United States. | National
characteristics, American. | Cultural pluralism—Political aspects—United
States. | United States—Politics and government. |
United States—Foreign relations.
Classification: LCC JC599.U5 (ebook) | LCC JC599.U5 M387 2019 (print) |
DDC 306.20973—dc23
LC record available at https://lccn.loc.gov/2018043848

Credits:
Frontispiece: J. M. W. Turner, *Rotterdam Ferry Boat*, 1833. Permission granted by the National
Gallery of Art
Figure 2.2: © Hulton Archive/Intermittent/Getty Images
Figure 4.5: Permission granted by Richard D. Lewis, www.crossculture.com
Figure 5.1: Robert Walter Weir (American, 1803–1889). *Embarkation of the Pilgrims*, 1857. Oil on
canvas, 48 1/8 x 72 1/4 in. (122.2 x 183.5 cm). Brooklyn Museum, A. Augustus Healy Fund and
Healy Purchase Fund B, 75.188
Figure 7.1: © Alissandra Petlin/New York Times Magazine
Figure 7.2: © Benjamin Lowy/New York Times Magazine
Figures 8.2, 10.4, 10.8, 10.9, 10.10, 11.1: © The Economist Newspaper Limited, London
Figure 11.2: © Philip Toscano/PA Archive/PA Images
Figure 11.3: © Jesus Blanco de Avellaneda/Associated Press
Figure 13.1: U.S. Navy photo by Mass Communication Specialist 2nd Class Kristopher
Wilson/Released
Figure 13.2: Permission granted by the artist, Boris Vallejo

For Kirt
"Am I my brother's keeper?"
(Genesis 4:9)

CONTENTS

PREFACE AND ACKNOWLEDGMENTS

Burdens of Freedom makes a simple but radical argument: The United States is an individualist country. By this I mean that most Americans think of life as an effort to realize their own goals and values out in the world. This may sound obvious, but almost no previous author, to my knowledge, has said this. Many have said that America is a free country, or a democratic country, but not an individualist one. The very idea has been, perhaps, too sensitive.

Worldwide, it turns out, individualism is quite unusual. That temperament was the chief reason why first Europe, then Britain, and then America came to lead the world. But today, our chief challenges come from groups within our society, and nations abroad, who are not individualist, who think of life in more cautious and collective terms. To continue to lead, America must come to terms with that world yet remain an individualist nation.

This is the first book to discuss America's prospects in cultural terms. I was driven to write it by three problems I've wrestled with for decades. To understand any of them I finally had to invoke culture—that is, differences in what different groups and nations think life is about.

The first problem is persistent poverty in the United States. How can a sizable minority of Americans remain jobless and deeply impoverished in the world's richest country—even when jobs are available? Most of my previous work has been about how to raise work levels among the poor and thus reduce poverty.

A second problem is the troubled assimilation of many recent immigrants to the United States. Since the 1960s, on average, these newcomers have had much more difficulty getting ahead and avoiding social problems than the immigrants we remember nostalgically from a century ago. Immigration in Europe has been similarly troubled.

The third problem is persistent governmental failure in many developing countries. I was taught in graduate school, in the 1970s, that the "new nations" that became independent in the 1960s when the European empires were dissolved would steadily converge to Western political norms, becoming well-governed and free. But most have failed to do so. How to cope with "failed" states in Africa and elsewhere has become one of America's greatest challenges.

In the orthodox view, all these problems reflect a lack of opportunity. The poor or recent immigrants remain disadvantaged because society has not done enough to help them to work, get through school, and avoid other problems. Scholars earnestly search out new "barriers" to explain these difficulties. And struggling nations are said to fail because the world economic system is unfair to them, or simply because the West has not saved poor countries from misrule. All these analyses are structural. There is usually no mention of culture, no suggestion that those suffering from hardship differ in any personal way from the more fortunate. Everyone, rich and poor, is assumed to be fundamentally *the same*, differing only in external conditions and resources.

I finally concluded that this consensus represents denial. Half a century after the War on Poverty, the expansion of immigration, and the liberation of the colonies, outside conditions no longer explain well why disadvantage persists. We must reckon with obvious differences in attitudes between the more and the less fortunate. While some scholars of poverty and development have been driven to speak of culture, none has yet invoked the research on world cultural differences that I cite here. These studies highlight the difference between Western assertiveness and the more passive mind-set of the non-West. That difference, I think, chiefly explains all three of the problems above. Individualism, it turns out, is simply better at both economic and political development than the mind-sets of nearly all of the non-West, despite its great diversity.

Yet Western culture is not simply to be praised. It does not serve all important values, and it imposes severe burdens on our "free" society. Freedom is not free but is ultimately a form of obligation. Thus, a cultural perspective casts an unsparing light not only on America's chief challenges but on our own society and the entire Western tradition.

None of this means that we should not help struggling people from the non-West, whether inside or outside our borders. Quite the contrary. America must still lead and assist a suffering world. But we have to give up sameness to know better how to help. Well-off Americans can no longer presume that others in need are fundamentally like themselves.

This book was difficult to fund and publish because it flouts the academic consensus against culture. I drafted it mostly during 2015 and 2016 when I was on sabbatical from NYU. I credit financial support from the university and also the American Enterprise Institute, where I was a visiting fellow. No academic center offered me support. AEI did offer, even though they did not espouse my argument, an act of notable magnanimity. They also supported my previous book. For me, AEI has been a better university than nearly all of academe.

I am especially grateful to Roger Kimball and Encounter Books for taking on the project. Encounter emphasizes the ideas that shape American politics and policy. This book is all about the fundamental difference in ideas between the individualist West and pretty much all the rest of the world. I also thank Encounter staff members and Will DeRooy, my able copy editor.

This book owes a great deal to Samuel Huntington and also to Francis Fukuyama, who, like me, was a graduate student of Sam's at Harvard. Sam was the first to link American primacy to world cultural differences, and Frank has written exceptionally wide-ranging books about world history and development. Frank gives less emphasis to cultural differences than I do, but I still rely heavily on his work.

This book also owes much to an undergraduate course on approaches to American primacy that I have taught at NYU since 2007. The course considers sixteen different theories that might explain why the West and especially America came to lead the world. The approaches come from several social sciences and include viewpoints from the political left as well as the right. I ask students to choose among the theories, playing no favorites. Many students differ with my emphasis on culture. Their feedback has greatly improved my argument.

I gratefully acknowledge helpful comments from Steve Balch, Mike Bernick, Bruce Bueno de Mesquita, David Curry, David Denoon, Madeleine Deschamps, Amy Elman, Adam Garfinkle, Robin Mead, Samuel Rothenberg, and Eugene Steuerle. Special credit to the members of my

NYU discussion group, to whom I presented the argument, and to Steve Balch, who not only read the entire manuscript but invited me to speak at the Institute for the Study of Welfare Civilization at Texas Tech University.

I am even more indebted to my twin brother Kirt. He was my leading partner in life. This book was born mostly in long conversations with him. He could respond because he was the opposite of the narrow specialists who dominate academe today—a true polymath, gifted in physics and math but also fluent in French and German, and deeply read in European history and culture. He persuaded me that European history could shed new light on America. When he died suddenly in 2017, he left a vast hole in my life. I can only hope that readers will engage with these ideas as deeply as Kirt did. I dedicate this book to him, in deep admiration and gratitude. He was indeed his brother's keeper.

Lastly, I thank my family. This book owes more to them than they know. My wife, Robin, read the entire manuscript and made many astute comments. She and our children tolerated my preoccupation with the book. Every day, I see them shoulder the burdens of freedom. We all strive to contribute to the great dynamism that has lifted America to world leadership. May it continue to do so.

Lawrence M. Mead
New York University
November 2018

CHAPTER ONE

INTRODUCTION

The great fact about today's world is cultural difference. Americans have long thought that they are no different from other people, only freer and more fortunate. They pride themselves on living independent lives in which they work out their personal destiny. They wish that everyone had these opportunities. But that individualist style of life is far less universal than most people think, and today it has come into question both at home and abroad. To recognize and address that huge reality is the leading challenge of our time.

All of America's toughest tests today involve groups or nations that, on average, are not individualist, but more cautious and collective-minded. At home, individualism is fading among low-income Americans, who are less able than they once were to take responsibility for themselves. Immigrants, too, are much less individualist today than they were a century ago, because they chiefly come from Asia or Latin America rather than Europe. That is, they tend to defer to the setting around them rather than asserting themselves and seeking change. Abroad, America must deal with poor countries much worse governed than we are. These countries require support but also guidance. We also face Asian challengers for world leadership, particularly mainland China, which again are not individualist. In all these struggles, cultural difference is the great reality.

Fear of racism has long suppressed discussion of these differences.

Our establishment insists that all Americans of whatever background are *the same*. But ever since his election campaign in 2016, President Trump has flouted that taboo. He often disparages minorities and immigrants in flagrant terms, inciting charges of racism. The defenders of sameness call him racist. But whether he is or not, he has made it clear that group and national differences in culture must be faced rather than denied.

In contrast to either Trump or his critics, this book questions both sameness and racism. Culture connotes what people think life is about, what we strive to do or be. Differences in culture are too important to ignore, but neither are they racial in any physical sense. Rather, they arise from differences in attitudes and ways of life. Most Americans descend from the strongly individualist ethos of Europe, but minorities and most recent immigrants reflect the more cautious, collective-minded, and deferential societies of other parts of the world. Research on world cultures and from other sources shows that these differences are large and important. They enrich our culture, but they greatly complicate integrating our society at home and maintaining American primacy abroad.

Yet cultural difference has been ignored in virtually all scholarship on public affairs, both foreign and domestic. We say that America has become multicultural, but to discuss cultural difference is forbidden. Orthodox commentators downplay differences. The world is said to be globalizing, all countries seek economic affluence, and since the Cold War most deep divisions among nations have faded. There are of course some conflicts, such as between radical Islam and the West, but these are relatively minor; the national and ideological divisions of old were far more serious. Within the United States, observers tend again to minimize difference. Since the civil rights movement and the expansion of immigration, citizens of all backgrounds have become officially interchangeable. While there are still divisions over treatment of racial minorities, the establishment and the media celebrate a generalized diversity.

It is true that old-fashioned ideological and racial hierarchies have faded, but they have been replaced by distressing cultural divisions. Groups and nations that are Western are set against others that are non-Western. The former are individualist; the latter far less so. Worldwide, Cold War divisions have diminished, but a gulf still separates the West—with its assertive, individualist style—from the rest of the world. And at home, the old hierarchies of empire, class, and caste live on in painful identity politics focused on group differences. If nothing else, Trumpism demands a more candid discussion of these differences. In order for American world leadership to endure, a *cultural* battle to reaffirm an individualist America must first be fought and won.

CULTURAL CHALLENGES

An individualist culture was the making of America, but it has too much been taken for granted. That is perhaps why, to my knowledge, no previous author has stressed it.[1] A lifestyle in which people pursue their own goals and values has been assumed to be normal, even universal, but it is in fact exceptional. Only in Europe and its offshoots, including America, did entire societies take on that confident mind-set. Our political rhetoric stresses freedom as if it were simply a gift, yet freedom American-style is actually demanding. The burdens of freedom are heavy, and only if ordinary people bear them can they "make it" in this country. And only then can the United States still generate the wealth and power that have empowered it to lead the world.

Culture defines the chief foreign challenge to American primacy, which comes mostly from Asia. Commentators usually treat China as an economic or military rival, but its defining quality rather is a much more collectivist ethos than the West's. People in China typically take orders from above rather than take initiative. In China (and in most of the world), people are less free than they are in the West, but they are also less responsible for themselves. So America's contest with Asia is a contest not just between countries but between entire ways of life. For both the United States and Asia, furthermore, opposition abroad is less threatening than cultural change at home. In China, the upper class presses for greater freedom, although this threatens the regime. In America, conversely, the less affluent are abandoning individualism, weakening the original basis of American wealth and power.

Cultural difference also chiefly explains our deepest domestic challenges. It is the principal reason why the United States has not yet achieved the color-blind society its values prescribe. Racial divisions now run much deeper than economic ones, because they reflect differences in lifestyle more than differences in income or wealth. A half-century after the civil rights reforms, we can no longer attribute poverty and inequality in America to racism or to impersonal deficiencies of opportunity. We must consider the fact that American society derives mostly from Europe, where individualism arose, whereas most of our long-term poor derive from the non-West, where most people have a more passive and less competitive temperament. The collision between this cautious worldview and mainstream individualism has come to dominate American politics. It causes advocates for disadvantaged groups to claim that they are oppressed even in a free country—something that most Americans who stem from Europe cannot understand.

Heavy immigration has recently deepened those divisions, both in the United States and in Europe. The great difference between the immigrants of today and those of a century ago is that these new immigrants are mostly *not* individualist, making it much more difficult for them to adjust to Western society. How to integrate non-Western newcomers yet remain Western is a central challenge faced by America and many European countries. Resistance to that task has produced turmoil in both America and Europe, helping to explain both Trump's election and Britain's recent vote to leave the European Union.[2]

Despite fearful commentators, cultural differences are simply too important to ignore. They explain too much about world power and development as well as important domestic issues, including poverty and immigration. Trump has forced them out into the open; we now must face them. We cannot reckon seriously with where we are as a country unless we ask *who* we are—unless we address culture.

WHAT IS NEW HERE?

This book breaks with the sort of arguments other authors have made about America's prospects, both abroad and at home, in several important ways.

Cultural Difference vs. Sameness

Discussions of world power by international relations specialists usually make no reference at all to culture. Some scholars say that states seek security by dominating rivals in a chaotic world without central authority;[3] others that they seek to build international institutions and so achieve order.[4] But either view assumes that the psychology of all countries is essentially the same. That assumption has long been orthodox in international studies, which looks back to the historic conflicts of similar states in Europe.

But in today's world, differences among states run far deeper. Most countries are non-Western. Few if any of them have the West's capacities to sustain an assertive foreign policy, let alone make war for any extended period. No other country approaches the international standing of the United States, with its elaborate alliances and globe-girdling forces. These differences are more than matters of degree. The main causes lie, I suggest, in the contrasts between Western and non-Western worldviews. The Western mind-set simply generates not only the greatest will for change, but also the most governmental capacity to pursue it. In the rest of the world, by comparison, people typically seek adjustment rather than change, and states are weaker.

Still less do experts on social policy make any reference to worldviews when appraising America's domestic challenges. Everyone, rich and poor, is assumed to be an individualist seeking to get ahead. Thus, the problems of poor people and minorities are attributed entirely to adversities that they suffer within America. Experts ignore the huge differences in temperament between Americans who come from Europe and those who come from Africa, Latin America, or Asia. On average, as chapter 4 shows, people with Western origins are simply much more assertive. In the non-West, life is far more about survival and less about the pursuit of personal goals. Studies show that those differences endure for generations after people from non-Western countries emigrate to America.

Cultural Difference vs. Resources

Observers typically rate American power against that of rival nations in terms of concrete resources. They ask whether American primacy can endure, given growing wealth in Asia.[5] The West has long dominated the world, but some think that the economic "rise of the rest" will end that.[6] Particularly, some think that China must eventually take over world leadership, simply because it will soon have the largest economy.[7]

Less-alarmist observers concede that China is growing but argue that America's resources still dominate.[8] As of 2017, China's gross domestic product (GDP) of $23.1 trillion already exceeded America's $19.4 trillion (when calculated based on purchasing power parity), and both countries were far ahead of India ($9.4 trillion) and Japan ($5.4 trillion).[9] The United States still ranks first in GDP when calculated in current dollar terms, and it is still far richer than Asian nations in terms of GDP per capita.

Experts also note that, in 2017, the United States spent $610 billion on defense, which was more than the next seven countries combined and nearly three times as much as China ($228 billion).[10] Finally, they note that the United States dominates in "soft power," or the unforced admiration of other countries for American institutions and values.[11] In a recent assessment of soft power among thirty leading countries, America ranked third; China ranked twenty-fifth.[12] Worldwide, millions of people aspire to study in America or emigrate there; China has no comparable appeal.

But these assessments overemphasize the details of power, which can change. They also say too little about the underlying societies. The United States is an exceptional nation that draws power from many sources.[13] Yet at the heart of American power is nothing material, but rather an individualist and civic worldview, drawn from Europe and especially from Britain. Similarly, at the core of Asia's challenge is not its scale or its huge population but a collective society that largely takes orders from above. America and its rivals today are not comparable, as Europe's strong states were in previous centuries, but radically different. Today, such contrasts have become central to world politics.[14]

Cultural Difference vs. Race

Many assume that to speak of culture is implicitly to speak of race. Fear that any discussion of cultural difference must be racist is the chief reason why it has been proscribed. The orthodoxy that everyone is the same has smothered all treatment of national or group differences. It is permissible to contrast groups or nations only in terms of impersonal attributes such as income, wealth, or education; to say anything about personal lifestyle or attitudes is assumed to be invidious.

But not all criticism of groups is improper. Properly understood, racism means the view that some races are superior to others and also that races differ in inherent, physical ways not subject to conditioning.[15] Assessments of groups or countries that avoid those implications can be heard. In contrast, sameness asserts that the races are really all alike, at least on average, or can be made so with appropriate compensatory policies; race is thus a social construct that should be ignored.

Racism is, of course, morally indefensible. Just as important, it no longer explains human differences well. The rising affluence of some Asian nations relative to the long-dominant West shows that, with the right policies, societies of any race can attain greater wealth and influence. In addition, the success of many members of minority groups in the United States since the civil rights reforms a half-century ago shows that the idea of white superiority is mistaken.

But sameness is also implausible. Although nations and individuals of any race can and do get ahead, on average the mostly white societies of the West are still much richer, more powerful, and better governed than the non-West. Within America, most minorities on average have much lower income and suffer more serious social problems than the white majority. Expert attempts to account for group inequality solely on the basis of impersonal differences in opportunity have failed (as I show in later chapters). No structural feature of America really explains our social problems. Some social policy experts already tacitly admit an important role for what I call culture—distinctive attitudes and lifestyles.

Cultural difference is more realistic than either racism or sameness. It improves on structural accounts of poverty or inequality by pointing to differences in ways of life between nations or between groups that strongly affect their relative advancement. At the same time, these differences have no inherent tie to race, as world cultural researchers make clear. Rather, culture depends on socialization: people display the attitudes in which they are raised. Culture also changes over time, and is changing, which again makes racial causes implausible. Thus, Asian dominance is not inevitable; neither is American decline. Cultural change, in fact, is likely to decide the contest for world primacy between the United States and Asia. I address culture versus race further in chapter 4.

West vs. Non-West

Some previous scholars, including Samuel Huntington, recognized the role of culture in world affairs. They found that nations' concept of themselves varies greatly over time and place and that there are different world cultures.[16] But these accounts did not focus on the general contrast of Western and non-Western worldviews, as I do here. Nor did they stress the widespread assumption that the West, particularly the United States, will take responsibility for world problems. The world system is becoming multipolar in some ways, but it still assumes a radical moral imbalance whereby some nations—especially America—bear burdens for others. Those differences largely reflect the very different ways in which the West and non-West achieve moral order.

Something beyond wealth and arms, and even soft power, explains why American primacy continues unabated, even as many non-Western countries grow richer. Recently, the United States led a coalition of Western and Middle Eastern nations in the fight against the Islamic State in Syria and Iraq. The principal reason America led was not only or even mainly our superior military, important though that is. Rather, it was widespread trust that America will "do the right thing" for others as well as itself. China does not yet approach the American capacity to project power or gain trust abroad. More important, it lacks any tradition of care for the world order. America inherited that mission from the British, and the willingness to assume it reflects the earnestness of Western culture. Although President Trump has questioned some of our commitments abroad, any wholesale US retreat from international affairs is unlikely.

Some critics overreact to recent American reverses in Iraq and Afghanistan or to Trump's controversial words, saying that presidential mistakes have damaged our influence.[17] The United States, however, tends to recover from such missteps, because of the deep trust it commands abroad and because of its irreplaceable global role. These same factors helped it to outlast previous rivals for world leadership—Nazi Germany, the Soviet Union, and Japan. Because Trump has cut back American commitments abroad while China is expanding its role, Chinese hegemony may seem inevitable.[18] But to assume that is to overlook China's deep-seated internal problems, which I discuss further below.

In the rest of this introduction, I reinterpret America's power and challenges using cultural difference. In later chapters I elaborate and document these themes more fully.

HISTORY

The past already suggests that America and Asia have very different ways of life. Typically, scholars assess the power of these two giants only in the present. Yet America and its Asian rivals are not just nations in being, but in motion.[19] What they are today reflects developmental processes that go back centuries, even millennia. The great fact about the United States is that it is the child of Europe, which, at the American founding, was already the world's richest and most powerful civilization. Our Asian rivals are immensely older and far more inhibited by a premodern past.[20]

Historians tend to treat the progress of Europe toward wealth and power, and its expansion to America, as natural and inevitable, but it was in fact exceptional. Nowhere but in Europe and its offshoots do we find such a rapid ascent to dominance. And nowhere else do we find vast movements of people across an ocean to exploit a new continent. In Europe, somehow, a Promethean urge to seek new opportunities and found new societies took hold. The rest of the world showed nothing like this—until it came under pressure from the West in recent centuries.

This European heritage gave the new America an enormous running start in development. The fledging nation inherited the strengths of Europe while escaping its limitations. European settlers in North America appropriated a new continent with huge resources, far larger than any European state (except Russia).[21] They also escaped Europe's medieval past and embraced from the outset the leading institutions of modernity—the market economy and elected government. Such lavish gifts made it virtually inevitable, even two centuries ago, that America would one day lead the world.[22] By comparison, all of America's rivals for primacy began, in developmental terms, much further back. They all have had to build modernity atop traditional societies that were and still are deeply resistant to change.

Another crucial inheritance for America was robust public institutions. The American colonies were chiefly founded by Britain, which went on to become the greatest imperialist since Rome. (The Mongols controlled a larger area but were merely exploitative; the British, like the Romans, ruled relatively well and left viable governments behind.) Somehow, the British achieved strong government and a wide market economy centuries before any other large country. And they bequeathed these institutions to America. So the United States inherited both European dynamism and the world's strongest governmental tradition. That combination made it, in effect, Britain writ large. So when Britain laid down the burdens of primacy after World War I, America took them up. These Anglo nations have now led the world for two centuries.[23]

But although Europe and the Anglos have recently led, Asia in recent centuries has found ways to become rich and powerful while remaining non-Western. First Japan, then several smaller Asian nations, and finally China have employed collective societies and strong leadership as well as the market to achieve sharply higher incomes and—in Japan's case—military prowess. These Western and Asian ways of life have now become competitors for world leadership.

THE END OF HISTORY

Thus, history suggests large differences between Western and non-Western cultures. Equally important, differences in wealth and thus military power cannot be explained in noncultural terms. Especially, these differences are not due to politics or policy in any conventional sense. A generation ago, most of the non-Western world was Communist or authoritarian, so its relative backwardness could be attributed simply to oppressive government. If economies were liberated, dictators toppled, and elections held, many believed, poor countries would speedily converge to Western norms, becoming both affluent and free.

After the collapse of Communism around 1990, the world largely moved in that direction. Most countries accepted market economies and elections, at least in form. Francis Fukuyama referred to this fading of ideological divisions as the end of history. He meant that progressive change toward more egalitarian regimes was complete. It was no longer arguable that socialism, or some other ideal, would be better than democratic capitalism. No further fundamental change in politics was now likely, to either the right or the left.[24]

Yet the convergence of poor countries with wealthy ones has been limited at best. Market economics has indeed made many countries richer, notably in Asia, and most countries today possess some form of elected government. But on a per-capita basis, America and other Western countries remain vastly the richest, as well as the strongest in military and soft power. The best-governed large countries are also nearly all Western. Despite accepting democracy and capitalism in name, much of the non-West remains relatively ill-governed and poor. The First World is still confined mostly to European countries and their offshoots.[25]

Rather than effacing all differences, the end of history has reasserted cultural differences between rich and poor that are far older than modern ideological divisions. The fundamental restraint on non-Western development is not a lack of economic or political freedom but the relative weakness of economic and political improvement over centuries. Civic values such as law and consent are honored more in form than in substance. In the West, by comparison, moral beliefs have a stronger civic character, which helps institutions become stronger over time. That difference, again, long predates the end of history.

CULTURAL DIFFERENCE

Research into world cultures shows that substantial differences between Western and non-Western cultures are indisputable. Despite great diversity among non-Western cultures, two differences dominate.[26]

First, Western culture is *individualist*, whereas non-Western cultures are much more *collectivist*.[27] Westerners take action largely to fulfill personal goals and values, if necessary changing the world to do so. In this sense, they live their lives from the inside out. In the non-West, by contrast, most people take their cues largely from without—from their immediate associates, higher authority, or tradition. They adjust to their environment much more than they seek to change it. They live their lives largely from the outside in.

Second, Western culture is *moralistic*, while non-Western cultures tend to be *conformist*. Westerners generally treat moral norms as principles that apply to all people, in all times and places. These values are not perfectly observed, but not to follow them typically generates inner guilt and outward criticism. In the non-West, by contrast, people tend to take moral cues from their environment. Moral behavior is shaped less by personal principles, goals, and values than by the immediate expectations of others. In a collectivist society, the sanction against misbehavior is external more than internal—shame rather than guilt.

Of course, the world displays a wide range of average temperaments. Latin American and Middle Eastern cultures are more emotionally expressive than Asian cultures, which are more taciturn.[28] Arab Islam can assert itself quite aggressively, as the West has painfully learned. *And neither Western nor non-Western ways are superior to the other in any general sense.* Nonetheless, the broad contrast I have defined still holds. Especially, the West has the only strongly individualist culture. That feature, above all, is what characterizes the United States. No other country shows that temperament so strongly.

Whereas conventional thinking about power ignores culture, the struggle for primacy should be seen as a contest of cultures more than nations. Among large Western countries, the United States is the most individualist, while China may be the most collective-minded country in Asia. In America, political or economic initiative chiefly begins with individuals seeking to improve their world or to realize some personal achievement. In China it usually begins with leaders directing their followers. Lately the Chinese have been told to seek greater wealth, so they are doing so. The master issue is whether celebrating or subordinating the individual is the best way to organize a society.[29]

OTHER ROOTS OF POWER

The bases of national power include not only culture but also a country's geographic position, economic system, and government. These latter features may seem to have little to do with culture, especially after history. Yet national attitudes strongly shape what each factor means in practice—to date, mostly to the advantage of the West.

Some recent authors say that the West derived developmental advantages from its geography, thus explaining its current power with little reference to culture.[30] One may also argue, in the tradition of geopolitics, that maritime nations such as Britain and America gained advantages from their geographic isolation and security. But what geography cannot explain is why the Anglos used their security to assume a general responsibility for the world order. They took the lead in forming coalitions to oppose aggressors and in building an international system based on peace, order, and open trade. Those actions served not only their own interests, but also those of many other countries. This instinct to assume responsibility, again, stems from the moralism of Western culture.

The same with economic systems. Free-market policies have shown a capacity to raise wealth in virtually any country. The freeing of markets is chiefly responsible for Asia's rapid ascent to power. Yet individualist countries still gain the most from capitalism, because their culture best tolerates the insecurities that the market brings. The United States, like

Britain before it, was once protectionist, but then accepted increasingly free trade. Both countries exposed their economies to competition more fully than rival nations did, and from this came the exceptional wealth needed for primacy.[31] Trump's questioning of free trade is hardly likely to restore protectionism.

In government, we might imagine that an individualist society would have more trouble establishing strong institutions than a collectivist one, where authority is less questioned. But government has typically been more honest and effective in Western nations than in non-Western ones.[32] A central reason, again, is the principled, moralistic character of Western culture, which deters corruption better than the less civic culture of the non-West. Unusually strong government at home has empowered the Anglo nations to project power abroad as no others can do.[33]

FREEDOM AS OBLIGATION

To see the importance of culture, we must transcend conventional ideas that America and the West are "free" while much of the rest of the world is "unfree." The truth is that freedom by itself never generated wealth or power. Becoming a rich and strong country requires discipline. A nation must motivate its citizens to put out the effort to generate wealth and then use it to create and project power abroad. All strong countries do this, but America and its Asian rivals do it in quite different ways.

Americans think of their country as free, but it is also demanding. In part, this means only that the rights guaranteed by a free government always imply obligations. The US government must expect citizens to obey the law, pay taxes, and serve on juries (or in the military, if there is a draft or a service requirement). Less formally, Americans also expect each other to display social capabilities such as working for a living, getting through school, and speaking English.[34] And aside from the demands of others, people must strive to achieve their own goals by competing for advancement in the meritocracy and in a competitive economy. Finally, they must grapple, with little guidance, with the many confusing political and moral issues thrown up by our free press and open politics. In all these ways, Americans *work hard* at freedom.

The more radical idea is that freedom actually *requires* obligation. At the core of American power is an individualist culture that transmutes freedom into obligation. At a psychological level, to say that I am free is not to say that I suffer no constraints. Rather, I *internalize* my constraints, making them *my* responsibility rather than others'. Only by shouldering those burdens does one become fully free. In politics, our leaders debate how to push back the barriers around people. But if freedom means only liberation at the hands of others, my fate is still determined by outside forces. The deeper meaning of freedom is autonomy, and autonomy requires that I *take on* my challenges. Only then am I in charge, and really free. Paradoxically, we are free only when we accept these inner responsibilities. Those who would be free must first be bound.

The alternative is to assume the burdens of necessity. In the more traditional and controlled non-Western world, material scarcity and social conventions largely dictate how people live. Competition for careers is limited, and the authorities settle most moral and political issues with little public input. An establishment governs, and that is consistent with the relative passivity of non-Western culture. That is the system that Asia has chiefly used to generate the effort needed for modernization and thus to close its gap with the West. Americans may call such a life "unfree," but the ordinary people who live it are also less responsible. They must do and decide much less in a collectivist society than they would face in an individualist one. In this sense, they are *more* free than we are. To them, life is not a project, as in the West. It is, rather, an experience to be endured. Viewed culturally, world primacy is a contest between these opposing views of life: Is life chiefly about self-realization—or acceptance?

THE POLICY ARENA

A cultural perspective offers fresh insights on many policy issues, both at home and abroad. The main threat to American primacy lies at home, in the current decay of an individualist way of life among low-income groups. Adverse trends include the withdrawal of many low-skilled workers from the economy, as well as the worsening of long-standing social problems among the poor. Government is already moving to enforce work where it can and otherwise reduce social disorders.

Another frontier is immigration. While historically immigration has strengthened America, it is currently creating social problems. Many of today's newcomers arrive from more collectivist societies, where they never had to compete and innovate as they must do here. Although still valuable, non-Western immigration should be reduced, to maintain the individualist character of our culture. America must accept and lead a multicultural world while still remaining a Western nation.

In foreign affairs, a cultural perspective regards the Chinese threat as smaller than many imagine. Most likely, Beijing is too weak institutionally to challenge the United States worldwide, although it may well dominate East Asia. Elsewhere, a cultural perspective counsels caution. America and the West probably cannot cultivate good government in the non-Western world unless and until local cultures there become more moralistic. Nonetheless, the United States will have to participate in the rescue of "failed states" in regions where governments are the weakest, particularly Africa.

Thus, American primacy will likely endure, but it will also become more sacrificial. The "rise of the rest" has spread world wealth more widely, yet the United States cannot expect newly rich countries to share its world burdens as our traditional European allies have done. Within the West and within history, America has been a beacon of freedom. But after history, what most poor countries need above all is order. In the worst cases, providing that may well become, for the United States, the heaviest burden of freedom. We must offer struggling nations governance and compassion, as no one else can (more on this in chapter 13).

THE MORAL ARENA

More central to American primacy than any specific policy is the moral arena, in which it is decided who bears responsibility for world problems. On this level, the great fact is how little debate there is. Liberals and conservatives may differ about how assertive America should be toward other nations, yet both tend to assume that America bears the largest responsibility for the world order. President Trump has vowed a policy of "American first," but even he cannot ignore the many nations that look to the United States for leadership.

That deference is not simply a reflection of America's power today; again, it reflects culture. An individualist worldview is steeped in the idea that nations, like individuals, are responsible for themselves. They cannot expect others to save them from their problems. The United States displayed that temperament even two centuries ago, in its infancy. Trump has reasserted that view. But due to America's enormous growth, we inevitably took on burdens for less individualist and assertive countries.

American commentators scarcely perceive the pervasive influence of individualism on our entire outlook. It is the medium in which we live and move and have our being. We end up displaying that influence rather than understanding it. American leaders and experts who debate policy sit on a mountaintop, looking out over a world very different from theirs. British leaders did the same in Victorian times. That such a separate, privileged, but isolated setting even exists is the surest sign that American primacy endures. But the very moralism of American culture conceals that reality from us. Our leaders generously attribute sameness to their peers from other cultures, treating them as they would themselves. They then are perpetually surprised when the others act differently than Americans would.

Due to free speech, American government is awash in criticism like no other regime. Americans are the first to bemoan any decline in their influence, even more than foreigners might do.[35] Donald Trump revived that theme during his presidential election campaign. Many share his determination to "make America great again." But self-criticism causes us to underestimate our own capacity. The truth is that, by calling attention to our shortcomings, we have already taken the first step in overcoming them. Wherever there is debate in American society, improvement usually follows. As many note, this "resiliency" has allowed the United States to adapt to challengers and, in the end, defeat or exceed them.[36]

There is much less self-criticism in the non-West, where power is more self-justifying but also less confident. The usual fear is that the regime must be defended, at least publicly, lest it be weakened. In societies where public norms rest more on outward than on inward authority, that fear may be realistic. Thus, self-criticism is usually hidden, if it occurs at all. But denial means that these countries forfeit opportunities to learn and grow. A free country like America fearlessly embraces those chances, confident that the truth is our friend and not an enemy. Thus, criticism ultimately expresses power rather than weakness. It is the mood music of power.[37]

A LOOK AHEAD

In the chapters following, I work out more fully the themes already sug-gested. Chapter 2 addresses history. The United States does not arise out of nowhere. Rather, it expressed the vitality of first Europe and then Brit-ain. I contrast this exceptional story with the very different history of the non-Western world, especially the Asian powers that now challenge the West. Europe and its offshoots rose to wealth and power spontaneously, while Asia modernized largely at the will of government. This major dif-ference, I believe, largely reflects the difference between an individualist and a collectivist culture.

Chapter 3 considers the end of history. That term, for me, connotes a change in political division—from issues that assume a Western culture to deeper divisions that pit Western against non-Western culture, both within and between countries. Traditional debates in the United States and Europe about how to realize freedom or equality assume that every-one involved is an individualist. Those issues are, thus, largely irrelevant to our struggles to come to terms with non-Western groups and nations, which have a very different formation. Our traditional political thinking is passé. A new politics, focused on human nature rather than justice, is struggling to be born.

In chapter 4, I describe the research on cultural differences among nations in some detail, and in chapter 5, I consider several explanations as to how those distinctions arose. These include the early settlement of Europe, the classical world, and religion. I go on to analyze the other roots of power—geography (chapter 6), economics (chapter 7), and gov-ernment (chapter 8)—showing how, in each case, the influence of these factors is mediated by culture. The formula—democratic capitalism—that has made the Western world dominant simply does not translate well to societies that are less inner-driven. That is why Asia has chosen a very different path.

Next, I go more deeply into why freedom requires obligations, first in theory (chapter 9) and then more concretely. The current threat to Amer-ican freedom comes mainly not from any foreign country but from the decline of individualism within America. That decline is apparent in the recent demoralization of the working class and also in the long-standing problem of entrenched poverty (chapter 10). Recent immigration is also weakening the individualist character of American society. Non-Western newcomers bring valuable assets to America, just as past immigrants did, but they must also join a mainstream culture that still shoulders the burdens of freedom. An ideal America is a multicultural society that remains individualist (chapter 11).

In the two final chapters, I consider the implications of this cultural perspective for American policy both at home and abroad. I contrast the United States with other centers of power, especially Asia. American primacy seems likely to continue; Asian culture is too cautious and too centered on immediate interests for these countries to lead the world as the West and America have done. Against all its rivals, only the United States possesses both the will and the capacity to lead. That potential, however, depends on the maintenance of an individualist way of life at home.

THE ESSENCE OF AMERICA

To restate this book's main theme: The contrast between Western and non-Western ways of life is the great division in the world today, both within and between countries. On one side of that great divide, America—due chiefly to the world's most individualist culture—has leapt to wealth and power. In such a society, particularly, power grows from the bottom up. It begins with ordinary people who take action toward their own goals and, in so doing, enrich and empower the nation.

The frontispiece to this book dramatizes that striving. This painting, by the great British artist J.M.W. Turner, is of a harbor in the Netherlands, in Europe, where America began. The wind is whistling. As any sailor knows, Western Europe is a lee shore. The weather mostly blows off the ocean onto the land, and is often severe. Given such conditions, Europe never was the Elysian Fields. It could never have become powerful but for its people and their ways. The painting shows a few of them in a ferry daring to cross the harbor. Despite the tempest, the vessel has moved from darkness into light, a symbol of the hope—the optimism—that has marked Western culture from the beginning.

The passengers are looking up, searching for the sun. It is a symbol of the meaning that Westerners always seek behind and beyond the appearances of the moment. To achieve meaning requires that outward reality conform to the visions in their heads. These Europeans are merely crossing a harbor. But in a like spirit, the Pilgrims left England for the Netherlands and then crossed the Atlantic to found a New Jerusalem in the American wilderness. As much as anyone in history, they shouldered the burdens of freedom.

Myriad other adventurers would follow them, pursuing other visions— or mere self-interest. No one was thinking of power. Yet the daring of those individual efforts, channeled through economics and politics, would finally build the hegemon that leads the world today. American power is not just a by-product of wealth or the scale of a large country. Rather, it is the *achievement* of individuals who determine, in Tennyson's words, "To strive, to seek, to find, and not to yield."[38] For America to continue to lead the world, it must, above all, retain that buccaneering spirit. Americans must continue to bear the burdens of freedom.

PART ONE

HISTORY AND CULTURE

INTRODUCTION TO PART ONE

HISTORY AND CULTURE

Cultural difference is the great fact about the world today. In the next chapter, I set out the history that suggests that individualism, though largely confined to the West, largely explains Western and American primacy. In chapter 3, I explain why cultural difference eclipses political differences in accounting for world inequality today. In chapter 4, I explain cultural differences in more detail, and in chapter 5 I consider how they might have arisen.

Paradoxically, the very triumph of the West, currently led by the United States, reveals the limits of individualism. Our way of life is far from universal. Not only has Asia found a different, more collectivist path forward, but both Western and Asian cultures are deeply rooted in the past. In addition, individualism makes far greater demands on rich countries than we usually assume. Poorer countries simply cannot adopt that style of life (and reap its historic fruits) in the same way they might change their style of government or their policies. Freedom brings heavy burdens that most non-Western societies have been unable or unwilling to bear.

Given our current multicultural world, and the manifest value of all world cultures, it may seem nostalgic to say that individualism was the root of Western primacy. To say that is no argument against a diverse America today, which remains valuable. It does imply, however, that maintaining American world leadership requires maintaining an individualist culture at home. If the United States were no longer individualist, it could not remain the dynamic and civic paragon it has become.

CHAPTER TWO

HISTORY

History already suggests that an individualist culture underlies American wealth and power. That ambitious view of life is the best explanation we have for why Western countries—and currently the United States—have come to lead the world. Since medieval times, Europe and its offshoots, including America, steadily grew richer until (largely as a result) they came to control much of the planet. Although the West today has given up formal empires, it remains by far the wealthiest region and also the strongest in military and soft power. The challenge posed by Asia is recent, and its potential is unclear.

We cannot understand American power in isolation. Even though today it encompasses peoples from every nation, the United States was largely created by Europeans, especially the British. Thus, the sources of American power and primacy lie largely in the European past. When Henry Ford declared that "History is bunk," he meant that all that matters is what we can make of ourselves *today*, and probably most Americans would agree. Yet, to understand ourselves, we must give up the idea that America sprang full-blown into being in 1776 when it declared independence from Britain. Within Western history, the United States did break with our mother country over important issues, but viewed today—after history—its *continuity* with the British and Europe is far more notable.

Westerners used to study chiefly their own history, as if the rest of the world did not matter. Admonished by our moralistic culture, today world historians accept that all traditions have in some way shaped the world we live in.[1] But though all cultures are valuable, not all are equally influential. To understand what the West has done, we must recover a sense of wonder at the striking advance of Europe from obscurity to world dominance in a few short centuries. To consider other civilizations alongside the West only dramatizes this remarkable story.

History poses the central mysteries of that development. In classical times, human civilization centered on the Mediterranean and China. By all odds, those regions should have continued to dominate, with the rest of the world remaining their tributaries. But Europe changed all that. Somehow, this afterthought of Rome became more powerful than the rest of Eurasia combined. And then the still more obscure British came to lead Europe and became the greatest imperialists since Rome. And finally, North America, hitherto scarcely developed in economic terms, came to host the most powerful nation in history.

America's self-conception was also radically different than that of most of humanity. What earlier nation was ever "conceived in liberty," as Lincoln put it? As I show below, most previous nations were dedicated to some vision of order, not freedom. And what other country, until that time, stated its social ideals in terms of the rights and fortunes of ordinary people, as against elites claiming special authority? Those features already suggest how central individualism has been to everything that America has achieved.

The striking rise of Europe, then Britain, and then America can best be explained by the strange appearance of an individualist culture that was unique to the West. That ambitious mind-set motivated ordinary people to shoulder far more responsibility for themselves and for change than the world had seen before. Above all, it was this vast dispersion of initiative and problem-solving across an entire society that drove the emergence of unimagined wealth and power, first in Europe and then in the Anglo countries.

There were also more material, worldly forces behind Europe's advance, but the fundamental cause was psychological. Somehow, human beings in Europe, more than anywhere else, came to believe that they had the capacity to shape their own fate and improve their fortunes, either

FIGURE 2.1 **The Resurrection**

Matthias Grünewald, Isenheim altarpiece, 1515

through ingenuity or through plain hard work. This gave birth to radical notions of what mere mortals could achieve. History, mostly driven by the West, has pursued "a series of breakthroughs toward the realization of greater and greater power." It is a tale of expanding control and ultimately "a story of consciousness."[2]

EUROPE

In the world of the Roman Empire, Europe was a backwater. It was that forested region mostly north of the Alps that Rome never fully civilized, where the barbarians reigned. Tribes from those regions finally invaded the Western empire and, in 476 AD, put an end to it. Europe thus formed atop the ruins of Rome. It might have remained dormant for centuries, but it rose like a phoenix to new life. And, as figure 2.1 suggests, the chief impetus for this rise was the Christian church. Despite the collapse of the empire, the church became the "legatee of Rome," with churchmen now ruling where Roman officials had before. The church retained Rome's ambition to lead and to inspire civilization on the grandest scale.[3] That vision rings out from the bold statements of early popes and saints, including those who converted Europe to the new creed.

Saint Benedict, who founded monasticism in the West, proclaimed in the sixth century that "The time has come for us to rouse ourselves from sleep. Let us open our eyes to the light that can change us into the likeness of God. Let our ears be alert to the stirring call of his voice crying to us every day.... Run, while you have the light of life."[4] Note that Benedict wrote this from an isolated monastery in early medieval Italy. He was writing for monks, men dedicated to lives of prayer who shut themselves away from the world. Yet this was a call not to escape the world, but to transform it. It was the primal cry of a new civilization with ambitious goals for this life as well as the next.

So, the early church was strongly led. Yet on the whole, the revival of civilization in Europe was not the doing of leaders. Rather, a process of spontaneous improvement took hold across the continent. Towns grew up, and trade arose between them and with regions beyond Europe. Equally important, political order revived, based initially on a feudal system in which kings ruled through vassals, who held lands in return for military service. Intellectual life also arose, first in the monasteries and then in newly founded universities in Paris and other cities across the continent. By all these routes, Europe grew richer and more organized. Its leading thinkers already looked to the future, with ambitious goals and visions.

Of course, during these centuries, growth also occurred in Asia, with China becoming by far the richest and most urbanized region. Yet Europe showed much more will and ability to project power. In the eleventh through thirteenth centuries, that impulse spawned the Crusades. These expeditions aimed to wrest back control of the Holy Land from Islam, which had built a large empire in the Middle East and beyond. In the fifteenth century, the same impetus took the form of voyages of discovery to Africa, Asia, and the Americas. These explorations were initially led by Portugal, a tiny, poor country that, as one scholar notes, "lacked just about everything one would expect in a nation about to embark [on] the exploration of the world."[5] Although governments helped sponsor the expeditions, the initiative came chiefly from enterprising individuals. In 1492, Columbus set out to reach the Orient by sailing west across the Atlantic—an outrageous idea—and in doing so he discovered the New World.[6] Settlement of the new continent by the Spanish, French, and British would make Western power even more dominant.

From the start, the keynote of European history was ceaseless change. An endless urge to make things work better prevailed, even if change often met resistance. The many economic innovations included more efficient agriculture, improved rules for private ownership, and the technical revolutions, such as the steam engine and electric power, that drove the Industrial Revolution. In government, reformist monarchs developed legalized and bureaucratic forms of rule that later evolved into representative political institutions. Although inspired by the memory of Rome, almost all the European innovations were home-grown, relying very little upon examples from the rest of the world.

A drive for improvement was evident in the entire society, not only among the elite. Europe's defining quality was "a culture and institutions that routinely applied effort to solving problems of all kinds."[7] The energy for development was expansive and uncontrollable, with no one in charge, and no one could stand in its way. No other culture showed the same protean quality.[8] In 1500, according to J.M. Roberts, "Europeans stood...at the beginning of an age in which their energy and confidence would grow seemingly without limit." He asks, "What it was in the European mind that pressed...forward," always seeking to overcome limits?[9] That something, I suggest, could only be an individualist culture.

Progress was not continuous, however. Europe suffered setbacks from the Black Death, famine, and other natural disasters. Above all, there was near-constant war, as Europe's growing states fought over territory, trade, religion, and politics. But even as European countries failed to dominate each other, they came to control much of the rest of the globe, either through trade or conquest. European assertiveness encountered many more checks inside the West than it did outside.

THE NON-WESTERN WORLD

Compared to Europe, some regions of the world—including Africa and the Americas before the arrival of Europeans—saw very little development.[10] The reasons were often environmental, such as a hostile climate or a lack of resources. (I consider these factors in chapter 6.) When we look back on early civilizations, we note the birth of cities, agriculture, and written languages not only in the West, but across Eurasia. Viewed from a distance and over many centuries, growth in the West and in Asia were broadly the same, as some scholars emphasize.[11]

Nevertheless, development that occurs outside the West has a different character. It is typically slower, and it less often involves fundamental change. There may be growth in wealth and population, but it is incremental and seldom involves major shifts in the economy or other institutions. Above all, no non-Western country spontaneously experienced the explosive growth in wealth that came with the Industrial Revolution in Europe. The norm, in short, is "growth without development."[12] Only since the mid-nineteenth century have several countries, mainly in Asia, found ways to industrialize and open themselves to trade, thus becoming far richer and more powerful, as I note below. But they did so chiefly in response to pressure from the West.

Political change, like economic change, is typically faster in the West. It is also more progressive, in the sense that regimes become stronger and more modern—that is, legal, democratic, and rational—over time. Since the Dark Ages, European states gradually increased their authority and changed their political basis, from feudalism to monarchy and then to representative government. Governments also became more law-based and bureaucratic, in the sense that officials increasingly were appointed on grounds of personal ability rather than political influence, and they also operated more by impartial rules.

In the non-Western world, political change—even turmoil—has also occurred, but any sense of progressive improvement is far weaker. Compared to the West, revolutions of the sort that took place in Mexico in

1910, China in 1911 and 1949, and Cuba in 1959 are due less to progressive change in the background society than to the weakness of the regime or to outside pressure. Latin America, for example, has mostly adopted the form of Western politics, but the underlying society is far less dynamic. In Latin America and other parts of the non-West, even after centuries, regimes remain weak, and norms of consent, legality, and efficiency are far less fully achieved than in the West.[13]

Another key difference is that non-Western development lacks the same popular character of development in Europe and its offshoots; it is typically led by elites. Change is usually an act of policy, driven from the top, whereas in the West it is driven mostly by lower echelons seeking to make money and get ahead. In Europe, it is chiefly Adam Smith's "invisible hand" that converts widespread striving into greater wealth for the wider society. Of course, non-Westerners have historically made remarkable breakthroughs. China invented gunpowder and the horse collar centuries before Europe acquired these things. But in Asia, creative change typically has shallow roots: innovation is not well supported by government, let alone by the wider society.[14]

STATIC CIVILIZATIONS

From its origins at least until the mid-twentieth century, Europe seems to have changed continuously. There was constant struggle, but it generally led in a progressive direction, toward both economic and political improvement. Dr. Martin Luther King, Jr., famously said that "The arc of the moral universe is long, but it bends toward justice."[15] That idea captures the West's conviction that its history realizes its ideals over time, even if it still falls short.

Other civilizations, however, formed their essential character early and then changed little for many centuries. These cultures did not generally experience the cataclysms—the Renaissance, the Reformation, the Enlightenment, or the industrial, democratic, and socialist revolutions of more recent times—that forced rethinking and change in Europe and its offshoots. Those changes arose mostly spontaneously from within Western societies. Outside the West, in contrast, change came slowly or did not last. Regimes typically endured with little change, or they collapsed due to outside pressure. It was chiefly economic and military challenges from the West, beginning in the nineteenth century, that led to the revolutions in Russia and Asia in the last hundred years or so. Although mostly undertaken in the name of democratic or socialist values, those upheavals usually led to continued elite rule. Consider the following examples.

BYZANTIUM was originally the eastern half of the Roman Empire. It survived for nearly a thousand years longer than the Western empire—until 1453—largely by becoming an efficient autocracy. A dominant emperor controlled the military and the Orthodox church, supported by a clerical culture that strongly resisted change, as that church still does today. The culture was backward-looking, focused on preserving old values and institutions, not improving them for the future. Since Byzantium was under siege by foreign powers (Persians, Arabs, Ottomans) for much of its history, this defensive mentality is understandable.[16]

ISLAM, after erupting from Arabia in the seventh century, built a vast empire covering the entire Middle East plus North Africa and Spain. For several centuries it was also an intellectual power, achieving breakthroughs in mathematics and astronomy, and it transmitted classical learning to Europe. Yet Islam never developed a "questioning and self-critical culture" such as appeared in the cities and universities of Europe.[17] Religious authorities finally discouraged questioning and science for fear that they would threaten Islamic beliefs. As orthodoxy advanced, the vigor of Islamic intellectual life declined. Under the Ottoman Empire, Islamic thinking was dominated by the legalism of Moslem clerics and Sufi mysticism. So the mantle of scientific progress passed to Europe and the West.[18]

INDIAN society built its essential character around the caste system and Hindu religion as early as the fourth century AD, but it then changed little. Those beliefs taught Indians to accept given roles in the existing society, rather than to rationalize it or seek personal advancement. The resulting society was highly stable, strongly resistant to changes pressed by government, but also profoundly passive. The Moghul regime, imposed by Islamic conquerors in the sixteenth century, had little influence upon it. Later, by dint of ruling India for almost two centuries, the British managed to implant some Western institutions—a capable military, bureaucracy, courts, and representative government—so that today India is developed in some ways. Its economy, for example, has a high-tech sector. But modern life still touches little of the wider society. Most Indians still live in rural villages, where little has changed for millennia.[19]

CHINA—well over two thousand years ago—formed a society based on strong families, a landed aristocracy, and an imperial regime. The country was unified as early as 221 BC, and it was the first to develop a strong state, able to rule despite parochial loyalties to families or tribes.[20] But the regime was an autocracy that improved little over time. Although its dynasties were repeatedly overthrown by revolts, there was scant evolution toward more advanced forms of rule, as seen in Europe. The culture was dominated by Confucian thinking, without much openness to new ideas.

China did experience a period of rapid economic growth under the Song dynasty, from the tenth through thirteenth centuries. Some scholars think that during this time China might have industrialized, centuries before Europe did. And in the fifteenth century, Chinese explorers voyaged to other parts of the world. But openness to change or discovery was never deeply rooted in the culture—the Ming dynasty (1368–1644) reined in innovation and exploration.[21] China then changed little until torn apart by Western pressure and internal rebellion beginning in the mid-nineteenth century. Today, a Communist regime using market tactics is rapidly developing the economy and has made China a world power. But the state remains highly resistant to change and vulnerable to rebellion. And economic progress is still driven from the top, as is typical in the non-Western world.

LATIN AMERICA has generally seen only limited development, because a traditional elite with origins in Spain and Portugal continues to dominate in most of these countries. In most of the region, wealthy rulers preside over societies composed largely of the disadvantaged descendants of Native Americans and slaves, people who lack the individualist temperament of the West.[22] Leaders have faced little pressure to improve education or promote advancement for the masses. There is much less commitment to equal opportunity for ordinary people than in the United States and other Western countries (imperfect though that commitment remains). The people's main response to the common lack of prospects has been not pressure for reform, but rising emigration to the United States.

What seems missing in all these cases is the spontaneous innovation seen in the West. In Europe—and, later, in America—a will to advance and improve somehow welled up within the society, leading to constant change that nobody in particular controlled. Ordinary people simply took it on themselves to change things, and nobody could stop them. They were usually free to do this, but they also used freedom well. They bore, that is, the burdens of freedom.

THE ASIAN WAY

Nevertheless, the West has recently learned that individualism is not the only way to become rich and powerful. The first non-Western country to seriously compete with the West was Japan. In medieval times, towns and trade developed there much as in Europe, a middle class grew up, and spontaneous economic growth occurred. Some scholars believe that Japan might well have industrialized on its own, even without Western pressure to do so.[23]

Japan was also politically precocious. The island nation possessed a strong sense of national unity, expressed by an emperor and the shogun, the chief military ruler. But, unlike in China, much power was dispersed among local warlords served by knight-like samurai, in a feudal system akin to Europe's. Although this led to constant conflict, political contention became more accepted than in China, and this led eventually to a stronger, more legitimate regime.[24] The Japanese government became the most effective in Asia. Still today, it is the only government of any large country outside the West that performs at Western levels.[25]

Yet culturally, Japan is far more collective-minded than the West. That temperament powered its response to the Western challenge. When American commodore Matthew Perry, with a show of force, entered what is now Tokyo Bay in 1853 and demanded that Japan open herself to trade, the island nation responded with unusual vigor. The Meiji Restoration of 1868 overthrew the shogun in the name of the emperor, and a samurai elite proceeded to modernize the country; they adopted Western technology and institutions with none of the hesitation shown elsewhere in the non-West. In a single generation, Japan became a world power, building a large navy and conquering a vast empire in Asia. It is the most striking transformation in the entire history of development. Although beaten by the United States in World War II, Japan reemerged afterward as a major economic power, as it remains today.

The spirit of the Japanese advance was not individualist competition, as in the West, but rather militant dedication to the nation. High and low, a Spartan people pulled together to build wealth and power with fewer internal differences than might be encountered in an individualist society. Although Japan has relied chiefly on the market to motivate its economy, government has also strongly shaped investment and otherwise guided industrial and technological development. The Japanese success inspired other Asian nations to follow suit. South Korea, Taiwan, Hong Kong, Singapore, and most recently China have all become much richer through similar combinations of public and private enterprise.

CONTROL VS. FREEDOM

A major contrast in history is between the few, Western nations that became "free" and much of the rest of the world. Since ancient times, most peoples have lived under political and religious authorities that were not accountable to their subjects. Elites lived off an economic surplus generated by their societies, justifying their privileges in the name of higher values. Rulers and the military claimed to defend the nation, while the clergy sought the solicitude of the gods. Government was a "plunder machine" that existed chiefly to fund itself.[26] This was the character of all the static civilizations surveyed above, and much of humanity still lives under such regimes today, despite the superficial spread of democracy.[27]

An autocratic government, however, is weaker than it appears. Above all, it cannot allow individual questioning, because any dissent might snowball and destroy the system. Autocracies rarely attempt the total control of their subjects' lives, but they must crush internal opposition to their authority. Leaders in Russia, China, and the Middle East still today often sanction ruthless government crackdowns to uphold their rule, because to tolerate dissent can indeed bring down an authoritarian system, as evidenced by the collapse of the USSR. A similar fate might have befallen China in 1989 had the Communist government not brutally crushed the demonstrations by democratic reformers in Beijing's Tiananmen Square. Ultimately, in an autocracy, there can be no rights against the state.

Aside from bloodletting, the cost of top-down government is that personal initiative is suppressed. Ordinary people cannot act to change or improve things without the approval of higher officials. They may even be afraid to express criticism. In an autocracy, all statements about reality must in some way defer to the authorities; discourse must be "multi-stranded." This is why the Chinese regime, over two millennia, has never permitted the intellectual fermentation and innovation seen in Western cities and universities.[28] One can still sense that deferential temperament in Asia today.[29] Due to the lack of initiative and the emphasis on control, such a society must limit economic development. Indeed, autocratic rulers sometimes oppose development because it might spawn new economic elites who could threaten their control.[30]

For these reasons, over history and worldwide, tightly controlled societies are the norm. Yet somehow Europe escaped. Although autocrats arose in many European countries, few of them were despots by non-Western standards. In Europe, some rights against government always existed, even in feudal times. Rulers could not prevent all political and economic change, and they could not restrain all new thinking. The canniest of them—as in Britain—took to promoting development rather than opposing it. Government became not just a "plunder machine"; it also provided key public goods and services.[31] And from the fifteenth century onward, the strictures of European authority loosened. People could increasingly do or say things freely, unless the law specifically forbade it. Expression of personal judgment, even about politics and religion, was increasingly accepted. This happened first in the most advanced nations—Britain and the Netherlands—and then, more slowly, in the rest of Europe.

In Western experience, the growth of freedom stimulated a vast increase in wealth and power. Mentally, individuals needed no longer to defer explicitly to authority. Their thinking became more "single-stranded," meaning more resolute, more focused on the problem at hand, whether it be to make money, advance science, or improve government. Hence the relentless innovation that swept through Western countries, especially after the Reformation.

Americans take this story as the norm. But it is in fact exceptional. It occurred "once only," in Europe.[32] The rest of the world did not follow. Regimes of control, that distrust freedom, still dominate most of the non-Western world. Even highly developed Asian countries tend to discourage openness in politics or the market. In those countries, development has meant greater wealth and influence but not greater freedom (although, as I note later, that may be changing).

Some Western scholars conclude that freedom is in fact the secret to development. Supposedly, the West grew rich precisely by reversing the controls that government had previously exerted over the economy.[33] The implication is that repressive societies today should do the same (see further in chapter 7).

However, the Western secret was not freedom in any simple sense but a refounding of authority. An individualist society proved to have its own, internalized bases of order. Authority, which hitherto had largely been external, came to be located mostly within individual psychology. As Ernest Gellner put it, "The crucial fact is that a society emerged in which single individuals could apparently carry the entire culture within themselves, unaided, and if need be reproduce it single-handedly."[34] Westerners generated from internalized principles a civic culture that permitted freedom while also enforcing good behavior, such as obeying the law and paying taxes. By bearing these *internal* burdens of freedom, people gained an *outward* freedom that was otherwise impossible. Thus freedom and order were reconciled. That is an alchemy that, still today, is possible only in an individualist culture. That is the innermost secret of Western and American primacy, as I explain more fully in later chapters.

BRITAIN

Britain is the exemplar of freedom and civility that, in history, stands between Europe and America. The remarkable island kingdom came to be the richest and best-governed large country in the West, and hence the one that would chiefly found the United States. The spirit of a strenuous freedom that was later to mark America was already visible in the mother country.

Britain's ascent, however, was at least as surprising as Europe's. Following the Iron Age, the British Isles had stood at the outer edge of the Roman Empire. Britain was not even conquered by Rome until the first century AD. And almost all traces of Roman rule were obliterated by the subsequent Anglo-Saxon invasions. For centuries thereafter, no one ever supposed that this "miserable rainy island on the edge of the world" would become a world power.[35] That is why, as historian Niall Ferguson remarked, "How an archipelago of rainy islands off the northwest coast of Europe came to rule the world is one of the fundamental questions not just of British but of world history."[36]

The simplest explanation is that Britain turned out to have the qualities of Europe, only more so. It developed an individualist society that promoted both a dynamic economy and strong government, and it achieved these things sooner and more fully than any other country (with the exception of the Netherlands). Both wealthy and well-governed, Britain also proved to have a highly effective military. These assets and victories gradually lifted the island kingdom to the leadership of Europe, a position it commanded for a century after the defeat of Napoleon in 1815.

Furthermore, the British displayed a prowess in politics and economics that defies explanation.[37] Their political precocity is the most remarkable (as I explain more fully in chapter 8). From the first unification of England in the ninth century, the monarchy was unusually strong, both ruling well (most of the time) and building an unusual bond of trust with English society. England inaugurated the rule of law in the twelfth century and government by consent, through parliament, in the thirteenth century. Thus, it achieved the essentials of good government deep in the Middle Ages, centuries before most of the rest of Europe. Much of the world still lacks such institutions even today.

Political change was mostly led by British rulers themselves, rather than being forced upon them as in other countries. Most European monarchs clung to power until violence from below convinced them to share it. But in England, trust between rulers and ruled allowed the political class to broaden over time without threatening royal authority. The seventeenth-century English Revolution against the Stuarts, which subordinated the monarch to parliament, scarcely breaks the smooth progress of British political evolution. Later revolutions in France, elsewhere in the Continent, and in Russia were far more disruptive.

Partly thanks to effective government, England became unusually wealthy. A national legal system helped it create the largest internal market in Europe, unhampered by local tolls and restrictions. Much of the Continent did not realize such changes until Napoleon. British society was also productive, because the aristocracy was more engaged in "trade" and less resistant to absorbing new blood from the middle class than in many Continental countries. Men of rank often became "improving" landlords who developed British commercial agriculture. By the fifteenth century, "England" was a byword for wealth, a place where even common people lived unusually well.[38]

England, like many poor countries today, began as a supplier of raw materials to advanced economies—it shipped wool to the cloth trade in the Low Countries. But it soon began weaving its own cloth and became the dominant textile producer.[39] Before long, it was producing many other goods and competing with the Dutch to dominate European trade. In his *Wealth of Nations*, Adam Smith (1723–1790) deprecated the mercantilism of both countries, their efforts to control trade and amass gold at the expense of real wealth. But England's open and competitive market nonetheless became the model for Smith's laissez-faire economic ideal.

Even today, the British treasure continuity with their past. Their institutions are encrusted with medieval holdovers, such as the monarchy, that conceal how functional they are. In fact, the nation came to exemplify what we today call modernity—a society largely open to talent and competition, dedicated to progress, and governed by a regime of great authority coupled with the restraints of law and consent. Historians may marvel that the British still "term themselves *subjects* of the crown, although they have long—longer than anywhere—been *citizens*."[40] Britain's role in world political and economic development thus exceeded even that of the rest of Europe.

BRITISH PRIMACY

By the seventeenth century, Britain's matchless combination of a precocious government yoked to a powerful capitalist economy drove it toward primacy within Europe. The British led other nations, which were weaker and less secure, in resisting efforts by Spain and then France to dominate the Continent. Britain fielded the world's largest navy and a small but effective army, and it bankrolled its allies in the Low Countries and Germany. All this it paid for with ferocious taxes and borrowing, which the British public accepted because they trusted the government. During the long struggle against Napoleon, Britain dedicated as much as 30 percent of its national income to war—twice the level of France, even though its population was much smaller.[41]

In the late eighteenth century, the growth of manufacturing in Britain finally precipitated the Industrial Revolution. Steam-powered factories brought about a wholly new level of production, first in textiles and iron and steel and then in many other fields. This transformation was as pivotal for humanity as any event in history.[42] As the first industrial nation, Britain became the workshop of the world, and its wealth soared to incredible heights. The figures are staggering: In 1850 the United Kingdom owned half the world's ocean-going ships and contained half the world's railway track. As late as 1870, it produced as much pig iron as the rest of the world combined.[43] These vast resources empowered Britain to become the main guarantor of the peace (at least in Europe) that prevailed between the Napoleonic wars and World War I.

Another marker of British primacy was empire. Even more than the rest of Europe, Britain excelled at projecting power abroad. Figure 2.2 shows British forces going ashore in Canada in 1759 to defeat France for the control of North America. The scene resembles D-Day in 1944, but it occurred almost two centuries earlier. The British prevailed even using sailing ships across thousands of miles of ocean, as they also did in India, the Caribbean, and South Africa. At the time, no other nation approached this capacity.

The British had accumulated territories overseas since the seventeenth century. By the late 1800s Britain governed an empire that was three times the size of France's and ten times that of Germany, encompassing nearly a quarter of the globe and ruling a quarter of its population.[44] So formidable was tiny Britain that it took over huge regions much larger than itself. It conquered the entire Indian subcontinent "like a toad swallowing a cow."[45]

Britain's primacy faded only in the late nineteenth century, when several other European countries, preeminently Germany, grew rich and unified enough to challenge her. Tensions, chiefly between Germany and the rest of Europe, led to the great wars of the twentieth century, which consumed much of Britain's accumulated wealth. Afterward, shorn of her empire and no longer a military giant, Britain depended on a close alliance with the United States to defend the values of law, peace, and open trade in which both nations believed.

FIGURE 2.2 **British Landing Troops before the Battle of Quebec, 1759**

Hervey Smith, 1734–1811

AMERICA

The United States arose on territory that once was even more obscure than Roman Britain. In the New World, Native Americans had built a civilization of enduring interest and value, but—like the rest of the non-West—it was far less oriented to development than Europe was. So it could offer little resistance when settlers from Europe streamed into the newly discovered continent starting in the seventeenth century.

The United States was to take European accomplishments to even further lengths than Britain, and this is the simplest explanation for American primacy. The country inherited Britain's leading attributes—a dynamic society coupled with strong government. It also vastly exceeded the small size that had, in the end, limited British power. A country with an individualist society and British institutions but continental scale would inevitably lead the world. Otto von Bismarck (1815–1898), the brilliant statesman who unified Germany, famously remarked that the most important fact about world affairs was that the North Americans spoke English.[46]

The British who settled America were particularly daring and ambitious. Americans today think it natural that ordinary people should cross oceans to pursue a better life on these shores. But that was not something that anybody but Europeans did on any large scale during America's formative centuries. The prospect of crossing the Atlantic in sailing ships and then settling in the wilderness intimidated most people, if they thought about it at all. Yet between 1620 and 1642, close to sixty thousand English, almost 1.5 percent of the nation's population, left Britain for North America.[47]

And, largely freed from the European class system and religious prejudice, most of these immigrants, from the moment they stepped ashore, set about making themselves richer. The result was economic growth and dynamism even more striking than in the old country. By the time of their revolt against British rule, the American colonies had already achieved the world's highest standard of living.[48] And this was before settlers had reached the far richer farmlands of the Midwest.

Another feature of the early United States was the remarkable self-assurance of its new regime. Even during the Revolutionary War era, American envoys—among them founders John Adams, Benjamin Franklin, Thomas Jefferson, and John Jay—negotiated as equals with Britain and France. In the decades that followed, as befitted a still-small and weak nation, America's foreign policy was at first cautious, eschewing involvement in European wars and alliances. Nonetheless, the young nation showed a willingness to fight over specific issues, such as trade and the impressment of American sailors, in the Quasi-War against France from 1798 to 1800 and in the War of 1812 against Britain.

Other countries steered clear of the British navy, which at this time was absolutely dominant at sea. The Americans knew that their tiny flotilla could never challenge the British in a fleet action. So they built warships, such as USS *Constitution*, that were designed to beat individual British ships, and did so. Figure 2.3 shows the *Constitution* defeating the British *Guerrière* in 1812, the first of her several victories. It was on that day, according to historian Charles F. Adams, Jr., that the United States emerged as a world power. Although still weak by any objective measure, the new republic already exhibited an assertive temperament. One British commentator extolled "the rising greatness of this distant empire." Even this early in US history, the national government was "confident, progressive, and expansive."[49]

FIGURE 2.3 **USS *Constitution* Defeating *Guerrière*, War of 1812**

Michel Felice Corne, 1752–1845

By the early nineteenth century, indeed, some observers already predicted that the United States would dominate the world. The American founders, of course, acclaimed the nation they had created. Jefferson foresaw that America would become a "colossus," while Hamilton called it "the embryo of a great empire." More telling, however, was that foreign observers said much the same. The Venetian ambassador to Paris predicted that the United States might become "the most formidable power in the world." And French observer Alexis de Tocqueville (1805–1859) wrote in *Democracy in America* that the country would become the world's "leading naval power," destined "to rule the seas, as the Romans were to conquer the world."[50]

No doubt, these observers were responding to the nature of the young country, rather than to anything it had yet achieved. They noted the ferment of American society (which at that time was racing across the continent) and also the capability of the federal government. It was clear that American leaders would, in time, harness that vast energy to generate unequaled wealth and power. The South American nations that won independence from Spain and Brazil in the 1820s made quite a different impression. Those countries were not oriented to development in the same way; rather, they were invested in the status quo. In contrast,

"America by 1820 was a Prometheus unbound, ready to bring knowledge and freedom to the world."[51]

AMERICAN PRIMACY

Like Britain, the United States was swept toward primacy on a wave of wealth such as the world had never seen, as well as by an effective government. By the mid-nineteenth century, the country was already an "economic giant." It possessed not only the world's most productive agriculture but also an expanding industry, rivaling that of several European powers. From 1873 to 1913, American economic growth averaged 5 percent a year, producing prodigious increases over time. Output of major products (see below for examples) grew by multiples. By the end of the century, American industry had eclipsed that of every other country. The American magnate Andrew Carnegie alone produced more steel than the whole of England. By 1919, America's total production exceeded that of the whole of Europe.[52] Despite the vicissitudes of depression and war, in the twentieth century US economic dominance grew even further. After World War II, with only 7 percent of the world's population, the United States disposed of 42 percent of the world's income and half of its manufacturing output.[53]

Such figures confirmed that America was a radically different society from nations to its south. In the early nineteenth century, Mexico had nearly half the per-capita income of the United States, and Mexico City was the largest in North America. But in the decades that followed, there was massively more development to the north of the Rio Grande than to the south. The American victory in the Mexican-American War (1846–1848) was too brief to have large economic effects; more important might be the new resources America gained from conquering Mexico's northern territories. But in the main, Mexico was simply outdistanced by American growth. America went from strength to strength; all the while its southern neighbor was largely wrapped up in political turmoil. By the 1870s, American national income was thirty-five times that of Mexico.[54]

Politically as well, the United States grew steadily more formidable. When early nineteenth-century observers noted its vast potential, the one doubt they had was whether it would break up over slavery. The founders

had left that great question unresolved. The issue led to decades-of political struggle but then was faced and resolved through the Civil War. Of
course, a great president—Abraham Lincoln—emerged to lead the North
to victory, but the ultimate credit for maintaining the Union goes to the
strength of the nation's political institutions. The national government
formed a will to fight and then mobilized millions of citizens for a civic
cause, which prevailed. The triumph solidified America's commitment
to democracy, thus fortifying its moralistic sense of mission and its influence in the world.[55] And from the late nineteenth century through the
Progressive era, major governmental reforms strengthened America's civil
service, its federal administration, and its military.[56]

Backed by these resources, American foreign policy became steadily
more ambitious. In its early decades, the United States sought mainly
to keep European powers out of the Western Hemisphere (under the
Monroe Doctrine), then to take territory from Mexico. It later exerted
influence more widely with "gunboat diplomacy" in the Caribbean and
the Open Door policy in Asia, as it built a navy even larger than Britain's.
Then, starting with the Spanish-American War in 1898, it demonstrated
a peerless power to project force at a distance, easily conquering Cuba
and the Philippines.

By the First World War, American primacy had arrived. The United
States helped the Allied powers win that war but then withdrew from
efforts to keep the peace, including the League of Nations. American
recalcitrance was thus one cause of World War II. In that epic conflict,
however, the United States mobilized as never before to defeat both
Germany and Japan (with much help from the Soviet Union, China, and
others). From 1941 to 1943, American arms manufacturing grew by a factor
of eight, until it was three times that of the Axis powers, and the nation's
physical plant and output grew by 50 percent or more.[57]

After its victory, America did not withdraw from global affairs, as it
had done previously. Instead, it led the construction of a new international
order based on the United Nations, institutions to oversee world finance
and trade, and military alliances. During the Cold War, America again
took the reins, this time in opposing Communist expansion, leading finally
to the collapse of Communism and today's more pluralist world order.

In current worldwide struggles against terrorism and Islamic radicalism, the United States is yet again at the fore. President Trump has

questioned the scale of America's world commitments. But there appears to be no alternative to continued American leadership around the globe, although its burdens will be heavy, as later chapters show.

Some critics say that the United States has become a latter-day imperialist. For a hegemon that controls only Puerto Rico and a few Pacific islands, that is an overstatement. Like Europe and Britain beforehand, America's worldwide sway is due less to formal, governmental power than to the vast vitality of its society. The United States exerts power not only militarily, but also through trade, its exemplary educational institutions, and its entire way of life. To a great extent, "empire" today connotes not direct power, but the soft power of example. Very substantially, American primacy reflects the vast impact of American culture.

CONCLUSION

The history of Europe, Britain, and America strongly suggests that the chief force behind the dominant wealth and power of the West is an individualist culture. Strictly speaking, there is no way to prove that connection. We cannot rerun history without individualism and see whether the regions and nations that rise to power turn out to be the same. The association between individualism and high development is strong simply because all Western countries are, to varying degrees, individualist, and all became rich and powerful (at least by world standards).[58] Concretely, the connection is that individualism promotes both a dynamic society and strong government, and those features together generate rising wealth at home and power abroad.

Like yeast that is mixed with dough, an individualist temperament leavened Western society, producing growth and improvement first within Europe and then in its offshoots. Ordinary people seeking to better themselves and others found better and better ways of doing so. An impatient mind-set that never stood still drove Europe, then Britain, then America to seek to change the world. Until recent times, most other countries were fundamentally different from the West, dedicated mostly to conserving the society they had.

Western primacy has noncultural roots as well, such as natural resources and geographic position. But, as I show in later chapters, the influence of these factors is also shaped by culture. If these forces were truly decisive, then wealth and power would not be so strongly correlated with culture. We would see rich and poor countries of varying worldviews scattered randomly around the world depending on favorable physical conditions. Japan is the one major case of a country that became rich and powerful before the twentieth century without an individualist culture. In general, however, individualist culture rules, and therefore the West has ruled.

High development might also be a matter of chance, occurring wherever pivotal events were favorable and leadership competent. There might be "critical junctures" in history where some countries took positive steps toward a more progressive society, while others turned away. For example, perhaps Western individualism would have been strangled in its cradle if the ancient Greeks had not repulsed the Persian invasions in the fifth century BC.[59] Again, that is not the main lesson of history. Systematic causes matter more than chance. Chiefly, we see that countries of a certain kind become rich and powerful while others do not.

One might go further and suggest that the real winners in development are the English-speaking nations. After all, it was chiefly Britain and her offshoots, preeminently the United States, that became the world's richest and mightiest countries. They eclipsed all competitors, first within Europe and then beyond.[60] There is no denying that the British had an unequaled gift for political and economic improvement, which they bequeathed to America. But the British achievement is not fundamentally different from that of the rest of Europe. What triumphed within Europe as a whole, and then beyond, was an ambitious vision of life in which individuals dared to embrace both freedom and its burdens.

The major qualification to this conclusion is that several Asian countries besides Japan have recently become rich and strong without individualism. The proper inference, however, is not that culture does not matter. Rather, it is that *either* an individualist or a collectivist ethos may generate the social discipline needed for high development, but they do so in quite different ways, as I explain further below. Success is associated with the *extremes* of culture—with the *most* individualist countries (preeminently the United States) and the *most* collectivist countries (notably Japan and China). Most of the world, however, lives in a muddled middle, under unaccountable authorities, without a strong will to change on either an individual or a collective basis.

It is also likely, because of the West's greater capacity for innovation and greater sense of responsibility for the world, that American and Western primacy will endure despite the advance of Asia. As I elaborate in later chapters, an individualist culture accepts self-seeking. It celebrates the will and capacity of ordinary people to achieve what they want. But individualists also internalize moral principles that make them attentive to wider interests. And as they get richer, this moralism strengthens (see chapters 12 and 13), until people expect that everything they do, or everything their government does, will be justified by some higher end. Self-seeking never ceases, yet individualism also achieves collective good.

This widening of moral vision was already visible early in Western history. Individuals sought to advance themselves, but the moral teachings of the church, and the market's "invisible hand," promoted concern for a social interest as well. By the nineteenth century, Western states that had previously fought over territory, religion, and trade had accepted some collective responsibility for the peace of Europe. That vision was shattered in the great wars and other conflicts of the twentieth century, but it gradually revived and is today exemplified by the European Union, the United Nations, the World Trade Organization, and other global institutions. President Trump has challenged some of those institutions, but he is unlikely to destroy them.

Already by the sixteenth century, Western thinkers began to extend their moral concerns beyond Europe. As they discovered the non-Western world, they conceived that there was a universal humanity embracing all persons. There were natural laws that applied to everyone, and there were universal rights that everyone should have. There thus could be a world citizenry, even if world government was but a distant hope.[61] That is the universal vision that, with or without Trump, American primacy still serves today.

CHAPTER THREE

THE END OF HISTORY

Viewed from the present, history strongly suggests that an individualist culture was the deepest driver of Western dominance. Europe, then Britain, then America rose to primacy because they embodied such a society most fully. The actions of ordinary people toward their own goals finally empowered whole nations to generate wealth and power on a scale never before seen.

However, it is easier to draw this conclusion today than it was during the many wars and other conflicts that litter Western history. At the time, the antagonists were most aware of the values they fought over. Whichever political or religious persuasion won out would have changed their future. Norms that we today associate with freedom finally won out in the West. Market economies overseen by democratic polities prevail. No one was thinking of individualism as a way of life—it was assumed by all.

But today, to a long view, cultural difference is, in fact, more important than the differences fought over during history. In some form, it was probably inevitable that institutions based on individualism would arise in Europe and its offshoots. Far more significant is the fact that those institutions have not traveled well to non-Western societies. Since the collapse of Communism, much of the developing world has adopted elected government and market economics, at least formally. The effects have clearly been positive—notably in the former Soviet satellites of Eastern Europe, parts of Latin America, and the newly rich economies in Asia. Yet the West's "free" institutions clearly are an ill fit in most of the world. They have left many people only a little less poor and ill-governed than they were before.

What the victory of "freedom" really did was expose cultural bases of development and underdevelopment that are far older than modern ideologies. As suggested in the last chapter, development has come most easily to countries at either cultural extreme—not only the most individualist but also the most collectivist. Political differences are quite secondary to culture. Ways of life have proven more powerful than any ideology.

FUKUYAMA'S THEORY

The ascendancy of culture over ideology is best understood in terms of what Francis Fukuyama called the end of history. He meant the recent eclipse of deep ideological divisions in international affairs. The idea is often misunderstood or dismissed too facilely, but it captures quite well the shifting of politics, both at home and abroad, away from impersonal theories toward a much more personal focus on culture. Not ideology but mass psychology—really, human nature—is what truly differentiates most rich and powerful countries from most poor and weak ones today.

Fukuyama first wrote that history had ended in 1989, just as Russia's Communist empire in the Soviet Union and Eastern Europe was crumbling.[1] Under Communism, an elite calling itself the "vanguard of the proletariat" had monopolized politics and imposed bureaucratic planning on the economy. In a matter of decades, that system proved to be too authoritarian and inefficient. Russia was forced to abandon Communism for a regime that was at least somewhat free in both political and economic terms, although still authoritarian and corrupt. Meanwhile, China and Vietnam kept their Communist governments yet allowed their economies to operate more freely.

Fukuyama judged that not only had the West won the Cold War but a consensus had jelled in favor of the central Western institutions—democracy and capitalism. A struggle between these institutions and various forms of socialism or collectivism had dominated politics for two centuries, ever since the French Revolution, first within Western countries and then—for much of the twentieth century—within world politics as well. Fascism, another mid-century foe of freedom, had also been vanquished. Fukuyama believed that the superiority of representative government and the market economy was now recognized worldwide. He did not deny the limitations of these institutions, yet he concluded that they were the best that humanity could devise.

Behind that theory stood the thinking of G.W. F. Hegel (1770–1831), the great German Idealist, as interpreted by the French philosopher Alexandre Kojève. Hegel saw history as revealing a growth in consciousness toward freedom, meaning a condition in which individuals were truly able to act autonomously. To Hegel, "The History of the world is none other than the progress of the consciousness of Freedom."[2] History in this sense reveals conflicts between opposing moral or political systems. Each impasse was resolved by some new synthesis that brought consciousness to a higher level. Kojève and Fukuyama interpreted the contest between free institutions and collectivism as such a conflict. It had now been resolved in favor of freedom. Since there appeared to be no further fundamental political divisions, there were no more contradictions to resolve. Thus, history—at least in Hegel's sense—had ended.

That did not mean that change in more prosaic senses ended. It did not imply that unfree institutions would immediately disappear. But they could no longer be *justified*. They were no longer on the march. Few Americans today, as *The Economist* remarked, can remember the era when Communists "took themselves and their words seriously."[3] In 1956, Nikita Khrushchev, the Soviet leader, promised the West that "We will bury you." Today, advocates for socialism or Communism can no longer hold such conviction. A governmental polity and economy no longer represents the future, but the past.

As if to vindicate Fukuyama, the collapse of Communism did indeed accelerate the growth of democracy and capitalism in much of the world, especially Eastern Europe. Now that the Communist threat had vanished, there was also much less reason for countries to fight one another. A "democratic peace" prevailed, in the sense that rich countries with elected governments no longer made war on each other. The primary difference between nations now was not their ideological identity but how rich and powerful they were. In comparing societies, commentators focused less on politics and more on ways of life and levels of productivity.

One criticism of Fukuyama is that the world consensus in favor of democratic capitalism is not unanimous. As shown by Venezuela's Hugo Chavez, some politicians in poor countries can still gain power by selling a socialist platform to the masses. History has, perhaps, ended more clearly *within* the West than outside of it. The more serious criticism of the end of history is that new conflicts speedily arose. No sooner had Communism collapsed than Islamic radicalism threatened several Middle Eastern countries and launched a terrorist campaign against the West.[4] The 9/11 attacks using hijacked airliners to target New York and Washington were dramatic proof that America still had fundamentalist enemies in the world.

CULTURAL CONFLICT

In apparent contrast to Fukuyama, Samuel Huntington portrayed the world as divided among seven or eight different civilizations, of which the West and Islam are those most obviously at odds.[5] But if cultural difference may lead to conflict, it is not historical conflict in the sense meant by Fukuyama or Hegel. Historical conflicts were ideological rather than cultural. The competing political values were chiefly different meanings of freedom and equality, the West's dominant values. Ideological systems have differed from one another mainly in how they interpreted those norms. That is one reason why the conflicts have been resolved over time. Western polities were able to transcend the contest between capitalism and socialism by combining essentially market economies with welfare states. Capitalism and socialism were merely different points on an ideological spectrum—and somewhere the two could meet.

But conflicts between the West and Islamic radicalism are cultural, rather than historical or ideological. Islamic political ideals do not align well with Western ones, whether liberal or collectivist. That is because, having originated in the non-West, Islam posits a non-individualist personality that—as I show later—depends on external authority for social order. That makes Western ideological visions, whether of the right or the left, unacceptable to Islam. Rather, the issue within Islam is how fully Muslim societies must live by the literal strictures of the Koran or Islamic tradition. No Western ideology today allows the same unquestioned authority that is accepted in Islam. Conversely, no version of Islam gives freedom the primacy that it has had in the West. Political ideologies compare to each other as hot water to cold, so compromise is possible. But cultural conflicts are like oil and water—battles of opposed worldviews that cannot be made commensurable.[6]

Thus, the end of history means, not the end of all conflict, but the shifting of conflict from ideological differences within the Western world to cultural differences between the West and the non-West. (I emphasize here the basic division between the individualist West and the more cautious and collective-minded non-West, rather than Huntington's more complex scheme.)

From one point of view, cultural conflict is less threatening to the West than the ideological conflicts of the past. However disturbing Islamic radicalism is, it has nowhere near the potential of Communism or fascism to challenge the very basis of Western societies. Those ideologies were not only external threats but had substantial appeal within Western societies. In the 1930s, for example, many thoughtful Americans as well as Europeans believed that capitalism had failed. There was a sort of national identity crisis that fostered visions of a new society, notions that incorporated some version of state planning. Islamic radicalism, by contrast, has no such attraction to Westerners. It may threaten our national security but not our traditional ways of life.

On the other hand, as Huntington and others have argued, Western values are receding in the world as a whole, even as Western institutions seem to dominate. The end of European empires allowed many former colonies to return to non-Western political ways.[7] Thus, relations among countries will increasingly involve cultural conflict, or at least cultural difference. (This is apart from cultural change within the United States, which could attune our society more to non-Western ways of life, as I discuss in later chapters.)

Aside from Islamic radicalism, for many Americans the chief threat to our nation today is economic competition with Asia, especially mainland China. That contest, as shown above, is ultimately a contest of cultures. The great issue is whether an individualist society like the United States or a collectivist one like China will produce the most wealth and power in future. The earlier contest raised impersonal issues, while the current contest raises far more personal ones: in essence, can a society in which people mostly think for themselves be outproduced by one in which they mostly take orders from above?

FIGURE 3.1 **Ideological Blocs during the Cold War**

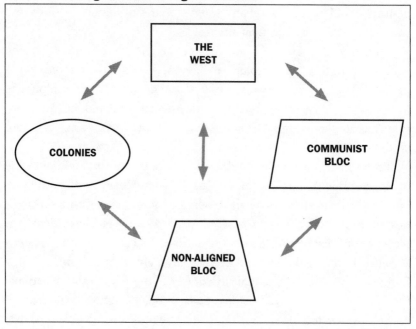

Figure 3.1 portrays the world as it was during the Cold War. Blocs of countries were defined chiefly in ideological terms, and there was overt conflict among them. The West, led by the United States, opposed Communism, but some countries were non-aligned, while others were still colonies of the West.

In contrast, figure 3.2 portrays the world as it is today, with nations ranked chiefly in terms of wealth and power. Conflict is now chiefly economic and is less overt. On that basis, the United States stands first, but its principal Asian challengers—China and India—loom much larger than they did before history ended.

This cultural contest may appear to be recent. It gained prominence only after the fall of Communism and the economic reforms in China and India that liberated their economies to accelerate. But in truth, it has been brewing for far longer. As early as two centuries ago, Asia faced pressure from the West to become richer and stronger. It has done so by combining its collectivist ethos with market elements. This jousting between East and West has, so far, been less violent than Fukuyama's historical conflicts, but in some ways it is more far-reaching, because it pits entire ways of life against one another.

FIGURE 3.2 **Relative Standing of World Nations and Regions Today**

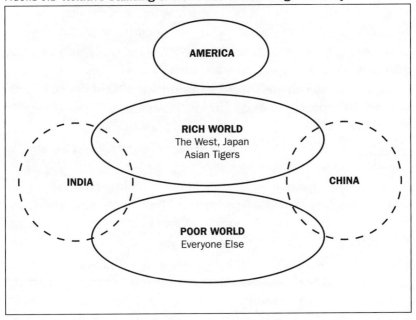

THE DOMESTIC ARENA

As is less commonly noted, history has also ended in domestic politics. Just as in the international arena, the deepest political divisions within Western countries are no longer over ideology but over questions of culture or human nature.[8]

In European politics, the chief divisions until recent decades were between different classes representing different political visions. The oldest elites, with origins in feudalism, favored a backward-looking society that would serve traditional values, often rooted in religion. They were opposed by newer, middle-class elites who had developed the capitalist economy; these favored a regime of classic liberalism based on the rule of law, economic freedom, and representative government. They, in turn, were opposed by the labor or socialist movement, based mainly in industry; it sought to use government to protect workers against the insecurities of capitalism, as well as to distribute opportunity and reward more equally. The United States added to these class divisions the important issue of race. When and how blacks could become equal citizens has alternated with class as the dominant issue in American politics ever since the birth of the nation.

While the radical left hoped for socialism and other radical changes, what in fact occurred were reforms to achieve some of the aims of socialism within a still largely democratic and capitalist society. Workers received some protections on the job, and a welfare state supported groups, such as the jobless and elderly, who were unable to support themselves through employment. The United States also established formal citizenship for blacks and the abolition of open discrimination against them. Full integration is still distant, due chiefly to the disproportionate involvement of blacks and other minorities in poverty and other social problems, as discussed further in chapters 10 and 11.

History has ended in domestic politics, in the first place, because of broad consensus behind this outcome. In Western countries today, few leaders propose to abolish the market, as socialists once did, or to abolish all workplace protections or the welfare state, as some rightists still seek. Disputes are confined to marginal changes toward more government or less. Some may doubt that consensus, pointing to the recent sharp polarization of the two major American parties: Republicans, who seek drastic cuts in government, oppose Democrats, who defend existing social programs while advocating some new ones. But even today, few on the right totally oppose the welfare state, nor would those on the left any longer override the market economy with government planning. Partisan combat is far sharper than substantive differences.

Donald Trump's upset victory in the 2016 presidential election does not much change this picture. In ideological terms, Trump is an ill-defined moderate rather than a radical or a reactionary. His political appeal is more populist than ideological. That is, he represents protest by groups that have been marginalized economically, especially former industrial workers who saw their well-paying factory jobs lost to Asia. But his supporters seek to restore an imagined past of good jobs for workers like themselves, rather than to realize any ideal vision of either the right or the left.

Budget problems also overshadow ideological differences. Current spending on pensions for the elderly and, especially, on health care is far larger than anyone imagined when these programs were inaugurated. All by itself, that makes fundamental change unlikely. Funds are lacking for major new benefits, as the left might want; at the same time, so many interests are served by current social spending that major cutbacks are impolitic, as Republicans recently rediscovered when they tried and failed to repeal the Affordable Care Act.[9]

HOW SOCIAL PROBLEMS END HISTORY

So far, one could still view the issues in Western politics as structural, all about economics rather than human nature. But one reason behind the soaring costs of social programs is that dependency on government has vastly grown, and that, in turn, reflects a weakening of individualism within Western publics. Many Europeans and Americans have become less self-reliant. They are less willing and able to bear the burdens of freedom than they once were.

The same message emerges from growing social problems in Western countries. Families have weakened, with a sharp growth in births out of wedlock. Work levels have declined, as many adults have left jobs for welfare, unemployment, or disability benefits. Schools are more troubled, and crime has risen in the last several decades (although in the United States it has recently declined). Many disadvantaged youth are mired in dysfunctional lives in which they fail to get through school and then fail to work regularly, and in which they have children mainly without marriage. Despite much research, it has proven impossible to attribute these problems to the impersonal external conditions that political debate turned on before history ended.

Furthermore, poverty is most prevalent among racial and ethnic minorities with non-Western origins. In the United States, blacks, Hispanics (particularly Mexican-Americans and Puerto Ricans), and Native Americans are most likely to suffer from broken families, low work levels, high crime, and drug addiction. In Europe, the same problems are commonest among families of immigrants from South Asia or Islamic countries. These racial and ethnic differences, which are relatively new to Europe, now crosscut and complicate the older politics of class.

Some will say that history has not ended insofar as intellectual elites remain strongly left of center, still seeking a more egalitarian society at the hands of government. Recent alarms about growing inequality have momentarily strengthened their hand. Yet, even for them, the traditional leftist concerns for workers have largely been displaced by advocacy for racial and ethnic minorities, among whom social problems are far more salient. For those on the left, this "identity politics" is far stronger than the older appeals of class. Many workers who once voted liberal now vote conservative in order to oppose preferential treatment for minority groups. Even Trump's triumph in the 2016 election did not restore a class politics, because the whites who voted for him also asserted a cultural identity.[10]

POVERTY POLITICS

Since the 1960s, poverty has disrupted politics in America and in many European countries. Traditional Western politics, which largely focused on class, presumed an individualist psychology. It assumed personal competence—that ordinary people were at least able to advance their own self-interest, if not society's. They might be self-serving. Government might have to limit their demands or advance collective interests at their expense. But overall the public shouldered the burdens of a free life.

Especially, it was presumed that the less privileged, who needed protections and benefits from government, were employed. It was precisely their status as workers that gave them the moral standing to make demands on society. Generally, they worked harder than the affluent. Their leaders could rebuke the rich as parasites on the working class. Such was the war cry of the union organizers and labor politicians who largely built the welfare state starting in the late nineteenth century, although some more conservative leaders and parties also contributed. The "deserving" poor largely meant those who worked, while the "undeserving" were those who did not.

But as social problems and dependency increased, the "undeserving" became more salient. In America, poverty had traditionally been a local concern, but from the 1960s, it dominated national politics much of the time. Welfarism, crime, and nonwork became chronic issues. The poor now typically worked less, not more, than the rich. And the politics of poverty proved to be quite different from the traditional politics of class. Individual competence could no longer be presumed. Instead it became the chief issue, the great problem that government needed to address.

Earlier, the deservingness of the less privileged had driven history toward progressively more egalitarian regimes. But now the lifestyle of the disadvantaged became more dysfunctional, meaning contrary to the interests of the poor themselves. In the 1960s, even as the civil rights reforms were enacted, riots broke out in poor neighborhoods of major cities. The rioters, whose goals were unclear, caused great damage to their own neighborhoods. Around the same time, millions of poor families went on welfare, and work levels among them plummeted, even as the economy boomed and a black middle class arose. This was quite unlike the radical popular politics of the past. *The Economist* commented:

> [T]he most striking contrast between 18th-century England and 20th-century inner-city America (and, come to that, 20th-century inner-city England) concerns the adaptation of means to ends. Violence in the 18th century was almost never savage or anarchic. Looting and arson were rare. Loss of life, by the standards of the time, was minimal. The 18th-century mob usually had goals and directed its violence to the achievement of those goals. It was aware that too much force would provoke counterforce and end up being self-defeating.[11]

That is, the old politics had been individualist in spirit. It represented collective, not individual, action, but all the same it focused on achieving practical change in the outside world. The new poverty politics was simply anarchic, expressing not power but the lack of it.

Of course, the welfare state had recognized that sometimes the poor could not work for structural reasons, especially lack of jobs during economic downturns. If nonwork or other social problems could be explained in such terms, then the new poor might have seemed as "deserving" as the old. But in general, efforts to do that failed. Social barriers, such as lack of education, might explain why poor adults earned little if they worked, but not why they often failed to work at all when jobs were available. Instead, antipoverty programs had to focus on the poor themselves and attempt to change their way of life. In this sense, the focus of politics shifted from structure to culture.

As a result, after the 1960s, leftist politics faltered. Labor organizing fell off. Academia became more interested in minority groups than workers. Unemployment lost much of its political punch. Today, when the jobless rate rises, the sense of urgency to do something about it is far weaker than it was decades ago. The Great Recession of 2007 to 2010 was the worst downturn since the Depression, yet its politics were surprisingly conservative. The better-off public no longer identified strongly with the jobless, and even intellectuals gave them little attention.[12] On the other hand, conservative attempts to slash welfare were also stymied, by a widespread sense that the poor could not cope on their own. Both left and right had presumed an individualist psychology that was now obviously lacking.

Traditionally, Western politics have been most deeply about justice. The contest between competing class visions has been, fundamentally, about what citizens do or do not deserve. It has been a structural battle about the basic values and institutions of the society. It made little reference to the personal qualities or private lives of citizens, who again were assumed to be employed and functional. This was historical conflict in Hegel's sense.

With poverty, however, social policy turned to promoting individual competence, and issues of justice fell into the background. The aim was no longer to redistribute advantages but to heal broken families, get poor children through school, and above all raise work levels among poor adults. The issue was no longer what social values should be but why the poor so often violated values that everyone accepted. The focus was no longer on the good society but on good behavior. Again, politics shifted its focus from structure to culture. Amid such issues, politics moved solidly beyond history.

Recently, some Western countries have reduced their welfare caseloads. In addition, since the 1990s, crime has fallen sharply in the United States. For a time, that alleviated concerns about urban disorder, allowing issues of class and justice to return to prominence. That is one reason why the American welfare state grew, with expansions of health programming and greater subsidies for the working poor. In recent US elections, as mentioned, rising inequality in income and wealth has become an issue.[13] Still more recently, however, the issue of police violence against poor black men has once again pushed race and crime to the forefront—as before, easily eclipsing concerns about economic inequality.

As shown more fully in chapter 10, the new disorders are not due to race in the civil-rights sense of denied opportunity but rather to a defeated subculture with non-Western origins that struggles to maintain order in a free society. The only real solution is the fuller assimilation of minorities into the individualist culture of mainstream America. The black middle class, which has achieved assimilation, shows that this—not further claims on society—is the way forward.

FIGURE 3.3 **Divisions in Domestic Politics before History Ended**

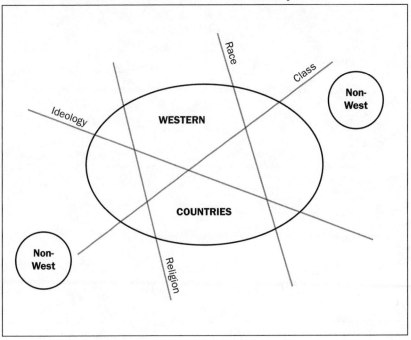

Figure 3.3 represents divisions in Western domestic politics as they were before poverty became a dominant issue in the 1960s. The major fissures were those of class and ideology, which were closely linked. American politics added the issues of race, region, religion, and others. All these crosscut mainstream society and became the stuff of electoral contests at all levels. Leaders paid little attention to the non-West, which had few contacts with rich countries.

Figure 3.4 represents domestic politics after history ended and poverty replaced class as the dominant division. Previously, the fissures lay in the heart of the society, because they were rooted in the economy, in which all classes had some function. Now, after history, these divisions are muted, and conflict has shifted toward the fringes of society. It chiefly concerns the poor, immigrants, racial minorities, and other groups that are marginal to the economy and where the major issues concern order, lifestyle, and, ultimately, culture. The immigration issue, which I treat in chapter 11, is especially virulent. On all these fronts—as well as in trade, globalization, and terrorism—threats come primarily from the non-West.

FIGURE 3.4 **Divisions in Domestic Politics after History Ended**

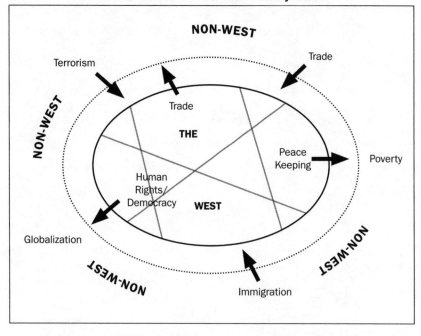

Before history ended, domestic politics largely concerned structural issues within Western countries, in which an individualist culture was taken for granted. Those decisions might greatly affect non-individualist groups, but the latter received little attention. The bright lights, so to speak, were all on the mainstream groups, while non-Westerners were largely spectators who sat in darkness. Since the end of history, however, the spectators are climbing into the bright lights themselves, and the great question is how an individualist society should relate to them, both at home and abroad.

In *Democracy in America*, published in 1835, Alexis de Tocqueville focused on how American society differed from the far more aristocratic society of France, his own country. His main focus was thus on structure and values. Having toured the United States extensively, he made prescient comments about blacks and also women, who are central to the new identity politics. But he paid much more attention to the frenetic "activity and bustle" he found in mainstream male society, where everyone strove to get ahead in an individualist manner.[14] That goal-oriented quality is precisely what is most lacking in disadvantaged society today. How to make the less favored *more* active is now far more salient politically than what equality should mean.

OPTIMISM VS. TRAGEDY

A related reason why history ended is that poverty ushered into American politics an unprecedented pessimism. As I explain further in the next chapter, Western culture is more optimistic than any other. It embodies a deep belief in the possibilities of both individual and collective action. That is one reason why, ever since the ancient Greeks, politics holds an exalted place in what Westerners think life is about.

One reason why Tocqueville's picture of early America is so charming is its upbeat character. He describes a society in which ordinary citizens busily make their way in the world and work together with others to accomplish joint tasks. This vision is a hopeful one, in which there seem to be no losers. Of course, both politics and the economy are competitive arenas, and not everyone wins in relative terms. But few Americans, in Tocqueville's view, seem to have been defeated or depressed. This positive atmosphere reflects the masterful temperament of Western individualism, the conviction that ordinary people can accomplish, alone or together, pretty much anything they set their minds to.

Some Western groups well-represented in America have in fact suffered great adversities. The Irish faced centuries of mistreatment by the English and mass starvation in Ireland in the 1840s. In Europe, Jews suffered anti-Semitism for centuries before being rounded up and exterminated by the millions in the Holocaust. Both groups initially were hostilely received in America, due largely to religious intolerance. But today neither one exhibits a strong sense of victimhood. These groups came from Europe, so they partake of the West's optimistic and activist temperament. The Irish got ahead by way of politics and municipal employment; the Jews, by way of education, business, and the professions.[15] Looking forward, as most Westerners do, they focus on achieving current goals and have largely left their adversities behind.

Optimism also makes for constructive politics, because most people look chiefly to themselves for progress rather than to outside forces. So the claims they make on government are limited. Those who fail to win elections or to gain public benefits can still maintain themselves until the next turn of the wheel. The political stakes are not total. In traditional American politics there can be defeats, but no tragedies—no loss that makes ordinary life impossible.

Poverty, however, shifted the political focus to groups among whom optimism faltered. The poor, by definition, have a limited capacity to take care of themselves, and racial minorities descend from a far more tragic history than the Europeans who initially formed America. Blacks came from Africa, a severe environment; in America, they then endured slavery and Jim Crow. Understandably, most disbelieved the image of innocence and progress in Tocqueville's *Democracy*. The race question became "the chief generator of doubt" about the nobility of the entire American enterprise. Hispanics, with their own history of adversity, brought that same tragic sense of limitation with them as they emigrated *en masse* to America.[16] Other groups favored by "identity politics" show the same pessimism.

These minority groups had faced more hardship than the European groups. But just as important, they came from the non-West, where most people feel far more vulnerable to their environment than able to control it (as discussed further in chapter 4). For both of these reasons, the claims of blacks and other minorities have greater force than any others. Race has a profundity that class cannot match. It exhibits a deeper powerlessness. Nothing government does, or fails to do, feels like a sufficient response. Nor do minorities' claims diminish with time. Perceived further offenses by society keep grievances fresh. Most blacks remain attached to these injuries as their principal identity. Most have not yet moved on to simply work to advance themselves, as other groups have. The burdens of necessity continue to dominate their lives, even in a free and prosperous society.

This impasse over race has undercut optimism about politics even among whites. The failure of many antipoverty programs has allowed conservative critics to cast doubt on the very efficacy of government, so different from the bullishness in Tocqueville's time. So again, history in Fukuyama's or Hegel's sense has ceased. Without confidence in government, further positive change in politics cannot be imagined. Our task, rather, is to restore that sense of individual mastery which, at America's founding, no one ever questioned. Only then might history resume.[17]

CONCLUSION

In chapter 2, I argued that an individualist society is the main reason why the West, and lately America, has led the world. Hitherto, world primacy was determined chiefly by struggles within the West. British and then American primacy emerged chiefly because these nations bested their rivals among other strong states, nearly all of them European. Yet due to the end of history, America's main challenges no longer come from within the West, with its individualist ethos. Rather, they come from nations and peoples from outside who reflect a far more cautious disposition. They come from cultures in which life usually centers on the burdens of necessity, not of freedom.

America is less directly threatened by cultural difference than it was during our historic struggles against fascism and Communism, but we are unsure how to respond. That is because the Western tradition has been surprisingly insular, despite its world influence. Within history, Western leaders and thinkers paid little attention to the particulars of non-Western cultures. They simply assumed that Western categories and goals, such as seeking to maximize wealth, power, and freedom, applied universally. Third World societies were seen simply as less developed than the West, and, over time, it was reasoned, they would "catch up." Non-Western cultures were too distant or too weak for Westerners to perceive how deeply different they really were. Only Japan, and recently China, seriously gained Western attention, chiefly as adversaries.

In domestic politics, America has long grappled with racial differences, but the idea that minorities are culturally distinct from the individualist mainstream has been suppressed as unconscionable. In Europe, cultural difference is even harder to conceive of, because until recent decades the influx of non-Western immigrants was small. On both sides of the Atlantic, elites have misinterpreted cultural difference as racial and for this reason suppressed all serious discussion of it.

The time for assuming sameness among all peoples is over. We must abandon the idea that our own Western tradition contains the answers to cultural difference. Internationally, most countries neither compete nor cooperate in the same ways Western states once did. In domestic affairs, both those on the right and those on the left seek to address social problems through expanding freedom, the former through smaller and the latter through larger government. Conservatives find inspiration in the thought of the American founders; liberals, in European welfare states.

But all these visions take individualism too much for granted. Americans look out on a world in which the tendency is toward order rather than freedom, in which states and peoples typically seek only to survive rather than thrive. Nor, in domestic affairs, have assumptions of sameness help us integrate groups from non-Western origins (both immigrants and many Americans of color). These groups need first to take freedom American-style to heart (as discussed in part 3). That is, they must become more individualist themselves, for only then can they be secure and successful in a free society.

Trump's victory signifies, if nothing else, that the myth of sameness no longer dominates politics. During his election campaign and since, he has spoken of the poor, minorities, immigrants, and failed states in scathing terms. His language is indefensible, yet his subtext is sound—the need to deal more realistically with our challenges. Our chief problems now arise from cultural difference rather than ideological conflict.[18]

The Western political tradition, in fact, is antiquated. It explicates the issues that have been resolved in history, but not the deepest struggles that confront us after history. To address them, we need a new intellectual tradition. It must focus on cultural difference, not sameness; on human nature, not freedom or equality. It will inevitably give greater place to values of order and authority, and a lesser place to freedom or autonomy, than intellectuals favor. To reinterpret individualism as a culture of obligation rather than freedom, as I do in this book, is already a step down that road.

Confusion is inevitable. In Victorian times, the poet Matthew Arnold described hearing waves sweep up and down an ocean beach in England (at that time, the world's strongest country). He wrote:

> The Sea of Faith
> Was once, too, at the full, and round earth's shore
> Lay like the folds of a bright girdle furled.
> But now I only hear
> Its melancholy, long, withdrawing roar,
> Retreating, to the breath
> Of the night-wind, down the vast edges drear
> And naked shingles of the world.[19]

Arnold here mourned the loss of the unquestioned religious faith that had anchored Western culture since its inception. Today, America remains a largely religious nation, yet our political traditions have suffered a comparable obsolescence. This has happened despite American primacy and even because of it. A new political tradition that truly addresses culture must be born.

Americans of European descent lead a world most of whose people are quite unlike them. Less favored peoples clamor for our attention. Many also seek to enter our society. On average, they *are* less fortunate than us, but they are also less forthright. They bear the burdens of necessity, not of freedom. How to get them to forget past adversity, to consult their own goals—the better to pursue them? That now is America's great challenge.

CHAPTER FOUR

CULTURAL DIFFERENCE

I t seems likely that an individualist culture chiefly drove the emergence of dominant wealth and power in Europe and, eventually, in America. We cannot prove that historical connection rigorously, but we can ask whether such a culture differentiates the West from the rest of the world today. There is ample evidence that it does, although there are important variations within both the West and the non-West. In this chapter, I set out that evidence and its implications.

Discussions of world power have seldom addressed culture. Before history ended, the dominant language of politics was class. After history, culture is just as central, but its role is unacknowledged. Our political principles teach us to define human nature abstractly, to assume that human beings everywhere have the same attributes and claim the same rights. Yet more than we admit, politics—both within and among nations—is overshadowed today by different ways of life. Groups and societies have different mind-sets, and as a result some are far more likely than others to become rich and powerful.

Karl Marx (1818–1883) wrote that class was the unacknowledged reality that prevented Western societies from seeing their politics honestly. The rich who controlled the economy were so dominant that a democratic politics became meaningless. Within history, politics tamed that reality somewhat. After history, however, cultural difference plays the same hidden role as class once did. To address difference seriously, we must break through the ideology of sameness and admit that humanity's ways of life differ.

The discussion below focuses on three attributes of Western culture that differentiate it clearly from the non-West: individualism, moralism, and theoretical thinking.[1] Western peoples tend to take initiative on their own, yet they are guided by internalized norms and tend to think in abstract terms. Such a mentality is symbolized by Prometheus, the Titan of Greek mythology who stole fire from heaven and gave it to humans (figure 4.1). He thus gave them godlike power (including science), which displeased the gods. Such a mentality generates restless innovation motivated by inner goals and values—even at the expense of other values. It is a recipe for mastery and achievement, but not for the contemplative, the aesthetic, the communal, or endurance amidst life's reverses.

Note that the contrasts I draw below between different groups and societies are all matters of degree. The West is not absolutely individualist, nor is the non-West not individualist at all; rather, the two differ by degree. In addition, the contrasts are based on research, but they are also generalizations, and therefore their usefulness is limited to broad discussions. We cannot assume that they apply to a group uniformly; many individuals from any group will differ from the norm. And, as I stress later, all cultures have value. The emphasis here is simply on average cultural differences. We must question the current ideology that tells us to ignore culture and insist that everyone is *the same*.[2]

INDIVIDUALISM VS. COLLECTIVISM

Individualism connotes the idea that people can and should guide their own lives. That is, they should pursue goals and values that they themselves have chosen. In contrast, collectivism connotes the idea that society must decide most matters for its members, who should defer to others. Typically, Westerners think of themselves first as individuals, whereas Asians conceive of themselves first as members of a group. That mental difference is supported by research.

In psychological studies, Richard Nisbett juxtaposed Western culture as seen in the United States to the non-Western cultures of Asia, particularly China. He found that Westerners typically see themselves

FIGURE 4.1 **Prometheus**

Heinrich Fieger, 1817

as willing and able to act autonomously, while East Asians see themselves as submerged amidst social pressures that largely tell them what to do. "For Westerners, it is the self who does the acting; for Easterners, action is something that is undertaken in concert with others or that is a consequence of the self operating in a field of forces."[3] As this implies, Westerners typically have more sense of agency. "Surveys show that Asians feel themselves to be in less control than their Western counterparts. And rather than attempting to control situations, they are likely to try to adjust to them."[4] This difference is deeply rooted. Western languages typically attribute events to individuals who cause them, while Eastern tongues adopt the passive voice, with events simply *happening to* people.[5]

The relatively passive and reactive manner of Eastern culture does not imply a lack of energy. Asians may still work hard. The difference from the West rather is that they are less autonomous. They usually follow outside direction—whether from tradition, from the society around them, or from public authorities.

Japan is an Asian society of legendary force, first as a military and then as an economic power. Yet individual Japanese cannot imagine themselves living independently of their myriad obligations to others.[6] By contrast, Westerners more often act for themselves. What is right or rational is not something to be imposed "from the outside," Hegel wrote, but rather something discovered by individuals seeking to realize their own will in the world.[7]

In Western usage, "collective" usually connotes a society with an ambitious government that seeks to control or displace the economic market, as socialists aspired to do before history ended. Here, rather, it connotes a popular psychology in which individuals identify themselves with groups and not as distinct individuals. In the West, even "collective" societies remained largely individualist at a psychological level. In the non-West, societies are generally collective-minded, whether government is large or small.

In the late 1960s and early '70s, the Dutch social psychologist Geert Hofstede surveyed IBM personnel in sixty-six countries to describe differences in their attitudes. As figure 4.2 shows, workers in Britain and the United States scored highest in individualism, which comprised desire for freedom, personal time, and challenge on the job. Canada also scored high, followed by other European countries and then Latin America, with Asia at the bottom.[8]

Hofstede found that workers in Anglo countries were also high in assertiveness, relatively averse to hierarchy, but highly tolerant of uncertainty. In Anglo culture, people largely make their own lives. They do not expect much direction from others, and they tolerate the constant uncertainty that such a society brings. In other cultures, people tend to

FIGURE 4.2 **Nations on Hofstede's Individualism**

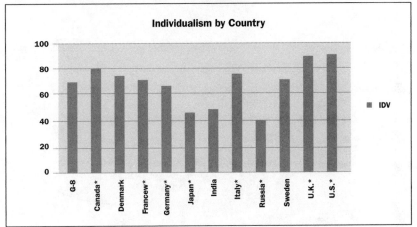

Source: Anthony J. Culpepper and J. Goosby Smith, "To Tell or Not to Tell: How Does Culture Impact Corporate Disclosure of Non-Financial Metrics?" *Graziadio Business Review* 10, no. 3 (2007), https://gbr.pepperdine.edu/2010/08/to-tell-or-not-to-tell. (IDV = individualism.)

be less assertive, more hierarchical, or more afraid of uncertainty. They, too, can be productive if led in ways consistent with their attitudes, yet their focus on goal attainment at the individual level is weaker.[9]

The World Values Surveys developed by Ronald Inglehart and his associates mapped countries in terms of whether they were "secular" versus "traditional" and whether they were oriented toward "survival" versus "self-expression," the latter term connoting individualism. The results (figure 4.3) show that the United States is only moderate in secularism, because it remains a highly religious society. But it is strongly individualist. Other Anglo countries and Protestant Europe rank similarly, while Catholic Europe, South Asia, and Latin America are less individualist, and Asia and Africa are the least individualist of all.[10]

These sources confirm that Westerners typically live life from the inside out. They begin with their own internal goals and values, then act to realize these in the world. In contrast, non-Westerners more often live from the outside in. They first seek to know what the outward environment expects of them, and then adjust to it. In the West, life is a project, led with some goal in mind, with one's eyes on the horizon. In the non-West, typically, life is rather something to be endured, to get through day by day. The focus is more on the immediate, less on distant goals.

FIGURE 4.3 **Culture Map of the World, 2010–2014**

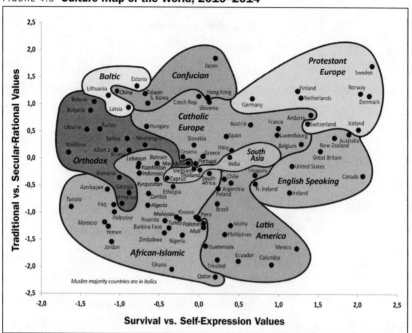

Source: World Values Survey Webpage, downloaded Dec. 12, 2018. http://www.worldvaluessurvey.org/WVSContents.jsp

The Western style begins in freedom but ends in obligation. One is free to choose personal goals, but to achieve them entails responsibilities beyond those borne in more closed societies. One must organize one's life around the mission. Conversely, the non-Western way begins in obligation but ends in freedom, or at least latitude: One must respect the outer expectations one faces, but one has no other responsibilities. One's goal is usually something less ambitious than what most Americans understand as "life, liberty, and the pursuit of happiness."

This difference helps explain why the West was so much more dynamic in history. Westerners have shouldered the burdens of freedom to undertake improvements that produced constant change, usually in an improving direction; in the non-West, most change has been forced from outside or above. Leaders in the West have followed change as much as guided it, while in the non-West leaders have usually controlled it, if they permitted it at all.

MORALISM VS. SITUATIONAL ETHICS

A second central feature of the Western mentality is moralism. In deciding whether something is right or wrong, Westerners typically consult principles that they internalized early in life. These they construe to be universal and timeless. Westerners thus may issue moral judgments entirely on their own authority, without reference to the society around them. In the non-West, by contrast, such judgments are typically more situational; that is, more dependent on social context. What is right or wrong usually hinges on what one's immediate associates—including family members, neighbors, and coworkers—expect.

Thus, in the West, moral structure is largely internal to the individual, and external enforcement by the legal system is secondary. In the non-West, morals are largely external, residing in the expectations of the society from which individuals take their cues; external enforcement is more important than in the West (although it may occur informally through the expectations of one's family or neighbors, rather than state action). A Western individual often can stand apart from his or her society and judge it. In the non-West, individuals are more likely to be judged by the society, which subsumes them.

Western moralism presumes that people can be held individually responsible for observing key values, rigidly defined. That presumes that they feel free enough to have choices. In the non-West, however, there is little sense of freedom or responsibility in this individualized sense. Rather, people orient to others' expectations and the conditions around them. Mostly, they do what they have to do. As long as society is stable, a moral order is still achieved, but it depends more on conformity to social conventions than on individual choice and commitment.

In the West, the psychic sanction behind good behavior is typically guilt, the sense that one has violated some universal moral norm. In China or Japan, it is mostly shame, the sense that one has lost face or standing in the eyes of one's peers.[11] Because Eastern ethics involves this relational element, it is never as absolute as Western ethics. Some have suggested that the norms that China derived from the teachings of Confucius (551–479 BC) are equivalent to Weber's Protestant ethic in motivating development.[12] But Asian ethics does not produce rigid rules; largely, people do what others expect them to do, not what any religious doctrine says. In the West, people must be persuaded to obey authority by reconciling it with the principles they hold. But in the East, people mostly obey simply because they are commanded. Moral direction is something that resides largely outside, not inside, the self.

These differences produce a conflict of moral styles. To Westerners, Asians may appear unprincipled—that is, lacking any inner commitment to moral truths. Devoid of an individualist psychology, they are unable to express inner obligation in a way that, to individualists, conveys conviction. In the West, that "uptight" quality is what certifies a person as responsible, meaning accountable for moral probity and hence trustworthy. But to Asians, that very quality may seem self-centered: it gives Westerners license to impose their will on others without considering them. The novelist Joseph Conrad (1857–1924), who had much experience in Asia, wrote that in the East, Westerners appear as "arbitrary and obstinate men who pursue inflexibly their incomprehensible purposes."[13]

Still, the West's moralistic style has brought huge benefits to government and politics. Objective standards embodied in laws have given the West a kind of moral authority that other cultures lack—what Conrad refers to as "the sovereign power enthroned in a fixed standard of conduct."[14] By internalizing objective standards, Westerners reconcile order and freedom as non-Westerners can seldom do. They are relatively free to act, which favors innovation and wealth for their society, yet most of them obey social norms without the need for a heavy-handed state. Since the non-West is more dependent on external enforcement, it more often must choose between freedom and order. A moralistic culture also promotes the rule of law in a way that situational ethics cannot. Most people in the West obey the law and pay taxes because they believe it is right and they would feel guilty if they did not. In the non-West, a more flexible and relational ethics offers only weak defense against private dealing at public expense, such as corruption.[15]

A moralistic ethic also motivates Western countries—preeminently the Anglo countries—to assume an ambitious responsibility for the world. Many Americans feel morally obliged to help less fortunate people and nations, and government often acts on that wish. The emerging Asian powers, China and India, feel far less driven in this way. They do not act by any definite moral code, and they are not trying to save the world. Their foreign policy is thus more practical than ours in the short term.[16] But they are also less trusted by other countries. America's moral earnestness generates soft power, as mentioned in chapter 1. Weaker countries—even countries that are not moralistic themselves—are reassured that the United States will seldom behave in narrowly self-interested ways. President Trump has moved to put "America first" on trade and other matters, but the hostile reaction of the establishment shows how unusual this is.

Citing Trump, some critics of American power scoff at the idea that our policy is animated by *any* moral concerns. However, this criticism reflects the presence, not the absence, of a moralistic culture. It comes most strongly from within the society, and it has the contradictory character of all moral criticism: it asserts shortcomings, which are often indisputable, but it also assumes that everyone involved takes the same moral values seriously. So, indirectly, moral criticism is a compliment to the American regime. Whereas against a nonmoralistic regime, criticism is often pointless—or risky.

Research shows that values differ somewhat between West and non-West. In the West, the leading political values are to care for the public and the most vulnerable people, to defend liberty against oppression, and to insist on fairness in government rather than to tolerate cheating or favoritism. In non-Western politics, however, greater attention goes to defending the loyal against betrayal, safeguarding authority against subversion, and protecting what is sacred against degradation. Those values reflect the more hierarchical and deferential character of most non-Western societies.[17]

But the major difference between Western and non-Western cultures is not one of values. It is one of how people live in order to realize their values. Americans largely agree about political principles like those just mentioned, but disagree about how to achieve them. Individualists typically take action to achieve personal goals in some way, while groups with non-Western origins more often defer to the environment and take less initiative.

At a psychological level, the great difference between Western and non-Western cultures is that Westerners simply have far more packed into their heads than non-Westerners. Their minds are full of purposes and ideals derived from their early lives. Their actions are largely driven by the desire to realize those goals and purposes in the world. For them, life is all about inner vision becoming outward reality. Non-Westerners also follow goals and values, but those norms reside far less in their minds than in the society around them. So, for them, life is mostly about going with the flow, about maintaining harmony with their surroundings.

THEORY VS. EXPERIENCE

A third central feature of Western culture is a penchant for abstract thinking.[18] For Westerners, typically, what is true or real does not always mean what they experience directly. Rather, what is "real," often, is something theoretical, beyond what is immediately apprehended. What is sensed is only an instance of something universal. The non-West, in contrast, is more empirical and less theoretical. What counts are the immediate facts of life, not what the mind dreams up about them. The "real" is the tangible and practical, and anything beyond that is useless or illusory.

In the West, ever since the classical Greeks, truth has usually been seen as an attribute of mind rather than sensation. Early philosophers and scientists attempted to determine profound truths by debating the fundamentals of reality—the hidden rules and order that governed the nature of everything one perceived. Just as individuals stood apart from the mass, the intellect stood apart from the senses. Plato's conviction that abstract "forms" were more real than their empirical expression in sensed reality is one example of this. Distinct objects and phenomena in the sensory world could be explained and related to other objects and phenomena in ways that were discoverable through reason. This book's frontispiece, showing people in a ferry searching for the sun, captures the way in which Westerners seek meanings that transcend their immediate reality.

In the non-West, the mind's power to penetrate reality is more doubted. In Asia, the world is seen as endlessly complex, beyond human comprehension. Objects and people are not distinct from one another but, rather, related by myriad ties. Individuals are not distinct from society but bound to it by many duties. The wisest people seek not to unravel this complexity but rather to sense it, to come to terms with it psychologically. There is no reality that we cannot see, hear, touch, taste, or smell. To search for any "deeper" truth is hubris.

While the West seeks mastery through reason, the East seeks harmony through sensibility, as the painting in figure 4.4 shows.

FIGURE 4.4 **Chinese Sage Contemplating Nature**

A belief in abstractions was key to the birth of science in the West. Scientists search out laws that state causes and relationships between phenomena in general terms. Scientific theories are not more true in any absolute sense than immediate sensory impressions, but they are more useful. They give humans the power to change reality by finding and manipulating its causes. A desire to demonstrate and exercise control over nature is one reason that human intellectual achievement in all fields has so often occurred in the West.[19] However, Western theories tend to go beyond the data at hand. They are forever vulnerable to disproof by some new theory that fits the evidence better. Thus, the edifice of Western culture is imposing but unstable.[20]

Abstraction also gives force to the other two leading features of the Western mind—individualism and moralism. Much of Western political theory struggles to reconcile the individual with political order: how can people remain true to themselves and yet enter into relationship with government, both obeying it and holding it accountable? Thinkers such as Thomas Hobbes (1588–1679), John Locke (1632–1704), and Jean-Jacques Rousseau (1712–1778), each in a different way, supposed that governmental authority is based on agreement by the citizens. In the non-West, however, there is little such theorizing. Chinese authors comment on Confucius or other classics, but any general conclusions are elusive. What emerges is closer to wisdom than theory, as with non-Western morals in general. Some Western scholars say that we should pay more attention to this type of thinking, but they say this in an assertive, Western style that is foreign to the very thinking they espouse. The non-West's own voice is much closer to silence.[21]

As for morals, Westerners typically have stated the principles that they believe should govern the world in general terms—going back, for example, to the Ten Commandments. Western ethical systems proclaim norms that should apply to everyone, everywhere. Immanuel Kant (1724–1804) famously defined as "moral" whatever we can will to be a universal law for all humankind. Whatever is mandatory must first be general.[22] Western philosophers presume that to state principles abstractly can be meaningful even if they are never perfectly realized in the world—the very enterprise that much of the non-West denies.

VARIATIONS

A general contrast between West and non-West is clear, yet internal differences are also important. Within the West northern, Protestant Europe and its offshoots—chiefly Britain and her settlements (especially the United States)—are the most strongly individualist countries, followed by Continental and southern Europe, then Eastern Europe and Russia. Meanwhile, East Asia, including China and Japan, exhibits the most strongly collectivist cultures. Hofstede's and Inglehart's results (figures 4.2 and 4.3) show much the same. There is a general tendency for worldviews to become less collectivist and more individualist as one moves from the eastern to the western end of Eurasia. As Nisbett remarked, echoing Hegel, "The Idea moves west."[23] That is, belief in a universal moral order that individuals can possess grows stronger as one travels westward from East Asia, to the Middle East, to Europe, and finally to North America.

The non-West is highly diverse, exhibiting strong religious and other differences. In fact, leaders and intellectuals from regions that are often critical of the United States, such as the Middle East and Latin America, frequently write and act in assertive ways that seem individualist. Their speech may sound as moralistic and abstract as any of their Western counterparts. One reason for this is that many people from the non-West have been educated in the West. That fact may seem to confirm the sameness assumption, the idea that everyone, in a globalizing world, is essentially the same. But typically, these leaders sit atop societies that are far less Westernized than they are. Overall, the Middle East and Latin America fall between those extremes in individualism and other Western features represented by the United States and collectivist East Asia.[24]

Figure 4.5 shows a diagram of world culture derived from business research. It contrasts the Western "linear-active" style, with its strong orientation to the task at hand, to the Asian "reactive" style, in which the priority is to maintain social harmony and defer to leaders. A third, "multi-active" style is found especially in Catholic Europe, Latin America, the Middle East, and Africa, in which the emphasis is on maintaining good relationships with people in the workplace (rather than on keeping to a schedule, giving honest feedback about performance, or getting things done). The multi-active regions are more expressive than Asia, which tends to be reticent emotionally, but both emphasize deference to others. The linear-active style is the one most focused on outward forms of achievement.[25]

Despite this diversity, however, the big picture still is "the West" versus "the Rest."[26] That is because individualism and other Western features are simply stronger in Europe and its offshoots (especially America) than anywhere else. Western countries all derive from Europe; no other region

FIGURE 4.5 **Cultural Types: The Lewis Model**

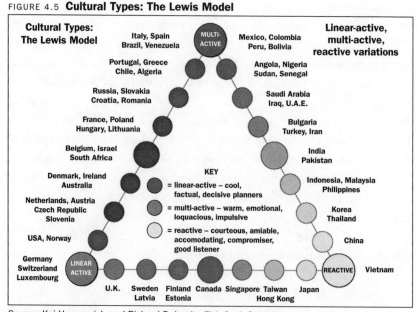

Source: Kai Hammerich and Richard D. Lewis, *Fish Can't See Water: How National Culture Can Make or Break Your Corporate Strategy* (Chichester, UK: Wiley, 2013), diagram 2.1.

ever displayed an individualist temperament on any wide scale, although there may be minorities in the non-West that do so.[27] And that mentality is strongly linked to the dominant wealth and power of Europe and the Anglo countries in recent times, as I show in later chapters. The great question (which I address in chapter 5) is *why* this masterful mind-set arose only in Europe.

Individualism, moralism, and abstract thinking also vary within the United States. The more strongly a group descends from Western Europe (especially Britain, Scandinavia, or Germany), the more strongly it shows these features, on average. In Nisbett's studies, white Protestants appear to be the most Western group, with Catholics, blacks, and Hispanics "shifted somewhat toward Eastern patterns."[28] Triandis found that Hispanics are "much more collectivist" than Americans from "Northern and Western European backgrounds."[29] Some scholars portray Italians as displaying rather non-Western ways of life, both in Italy and in the United States.[30] Blacks have non-Western tendencies because most of them descend from Africa, whose culture historically has been strongly collectivist. Slavery and Jim Crow, in addition, promoted in American blacks a similarly passive, reactive mind-set not oriented to practical achievement.[31] But as I note later, a black middle class—with a more individualist, achieving style—has also emerged. These contrasts shed useful light on the causes of the poverty problem, as chapter 10 shows.

A MASTERFUL MENTALITY

Together, Western attributes all promote mastery of the outside world. Individualism leads people to pursue their own inner goals, while moralism motivates them to find shortcomings in the world as it is, and theoretical reasoning gives them mental tools to improve things. The theme is confidence and control. This Promethean mind-set appeared very early in European history because, as Nisbett remarks, "Europe had created a new sort of person—one who conceived of individuals as separate from the larger community and thought in terms imbued with freedom."[32]

As early as the fourth century BC, scholars noted differences between Europeans and Asians. Aristotle wrote that Europeans were "full of spirit" and hence difficult to rule, while Asians had "both brains and skill" but were "deficient in spirit," which was why they had remained "subjects and slaves." In addition, Europeans were "deficient in skill and intelligence" and showed "no political development" and "no capacity for governing others."[33] Those latter features clearly changed after Aristotle's time, as Europe became the exemplar of strong government and imperialism. Asian cultures did not, conversely, become more individualist (although, as I note below, there has recently been movement in that direction).

This ambitious outlook has allowed the West to embrace radical and continuous change as almost no other culture has done. The very notion that change and improvement were possible and desirable was, perhaps, the most revolutionary idea to come out of Europe. By the end of the Middle Ages, the world seemed "less mysterious" and "less tragic" than it had seemed before. With the Enlightenment, Europe gained "a conviction of intellectual power." Humanity need not resign itself to timeless hardship, because now "indefinite improvement was possible."[34]

In psychological studies, David McClelland defined the "will to achieve" as the desire to excel by some external standard. His results showed that a society's will to achieve is not clearly associated with development at a certain point in time, but it is linked with development over time. Societies with a stronger drive for achievement tend to show more economic growth, and this is true in both the West and the non-West. Entrepreneurs, people willing to take risks, are crucial agents of change. Both Britain and the United States were lifted toward primacy by periods of passion for progress.[35]

Outside the West, in contrast, people are typically more cautious. Fukuyama wrote of *thymos,* or the will to assert oneself, as a universal human trait,[36] but it does not appear to be so. People in poor countries do rebel against unjust rule, yet they less often undertake risky ventures on their own than people do in the West. It is not enough to have opportunity—one must also be motivated to take advantage of it. To do that takes a "character structure" that is more common in the West.[37]

All this research implies that the world is divided between those who are *responsible* for things and those who are *responsive* to them. Largely, the former create conditions and structures to which the latter then adapt. There are, of course, many grades and degrees between these extremes. Every society—indeed, every individual—is assertive in some situations and reactive in other ones. But the distribution of the two extremes around the world is very uneven. Most individualists apparently live, and have always lived, in the West. And a significant number of the most ambitious people have been Americans, largely because the country was settled mostly from Europe, especially Britain. That is the core reason why the United States became the world's dominant country, as perceptive observers predicted even two centuries ago.

Of course, several Asian countries have embraced change quite radically since the nineteenth century. That move, however, came at the initiative of leaders, not ordinary people. For collective achievement, the very caution of non-Western culture may be an asset. The capacity of millions to take orders and sacrifice for the nation empowered Japan (and its later Asian followers) to make prodigious advances. Whether a collective approach can similarly challenge the West in future, however, is unclear, because it does confine problem-solving largely to the top of society.

Figure 4.6 is a map of world cultural differences based on surveys assembled by Shalom Schwartz. The chief dimensions contrast countries where people feel autonomous versus embedded in the society, where societies are egalitarian versus hierarchical, and where people seek mastery

FIGURE 4.6 **Map of World Cultural Differences**

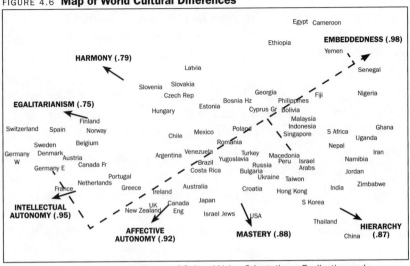

Source: Shalom H. Schwartz, "A Theory of Cultural Value Orientations: Explication and Applications," *Comparative Sociology* 5, nos. 2–3 (May 2006): 137–82. (figure 4 shown)

over their environment versus harmony. The results show (as expected) that the West stresses autonomy, while non-Western societies are more embedded or collective-minded. China is strongly hierarchical, while the United States orients more to mastery than any other country.

A DEMOCRATIC SOCIETY

An assertive, confident style tends to characterize Western individuals, and it can also produce a democratic society. Democracy, of course, means that ordinary people have political rights and that the government is accountable to them. There can be non-Western democracies, but in the West there is much less deference to other people in general than in the non-West. Typically, Westerners already know who they are and what they want before they enter into any interaction with others; so, to cooperate with others, they must first agree about how everyone's purposes will be served. Hence the constant bargaining that goes on in the marketplace and also in politics in Western countries. Only authorities with clear legitimacy based on prior consent can order anyone around. Non-Westerners defer to authority figures far more. In politics outside the West, there may be adjustment among people, but it is usually far less overt, because individuals are less distinct from the mass. So people may be ordered around without their consent, in a manner surprising to Westerners.

An individualist society may also become democratic in the wider sense that it refuses to accept a settled upper class. All of life is oriented to the mass rather than the elite. Above all, a individualist society is competitive, as people vie to reach their own goals and to achieve success in a contest against others seeking the same. Such a society generates uncommon energy, which in turn promotes wealth, power, and influence abroad. Thucydides (d. 401 BC) first described such a society in Athens during the Peloponnesian War. Athenians of the time were known throughout Greece for ambitious risk-taking. They always sought out chances to expand their city's wealth and power or simply to make money. They were "addicted to innovation" and "adventurous beyond their power"; "daring spirits" to whom "an enterprise unattempted was always looked upon as a success sacrificed."[38] This was the vibrant society that Pericles (c. 495–429 BC) lauded as the "school of Hellas [Greece]." He claimed that it could celebrate the individual and at the same time show the military prowess needed to defeat its rival Sparta. The Athenians lost the war—chiefly because, in attempting to conquer Sicily, they came up against Syracuse, which was a democratic society much like their own.[39]

In subsequent European history, most societies were not so democratic, because they were more divided by class, even though they were dynamic. During Europe's brief moments of revolution, however, visions of a more ambitious individualism erupted. In England, the Civil War in the 1640s led briefly to a Commonwealth, in which religious visionaries flourished. We remember the Levelers because they advocated expanded *rights*—even democracy—for the lowborn. But they also claimed greater *obligations*: ordinary people were supposed to work out their own relationship with God, that supreme determinant of their salvation. The Quakers and their ilk gloried in the abolition of all higher religious authorities because "[w]hat was left was freedom—the precious freedom for them to find their own way."[40] It was formidable individualists like these who were, at the same time, leading the early settlement of North America, where their descendants would fight for American freedom.

In European politics, from the eighteenth century onward, democratic politics often implied class solidarity. Middle-class groups allied with each other to oppose the upper class, as working-class groups did later to oppose the capitalist class. In the United States—as in Athens—however, ordinary people were dominant enough politically that they competed mostly against one another. Like Thucydides' Athenians, early Americans "were in a permanent state of restlessness, driven ever forward and onward by the search for opportunity."[41] Individuals vied for success, largely on their own, in every line of work, including politics. The goal was not just wealth but personal distinction of the sort that elites had formerly sought through war. Thus, under democracy, an open society generated a popular kind of aristocracy.

In early America, most famously, Alexis de Tocqueville described the most democratic society the world had ever seen. An unfree country is "calm and immobile," Tocqueville wrote, but in individualist America "all is activity and bustle." Throughout the society, there was "a restless activity, superabundant force, and energy never found elsewhere." More traditional societies might regard "a restless spirit, immoderate desire for wealth, and an extreme love of independence as great social dangers. But precisely those things assure a long and peaceful future for the American republics."[42] Democracy means more than popular government—it is a whole way of life, in which individuals assert themselves for their own reasons, seek advancement, and accept constant rivalry with others. Recent scholars confirm that early America did display such attitudes and they have remained central to the culture.[43]

NEGLECTED VALUES

Despite all these virtues, however, we should not regard the Western mentality as superior to that of the non-West in any general sense. The emphasis in Western culture is strongly on individual and societal mastery of the outside world—so strongly that other values are slighted. One of these is simply the contemplation of reality for its own sake. As figure 4.4 suggests, that emphasis is strong in Asian culture. It also appears in many religious traditions, including Christianity. In medieval Europe, monasteries were centers of culture. Contemporary Western society, however, seeks principally to understand and manipulate reality in order to attain wealth and power.

The West is also relatively weaker in aesthetic sensibility than the non-West. There is, of course, great art in the West, but there is little general sense that to experience beauty in one's everyday surroundings is an important goal. In the non-West, especially in poorer countries, music and the other arts are more central to people's lives. Life is more colorful than in the West, both literally and figuratively. In contrast, McClelland remarks that people who are high achievers typically favor somber colors. They are not ascetics who oppose material rewards, but they seek satisfaction through practical achievements, not through the senses.[44]

Similarly, the West has a relatively weak sense of community. It does have a capacity for collective effort; a moralistic culture, in fact, generates stronger government than the non-West, including social programs for the needy, as I note further below. But that capacity is still limited. Advocates for new programs must appeal to the moral principles that individuals have internalized, and they do not always succeed. In the non-West, community is more deeply rooted, because society is less individualist in the first place. People see themselves as less distinct from the mass. This more communal society is closer to the tribal form that human social organization first took. By becoming more open and individualized, the West has attained much greater wealth, power, and security, at the risk of greater isolation and meaninglessness for many people.[45]

Most of all, the West's heavy emphasis on mastery leaves it less able to cope with tragedy—the things that cannot be mastered. In Mexican culture, a leading value is *aguante*, or stoic endurance in the face of adversity.[46] The West has no similar value, perhaps because its history has been relatively untroubled. Since its origin in Roman times, Europe has endured much conflict but only brief periods when tragedy seemed to extinguish all hope—the Black Death in the fourteenth century, the Thirty Years War in the seventeenth century, and World War I in the early twentieth century. These were all terrible trials, but none lasted long enough to challenge the underlying optimism of the culture. So, hope rebounded. In American history, the only tragic event for the *white* population was the Civil War, in which more than 600,000 people died. The country still moved on to the triumphs of its later history. As Ross Douthat remarked, "In America we have education for success, but no education for suffering."[47]

For minorities, of course, American history was less fortunate. While most black Americans have realized higher income and status since the civil rights era, they have suffered sudden episodes of racist violence. Black churches in the South are still periodically bombed. Black parishioners of course protest, but they also accept the tragedy and forgive their attackers. At this magnanimity, other Americans can only marvel. That astounding capacity comes, in part, from blacks' historic experience of powerlessness: for centuries, they struggled with forces they could not control, yet they still regard life as meaningful.[48] It is one example of the huge and distinctive contributions that blacks have made to American culture, as I note later.

The value of these more accepting virtues helps explain why the United States, historically, has gained much from immigration. The presence of people with origins in the non-West has vastly strengthened many dimensions of American culture. That has greatly increased American soft power. But greater limits are needed to reconcile the flow of immigrants with maintaining an individualist mainstream culture, as I discuss in chapter 11.

WHY IT MATTERS

One might suppose that cultural difference would matter little for American power or primacy. Following the sameness assumption, most scholars believe, along with Ian Morris, that humanity is "much the same" everywhere, so differences in culture have little to do with development around the globe. Perhaps cultural differences are themselves the result of *structural* differences between countries and have no independent force.[49] That is also what we would *like* to believe, given the great sensitivity of any discussion of group differences.

But in light of the research above, sameness cannot be defended. There simply are large differences in ways of life between the United States and most other countries, as well as between Western and non-Western countries in general. These go far to explain why certain countries are rich and powerful while others are not. Largely, the most individualist countries are the most developed, although some collectivist Asian countries have made large recent gains. Similar contrasts prevail within the United States, between groups with European and those with non-Western origins.

Among nations, the most Westernized will likely remain the most assertive, as that is the bent of their worldview. Non-Western countries will likely remain more cautious and reactive—even the largest, China and India, whose mere size might seem to dictate their dominance. The

Anglo nations probably have already faced the greatest external threats in their history—from Germany and Russia, which were rival Western countries. Most likely, they will need no further "finest hours" in any military sense. Today, with history ended, their chief challenges are no longer to face down enemies like themselves but to help countries that are much weaker and poorer.

Within the West, cultural difference also matters. When non-Western peoples come to the West, "freedom" is simply given to them as a gift. So our rhetoric suggests. America and Europe do offer newcomers wealth, security, and opportunity undreamt of in most poor countries. But Western societies also expect individualized effort to compete for and claim these opportunities, a demand that newcomers have seldom faced in their country of origin. In addition, individuals must observe key civilities largely on their own, without the strong external authority typical of the non-West. These burdens of freedom have proven too much for many non-Western Americans. Not only do they not (on average) seize opportunity with the avidity that earlier European immigrants displayed, but also they are more likely to suffer from severe social problems. Cultural difference explains why these difficulties are so much more serious for today's immigrants, who are mostly non-Western, than those of a century ago, who mostly came from Europe (see chapter 11).

Some writers may admit that cultural differences exist between or within societies but attribute them entirely to structural causes. Perhaps non-Western nations or groups are less assertive than Europeans because they have received less opportunity, not because they are really different in temperament. But that belies the clear fact that cultural differences run very deep, long predating the recent centuries when equal opportunity became a widely held value, let alone a policy. Mostly, values have created structure, rather than the other way around. (I address this issue more fully in the next chapter.)

Traditionally in Western countries, the European population was individualist but unequal, generating the demands for democratic change that dominated Western political history. After history, the biggest division is cultural rather than economic, between those able and those unable to shoulder the burdens of freedom. Social problems now eclipse inequality. The great challenge is no longer to make individualists more equal but to create more individuals and families able to live a free life.

IS THIS RACIST?

My central argument is that cultural difference explains both America's power and its deepest problems. Individualism was the making of the United States, but groups and nations without that temperament now challenge us. But is to speak of cultural difference racist after all? Racism connotes the belief that some social groups are superior to others in a general sense and that the differences between groups are inherent and immutable. White Americans often voiced such views about blacks before the civil rights era (though few will admit to holding them today).[50] White Europeans also condescended to the nonwhites they ruled over in the non-West before the dissolution of their empires after World War II.

Although today we may value all cultures, Western culture still dominates the richest part of the world and especially academe. It thus commands prestige. Students from every group and country stream to American universities, lauded as the best in the world, hoping to claim that cachet. Especially appealing are the young illegal immigrants, brought here as children, whom President Obama allowed to study and work here provisionally, under Deferred Action for Childhood Arrivals (DACA). Even to suggest that these earnest suppliants are different from individualist Americans in any deep-seated way can easily seem outrageous.

Is talk of cultural differences only code words for indelible racial differences?[51] Racial groups differ in intelligence as measured by IQ tests, and some scholars believe that those differences explain which groups do well or poorly in economic terms.[52] But it is unclear how far differences in IQ arise from differences in physical makeup as opposed to the conditions in which people are raised. I take no position on that issue here. It is enough that genetic differences among the races appear trivial.[53] More important, such differences, even if clear, affect the outcomes of people's lives far less than do cultural differences in ways of life. The poorest, weakest societies and groups are those where life is simply about survival, not about getting ahead. Individual differences in personal capacity are far less important.

In my usage, culture means only what groups and societies think life is and should be about, nothing more. The link between race and Western or non-Western *culture*, in this sense, is loose at best. A Western temperament is associated with whites only because Europe was almost entirely white until recent immigration. Jews suffered discrimination in Europe for centuries and were persecuted by the Nazis. But otherwise race played little role in European history until immigration. McClelland found that the achieving mentality, although strongly associated with development in history, is today not clearly associated with either race or environment. Lawrence Harrison concluded bluntly, "Culture does matter. Race doesn't,"[54] and I agree.

As noted, racial and ethnic groups within the United States vary on measures of individualism, yet many people of all groups differ from the averages. Many with non-Western backgrounds have become individualist simply because that has long been the dominant American culture. The black middle class is a signal case of this. Although group averages differ, elites from all groups tend to be strongly individualist and moralistic, because that is the temperament that our society promotes at the top.[55] These realities argue against any idea of inherent racial or ethnic difference.

Culture, in my usage, is not indelible but the result of socialization, mostly early in life. People of any race or ethnicity can assume any worldview, depending on their formative experience. There may also be cultural change over time. Such change is typically slow, occurring over generations rather than single lives, but that it occurs at all flouts the idea that culture is rooted in any physical characteristic of a people. Such change is occurring—in opposite directions—in the United States and China, as I show in later chapters.

In light of research on world cultures, it seems tragic that race in America ever was defined in terms of physical difference, especially skin color. To present minorities that way makes racial or ethnic discrimination seem far more irrational and intractable than it really is. Far more plausibly, the main basis of distrust between whites and nonwhites has been *culture* rather than race in any physical sense—the fact that minorities did not display the individualist temperament of the rest of America. Integration requires that they become more individualist themselves, but it will take time. That minorities can accomplish this is, of course, far clearer today than it was centuries ago. Our founders never imagined that racial integration could succeed. Today we know that it can. The black middle class shows everyone the way forward.

IS THIS ORIENTALIST?

A stronger argument can be made that to differentiate Western from non-Western culture is "Orientalist." I refer to the criticism that Edward Said (1935–2003) made of Western writing about the Near East. Said charged that scholars—even recent ones who were careful to avoid obvious racism—portrayed the Orient as unchanging, backward, and inferior to the West. He advocated a more sensitive portrayal that conveyed how the non-West experienced life from the inside. Any culture, he wrote, should show such empathy toward another.[56]

"Cultural difference," as I use the term, does not typify the non-West as inferior to the West in any general sense. Rather, different ways of life have different strengths and weaknesses. At issue here is merely that the non-West has not produced—except perhaps recently, in Asia—wealth and power comparable to the West's, and cultural difference is a key reason. Said himself granted that much of the West's dominance of the non-West originated in its aggressive intellect, its tendency to reduce reality to a theory. To Said, as to Foucault, Western regimes dominate the world with mental frames or "disciplines" that they impose on societies—both their own and others. In the past, these imputations that the Orient was in some way different, or backward, were enough to justify Western control.[57]

This is more plausible than racism. Western ascendancy does indeed begin with intellect. Hegel believed that "the European mind...subdues the outer world to its ends with an energy which has ensured for it the mastery of the world."[58] A confident mentality initially seeks understanding, possibly progressing to control and change. The "sovereign Western consciousness," Said admitted, does assert "sheer egoistic powers" over all that it surveys.[59] Such a process did justify much of Western colonialism. European governments had their own ideas of correct rule, including religious freedom and intolerance for corruption. Countries in Africa and Asia often violated these norms in their dealings with Western merchants or missionaries. So the Europeans were gradually drawn into controlling and often exploiting those countries.[60]

The countries that the West reasons about have little *intellectual* defense, because their own cultures are so much less theoretical. They must rely on defenders like Said—who, though Palestinian by birth, was educated and employed in the West. He criticized academe from a tenured chair high in the American academic establishment, at Columbia University. To allow him that freedom is something that few if any non-Western countries could do. This is one example of how the West's moralism works to eventually counter the excesses of its own power.

Said became a Westerner in order to defend the non-West. He had to fight fire with fire. But the world he defended is radically unlike him—it is much more passive, much less moralistic. That makes answering the West's images of the non-West difficult, because the very enterprise shows how plausible those images are. The gulf in power between the West and "the rest" ultimately reflects an inward difference. A masterful culture must inevitably dominate a culture that has other priorities.

CONCLUSION

Those who make American public policy, and the experts who study it, are all individualists of the most inner-driven kind. Our society expects that of leaders. But they too readily assume that the people about whom they reason are like themselves. They project their rationalist and moralistic temperament onto foreign leaders and intellectuals as well as disadvantaged groups of Americans. Unconsciously, they award those others sameness with themselves. That is what their egalitarian moral commitments tell them to do. But for non-Western leaders and groups, sameness probably cannot be assumed. Those people probably do not calculate and moralize as Westerners do; more likely, they adapt and conform. Any political thinking that crosses the cultural divide must now assume deep difference. That is why history has ended.

To bridge that divide is difficult exactly because one side is so much more assertive than the other. Experts debate about non-Western issues and problems; meanwhile, those about whom they reason remain largely silent, mere spectators of a discourse that is largely foreign to them. How can they be heard in a world so different from their origins? For any individualist to speak for them, even sympathetically, is already to betray that silence. In America, in any case, the way forward for those with non-Western backgrounds must be for them to become individualists themselves. In a free country, only shouldering the burdens of freedom can finally make them free.

CHAPTER FIVE

THE ORIGINS OF DIFFERENCE

The great question raised by the last chapter is why the individualist personality distinctive to the West arose in Europe and essentially nowhere else. How does one explain the eruption of "a new kind of man—rational, ordered, diligent, productive"?[1] To account for the more collectivist mentality in the rest of the world is much easier: as shown in chapter 2, non-Western societies mostly took their characteristic shape early and did not change much thereafter, until pressured by the West in recent times. But to explain Western culture, one must explain a clear departure from the human norm.

The usual academic view is that people will live an individualist life only if there is opportunity. The world they face must offer them "inclusive institutions" that give ordinary people fair chances to "make it." Only then will individuals, or whole societies, organize their lives around achievement. But in most of the world, elites restrict opportunity lest it produce social change and threaten their power.[2] This view, that opportunity shapes social psychology, has some basis in Asia (as I show later), where growing wealth has led some of the elite to seek greater freedom.

But in the West, opportunity did not come before individualism. Rather, an assertive culture preceded and produced opportunity. An impatient, improving society generated growing wealth, which in turn generated new avenues of advancement for the less privileged. Far from stopping development, rulers supported it, or else they were brushed aside. The society's own principles forced regimes to serve interests broader than their own. Government then provided the conditions, including legal fairness and accessible education, that allowed the less favored to compete even more effectively. This happened long before any society produced wealth or opportunity on the scale we know today. Opportunity does not automatically produce optimizing attitudes. Rather, such attitudes make people create or seek out opportunity.[3]

Admittedly, such a society need not be inclusive. It need not be good news for everyone. The reason that some groups or nations fail to prosper under equal opportunity is not primarily that fairness has been denied to them. Rather, it is that an individualist society makes its own heavy demands. It takes an individualist psychology for granted. That is, it presumes that people are inwardly organized to compete and achieve—that they bear the burdens of freedom rather than necessity. That lifestyle is not native to groups or nations from the non-West, and adjusting to it is the main challenge they face today.

So, like much else that explains American primacy, the origins of individualism are not recent but lie in the premodern past. We must identify the early, formative influences that caused Europeans to adopt their distinctive way of life. The discussion below begins with material conditions but moves quickly on to demography, the classical world, and religion. Overall, an individualist culture seems to have arisen in Europe mostly because of the ambitious temperament of the people who settled there. That attitude, already clear in classical times, was later shaped by a religious tradition that promoted both personal initiative and probity. Those currents became strongest in the Anglo countries. And so American culture came to be founded by perhaps the strongest individualists the world has ever known.

MOVING WESTWARD

As noted in chapter 4, a basic fact about world cultures today is that they become less collectivist and more individualist as one moves westward from East Asia to Europe. The same is true over history. The regions in which civilizations first arose, such as China, India, and the Middle East, are today among the most collectivist, whereas the individualism that marks Europe and its offshoots arose much later.

In his *Philosophy of History*, from the 1820s, Hegel conceived of history as the gradual growth of conscience: what he variously called the "Spirit," "Freedom," or "Reason" appeared in the Western mind through "a severe and lengthened process of culture."[4] According to Hegel, Chinese society had little sense of moral judgment, because rulers simply imposed their will and the people complied with it, much as they would with the laws of nature. The emperor was to be obeyed in the same sense as one expects a dropped stone to fall. In India, similarly, morals rested on caste, a rigid system of unequal status that was justified as natural; morals, then, were seen as grounded in nature rather than in any inner judgment. Only in Persian culture did morals begin to be a feature of the mind rather than of some outward condition.[5]

True individuality first appeared in classical Greece. The Greeks claimed "a subjective independent Freedom, in which the individual finds himself in a position to bring everything to the test of his own conscience." That freedom, however, expressed itself indirectly—through great art—rather than in spiritual doctrines of right and wrong. Then, during the Roman Empire, Christianity was born; its believers claimed a new freedom to judge for themselves, even against the pitiless authority of the state. Now, for the first time, individuals could fully express the Spirit, and "infinite inward liberty" became possible.[6]

That fundamental conviction was carried to early Europe by the church, where it struggled for centuries to realize itself in the institutions of church and state. To Hegel, the Reformation was essential to reaffirm the primacy of individual conscience. He concluded that the German state of his own time had come to embody the Spirit, so that individuals must now obey the state (a conclusion that modern readers resist, in light of Nazism). His more fundamental argument, however, was that outer authority and inward conscience must finally align, and that they should do so is the goal of history. Such indeed is the ambition of Western moralism.[7]

After Hegel's time, the Spirit continued to migrate westward. Due to economic and social modernization, Europeans gave up their loyalties to the past (or to particular regions or groups) more readily than did the rest of the world. Europeans were now held accountable simply as individuals, for their own honesty and performance, as the capitalist economy required.[8] Many of them abandoned old contexts to seize new opportunities. Over centuries, the individualist spirit of the Reformation spread through Western culture, to the point where individual authenticity became more valued than any traditional authority. The Anglo countries—first Britain, then America—came to lead that movement. More fearlessly than any others, they urged individuals to pursue their personal convictions, to stand alone even at the edge of history.[9]

ECONOMIC AND SOCIAL CONDITIONS

But why did this drive toward individualism appear distinctively in Europe and not elsewhere? Could economic and social conditions explain it? Richard Nisbett suggested that ancient Greece became more individualist than China because Greek society was more complex. In Greece, he argued, people were more aware of social and economic differences, and there was more intellectual conflict. In China, by contrast, society became collectivist because social divisions were few, the economy demanded strong government, and Confucian philosophy emphasized harmony over difference. So people in Greece grew accustomed to standing apart from their society, whereas in Asia they accepted subordination to it.[10]

In the mid-twentieth century, Karl Wittfogel argued famously that "oriental despotism" arose in much of the world because agriculture depended on irrigation, which needed to be organized by government. In these "hydraulic" societies, the regime became absolute, without the limits on power that sheltered freedom in Europe. Thus, there is nothing universal or inevitable about the relatively free pattern of development seen in the West.[11] (A recent related argument is that people in the northern, wheat-growing regions of China are more individualistic than those in the more southern, rice-growing regions, because the cultivation of wheat requires less coordination.)[12] But Wittfogel admitted that some authoritarian countries, such as Russia, were not strongly dependent on irrigation. So despotism seems, in the end, to reflect an authoritarian culture rather than anything about the physical environment.

A more recent argument, following the academic presumption that opportunity breeds individualism, is that individualism is the product of affluence. As societies become more developed in economic and social terms, so the possibilities for human life expand. That strengthens "self-expression values" in the culture, causing people to think and act more for themselves and to defer less to authority. That change, in turn, drives the expansion of human rights and democracy. Something like that does seem to be happening today in Asia (see chapter 12).[13] But as an account of Western development, this theory is implausible. Individualism in Europe still clearly predates wealth and opportunity in any modern sense. To defend the theory, one has to believe that economic conditions even very early in Europe were rich enough to light the individualist fire, and that is unlikely.[14]

Thus, material or social conditions appear to say little about the origins of an individualist culture. However, they do influence how a society that has become individualist generates power (as shown in chapter 6).

DEMOGRAPHY

The best single explanation of individualism may be simply that this was the temperament of Europeans. Ricardo Duchesne argued that Europe's restless style, "charged with tension, always striving to transcend itself," goes back to Indo-European peoples who took over the continent in waves beginning around 4,000 BC. They did so in several stages, ending with the Germanic invasions that toppled the Roman empire in the west and recast the populations of Europe. These militant tribes were led by aristocrats who constantly vied for rank and distinction. Kings ruled, but they were accountable to their peers, who resisted subordination. This jousting for prominence promoted an assertive style, which persists to this day, across the whole society. Thus, ironically, aristocracy spawned an individualist culture that would eventually serve democratic ends.[15]

The invasions transformed a backward region into a world force. "The spread of these warrior cultures brought a great revolution in European life," because "[i]n place of peaceable villagers and remote hunters and fishers, Europe was now dominated by warlike barbarians.... [T]he warrior ethos of the Bronze Age gave European society a distinctive and enduring bias. Europeans came to be warlike, valuing individual prowess more highly than any other civilized people (save only the Japanese)."[16] Thus began a long quest for world domination.

> The expansionist aggression of the West is an inescapable expression of its roots in aristocratic men who are free and therefore headstrong and ambitious, sure of themselves, easily offended, and unwilling to accept quiet subservience.[17]

There was, of course, aristocratic rivalry for leadership in other roughly contemporaneous societies, such as the natives of North America, the Aztecs in South America, and the Zulu kingdom in Africa.[18] But these societies were less thoroughly aristocratic, and they arose outside the global centers of wealth and power. There were also later invasions of Europe by Asian groups such as the Huns and the Mongols, but they were more collective-minded and their impact was transient. Only in the West did a wide individualist culture take root and endure.[19] After the fall of Rome, an aristocratic style persisted in Europe for centuries, as feudalism continued to hold rulers accountable to their vassals.[20]

A further demographic influence on European development was slower population growth than in Asia. China struggled for centuries to expand its food supply fast enough to feed a growing population, but such pressures were weaker in Europe. One reason was that Europe tapped resources from the New World that were unavailable in Asia, as I note further below. Europeans consequently had a richer diet, and this was, according to Eric Jones, one of the forces behind the more assertive individualism of the West and its greater resistance to autocratic rule.[21] Only when the British population soared during the Industrial Revolution, leading to famine in Ireland, did Thomas Malthus write that population growth might forever outpace rising incomes.[22] But then the runaway wealth of industrialism enabled the British and European populations to become far larger and yet richer than anyone had ever imagined.

THE CLASSICAL WORLD

In cultural terms, the chief importance of classical Greece and Rome was that they reconciled Europe's primal combativeness with political order. Greek culture was sharply competitive, admiring of the strong and successful and without the care for the poor and weak later inculcated by Christianity. Homer's *Iliad* is a tale of godlike warriors who vied for distinction in war even at the cost of death. Such a society, if left unchecked, might have produced only endless feuds of egos in conflict.

Yet in the *polis*, or city-state, Greece found a way to reconcile assertiveness with community. In the *polis*—at least in those cities that were democratic—an entire community took on responsibilities for governance that only leaders had borne before. Even farmers were not passive, as in the Middle East, but active citizens.

This ideal of citizenship was a direct inheritance from the aristocratic ethos of an earlier age. In effect, the humbler social classes,
eager to imitate their betters, deftly put the old aristocratic ideal on
a polis basis by substituting the collective aggrandizement of the
city for the individual aggrandizement sought so eagerly by Homer's
heroes.[23]

In the arts, philosophy, and other fields, the classical Greeks made
quantum leaps that still awe commentators today.[24] One reason probably
was that the *polis* became a forcing house, an arena that actively promoted individual daring. Even those of low birth aspired to the sort of
outward excellence that only the elite had attempted before. Achievement
became what Hannah Arendt called action—a display of prowess before
one's peers. In other cultures, people might seek merely to survive, but
the Greeks aspired to something timeless.[25] The *polis* allowed ambitious
individuals to become, so to speak, audiences for each other. And so we
first see here those "individuals persistently searching for new worlds,"
which would become the *leitmotif* of Western culture.[26]

The ancient Greeks, however, achieved no political structure larger
than the city-state. The Romans did, expanding their rule from Rome itself
to all of Italy and then to most of the Mediterranean world. Superficially,
Roman rule came to resemble the despotisms of Asia. A republic governed
by elected legislatures ceded to an empire in which the rulers were largely
chosen and changed by the army. Yet Rome achieved the rule of law more
fully than any previous empire.

And the law came to be framed mostly in terms of individuals. Bonds
among individuals, and between them and the state, were understood in
contractual terms. Individuals bore legal rights that were seen as essential
to their dignity. Legally, they were separated from their social context far
more than in China, where much more deference was paid to the family.
Thus Rome institutionalized more fully than Greece an individualist notion of personality. That conception would live on in the medieval church
and in the political conceptions of Europe after Rome.[27]

The individualism of classical times, however, did not endure. "By 146
B.C., when Macedonia became a Roman province and Greece a Roman
dependency," William H. McNeill wrote, "most of the energy with which
the Greeks had begun...had evaporated; scientific, literary, and philo-
sophic creativity had largely worn themselves out. The Oriental view of

the subordination of the individual and the nation to supernatural powers...had come to prevail over the one-time rationalistic, curious, and
restless spirit of Hellas [Greece]."[28] Free inquiry ceded to the dogmas of
Orthodox Christianity, various Christian heresies, and finally Islam. For
the ancient East, the burdens of freedom proved to be too much. They
were given up for the burdens of necessity.

BIBLICAL RELIGION

Yet individualism thrived in northern Europe. Rome and the church
provided institutions to reconcile a fractious temperament with order.
Probably of equal importance was the inner influence that the church
conveyed. Both the Old and the New Testament express a faith that promoted and also disciplined individualism like no other. The religions of
the East, as noted earlier, lacked definite moral commandments; also, they
tended toward escape from the world. Islam, which became Christianity's
great rival in the West, does contain definite commandments yet resisted
individualism. Judaism and Christianity, however, both embraced freedom
while at the same time calling individuals to higher purposes and moral
behavior. More than anything else, that faith "defined Europe" and gave
it "a transcendent goal."[29]

In the Near East, other ancient faiths understood time as cyclical and
sought mainly to placate natural forces that humans could not understand. Judaism, however, conceived of a God who controlled the world
and stood entirely outside it, yet at the same time related to individuals,
both affirming and challenging them.[30] Jewish time was linear, heading in
a direction that God defined. And he summoned humans to advance his
purposes. To that end, he might rip them away from their social setting,
the very thing in which non-Western peoples usually find their identity.
In the Bible, God's first words to Abraham, the first patriarch of the Jews,
are to "Go from your country and your kindred and your father's house
to the land that I will show you" (Genesis 12:1).

In Jewish thought, God was to govern the world through his chosen
people. They were to be pilgrims, "a people voyaging in time, their eyes on
a future.... The chosen people of the Bible...were going somewhere; they
were not simply people to whom inexplicable things happened which had
to be passively endured."[31] God's will was paramount, early Jews believed,

but humans must determine what that will is. And this empowered them to identify their own purposes with God's. So the individual was strongly trusted and affirmed.

At the same time, biblical faith admonished individuals to live by a set of moral principles, first embodied in the Ten Commandments and further elaborated in later Jewish and Christian teachings. Over centuries, the church would impart these principles to Europe and thus inculcate the moralism that is a central feature of the Western mind. Fidelity to those inner values would—most of the time—enable Westerners to achieve social order with a minimum of external enforcement, and thus reconcile order and freedom, as the non-West is seldom able to do.

Moralism did more than constrain, however. Surprisingly, it also liberated. A defining moment in scripture occurs in chapter 22 of Genesis, when God tells Abraham to sacrifice his beloved son Isaac. Obediently, he is about to comply when God intervenes and gives him a ram to sacrifice instead. An angel then declares that because Abraham has obeyed God's will, "I will indeed bless you, and I will multiply your descendants as the stars of heaven, and the sand that is on the seashore. And your descendants shall possess the gate of their enemies, and by your descendants shall all the nations of the earth bless themselves, because you have obeyed my voice" (Genesis 22:17–18).

This passage expresses a profound insight that would be central to all of Western experience. To internalize God's will promotes social order, yet it is not contrary to freedom. Indeed, it is the *essence* of freedom. The moral principles that individualists imbibe steer them away from obvious faults, but also motivate their deepest endeavors, both for themselves and for others. A person possessed by a moral cause has the strength of ten who lack the same inspiration. A more conformist personality that adjusts to outward necessity has nothing like the same impact. This psychology goes far to explain the matchless energy that Westerners displayed in their historical march toward wealth and power.

EUROPE

One of the reasons Europe developed so rapidly was that the inspirations it drew from the ancient world were all constructive and remarkably complementary. The Jews were spiritual geniuses—they originated the Jewish and Christian faiths, which would inspire the West for millennia—but they were not equally gifted in philosophy or politics. In contrast, the religion of the Greeks was primitive and their politics never rose above the city-state, but their philosophy changed the world. The Romans, in turn, were second-string in both religion and philosophy, but they were the greatest governors the world has ever seen.

Together, the three traditions generated a culture that was remarkably strong and positive in all dimensions. It was inspired by faith, yet questioning; strong in authority, yet civic-minded; committed to timeless ideas, yet improving. It promoted individual initiative but was at the same time capable of collective action. And in all dimensions, the psychic energy came from an individualist personality that embraced all the burdens of freedom.

Crucially, European individualism developed slowly—over several centuries—without disruption. No higher authority emerged to impose a more collectivist style. The church might have done so, but it never had the temporal authority to do this. Nor did secular rulers. In much of the rest of the world, as noted earlier, the empires that arose limited initiative to leaders and stifled it below. But in Europe, power was always divided among different territories, none of which could dominate the others. Popes bestowed the title of Holy Roman Emperor on some German rulers, but none of these gained control even of Germany, let alone the rest of Europe. Farther west, power very early was divided between the emerging kingdoms of England, France, and Spain, along with the Low Countries. (I consider geographic explanations for this dispersion in chapter 6.)

Divided power, however, also reflected an assertive culture. Europe's rivalrous style prompted each country to resist any aggrandizement by the others. Attempts by Spain, France, and later Germany to dominate Europe were thwarted by coalitions of smaller states. Britain often led these alliances (as the United States was later to do on a world scale). The weak simply refused to bow to the strong, as they might have done more readily in a collectivist culture.

Power was also dispersed within each country. The feudal system forced rulers to consult their vassals in order to govern, a principle that led eventually to modern government by consent and representative democracy. In addition, in most countries, cities had some autonomy from local lords, and everywhere the church was substantially an independent institution. Rulers gained the power to appoint bishops, at the expense of the pope, but the clergy never suffered the total subordination to the state seen in Russia or Asia. Popes and bishops retained the freedom to criticize rulers for misbehavior, thus continuing the biblical tradition in which prophets rebuked the Jewish kings.

For all these reasons, ordinary people in Europe never faced the utter subjection achieved by "oriental despotism" in much of the non-West. Even in the Middle Ages, they had substantial room to innovate, and they did so, thus producing the constant change seen in Europe from its earliest times.

> Even in feudal Europe, or perhaps because Europe was feudal rather than fully centralized, there existed people who were more ambitious and more willing to take risks than most others—including the serfs who fled the manors for the freedom of the towns; the merchants and mariners who undertook long and perilous trading voyages; the devout who dared the pilgrimages, armed or unarmed, to Palestine or shrines closer by; and even the scholars who devised theological doctrines that skirted the limits of Catholic tolerance. The breakdown and diffusion of political and religious authority in postfeudal Europe widened the range of activities over which this minority could expend its energies, and beginning in the fifteenth or sixteenth century there followed what some have viewed as an attack of human hyperactivity—scientific, literary, musical, dramatic, military, political, and commercial—from which the West has never wholly recovered.[32]

PROTESTANTISM

Developments in religious belief further strengthened individualism. Although Christianity had always accepted individualism, in medieval times that impulse was restrained by the church's emphasis on penitence and the sacraments. A moralistic culture made people feel guilty about wrongdoing. The church promoted that feeling, at best helping people manage their guilt by offering forgiveness to those who accepted confession and penance. By doing that, and by doing good works, the believer could earn credits for heaven.

But this emphasis downplayed a more radical belief: One might be justified simply by faith in God, independent of penance or works. That idea appears even in Genesis (15:6), in which Abraham trusts in God to provide him an heir, and God "reckoned it to him as righteousness." The Old Testament prophets suggest similarly that fervent faith in God can set one right with the Almighty, independent of any righteous act. At some level, in the biblical tradition, it is faith that produces righteousness.

Saint Paul, in his New Testament letters, made justification by faith the linchpin of his theology. In his time (the first century AD), Judaism had become highly legalistic. For Jews, life was filled with myriad rules that they had to observe, many of them dietary, which Orthodox Jews still observe today. Jesus criticized this legalism in favor of the more fundamental commandments to love God and one's neighbor. Paul went further, identifying the "law" with all the obligations that weighed people down in a moralistic culture. To him, Christianity announced a new life of grace, over and above the law. God's commandments were still important, yet—by faith in Christ—one could be justified through God's grace alone. "For the law of the Spirit of life in Jesus Christ has set me free from the law of sin and death" (Romans 8:2). Indeed, only the faithful were truly able to observe the law, so faith was primary. "The law was a kind of tutor in charge of us until Christ should come, when we should be justified by faith" (Galatians 3:23–25).[33]

The Reformation, in the sixteenth century, was in part a rebellion against the abuses of the Roman church, such as the selling of church offices and "indulgences," which remitted people's sins in return for money. Long the chief moralizer of the society and a critic of power, the Roman church was now subjected to its own moral standards. Protestant and "Dissenting" churches arose independent of Rome, some of them established by states and some not.

But in addition, reformers rediscovered the idea of justification by faith. Martin Luther (1483–1546), the initial leader of the revolt, wrote like a latter-day Paul that "[f]aith is a living and unshakeable confidence, a belief in the grace of God so assured that a man would die a thousand deaths for its sake. This kind of confidence in God's grace...makes us joyful, high-spirited, and eager in our relations with God and with all mankind."[34]

The effect was to give much greater scope to individual conscience and action than the medieval church had allowed. Ordinary people could now step forward and believe more readily that God affirmed the purposes that *they* had chosen. Luther's rebellion against Rome was "just the first of many individualistic acts in the Protestant tradition." Fukuyama explained, "In the long run, the individual's ability to have a direct relationship with God had extremely subversive consequences for all social relationships, because it gave individuals a moral ground to rebel against even the most broadly established traditions and social conventions."[35]

The Reformation eased religion's grip on Western culture. That probably is one reason for the surge in energy that one senses in European society from the sixteenth century onward. Much of the effort once claimed by religious dutifulness now flowed into entrepreneurial activity of all kinds. Britain and the Netherlands were both the richest and the most Protestant countries in Europe, and this was no coincidence. With the Reformation, they surged to the forefront of Western development. Right through the seventeenth century, the two kingdoms dueled for the leadership of European trade and empire-building. Relatively speaking, the countries that remained Catholic—above all, France and Spain—fell back.

BRITAIN

Individualism strengthened further because of Britain's special receptivity to this way of life. Even before the Reformation, England had been a strongly individualistic country. Historians used to think that modern individualism was chiefly a product of the Industrial Revolution. Only then, they assumed, had a market society totally displaced the more communal attitudes of the medieval era. Later research has suggested, however, that England in many respects was already an individualist society, even deep in the Middle Ages. It was as precocious in economics as it was in politics. According to Alan Macfarlane, "the majority of ordinary people in England from at least the thirteenth century were rampant individualists, highly mobile both geographically and socially, economically 'rational,' market-oriented and acquisitive, ego-centred in kinship and social life."[36]

The Reformation only strengthened these tendencies. Both England and Scotland rejected Rome, and a majority of their peoples converted to Protestantism.[37] In both countries, religious revolutionaries briefly took power. Perhaps as a result, in the late sixteenth century, England entered an era of extraordinary creativity, in the arts and science as well as politics and economics.[38] Like no other country, Britain built its national identity around religious individualism, going to war against the Catholic powers of the Continent—first Spain and then France. The island kingdom became a warrior nation, defending individual freedoms against the pope, as the United States would later do against Communism.[39]

As would be true in America, the most extreme Protestants were Calvinists, who were the furthest thing from carefree. For them, the new freedom meant replacing the collapsing authorities of the medieval world with new, self-chosen obligations to a transcendent God. As Michael Walzer wrote in *The Revolution of the Saints*, "Discipline and not liberty lies at the heart of Puritanism."[40]

Around this time, and with England's 1588 defeat of the Spanish Armada, we begin to see that outpouring of vitality that marks a dominant nation on the rise.

> While the [Spanish] Armada was going to pieces on the rocks,
> England was at last entering on the wider spaces of her destiny; and
> the sense of adventure in untrodden regions of mind and matter
> inspired the rising generation, who went out in the spirit of free
> individual initiative to explore new worlds of land and water, knowl-
> edge and imagination.[41]

But as in the ancient world, this tide toward individualism eventually turned back, at least somewhat. The Puritans who took over England during the Civil War in the 1640s failed to consolidate their revolution. The English grew tired of Puritan perfectionism. They demanded government that was more accountable and relaxed. They asked of the Puritans, as Sir Toby Belch does of Malvolio in Shakespeare's *Twelfth Night*, "Dost thou think because thou art virtuous there shall be no more cakes and ale?"[42] So in 1660, the monarchy was restored, along with the Anglican Church, which was Protestant but undemanding about theology. And the flame of heroic individualism began to dwindle. Today Britain and Europe

FIGURE 5.1 **Embarkation of the Pilgrims**

Robert Walter Weir, 1857

remain strongly individualist, but the will to seek still greater freedom, and its burdens, no longer has the force of faith behind it.[43]

AMERICA

So the frontiers of freedom crossed the Atlantic. It would prove crucial to American culture that the country was chiefly founded not just by Europeans, not just by the British, but by Protestants of the most committed kind. They discovered in America their promised land, as they had failed to do in the old country. Figure 5.1 shows the Pilgrims as they embarked for the New World in 1620. Probably no small group has ever shaped history so profoundly.[44]

Of course, the original settlers of North America were the Native Americans, and Europeans brought with them Africans as slaves. Europeans came to the New World from many countries, including France, Spain, and the Netherlands. Nevertheless, the vast majority of these new settlers were British. That was because Britain had the military power to dominate the New World, as well as the most people willing and able to emigrate there. As David Hackett Fischer has shown, the British settlers were diverse, reflecting several distinct political traditions. The Puritans who settled New England differed from the Quakers of Pennsylvania, the backcountry pioneers of Appalachia, and the aristocratic planters of the South. Nonetheless, all of them were individualist, Protestant, and self-governing.[45] They brought with them, in other words, individualism of various kinds, as well as Britain's peerless political traditions.

By escaping to America, the most stalwart British Protestants founded a nation that was even more oriented to freedom, and its burdens, than the mother country. They formed a political culture that, strangely, combined fierce insistence on individual rights with potent public institutions. America would become a free country that nonetheless possessed one of the world's strongest regimes. This Protestant founding knows no parallel elsewhere: Huntington remarked that "Muslim, Buddhist, Orthodox, Confucian, Hindu, Jewish, Catholic, and even Lutheran and Anglican cultures have produced nothing comparable. The American Creed is the unique creation of a dissenting Protestant culture."[46]

Of the several British traditions in colonial America, the Puritans marked the culture most deeply. The sheer force of their convictions made them the nation's leading moral teachers. The Puritan way of life combined particularly strong moralism with ambitious public ideals. Puritanism was "a form of social striving which labored obsessively to close the gap between ideals and actuality," and that earnestness extended from private to public life.[47] New Englanders pursued a vision of "ordered liberty" that exalted individual conscience but also used government to address many public needs and problems and was willing to tax accordingly.

Puritanism proved more enduring in America than in Britain, perhaps because there it encountered less competition from other religious traditions. That ideal could be intolerant, although over time it became less so. American society accepted religious pluralism and more diverse ways of life, yet the heirs of the Puritans still strive to live out their inner ideals. The Puritan mind-set survives in the strong work ethic, the demanding public ethics, the strict sense of personal responsibility, and the somewhat prudish social attitudes of Americans today.[48]

We remember the American founding as the doing largely of Virginians—such as Washington, Jefferson, and their successors—who formed the national government and largely wrote the Constitution. But the new nation's social attitudes derived far more from New England. Tocqueville regarded the Puritans of Massachusetts as the true founders of the country. "New England civilization," he found, shone like "beacons" all across America. The Puritans had "torn themselves away from home comforts" and accepted the "sufferings of exile" to pursue "the triumph of an *idea*."[49]

That idea combined democracy with religious faith. In New England, the Puritans effortlessly achieved self-rule more fully than even Britain would do for centuries, let alone the rest of the world. But order in the colonies was also upheld by weighty inner convictions. Religion commanded that education be expanded so that individuals could think for themselves. But at the same time, as Tocqueville says, it was "the observance of divine laws" that "leads men to liberty."[50]

Although not a warrior people, the Puritans became a nation in arms in the showdown over British rule. In Massachusetts by the 1770s, they already governed themselves through local committees and militias, marginalizing the colonial regime. When fighting broke out in 1775, the settlers fought in highly organized units, not as a "rabble in arms." The British swiftly lost control of New England and had no hope to recover it.[51] They shifted their efforts to the south, where it took other American colonists quite a bit longer to defeat them. The matchless capacity of an individualist culture to combine freedom with collective force was thus already on display, even before independence. Except briefly—during the Commonwealth in seventeenth-century England—such a temperament had never taken power before. Once extended across a vast continent, it would inevitably come to lead the world.

CONCLUSION

Culturally, the Puritans were the point of the lance, the most extreme expression of the individualism that Europe and Britain had nurtured over centuries. Like an arrow shot from the British bow, this confident creed struck fertile ground in the New World, where it was not to be challenged until very recent times. All the eras and forces I have reviewed above conspired to produce a civilization in which, more fully than anywhere else, ordinary people claimed the license and the responsibility to rule themselves.

All the forces acted to shift the bases for action and moral judgment from outside to inside the self. First in Europe, then in Britain, and then in America, people increasingly acted according to their own goals and values rather than in deference to others. This produced the shift from the conformist East to the autonomous West that Hegel noted. In America, finally, ordinary citizens asserted the dignity earlier afforded only to aristocrats—the right to be reckoned as independent and important forces in the world, to be judged only by their peers and in the light of achievement.

No comparable development toward individualism arose outside Europe. Non-Western societies continued largely as they had always been, until the West forced change upon them starting in the nineteenth century. The deciding factor might have been that in Europe an individualist culture formed very early, so that it became self-sustaining. The cake of custom faced early challenges, and once it started to crumble, there was no stopping it. The upshot was the utterly rootless individualism that some Western countries display today. In the non-West, there was no such challenge, until the strength of the West became too great to ignore.

Ignorant of their own origins, many Americans today imagine that poor countries sunk in a collective despond could easily choose to be more like them. Simply accept freedom in personal and public affairs, they urge, and a better society will emerge. But does the capacity for such a choice even exist outside the West? The obstacle is that freedom is not carefree. It requires accepting many burdens for oneself and others that most societies avoid or collectivize. It means stuffing one's head full of mores and matters to decide—matters that, in non-Western nations, are usually settled externally. To be free, it is not enough to stand tall; one must also shoulder freedom's burdens. The urge to do so reflects a unique history and is not inherent in human nature. If we think that freedom is easy, we do not understand ourselves.

PART TWO

OTHER ROOTS
OF POWER

OTHER ROOTS OF POWER

Might American and Western primacy be attributable to factors other than culture? Perhaps the United States leads the world simply because it is a large country or because of its rich natural resources. Or perhaps because it is a capitalist country or a democratic one. Since the end of history, by some reckonings, market economics and elective government have swept the globe. So the world is getting richer and freer. That may be enough to explain why the chief exemplar of those institutions—the United States—has become the world's leader.

The next three chapters will question that conclusion. Although geography, economics, and politics do help explain American preeminence, none of them seems as important as the individualist nature of American society. And—just as significant—the very influence of these other factors is itself shaped by culture. The Anglo countries have taken their geographic advantages as a mandate to lead the world rather than retire from it. A free economy and democratic politics also function far better in an individualist culture than in a collectivist one.

As before, the connection of individualism to these other factors bolsters the case for defending it. If an affluent, well-governed society could be had on some cultural basis other than individualism, why preserve that mind-set? But Asia, despite its ascent, has not yet achieved the good society, at least as Americans understand that. Only a country where individuals bear the burdens of freedom can be both orderly and free.

CHAPTER SIX

GEOGRAPHY

To some, geography is the ultimate basis of wealth and power. It is true that economic and, with it, military power ultimately must have a physical basis. A nation's territory and material resources must be among the roots of its power.

And yet the connection between geography and wealth or power is surprisingly weak. Much depends on how countries *respond* to their physical situation. What to some nations might be a constraint becomes to others a challenge. In some nations, what Nietzsche called a "will to power" has overridden all the limitations of nature. Some authors also speak of geographic influences in the distant past, but these appear insufficient to explain the special dynamism of Western society.

Geography does make some countries more secure than others. A century ago, geopolitical theorists imagined that geography, rather than ideology, would increasingly structure international politics. Geopolitics was a form of realism. While we may interpret the actions of some countries as driven by their geography, the major nations were driven far more by their internal nature. Each sought to realize its domestic values in the wider world.

This was the contest in which the Anglo nations—first Britain, then America—triumphed. They did so without changing their geographic situation at all. It was fortunate that they did. Geography alone might predict simply a Hobbesian struggle of all against all. That we have avoided that is substantially due to the steadying influence of Western and Anglo moralism.

PHYSICAL CONDITIONS

First of all, geography connotes physical conditions. One basis of American primacy is sheer size. Earlier we considered material influences on individualism, but here we consider direct influences on power. A vast nation, like the United States, with continental scale and now more than 325 million people, has a potential for world power that smaller countries lack. America's Cold War rival, the Soviet Union, was also huge, as are its current economic rivals China and India. Clearly, future primacy must be contested among these massive countries.

In the fairly recent past, however, powerful countries have included Britain, the Netherlands, Germany, and Japan, none of which is large by current standards. Somehow, all these countries generated unusual wealth and, along with it, military power. We usually say that was because they were more "developed," but development hinged on unusually strong internal institutions, both economic and political. Eventually, all these countries ceded their dominance to the Soviet or American giant, but the USSR and the US became dominant only because they, too, became "developed"—and not due to size alone. Similarly, China could take over American primacy only if it becomes comparably developed. Whether it can do that, as I show below, is very questionable.

Physical conditions also connote the material resources necessary for wealth and power. Some nations have better farmland or more mineral resources than others. In these terms, Europe and Britain were well off compared to most other parts of Eurasia. The United States was still more fortunate. It became wealthy, in part, because of its matchless Midwest croplands, as well as its plentiful iron, coal, and oil. American oil reserves were once depleted but have recently recovered thanks to fracking. With the exception of a few "rare earths"—obscure minerals—the United States need not import resources to power its huge economy.

But as with physical scale, the connection of resources to power is weaker than it seems. China had agricultural lands comparable to Europe's but, until recently, never developed so strongly. The surplus generated by agriculture went to support a growing population rather than, as in Europe, more modern economic sectors. Europe was long more dynamic than Asia.[1] And some countries became formidable without significant internal resources at all. Japan and the Netherlands conquered empires in Asia, ruling over nations much larger and potentially richer than themselves. Both imported the resources they needed, as they still do today. In these cases, the society, rather than anything physical, was the entire basis of power.

Climate probably matters more than physical resources. The richest and strongest countries have always been located in the earth's temperate zones—never in cold, polar regions or the tropics. A moderate climate promotes the best agricultural yields and also the most human activity. In brisk conditions, neither hot nor cold, people work harder, and the urge to achieve is also stronger. In the jungles of Africa, Asia, or Latin America, effort is enervated by heat and also by tropical diseases such as malaria.[2] Such conditions go far to explain the lassitude of Africa relative to Europe or America. "Africa south of the Sahara," J. M. Roberts wrote, "seems almost inert under the huge pressures exercised upon it by geography, climate and disease."[3] Climate, however, does little to differentiate the many nations in the temperate zone.

GEOGRAPHY AND DEVELOPMENT

Some recent authors seek to explain Western dominance in the world by appealing to geographic forces in the distant past. Geography, they contend, promoted the development of some nations, while condemning others to backwardness. In *Guns, Germs, and Steel*, Jared Diamond contended that the early appearance of agriculture in Eurasia gave it an enormous lead in later development, which it never relinquished. That supposedly explains why several European powers and Japan became industrialized and constructed vast empires, while other regions—like New Guinea, where Diamond has done most of his research—remain primitive.[4]

Diamond, however, failed to explain well why some countries within Eurasia became powerful and others did not. In Diamond's terms, England was "not a homeland at all"—not a place where anything fundamental happened in human development. Why, then, did this obscure island, rather than Russia or China, come to govern a quarter of the globe? Still less can Diamond explain how North America, which also lacked early development, came to host the world's most powerful nation.[5]

Several scholars also say that European development benefited enormously from the resources that Europeans discovered in America. As Eric Jones summarized, "the store of grasslands and cleared forest in the thinly populated parts of the globe was broken into once and for all on behalf of European civilization." Martin Jacques and Kenneth Pomeranz claimed that New World resources were a principal reason why European development was able to get ahead of population growth; China, in contrast, was long trapped in a Malthusian slough, in which its growing population ate up the economic margin it might have used for development.[6] But New World resources were only one of many reasons why Britain, rather than China, was the first nation to industrialize.[7]

Ian Morris made the further argument that the "Atlantic economy" consisting of trade between American colonists and the Old World made Europe more questioning and innovative than it had been before.[8] But an individualist culture oriented to constant improvement arose in Europe, and especially in Britain, long before the discovery of America. The New World was surely a gigantic windfall, but to exploit its potential depended on a commercial, problem-solving culture that had already emerged in Western Europe.[9] Spain and Portugal also built empires in the Americas, but without showing comparable dynamism. Their settlers sought to preserve a medieval society, not create a more modern one.[10]

SECURITY FROM THREATS

A more plausible geographic influence on the trajectories of nations is how they relate to each other. Geographic position makes some countries far more secure from attack or invasion than others. During much of recorded history, one of the great perils was invasion by "horse nomads," who would sweep out of central Asia, subjugating peoples to both the east and the west. The Mongol invasions of the thirteenth century conquered China, while the Tatars conquered Russia. These facts may go far to explain the dominance of autocratic rule in those countries.

As shown earlier, invasions by Germanic tribes did much to create

Europe's individualist temperament. But equally important, that culture was not disturbed by later invasions from deeper in Asia that might have implanted a more collective mind-set. The Huns in the fifth century, Islam in the eighth century, the Mongols in the thirteenth century, the Ottomans in the sixteenth and seventeenth centuries—all reached Western Europe. But except for the Muslims in Spain, none remained there long enough to have much impact. Western Europe escaped mostly because it was so remote, at the far western end of Eurasia. Not for nothing did Europe and its offshoots, including America, come to be known as "the West."[11]

In these global terms, the Anglo nations were even more secure. Britain was strongly shaped by the Germanic invasions, which continued as late as the ninth and tenth centuries. But as an island to the far west even in Europe, it was untouched by any of the Asian conquerors. America, of course, was even farther west—across the Atlantic Ocean. The United States has never faced any significant threat of military invasion. We have invaded our immediate neighbors—Canada and Mexico—rather than they us. In fact, no Western country ever had to deal seriously with non-Western culture at home until recent pressures from immigration (see further in chapter 11).

Isolation may also, of course, make it more difficult for any nation to dominate others. It favors defense over offense. It is thus of greatest value to nations, like the Anglos, that combine isolation with unusual capacity to project power. The United States, for instance, might have been a bystander in World War II, separated as it was by oceans from the main theaters of conflict in Europe and Asia. American forces, however, crossed both the Atlantic and the Pacific to defeat Germany and Japan, thousands of miles from their own shores (albeit with much help from Britain, the Soviet Union, and China). The capacity to do that cannot be explained by geography.

SECURITY WITHIN EUROPE

Geography has also affected security within Europe. Some historians think that Europe's complex setting—divided as it is by seas, rivers, and mountains—helps explain why no one country attained dominance for long. Charles Montesquieu (1689–1755) remarked that no dominant empire could be built on such terrain, much in contrast to the open plains farther east in Eurasia, where czars and emperors reigned.[12]

More important was the fact that, within Europe, countries of roughly equal power long counterbalanced one another, as mentioned in the last chapter. "[A] long-lasting state system" was a "miracle," hugely favorable to European development, because no government ever had enough control to stop the flow of improvement.[13] Among academics, Europe's rivalries among roughly equal states generated the realist theory of international relations, according to which opposing countries constantly struggle for relative wealth and power and there is no overall world order.[14]

That concept, however, fails to credit the moderating force of individualist attitudes. One reason, already mentioned, why no hegemon ever dominated Europe was that, in an individualist culture, the weak simply refused to accept dominance by the strong. They banded together to resist first Spain, then France, then Germany. The British became the leaders of Europe largely because they headed these coalitions while never seeking dominant power themselves. By Victorian times, they had become the honest brokers of Europe, the guarantors of stability.

As an island power, the British might simply have stood aside from power struggles among rivals on the Continent, as Scandinavia largely did. Of course, it was in their interest to resist the would-be hegemons, but their motives went beyond self-interest. Over time, they developed and defended a moral conception that relations among states should be based on peace, international law, and open trade. After defeating Napoleon in 1815, the British promoted that vision for the next hundred years. Their heirs, the Americans, still promote it today.

This conception projected on a world scale the idea of "the good society," based on law and markets, that Britain had achieved domestically. One benefit of geographic security had been that Britain achieved remarkable freedom and economic development at home, little distracted by military needs. As G. M. Trevelyan said, Britain became a free society because it mostly fought wars "from behind the shield of the Royal Navy" and thus never became militarized.[15] Through world leadership, Britain promoted the same security for the rest of the world. This moral vision helped perpetuate its world leadership much longer than its own power could have justified.

A comparison to Japan is instructive. Japan, like Britain, was an island power made secure by isolation. It also was precocious in its domestic development, becoming richer and better governed than the rest of Asia by the nineteenth century. Like Britain, it became a potent industrializer, conquered a large empire, and became a great power. So similar was it to Britain that it could have been "towed away and anchored off the Isle of Wight [a small island on England's south coast]."[16] But unlike Britain, Japan served only its own interests. It did not advance or defend any wider vision of the world order. (One reason for this is that Asian culture lacks the West's capacity to imagine and promote abstract political conceptions.) Therefore, Japan did not enjoy much deference from other countries. Following its defeat by the United States in World War II, it has remained a major economic power, but little more. It is still distrusted, not followed.

GEOPOLITICS

Geopolitics was an early version of realism that resembles it in downplaying the force of morals in world politics. This late-nineteenth-century school believed that, with the decay of the Victorian world order, world politics would no longer be driven by religious or political differences or the ambitions of ruling dynasties. Rather, states would compete for territory, and they would use their geographical position to frame policy and assert power.

Geopolitical theorists feared that the United States, secure in its own hemisphere, might avoid involvement in world affairs and thus be at risk from powers arising elsewhere. In 1890, Alfred Thayer Mahan wrote that the country needed a large navy not only to defeat rivals in war, but also to defend its interests—such as free trade—even during peace. He especially worried that America would run down its navy following its easy victory in the Spanish-American War.[17]

Later, Halford Mackinder and Nicholas Spykman located the principal dangers to America in Eurasia. A threatening power might arise there, they feared, unless the United States maintained an active policy of defending the global balance of power, as Britain had done.[18] One may argue that America acted on this advice by helping to defeat Germany and Japan in the World Wars and then resisting expansion by the Soviet Union and Communist China during the Cold War.[19]

Geopolitics, however, oversimplifies American motives. In the twentieth century, the United States was surely tempted by isolationism, yet it finally opposed the fascist and Communist powers because these countries appeared to threaten America's interests and, even more, its values. Our rivals were oppressors who denied their citizens the freedoms that Americans revered. Our contest with them was most deeply about those stakes, not geography. America's crusade served much more than self-interest. Like Britain, we defended a vision of world order based on peace, the rule of law, and expanding trade, and we continued to do so after the war.

THE AMERICAN CENTURY

Following the defeat of Germany and Japan, the United States, under the Truman administration, collaborated with foreign countries—including its former foes—to construct a new international order. Some of these institutions defended our European allies from economic collapse (e.g., the Marshall Plan) or Soviet aggression (e.g., the North Atlantic Treaty Organization—NATO). But others—the International Monetary Fund (IMF), the World Bank, and the General Agreement on Tariffs and Trade (GATT), which later became the World Trade Organization (WTO)—aimed to manage the world economy for the benefit of all nations. The United States even sponsored, in the form of the United Nations, an incipient world government.

By these steps, the United States accepted that its withdrawal from world leadership following World War I (see chapter 2) had been a mistake. It recognized that market forces alone could not avoid another collapse of the world economy like that of the 1930s. The UN was the successor to the League of Nations, which the US had refused to join. America thus abandoned isolationism. The new institutions spanned its protective seas as if they did not exist.

Under President Truman, leadership came from a confident group of senior officials who had been blooded by the war—Dean Acheson, George Kennan, George Marshall, James Forrestal, and others. They acted in an "inner-directed" manner, responding less to other countries than to their own convictions about what America and the world required. They saw themselves as "disinterested, far-seeing, and patriotic public servants," even "missionaries of a gospel that could save the world."[20] The new institutions they framed thus reflected classic, Western-style action—the realization of an inner vision in the outer world.

In a noted essay of 1941, the publisher Henry Luce stressed the moral purposes behind the emerging "American Century." Regarding the war in Europe, which the US had not yet joined, Luce rejected a focus on America's interests alone, which might counsel isolationism. Rather, the United States must not only fight Germany alongside Britain, but also become the "powerhouse" of such higher purposes as "Democracy, and Freedom, and Justice." After peace, Luce said, it must reconstruct the international system and become "the Good Samaritan of the entire world." To do this was not only a service to others but essential to America's own goals. Because "this nation... cannot truly endure unless there courses strongly through its veins... the blood of purposes and enterprise and high resolve."[21]

Thus the United States escaped from the straitjacket of geopolitics. Such universalistic purposes carried its foreign policy entirely beyond what its isolated global position might have suggested.

THE PROJECTION OF CULTURE

As early as the sixteenth century, Western imperialism was an expression of values as much as it was a quest for territory. Britain, France, Spain, and the Netherlands all established colonies in the New World. Thus, these "maritime peoples on the Atlantic coast" took over leadership of the West from the Mediterranean nations and projected their way of life upon the wider world.[22] The British won that contest, largely because the Netherlands was too small to compete, while the French and Spanish were too backward-looking. Both more free and more modern, the British overwhelmed their rivals in much of the New World.[23]

US foreign policy has projected American values in several different ways. There is statecraft, aimed at organizing the world to promote peace and free trade; a humanitarian urge to save benighted countries from despotism and poverty; an isolationist impulse to avoid war as a danger to democracy at home; and a populist urge that relishes war as an assertion of American power. All of these themes, sometimes in conflict, shaped America's steady advance from its initial obscurity toward world primacy.[24]

In the postwar era, statecraft initially dominated. But today, after history, the humanitarian urge is probably the strongest. It provides the principal impetus for the United States to stay involved in overseas problems and crises where often its own material interests are, at best, unclear. That urge expresses the moralism of Western culture. Formerly, in many ways the British had aspired not only to rule, but to save their empire morally. They opposed the slave trade and the more backward aspects of native cultures, as in India. They dispatched missionaries to evangelize the Africans.[25]

That impulse was similarly strong in America from the beginning. A commitment to missionary work abroad appears in the United States as early as 1806, long before the country became a world power. From that point, Protestant American missionaries streamed overseas in growing numbers, reaching around 100,000 by the year 2000. The urge to help was broader than just evangelism to preach the Gospel. More secular efforts to help poor societies expressed the idea that the West had a positive duty to help the non-West. One instance was the Peace Corps, established under President Kennedy, which has sent idealistic Americans abroad to help developing countries ever since. Thus America should seek "to transform the world and to bring about a social, economic, medical, and religious revolution."[26]

At the turn of the twentieth century, the missionary call reached even to the most privileged in America. The leaders of establishment universities, such as Princeton, exhorted their graduates to dedicate their lives to uplifting the less fortunate, and many responded.[27] The impact of their efforts, of course, was at best uneven. Much of the initial support for democracy in the developing world came from missionary activity.[28] Yet missionaries, whether religious or secular, also confronted the deep resistance of non-Western cultures to liberalizing change.

The American philanthropic impulse finds expression at home even more than it does abroad. Already in 1835, Tocqueville noted the proclivity of Americans to found charitable societies to carry on all manner of good works.[29] That urge has only strengthened since, in part because as society becomes richer it can afford to devote more resources to *doing* good, as opposed to making good. The nonprofit sector now accounts for 13 percent of the American GDP, two-thirds the size of federal revenues, and it employs 7 percent of the labor force. Recently, between 1996 and 2004, the number of American charitable organizations grew by more than half. At the same time, the number of private foundations grew from 58,774 to 102,881. Many of these philanthropies were created by successful baby boomers seeking to leave an earnest legacy to posterity. No other rich country has seen such an outpouring.[30]

LOOKING DOWNWARD

America's proselytizing tone primarily reflects a moralistic culture, but it is promoted as well by our geographic isolation and our relative lack of focused national interests. Especially since the end of history and the fading of the Communist challenge, many foreign-policy issues no longer pose clear stakes for the United States. The question of how to advance American interests is often overshadowed by the question of what our interest is. The effect is to turn foreign policy principally into a moral problem. Far more than leaders in most other countries, American policymakers have to ask what they *should* do, not just what they *must* do for "reasons of state." President Trump has recently questioned some of these commitments, but in calling on other countries to do more to help themselves, he too is a moralist.

The American will to save or at least improve the world remains strong, at least in elite culture. American journalists routinely report on and write books about desperate countries in Asia or Africa where people are starving or oppressed. These reporters demand that their own government do more to help—or stop doing harm.[31] Other idealists, using their own money, have created schools and health clinics in remote villages in Nepal.[32] American academics travel abroad to study the most wretched of the poor, few of whose like can be found today in America.[33] Some brave Americans who recently ventured forth into war-torn Syria to provide relief or health care were taken hostage there for their troubles.[34]

In all these cases, well-meaning Americans do more than sympathize—they identify with those they help or observe. They imagine that, "but for the grace of God," they could easily be in the same predicament. Mentally, they assume sameness—that people in other countries are just like them. If those people are less fortunate, the fault must lie with us or our government. The victims could be liberated from oppression, destitution, or war if only America gave aid, or removed some dictator, or sent in the Marines.

The sameness assumption, however, elides the profound differences between Western and non-Western cultures. In truth, the victims of misfortune in Asia and Africa are not the same as their Western observers. The crucial difference is that Americans are usually vastly more willing to assume responsibility for difficulties in distant regions than are those who live there. The latter's chief impulse is simply to endure or, if possible, to escape. History has not confirmed for them, as it has for the West, the potential of individual or collective action.

That cultural gulf also has a geographic reference: From a secure redoubt, the do-gooders look down from a great height upon a world in which nearly everyone is less fortunate than they are. They sally forth to do good out there, but they can always return home. Few of those they aid can follow them, although a great many would like to. The United States has become a vast lifeboat for distressed peoples struggling to emigrate to the West. But, however inspiring that may be, newcomers seldom find an untroubled life here. The oppressive societies they came from at least told them what to do in some sense. Freedom makes demands on them to create and direct their own lives that they never faced before. Geography merely maps the more fundamental division: between lives of freedom and lives of necessity.

CONCLUSION

Some critics would prefer a more realist foreign policy, in which the United States makes deals with other countries, even regimes of which we disapprove, to advance mutual interests. Former secretary of state Henry Kissinger has long advocated this approach.[35] President Trump sometimes suggests the same. Yet one force that clearly has served the world order since the nineteenth century has been the willingness of the Anglo powers—first Britain and now America—to pursue a moral vision. They have defined their national interests very broadly to include the overall stability of the globe. Without that moderating force, a far more combative world order would surely have emerged.[36]

Geography still matters, yet culture matters more. America still gains security from the fact that hostile nations, such as North Korea, find it hard to physically threaten us. True, as 9/11 showed, terrorist groups today can sometimes attack America and the West without any geographic base at all. Such forces can organize their efforts online, so that location matters little. American policymakers now must take preemptive action against such threats, since they cannot be deterred like traditional nation-states.[37]

Yet the fight to keep America safe from twenty-first-century terrorists is not only a high-tech battle (involving hackers and electronic attacks), but a battle of ideas. After history, America faces no compelling ideological system like Communism, yet it still must defend liberal values against radicals with utterly opposed visions of life.[38] That is just one form of the pervasive contest America must face today, pitting Western against non-Western culture.

CHAPTER SEVEN

THE MARKET

The most noted basis of national power is economic wealth. It was burgeoning wealth that lifted first Europe and then the Anglo countries to world leadership. One key to this growth clearly was growing economic freedom. Western countries profited hugely from what we today call capitalism—economies where producers claimed the prerogative to decide production and prices, subject only to market forces. From the late Middle Ages, most earlier restraints on that freedom were cast aside.

Since the defeat of Communism and the end of history, many countries outside the West have also reduced the impediments to their own economies. That produced the recent "rise of the rest"—a worldwide surge in wealth that has reduced, if not ended, the preeminence once enjoyed by the richest countries, including America.[1] The gains have been especially dramatic in China and India, the rising powers that some believe might soon take over American primacy.

The magic of the market has made so many countries richer that it would seem to be totally independent of culture. Yet the "free" economy depends on social discipline in several respects, and these attributes are commonest in Western countries. Western individualism supports both the freedom of the market and the moral commitments that it presumes. That was probably why capitalism arose first in Europe, and why—even today—it comes easiest to the West. For the non-West, where action is typically neither so free nor so principled, the market as we know it is an awkward transplant. Despite appearances, "Capitalism isn't easy."[2]

Those who criticize developing countries for lacking the individualist virtues have a point, yet they fail to see that the culture they fault has its own coherence—that of the non-West. Max Weber's famous theory that Protestantism helped generate modern capitalism may be overstated, but it does capture the inner-driven quality that underlies personal achievement in individualist societies. The West, meanwhile, has recently scaled back social protections against the market in an effort to preserve its competitiveness. So, despite the end of history and the muting of ideological divisions, world cultural divisions seem destined to endure.

WEALTH AND FREEDOM

In chapter 2, I summarized the rapid ascent of Europe, then Britain, and then America to world leadership following the Middle Ages. The initial basis of their shared primacy was that each was the richest society of its time. Other forms of power—military force and soft power—largely followed from that.

That rise was spurred by an individualist temperament, which operated, above all, through economics. Since medieval times, Europe had been growing. It grew first in trade within the continent, then in trade with other regions, then in manufacturing within its towns, and less visibly in agriculture. Growth accelerated yet further in the cataclysm of the Industrial Revolution, which opened up vistas of affluence never before imagined. No other world region experienced anything comparable. The final result, by the late nineteenth century, was a global trading economy not unlike what we have today.

At least within the West, rising wealth was strongly linked with increasing economic freedom.[3] Capitalism connotes an economic system in which producers and consumers interact without direct government interference. Producers own the means of production, and they assert a freedom to set the prices and quantities of what is produced, restrained only by the impersonal forces of supply and demand. That they should do so was a radical innovation. In medieval times, European economies were hedged around with many restrictions meant to serve non-economic ends. Aristocrats treated land as the symbol of their status rather than as an economic resource, while town guilds controlled the production of goods, ostensibly to maintain quality. Above all, notions of "just price" influenced producers not to charge more for necessities than common people could afford.

In the early modern era, all these restraints were minimized or abolished. "Improving" landlords enclosed their fields to produce crops for the market, ending the rights to land that peasants had enjoyed. Manufacturing grew up outside the towns, where the guilds could not control it. Above all, restraints on pricing and production were abolished, and producers began charging whatever the markets would bear. Not all changes favored the producers. Monopolies that had privileged some companies were abolished, and restraints on foreign trade were loosened, forcing producers to compete increasingly with foreign rivals.

Critics indicted the changes as a betrayal of the moral values that the old order had served. The free market aroused "moral indignation."[4] And indeed, ordinary people faced great disruptions, as many peasants were driven off the land into towns, and artisans who had plied their craft independently were replaced by regimented factory workers. Repeated downturns in the new industrial economies threatened jobs and imposed hardship.

Above all, producers' freedom to set prices seemed unjustified. It did indeed lead to sharp inequality and huge fortunes for some new industrialists, while many workers suffered. Social historians still record that outrage.[5] That capitalism allowed such self-seeking was the "monstrous element" in modern liberalism.[6] Until the end of history, whether and how to subordinate the selfishness of capitalism, once again, to a wider social interest was the great struggle in Western politics. As I note below, a reaction did arise that sought to limit the market's impact on society—but its ambitions now seem exhausted.

Yet strangely, greater economic freedom finally produced greater wealth at all levels of society. The shifts toward open markets were greatest in Northern Europe, especially in Britain and the Netherlands, and these were the countries that became the richest and most powerful. Far from immiserating the masses, as Marx later predicted, industrialism in Europe led by the mid-nineteenth century to universally higher incomes. Wealth remained highly unequal, yet all classes gained. Across the Atlantic, the story was similar—capitalism, despite moral objections and some hardship, made America vastly the richest country the world had ever seen. The recent "rise of the rest" outside the West continues that same story.

How could capitalism's license for self-seeking serve the social good? As Adam Smith explained in *The Wealth of Nations*, even when producers are free from explicit restraint—provided that markets are reasonably open and fair—the pressures of supply and demand force them to serve the overall interest. They can produce only what consumers will buy, while competition among producers usually forces prices down close to costs. The market's "invisible hand" thus outperformed the more explicit controls of government.[7]

Until recent times, there was no comparable development outside Europe and America. In the Middle East, India, and China, merchants and artisans catered to the elite with luxury goods, rather than producing for a mass market. They sought protection from government rather than freedom from it. By comparison, Western merchants were far more "aggressive, ruthless, and self-reliant." And "The distinctive characteristics of subsequent Western history arise largely from this fact."[8] That difference, as I show further below, reflects the difference between an individualist society and a more cautious and collectivist one.

Westerners still largely believe today that economic freedom is the royal road to wealth. The Anglo countries once protected their economies against imports, but today they mostly believe in openness. As mentioned in the introduction, their willingness to expose producers to competition from abroad as well as at home is an essential reason why they have become so productive and rich. To the same end, the European Union has created a huge single market covering much of the continent, and the United States led the creation of what is today the World Trade Organization, which promotes free trade worldwide. Only recently have some workers in the United States and Europe begun to question how favorable trade is to them, producing a populist surge in politics.[9] President Trump has recently questioned free trade, but chiefly to challenge the unfair trade practices of other countries, notably China.

THE BURDENS OF ECONOMIZING

In Smith, the market sometimes appears simply as a *deus ex machina* that outperformed the medieval economy for technical reasons, as it later did

Communism. It is true that in Europe, land and labor were freed from medieval restraints so that they could be allocated to serve social needs more efficiently.[10] However, Smith downplayed the effort required to attain these benefits. The "free" market, just as Marx said, is a taskmaster that generates far greater effort than any previous system. Immigrants who come to America from traditional societies expect to find riches compared to most of the world, and so they do. But they are often unprepared for how hard they have to work to get that wealth. Affluence exacts a price in elbow grease.

More than in medieval times, today both producers and consumers must bear the burdens of economizing. Each buyer and seller must constantly shop and bargain to make the best deal he or she can. The balance of supply and demand shifts constantly, and so must the decisions of consumers or workers. And this constant adjustment is essential to the efficiency that the market achieves. It is precisely the free market's broad distribution of economizing across the entire society that accounts for its formidable efficiency. Any attempt to centralize control confronts prohibitive information loads and so is much less efficient.[11] In the last century, efforts to manage the economy for social ends made a comeback, but they failed. Some workers were guaranteed wages, and some nonworkers were guaranteed incomes, but this damaged the efficiency of the market too much, and these protections have been cut back.

INDIVIDUALISM AND THE MARKET

The main reason that Western countries have tolerated capitalism is that an individualist culture best accepts the insecurity that the free market brings. At least most of the time, European publics have been willing and able to economize, to adjust to the constant changes of a dynamic economy.[12] In feudal Europe, lords intervened less in the market than they did elsewhere.[13] And for obscure reasons, this tolerance for the market was greatest in Britain and its offshoots, including America. Compared to other European countries, in Britain the aristocracy was relatively small and most members of the upper class were engaged in the private economy (rather than seeking status in ways apart from it, as they did in France).[14] Anglo society accepted the uncertainty of ad hoc social processes rather than insisting that the authorities impose stability.[15] Historically, Continental countries have been more afraid of market forces. Still today, Latin Europe fears a ruthless, "Anglo-Saxon" economy.[16] Yet the market prevailed throughout Europe, making it by far the world's richest region.

Ambitious, maximizing attitudes were much less apparent in the non-West. Fukuyama remarked that China showed "enormous complacency" and lacked the "spirit of maximization" that created constant change and growth in the West.[17] In India, under the British Raj, the society "utterly lacked the economic habit of mind" presupposed by liberal theorists such as Smith. The Indian elite invested passively in land rather than showing enterprise and seeking out "untried economic potentialities," as they did in Britain. One reason why the Indian independence movement sought a more productive economy was that many of its leaders were schooled in European ideas.[18]

Social historians used to think that industrialization created a culture compatible with it. The new market economy tore apart the fabric of the medieval community and replaced it with ruthless capitalists who made money at the expense of society. But if in fact England had already long been an individualist society, as I have laid out, then the opposite was true: It was individualist, optimizing attitudes that created capitalism, first on the land and then in the factories. Other countries, such as China and India, possessed sophisticated cultures, but they simply could not compete with individualistic Britain or Europe as economic machines.[19]

If culture were not important to development, it would not be associated so strongly with wealth and poverty. National income would be determined mainly by structural factors, such as geography or natural resources, and both rich and poor nations would differ widely in temperament. But, as noted in chapter 4, Hofstede's studies of world cultures found that rich Europe and the Anglo countries were especially high in individualism. And the general correlation between individualism and per capita income was a "really remarkable" 0.82.[20]

Recent research by Gorodnichenko and Roland found that same relationship. Western countries typically are higher in both individualism and wealth per worker, while the non-West is lower in both. Individualism also predicts productivity and innovation. The association here is bivariate, but it holds up in analyses controlling for many other variables. Worldwide, individualism clearly has been the dominant way of wealth.[21]

THE NON-WEST

Asia, of course, has chosen a different path, with some countries achieving development more through collective authority than individual initiative. Some observers believe that the Confucian ethos of Taiwan, Korea, and Japan has supported economic growth because of its emphasis on education, frugality, merit, and social discipline.[22] Another view, however, is that Confucianism promotes ease over effort, the group over individual enterprise, and personal over market relationships.[23] Still, Asia's strong social cohesion, coupled with market reforms, has enabled some countries to make the extra effort required for rapid development, as exemplified by China and some other Asian countries.

Outside Asia, however, the non-Western world has not generally grown economically at a pace comparable to Europe or its offshoots. Most of these countries have not generated the social discipline needed for development on *either* an individualist *or* a collectivist basis. People within them either fear change or lack the capacity to impose it widely on the society. The impetus for spontaneous change is far weaker than in the West; there is no assertive middle class that promotes development. Nor is government usually strong enough to take the initiative. Regimes mostly fear change rather than promoting it.

We typically say that "tradition" is too strong in backward countries to permit modernization. But concretely what that means is usually that society is not individualist enough. In the West, ordinary people often sought change and achieved it, despite the disapproval of many around them. In the non-West, however, people typically have stronger ties to their social circle and are less willing to risk alienating those close to them. Their culture, including their religion, typically justifies things as they are and discourages questioning. There is strong resistance to economizing change, whether the impetus comes from individuals or the state. Elites, often swayed by the West, may seek development, but they face societies that are deeply resistant.[24] Even in Mexico, for example, where a good deal of development has occurred, rural areas remain deeply traditional, with peasants deeply attached to their land, their families, and the status quo. In their world, spontaneous change driven from below remains difficult to imagine.[25]

Producers in non-individualist societies typically fear market competition. One reflection of this is crony capitalism. Influential companies in non-Western countries receive various forms of protection from government. Insider practices ensure that these firms remain profitable, without serious accountability to consumers or competitors. Arab countries, for example, may "have capitalist economies, in which prices and private enterprise play a big role," *The Economist* noted, "[y]et it is a distorted, patriarchal capitalism characterized by a dominant state, kleptocratic monopolies, heavy regulation, and massive subsidies. This has fueled corruption, stunted growth, and left millions without jobs." Protections extend also to the public, which often receives subsidies for food, energy, and other necessities rather than, as in the West, trusting the market to provide them.[26] Such protections help explain why, in Brazil (for example), producers and workers are not as dynamic and productive as in richer countries.[27]

In Asia, despite recent growth, incestuous ties between government and the private sector limit the potential for wealth. Japan, Korea, and other countries continue to pursue industrial policies that, in theory, guide development, but in practice shield established firms. One reason that Japan has not fully recovered from its severe recession of the 1990s (although it remains a rich country) is its reluctance to allow many of its banks to fail.[28] The West has usually, if not always, been less protective. And although China's opening to the market in the late 1970s was the chief reason for its rapid growth, its economy still harbors a large and unproductive state sector. Although there are ambitious entrepreneurs in China, many people still prefer to work for government rather than private firms, due to the security it provides.[29]

These protections exact a cost. Cross-nationally, per capita wealth is strongly related to competitiveness, meaning the strength of countries' infrastructure, financial systems, flexible labor markets, and other institutions. In general, Western countries have the most competitive economies and are therefore richest. And the relationship is stronger at higher incomes than low. It is after nations reach a minimal level of wealth that explicit policies to promote or limit openness make the most difference.[30]

How, then, can non-Western economies be freed from the endless restraints on the magic of the market? Paul Romer has imagined "charter cities" that would be granted relatively liberal economies, like that of Hong Kong, one of the first Chinese ports to permit foreign trade. But Third World governments distrust the market too much to allow this.[31]

Of course, anti-market policies are not unknown in the West. In Italy and Greece, the economies are honeycombed with monopolies and other protections for various trades and industries. That shields many workers from insecurity but—in a classic case of self-defeating pluralism—makes those countries worse off overall.[32] Yet in general, the will and the ability to compete are strongest in the West, and this allows those countries to reap the greatest benefits from free economies. Broad support for market economics also makes it harder for determined minorities in the West to attain the protections they enjoy in less individualist societies.

THE SEARCH FOR OPPRESSION

Although the importance of culture for development is clear enough, academic reasoning has paid little attention to it. When attempting to explain a lack of development, experts typically seek out some impediment of an impersonal—usually economic—kind. Economists tend to assume that all societies are economizing and hence fundamentally alike; the differences are entirely in the resources and opportunities they command. And, in the Western experience, economic freedom did lead to wealth. Observers fail to see the discipline to accept the market that in fact makes freedom work in the West—and the lack of market discipline that keeps much of the rest of the world poor. In short, they are blind to cultural difference.

At one time, the legacy of colonialism was thought to doom formerly dependent territories to backwardness. Research now suggests, rather, that European influence *accelerated* development in former colonies by strengthening their public institutions (as I show in the next chapter). Several decades ago, some scholars argued for dependency theory, the idea that the global economy might condemn some countries to underdevelopment even if they were formally independent, as in Latin America. This theory has weak empirical support, however, and is belied by the recent growth in some Latin American countries.[33]

Today, international institutions actively promote development, and it is unclear whether bodies such as the World Bank could do any better in this regard than they have.[34] In the 1990s, international economists framed a "Washington consensus," the idea that developing countries should be more open to market forces, including foreign trade and investment. But—except in some Asian countries—the developing world typically shows less economic openness than the West.

The main impediments to these nations' development are likely internal. In the least developed countries, as in Africa, an obvious lack of infrastructure seems the culprit. Without investments in roads, ports, and so on, Africa can never compete with Asia, despite the lower cost of goods produced there.[35] But aside from this, it has been difficult to show that underdevelopment is centrally due to economics or in fact to any impersonal condition. Growing cities simply have not generated the growing wealth in Africa that they did in Europe.[36] Misgovernment is one clear explanation (as I show in the next chapter),[37] but why government is so weak outside the West is also a mystery. Behind both outcomes seems to be the sheer passivity of most non-Western societies, their lack of any strong impulse to improve either the economy or government. This would explain why—outside Asia—even elites have been unable to impose much change.

Western governments, led by the United States, have tried to promote growth in these countries—first through foreign aid, later through efforts to develop better markets, and then by efforts to improve governance. But none of these approaches has achieved much. Some economists, led by Jeffrey Sachs, believe that still more generous aid could at last jump-start Third World growth, but that view persuades fewer people today than it once did.[38] William Easterly concluded that all these strategies have, ironically, better served aid donors and international agencies than the poor countries they were supposed to help. Outside help can succeed only if a stronger commitment to improvement arises within poor countries themselves.[39] That is tantamount to saying that the lifestyle of these societies must change.

Journalistic and academic discussions of underdevelopment too often ignore culture. Many writers ask, for instance, why America has not produced development in poor countries in the same way it helped Europe and Japan recover from World War II. The difference, of course, is that Europe and Japan were already highly developed before the war. They already had highly skilled and disciplined labor forces, without the same evasion of the market seen in much of the Third World. All they needed was more resources, not a new way of life. If Third World countries were at all similar to Europe or Japan, many of them would have been taken off decades ago.

Why did the United States and Canada develop so much more strongly than Latin America? Economists suppose that the European populations in North America were more equal in "factor endowments" and "human capital" than those to the south, where European elites had ruled over vastly less fortunate slave or Indian populations.[40] But this ignores the huge cultural difference between the strongly individualist and largely Anglo populations of North America and the strongly collectivist cultures of Latin America, built on Native Americans and Africans. South Africa has a relatively high income for Africa, but that is chiefly because of the Dutch and English immigrants who led its development. The destitution still faced by common people in South Africa is typically seen as a legacy of colonialism and apartheid, ignoring the huge cultural differences between Africa and the West.[41]

Comparisons are often drawn between the United States and Mexico, its southern neighbor, as if nothing separated them but economic conditions that America has the power to change. *The Economist* wrote in 2006, for example:

> When the North American Free Trade Agreement (NAFTA) came into force in 1994, it was hoped that Mexico's economy would quickly converge with the United States. That hasn't happened. In the late 1990s, Mexico's GDP grew half as fast again as America's. No longer. China has partly displaced Mexico as a supplier of low-wage manufacturing. Nowadays, Mexico creates decent jobs for only around a quarter of the 800,000 who join its workforce each year.
>
> The main way to change that is for Mexico's next president...to push through long-delayed reforms of taxes, energy, labour and competition laws. But there is one way the United States could help. Lack of roads and railways mean that the benefits of NAFTA have been largely confined to northern Mexico, rather than the poorer centre and south where most migrants come from. A North American infrastructure fund—in which the United States matched Mexican investment—makes much more sense than spending money on a border wall. In the long run, a richer Mexico means a richer and more secure United States.[42]

But although Mexico has done better recently, there never was any prospect that it could "quickly converge" with the American economy under

NAFTA. That prediction ignored Mexico's chronic corruption, drug violence, and weak entrepreneurial talent, all linked to its far more passive
and collectivist mind-set compared to America's.[43]

MARKET MORALITY

So far I have emphasized the economizing burdens imposed by market
economies, which an individualist culture is most able to bear. The usual
analysis assumes that individuals' natural tendency is to directly serve
only themselves, and only the invisible hand of the market forces them to
serve any larger interest. But in fact, Smith's case for the market presumes
background virtues that are more humanist. In *The Theory of the Moral
Sentiments*, written before *The Wealth of Nations*, Smith posited that a
healthy society displays qualities of sympathy so that people can attend
to the needs of others, even before their own.[44]

A capitalist economy may free a society from medieval constraints
such as "just price," but that society must then develop a new, "market morality" appropriate to capitalism. Individuals must be honest, accountable
for their behavior to others, and—above all—willing to deal with everyone
impartially, even strangers. In the West, Protestantism strongly promoted
those values.[45] A readiness to trust relative strangers in economic and
political matters is a quality that sharply distinguishes most people in
Western countries from those in the non-West, where people tend to
trust only their immediate family or associates. Trust is higher in Britain
and Germany, the economic leaders of Europe, than in Latin countries,
and it is higher in Japan than in other Asian countries.[46] Statistical studies
support the idea that more trusting societies are likely to be richer, even
when controlling for many other factors.[47]

Earnest and trusting qualities are also essential to the nonmarket
side of the economy, which in the United States has become increasingly
important, as shown in the previous chapter. There are some tasks that
only nonprofit bodies can perform or that they do better than for-profit
ones.[48] To function, a nonprofit has to convince potential contributors
that it serves goals other than its own enrichment, and it must motivate
its employees to "do the right thing." The public and private sectors differ
in the motivations they assume, yet both must make moral presumptions
that surpass narrow self-interest.

THE CULTURALISTS

While economists typically ignore culture in explaining underdevelopment, another group of observers in a sense overemphasize it. These writers, whom I call the culturalists, include Lawrence Harrison, David Landes, and several others. Harrison is a former officer of the US Agency for International Development in Latin America. He became convinced that it was inhabitants' ways of thinking, rather than any economic factor, that largely explained the region's underdevelopment.[49] Landes is an economic historian who concluded, from an ambitious survey of world development, that "culture makes all the difference" to which countries have become rich or remain poor.[50]

These authors say that the main problem in poor countries is that their cultures tolerate bad behavior. In these societies, compared to the West, many people fail to work very hard, obey the law, adhere to moral principles, decide issues on the merits, behave fairly toward others, and—above all—accept responsibility for their problems. People typically attribute their personal difficulties to outside forces, including mistreatment by the rich world. In the West, by contrast, and especially in the Anglo countries, people typically behave better and do accept responsibility. That difference, rather than anything economic, explains the West's much greater wealth. This indictment is seconded even by some Third World leaders, such as Oscar Arias, former president of Costa Rica.[51]

Harrison is careful to say that these cultural differences have nothing inherently to do with race, nor is successful development entirely confined to the West. He celebrates Asian success stories such as that of Japan and those of Chinese transplants, as well as the successful Caribbean island of Barbados and the recent acceleration of growth in Brazil. He also argues, as I do, that culture can change. Through strong political leadership, better education, and religious reform, a poor society can learn attitudes that are more conducive to rational problem-solving, meritocracy, law-abidingness, and growth. Exemplars of such leadership are Kemal Ataturk in Turkey and Lee Kuan Yew in Singapore.

Nevertheless, most academic students of development reject the culturalist analysis. Most believe that poor countries are so handicapped that they cannot be expected to develop without significant accommodations by the international economic order. The West must give them more resources, and international trade rules must be changed in their favor, an idea once called the New International Economic Order.[52] The seemingly negative attitudes in these societies, most academics believe, simply reflect the hardships they have long endured, often at the hands of the West.

The culturalists, in turn, reject this sort of structuralism as enabling the same defensive attitudes that they criticize. "In this world, the optimists have it," Landes retorts, "not because they are always right, but because they are positive. Even when wrong they are positive, and that is the way of achievement, correction, improvement, and success."[53] The culturalists refuse to shift the responsibility for development to outsiders and thus deny the individualized commitments that liberated growth in the West.[54]

Both sides are correct, just not in the way they suppose. In some immediate sense, the culturalists' indictment of non-Western behavior is correct. In poor countries, practices that are dysfunctional from a Western viewpoint are indeed a worse detriment to development than any economic obstacles. The culturalists, however, moralize against these patterns of behavior as if they were the faults of individuals, as they would be in the West. In fact, the faults are collective—the product of the non-Western, often pessimistic worldview described in chapter 4. And in explaining that mind-set, the structuralists have a case. Distrustful attitudes that obstruct change may well have arisen from denials of opportunity over many generations. Thus, bad behavior may be the immediate cause of underdevelopment—but that behavior, in turn, has structural causes.

The culturalists sometimes suggest that unhelpful attitudes can be overcome by a mere act of will, whether by leaders or individuals. They seem not to realize how radical that change would be. Poor countries would reject the fatalism that often defeats them, but they would then have to bear the burdens of freedom, which may well be greater. For people to be individually responsible for their life outcomes, whether positive or negative, would be a huge change in these societies. It would require, J. M. Roberts remarks, nothing less than a "mental transformation."[55] The "trauma," Alan Macfarlane predicts, would be "far more intense" than it was for England during industrialization, where a precocious individualism eased the strain. Poor countries, therefore, "need to consider whether the costs in terms of loneliness, insecurity and family tensions...outweigh the economic benefits."[56]

THE PROTESTANT ETHIC

To summarize, the free market requires some elements of moral commitment by individuals toward each other, not simply pursuing self-interest. But economic freedom also rests on obligation of a more demanding kind. The energy behind the market comes not just from individuals seeking their own best bargain, but also from entrepreneurs who create economic activity. Their will to pursue enterprise requires commitments beyond those of the ordinary good citizen, worker, or consumer.

Where does that energy come from? Here we encounter Max Weber's famous argument that the chief force behind the rise of Western capitalism was the Protestant ethic. Weber accepted that mere desire for gain and even taking risks to obtain it were found in every society. But capitalism involved the systematic pursuit of enterprise over the long term so as to maximize profit. This rationalism was disciplined, even ascetic, contrary to the natural human wish for immediate fulfillment. Weber believed, accordingly, that it could be explained only through religious motivation.

He located that drive in the more extreme forms of European Protestantism. These creeds, especially Calvinism, denied believers the routine reassurance of God's acceptance which Catholicism had provided through penance and other sacraments. Thus, to be sure that they were "saved," Calvinists simply had to believe it, or they had to prove it through outward success, such as getting rich. Thus, spiritual insecurity drove them toward secular achievement. Protestantism's "valuation of restless, continuous, systematic work in a worldly calling," Weber wrote, provided "the most powerful conceivable lever" behind the growth of capitalism. In England, it became a basis for world power and even "a principle of general conduct."[57]

Historically, Protestants were more prominent than Catholics in the creation of the modern economy in Europe. Still today, within Europe, Protestant countries are generally richer, more modern, and better governed than Catholic or Orthodox countries,[58] but that does not establish that Protestantism produced this difference. In a more rigorous test, David McClelland found that an achieving temperament was associated with faster economic growth over time and that this attitude was linked to Protestantism in Britain just prior to its periods of rapid growth.[59]

Critics of Weber contend that he exaggerated the capacity of the more extreme Protestant sects to motivate capitalism. Perhaps Calvinists were too ascetic to have accepted worldly wealth as a sign of virtue.[60] Perhaps a rationalizing attitude really stemmed from medieval Christianity, which already endorsed the virtue of work and the efficient management of enterprise.[61] Perhaps religion was only a justification for the liberated individualism that rejected the social values that the medieval economy had served.[62] And perhaps the drive to succeed can be found in non-Western spiritual traditions, such as the Confucian ethos mentioned earlier.

Weber probably overstated the specific role of Calvinism in generating capitalism. But he was correct to say that a rationalizing attitude was crucial to Western development, and he characterized memorably the inner-driven psychology behind that.[63] The urge to calculate and rationalize is not a constant of human nature, as economists typically assume, but can vary widely for essentially cultural reasons.[64] Nowhere but in Europe and its offshoots do we find so strong a commitment to the disciplined mastery of external challenges. This was why, Weber suggested, Western culture had a "*universal* significance and value" not found elsewhere.[65] And that, in turn, meant, as shown in chapter 4, that science has been primarily a Western achievement.

Weber might as well have been writing about America. In the United States, attitudes favorable to both entrepreneurialism and science remain strong, more so than in Europe or Japan. And business innovation and science are also closely linked. The nerve centers of the globalized economy lie in places like Silicon Valley, where business and leading universities are closely tied.[66]

THE CALLING

Weber's capitalists were driven by personal religious fears, but more influential may have been the broader and more positive notion of the calling. The idea, born of Protestantism, is that one's life should proceed from inner goals. That idea has helped motivate much individualism in Western societies, especially in the Anglo countries.[67] In the world of the calling, it is not enough to work hard at a task given to you by others. Your work is not just a job but a vocation. You must set your own goal, to be achieved over time, and organize your life around it. Progress toward

FIGURE 7.1 **Maggie Doyne in Nepal**

Source: Nicholas Kristof, "The D.I.Y. Foreign-Aid Revolution," *New York Times Magazine*, October 24, 2010, pp. 49–53.

that goal gives your life meaning. Your task organizes your future. You are then in harmony with God, however God is understood; you have your eyes on the horizon.

Figure 7.1 depicts Maggie Doyne, a young American woman who, despite limited resources, founded a school in Nepal. She is staring straight ahead into the camera, exuding that inner direction that guides her life. Her students, around her, seem much more cautious. They are of course much younger than she is, but above all their largely traditional culture does not promote the individualized commitment she shows. To them, her temperament alone is enough to make her their leader.

FIGURE 7.2 **Charter School Leader Eva Moskowitz**

Source: Daniel Bergner, "Class Warrior," *New York Times Magazine*, September 7, 2014.

Figure 7.2 shows another American woman, Eva Moskowitz, who created a successful charter school network in New York City. Moskowitz has weathered numerous battles with the city and state to build her schools, in which students typically test better than in the public schools. Just like Doyne, she radiates direction. Inner conviction dominates her life. She is free to be a successful innovator, but only because she is inwardly unfree—totally dedicated to her calling.

As her example suggests, the world of the calling provides the psychic energy behind not only private entrepreneurship, but also the vast nonprofit sector. Only an individualist culture could create such a world. To achieve progress, an individualist society must produce motivated overachievers like these women. It must tolerate and even encourage what they do. As I show further below, that is possible only in an individualistic culture that combines personal freedom with strong institutions.

THE DEFEAT OF COLLECTIVISM

Though predisposed to accept capitalism, the West did not simply surrender to it. By the late nineteenth century, even as industrialism created new wealth, a collectivist movement arose to restore society's earlier control over the economy. Governments in various ways began to shield societies from the full rigors of the marketplace.[68] They tried to manipulate public finances and the money supply to prevent the economic downturns that periodically destroyed jobs. They also regulated the labor market to improve working conditions and stop employers from firing workers arbitrarily. They directly controlled some prices and wages so that more families could afford the necessities of life. They provided some essentials—education, housing, health care—publically. And they established a welfare state to support some groups, such as the elderly and the disabled, who could not support themselves.

More radically, socialists proposed to replace capitalism entirely with an economy run by government, which would supposedly be fairer. That vision was literally achieved only in the Communist bloc, where political as well as economic freedoms were denied, but it had strong appeal among intellectuals even in the West.[69] In Europe and America, socialism was mostly limited to public takeover of some industries; the rest of the economy, and its demands, remained private.

Social programs were enacted first in the late nineteenth century, with Europe generally leading the way. In the United States, some important social programs were enacted in the 1930s and 1960s, but America still lacks some public benefits that are routine in Europe, such as a minimum cash income assured to all and universal health care.

Collectivism in this sense weakened the public's accountability to the market. The welfare state and restrictions on employers created economic rights that complemented existing legal and political rights. This meant that the need for producers to compete in the market, or even for people to work at all, was reduced. Citizenship was separated from employment, and most intellectuals applauded.[70]

But by the 1980s, social democracy faced reverses. Overspending by governments to reduce unemployment had promoted inflation. Socialized industries turned out to be wasteful, so most were privatized. Price and wage controls also had proved inefficient, so they were reduced. Inability to match the productivity of Western capitalism was a central reason for the collapse of Communism in the Soviet Union and Eastern Europe.

Above all, in the 1980s and 1990s, the welfare state was reformed. Dependency on government benefits had come to seem excessive—allowing many work-averse adults who *could* hold jobs to avoid employment indefinitely. So some benefits were cut, while others were conditioned on employment. Social rights must now, Western leaders decided, be linked to social obligations—above all, employment.[71] The attempt to separate citizenship from economic function was rejected, and many intellectuals mourned.[72] These reforms were most associated with Ronald Reagan in America and Margaret Thatcher in Britain, but they occurred across most rich countries.[73]

Collectivism in the West meant a change in social and economic organization. It did not make these countries collectivist in a cultural sense. Western societies remained strongly individualist whether they moved toward or away from the market economy. Indeed, the moralism of Western culture generated much of the impetus behind collectivism. But at the same time, collectivism came to be seen as one cause of a general weakening of individualism in Western societies. The welfare state, especially, allowed nonworkers to claim the rights of a free society while ignoring its intended burdens—especially employment. So (as I show in chapter 10), more directive programs that enforce work and other civilities have become central to restoring individualism in America and Europe.

CONCLUSION

The market economy, first developed in the West, has made many nations richer. Yet the idea that the market works independently of culture cannot be sustained. The magic of the market is strongest where individuals interact autonomously, each of them seeking to optimize his or her utilities. Each must orient to *inner* goals and then seek to advance them in competition with others. Although the system presumes some moral commitments to others, these too are features of an individualist psychology. They promote, rather than impede, the efficient meshing of supply and demand. Even in the wake of recent collectivism, that still is the basic psychology of the West.

In a collectivist culture, on the other hand, the freedom to optimize is inevitably restricted by far more constraining ties to others. So in the non-West, the market is more feared. It is hedged around with more limitations, and much of its efficiency is lost. The richer Asian countries have overcome resistance to the market mainly by promoting development through government and (only later) incorporating market elements. Thus, in Asian capitalism, the market is the handmaiden of the state.

The culturalists mentioned above remark on how difficult it is for officials engaged in development to admit its dependence on culture. In helping poor countries, Landes noted, experts prefer to talk about impersonal things, such as interest and exchange rates. To criticize culture would "cut close to the ego" and "injure identity and self-esteem."[74] Harrison described international institutions as places "where both donors and recipients have a voice, and where it is much more interpersonally comfortable, and less threatening to self-esteem, to view the countries lagging behind either as the victims of the more successful countries or as merely having failed so far to find the proper mix of policies, incentives and institutions."[75]

The ultimate barriers to any nation's development today are psychological, not economic. Classical economists assume that people in every country will respond to opportunity in the energetic way Westerners do. But the problem in most underdeveloped countries, David McClelland remarked, is that most people do not have the "character structure, especially the motivational structure," that this presumes. "The model is like a combustion engine without gas to make it go."[76]

CHAPTER EIGHT

GOOD GOVERNMENT

After geography and the market, a final root of power is good government. Countries need strong regimes if they are to achieve efficient economies, convert wealth into military power, and project power abroad. Government is also the leading exemplar of the civic values that help earn the admiration of other countries and hence generate soft power.

Worldwide trends in government have lately been positive. In recent decades, many countries have inaugurated, or returned to, democratic regimes (in the sense that officeholders are elected). The gains were particularly large following World War II and again after the collapse of the Soviet Union in 1991.[1] The spread of democracy, like the market, appears to have drawn many countries closer to the West. And elected government, like the market, may appear to be a movement that owes little to culture; democratic elections have the potential to improve government in every country, regardless of the different ways of life.

But as with the market, appearances deceive. Although elected government is a step forward, it actually does little to improve the quality of government, in the sense of the regime's will and ability to serve the society. In government, Western countries continue to enjoy huge advantages, even more than they do in economics. And again, the leading reason is culture. An individualist mind-set promotes the qualities of good citizenship and also assertiveness that a society needs to develop good government and maintain it over time.

Some say that the confusions of the Trump administration have brought good government in America into question. Other policymakers and much of the public, however, have mobilized to defend public mores, and this shows how strong American institutions are.

In the discussion below, I first describe what good government means. The fact that good government is achieved most fully in Western countries appears due mainly to the moralism of Western culture—the fruit of its individualist psychology—and secondarily to the exceptional political gifts of the British, who founded all the Anglo nations, including the United States. Other explanations—which blame weak government in non-Western countries on a lack of freedom or on underdevelopment—are far less persuasive.

Parts of Asia have recently developed better government without an individualist culture, just as they have become wealthy. But except for Japan, no Asian regime is yet as formidable as those in the West. I conclude that the problem of weak government in the non-West is deeply seated. Misgoverned countries cannot improve their lot without becoming culturally more moralistic, more like the West. For this they would have to shoulder the burdens of freedom, and that is a distant prospect.

GOOD GOVERNMENT

Good government implies more than democracy. It connotes both the rule of law and government by consent. The rule of law—a complicated idea—means that government operates by general rules that are publicly justified as serving a public interest. Everything officials do, accordingly, is authorized by laws enacted by due process and subjected to public scrutiny. Rulers make decisions not in a personal or arbitrary way but rather in a general way that treats the relevant parties impartially. Especially, functionaries do not make private gains out of their offices, and bribery is rare. Legal offenses are adjudicated by courts that are independent of the regime.

Government by consent connotes that officeholders do not rule only for themselves or for those in government; rather, they are accountable to a political class wider than the government itself. Today that usually implies that leaders are elected under adult suffrage, but who can vote and when is less important than the regime's willingness to accept outside criticism. Together, the rule of law and government by consent imply that officeholders govern not solely in their own interest but as stewards of public institutions serving the whole society. More than any specific policies, these institutions embody the public interest.[2]

The deeper meaning of consent is that government must respect the autonomy of individuals. It cannot impose authority upon them without consultation. Even if a democratic decision goes against an individual, he or she has at least been heard. At least in this sense, as Vaclav Havel said, citizens of a democracy can "live in truth"—the truth in which *they* believe.[3] The need for consent can sometimes delay governmental action in times of crisis. But once consent is given, an accountable regime is more formidable than an autocracy, simply because its citizens are now more committed to the task. Both Britain and America, for example, hesitated to enter both World Wars of the last century, but they then fought with near-total resolution and prevailed.

THE WESTERN EDGE

The world's dominant nations have been distinguished by strong government at least as much as by wealth. Good government was a principal reason why they became dominant and have remained so. That was historically true of Europe as a whole and even more of the Anglo nations that have recently held primacy—first Britain and then America.

The World Bank measures the quality of governance worldwide. Most of its indicators are self-explanatory:

- Voice and accountability
- Political stability and absence of violence
- Government effectiveness
- Regulatory quality
- Rule of law
- Control of corruption

"Government effectiveness" connotes the perceived quality of the public service, its freedom from undue political pressures, and the quality of policy formulation and implementation.

FIGURE 8.1 **Ranking of Major Nations on World Bank Governance Indicators 2015**

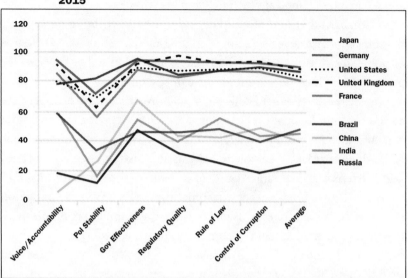

Source: World Bank web site, downloaded June 15, 2017, https://datacatalog.worldbank.org /dataset/worldwide-governance-indicators.

Figure 8.1 shows how the major nations rated on these variables in terms of percentile rank in 2015. On every dimension, the leading countries are nearly all Western. The sole exception is Japan.[4] The other non-Western countries—including China and India, which some expect to take over American primacy—all rank well below. The immediate question is—how could they lead the world with regimes so much less capable than those of their Western rivals?

The impact of governmental quality on wealth and power is profound. Economists have sometimes imagined that lifting a country out of poverty is just a matter of getting economic policies right. But as discussed in the last chapter, such efforts have achieved little. Many economists now realize that only a well-governed country can generate the trust and enterprise needed for growth. The big question is how governance in poor countries can be improved.[5]

Even Adam Smith, the prophet of capitalism, remarked that it was even more important for wealth that a country protect property legally than that its markets be free.[6] And the rule of law is associated chiefly with affluent, Western countries, as figure 8.2 shows. In these countries, corruption and bribery are rare, whereas in poor countries they are systemic.

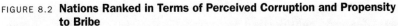

FIGURE 8.2 **Nations Ranked in Terms of Perceived Corruption and Propensity to Bribe**

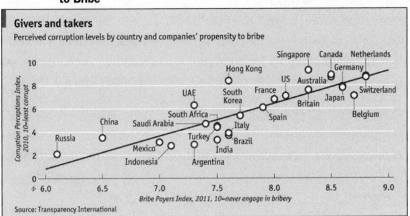

Source: "Supply Side," *The Economist*, November 5, 2011, p. 72.

Except for Japan and the Asian city-states of Hong Kong and Singapore, all the highly ranked countries are European or Anglo.

Governance problems in the non-West show up in recurrent political turmoil. Even in countries that have traded military rule for elected government, political violence may be chronic. Ordinary people are forced to pay corrupt functionaries to avoid mistreatment by them. Less visibly, the quality of public services is often abysmal; tellingly, in few countries outside the West is the public water supply safe to drink. For example, the foreign tourists who visit glamorous resorts in Mexico must buy bottled water. And when it comes to Central America, "Panama City's skyscrapers are dazzling," *The Economist* writes, "but look down and the pavements are often covered in leaking sewage."[7]

As Thomas Friedman lamented, in poor parts of the world, "hundreds of millions of people...have no hope...for two reasons: Either they are too sick, or their local governments are too broken for them to believe they have a pathway forward."[8] So, many people struggle to emigrate to the West, where government is immensely better. But that influx can also threaten the very civility that they seek (as I show in chapter 11).

WESTERN DEVELOPMENT

Western governance was not always so impressive. Rather, it improved over time, and this fact is even more significant than how well it performs today. Development occurred roughly in three stages. First, European ideas of government derived a strongly legal cast from classical Rome, whose legal system was the most highly developed of all ancient civilizations.[9] The Romans were the first to establish institutions that had some authority apart from the personal power of the officeholder. The feudal regimes of Europe were weak in the sense that power was dispersed, but they already, at least in form, embodied the cornerstones of good government—the ideas that rulers were to govern by law and accept accountability to their peers.[10]

Second, in much of Europe, medieval kings strengthened their regimes by centralizing power at the expense of their vassals. By the eighteenth century, some of these states had become bureaucratic, employing organized officials to perform growing functions. The rule of law was substantially achieved, but accountability suffered—because, in most countries, the kings downgraded parliaments dating from medieval times.[11] And in Germany, Italy, and much of Eastern Europe, national unity and independence were not achieved until the nineteenth or twentieth century.

Third, these powerful regimes then were democratized as their societies reasserted control over them. This happened through a messy process of uprisings and war, beginning in the seventeenth century and lasting through the late twentieth century. Today, Europe comprises mostly well-governed states, nearly all of them legal and democratic in character, and most of them now joined in the European Union. Political development finally has achieved that paradoxical condition in which the regime has enough authority to govern the society yet still is politically subject to it.[12]

European peoples who emigrated to distant continents mostly brought advanced institutions with them. Especially, the Anglo nations of recent settlement, including Australia, Canada, New Zealand, and the United States, inherited legal and accountable government from Britain. To be sure, these countries required further development before they achieved the fully legal, bureaucratic, and elected regimes they have today. The United States, notably, was born as a legal and democratic country, but only in the twentieth century did it develop the administrative capacity to respond to the demands of world wars, world leadership, and growing domestic needs.[13]

Thus, in the long term, the development of strong government in the West was steady and successful. In the short term, of course, political progress has suffered reversals of the kind that many judge Trump's presidency of the United States to be. And we have recently seen anti-democratic trends in some Eastern European countries. But viewed over history, advancement in Western government appears relentless—even inevitable. In Western politics, few governmental abuses, scandals, or weaknesses are endured forever. The will to improve is unceasing and, in the end, irresistible. That temperament is what only the moralism of Western culture can explain.

THE NON-WEST

In the non-West, political development has been much more tentative. For centuries, government outside Europe and its offshoots has been comparatively weak—not only more corrupt and less democratic, but also less able to govern in more elemental senses. The wide difference in capacity to rule between the West and other parts of the world (see figure 8.2) is echoed throughout history.

That might be partly because the non-West has different values from the West. Some scholars note that most of humanity has lived for most of history under remote empires that made no pretense of serving the society or answering to it. Rulers sought mainly to stay in power and serve themselves, justifying their power as morally above question. In most of the world, the modern, legal, and democratic state is a recent import.[14]

But today most of the non-West shows at least formal commitment to norms of legality and democracy. Amartya Sen has argued that countries outside the West also have a tradition of "government by discussion," and there has been some movement toward democracy in much of the developing world.[15] There is little reason to doubt that Mexicans, for example, desire good government as much as Americans do.

What differs, though, is Mexico's ability to achieve it. North of the Rio Grande, the United States is a law-governed country where government is generally effective and accountable, if far from perfect. South of the border, however, drug gangs essentially rule large areas of Mexico, murdering local mayors who stand in their way. Even leaders elected with a mandate to tackle the violence are unable to do so. Mexico has been forced to extradite many drug kingpins to the United States for trial because its own judicial system is so weak and corrupt. Legality is also relatively weak in Brazil and elsewhere in Latin America.[16]

Somehow, the civic values that buttress the regime in America are immensely stronger than those in Mexico, even though formal adherence to them is the same. In America, commitment to the proper and equal treatment of citizens is so strong that, over history, it has driven corruption down while flattening many of the differences that once divided the public. At least formally, the United States no longer allows discrimination on grounds of race, gender, or sexual orientation. A powerful and abstract idea of citizenship reigns.[17]

In the West, modern civic values have dominated older loyalties for centuries. In Mexico, however, as in much of the developing world, parochial attachments to family, locality, or tribe still compete strongly with obedience to the state and with more encompassing values. People enrich their friends or relatives through payoffs or private connections rather than upholding impartial rule. In the extreme case, in a failed state like Yemen, tribes and clans carry on endless feuds, as if society had never left the state of nature.[18]

A Latin American country may appear to have all the trappings of a modern state, including an ambitious welfare state. But the reality is far different. There is a formal sector to the economy in which workers are ensured job protections and benefits, much as in the West. But meanwhile, half the continent's labor force—135 million people—lives essentially outside the law. Millions work in an informal sector, unknown to government, in which firms rarely grow above family size for lack of any larger trustworthy institutional structure.[19]

There is, of course, change in the non-West. Elections occur, leaders are ousted, and wars are fought. But public institutions do not grow in strength and authority nearly as clearly as they did over European or American history. Almost two centuries ago, Hegel remarked that in Eastern empires there was "ceaseless conflict" but without moral progress, and the same is still true in most of the world today.[20] There has been notable economic development in many countries, but generally short of the Western level—and without comparable improvement in government. In this sense, we have what Fukuyama called "modernization without development."[21]

THEORIES OF MISRULE

The usual explanations for weak government in the non-West stress either oppression or underdevelopment, and fail to convince.[22] One of these theories fingers imperialism. For several generations, European powers controlled much of the non-West. Often they kept local despots in power and prevented evolution toward democracy or a more modern economy. They also imposed borders that cut across underlying tribal or ethnic divisions and thus weakened government, particularly in Africa and the Middle East.[23]

But, as mentioned already, research suggests that nonetheless colonial rule actually favored the development of countries after independence. That is probably because European settlement in the colonies strengthened their public institutions.[24] To varying extents, the European powers implanted their own institutions in their colonies. (This differentiated them from the traditional empires of the non-West, such as the Ottomans and the Chinese, who left no such legacy.) Above all, Britain gave India its "basic structure" by installing courts, an army, universities, and eventually representative institutions. According to Fareed Zakaria, India owes its very existence as a nation to British rule.[25] The main limitation of colonial rule was that it was too brief in most countries, notably in Africa, to have much impact.[26] The British impact on India was exceptional, but it required almost two centuries of Western control.

After independence in the 1960s, observers assumed that former colonies would speedily achieve Western norms of governance, including the rule of law and democracy. But in general they did not. Independence weakened rather than enhanced commitment to political modernity. The "new nations" often succumbed to one-party or military rule. Governmental quality often declined, particularly in Africa. Countries regressed toward the oligarchic, unaccountable rule that had prevailed prior to colonialism.[27]

Similarly, after the end of history, the former satellites of the Soviet Union were freed to govern themselves. Many had strong incentives to adopt Western forms of government in order to join the European Union, the better to become modern and rich. Around the same time, the end of military rule in many other countries, notably in Latin America, seemed to mean a worldwide victory for democracy.

But since independence or liberation, the actual quality of government has improved little. Elections in formerly unfree countries are often fraught with difficulties, requiring amnesty or concessions to the military or oligarchs who previously ruled.[28] Even elected governments are often fragmented or irresolute, unable to solve problems, or prone to some form of autocracy, leading them back to less liberal forms of rule.[29] The idea that a "transition" to democracy or legality is occurring is no longer tenable, despite hopes in the West.[30]

This pattern repeated itself again with the recent Arab Spring. Starting in 2010, a wave of protests against autocracy toppled dictatorships in Tunisia, Egypt, and Libya and seemed to threaten similar change elsewhere in the Middle East. Commentators drew parallels to past revolutions in Europe and to the American Revolution. But in most Arab countries, autocratic rule survived—or returned. Open government has survived—precariously—only in Tunisia. Again, to achieve democracy seems to require something more than the mere end of oppression, contrary to what many Americans believe.

A related idea, suggested also in the last chapter, is that governments in poor nations overcontrol the society. Whether or not they are democratic, regimes in these countries often have ambitious goals that impose too much change. That leads to the politicization of other institutions, causing political breakdown as well as economic stagnation. In one recent example, Hugo Chavez's attempt to institute socialism in Venezuela triggered a downward spiral of destructive conflict.

But the scope of government, in this sense, is quite different from its capacity to govern. As figure 8.3 suggests, Western regimes, including American government, are far stronger and more effective than most non-Western governments, even though they seek to impose less change. Even if most non-Western governments attempted less, they would still be far weaker than their Western counterparts.

A final approach has been to interpret political development as part of general modernization. As poor countries grow richer—many observers hope or assume—they will also become better governed. That idea has a long pedigree in social science.[31] Bill Gates, the software entrepreneur, once remarked that the tragedy of poor countries is that "they may never get into the virtuous cycle of more education, more health, more capitalism, more rule of law, more wealth," as if all these good things somehow

FIGURE 8.3 **Strength vs. Scope of State in Various Countries**

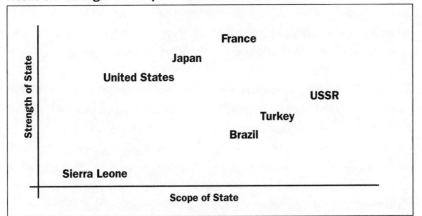

Source: Francis Fukuyama, *State-Building: Governance and World Order in the 21st Century* (Ithaca, NY: Cornell University Press, 2004), figure 5.

run together.[32] But modernization's connection with good government is ambiguous at best. It provides more wealth to invest in public institutions, but it also generates social change and thus builds new pressures on government, often causing breakdowns in weakly governed countries.[33]

It is true that economic and political modernization went together in the West, thus suggesting that one causes the other. But that was because both processes were driven by the background dynamism of the society. An ambitious middle class largely created both a modern economy and modern government. It shoved aside traditional powerholders in both domains. And, because of a disciplined individualist culture, fundamental order was also achieved. The great fact, as shown in chapter 2, is how much weaker that dynamism is in the non-West, in both economic and political spheres: on all fronts, most societies are simply more passive than the West, and in most places an entrenched oligarchy rules.[34]

A MORALISTIC CULTURE

Thus, the problem of bad government is not a problem of freedom in any simple sense. To achieve good government, it is not enough to overthrow oppressors. Rather, autocracy must be replaced with a new kind of order where government is more accountable to the society yet still has the authority to govern. Revolution cannot just be destructive; it must be followed by constitution-building if the hoped-for new order is to emerge.[35] To explain why democratic yet secure regimes have arisen chiefly in the West, we must identify some feature that unites its well-governed countries, despite their diversity, and which also separates them from the less fortunate non-West.

That feature is apparently the West's individualist culture. When Europe is defined geographically, this is the only feature that virtually all its countries share. And no individualist culture exists on any large scale outside the West. If culture did not matter, then good government—like economic development—would have occurred more randomly around the world, amid varying cultures. It would be determined entirely by structural conditions or idiosyncratic factors. But the fact is that the Western edge in governmental quality is enormous.

What, concretely, is the connection between individualism and good government? As explained in chapter 4, individualist psychology licenses self-seeking, but it also includes internalized commitments to moral values that are understood as general rules rather than social conventions. Those scruples seem to explain best why civic values are typically strongest in the West and why governments, as well as citizens, usually obey them.

In Western countries, most people display good citizenship, at least in that they generally obey the law and pay their taxes. That allows government to govern. But at the same time, moralism empowers society outside government to criticize officeholders so that they also mostly behave well. Those in power cannot rule without serious check, as they typically do in the non-West. The fact that moralism disciplines both leaders and led allows a shared culture of civility to arise.

This ethos seems to explain not only why Western governance is good today, but also why it has improved over history. One might imagine that a more collectivist culture where authority is less questioned would support government more strongly, but the opposite has been true. Apparently, as rulers instituted structures of law, bureaucracy, and consent, those arrangements quickly became the focus of moralistic attitudes both inside and outside of government. That increased the institutions' authority, as well as reformed and improved them over time. And eventually, public institutions became morally unassailable, entrenched in the dutiful attitudes of both leaders and led. Good government in the West ultimately resides in the conscience of Western publics.

And Western public institutions grew up despite serious political divisions and conflicts, even revolution and civil war. In the main, these disputes were about who should rule and what government should do, not about its basic authority. The institutions' very strength allowed most differences to be resolved or transcended over time, rather than becoming chronic, as they so often have in the developing world.

Francis Fukuyama has written that the main challenge in political development is for the state to overcome the more parochial loyalties with which human organization begins. Primitive peoples typically are loyal first to the family and village, then to their tribe. But in order for the state to arise, leaders must somehow transcend these patrimonial attachments. This China first achieved when the country was unified in 221 BC. But that state was soon toppled, and in China's later history, the state fought a constant battle against patrimonial tendencies, as it still does today. The same was true in other non-Western empires.[36]

Yet somehow in the West, societies achieved the leap from the tribe to the larger and more impersonal state far more securely. F. S. C. Northrop wrote in 1946 that only the West had a principled sense of morals, and thus only it could achieve strong states.[37] Few might have believed that bold assessment then, when many African and Asian countries were still colonies of the West, but it has proven true. Compared to Western moralism, the less principled, more situational ethic of the non-West simply does not provide the same support for public institutions.

Western politics, as a rule, simply has more moral content. Politics in the non-West is mostly about power—who governs and who gains from that. In the West, by contrast, both rulers and followers have to argue to a public interest more clearly. Politics also entails more legal content, with legislatures and courts clearly limiting the pursuit of narrow interests. Government provides more public benefits to the society, protecting property and supporting the market. All these differences between West and non-West were evident even in medieval times.[38] And in the West, government improves more clearly over time.[39]

CIVIC VIRTUE

Moralism's primary contribution to good government is to motivate good behavior by the citizenry. Hobbes, Locke, and other Western political theorists present government as a deal struck between autonomous individuals to serve their mutual interests. But on a strictly contractual basis like this, there would never be enough civic spirit to maintain a community. Citizens must both give and receive more than strict exchange requires. We must possess some ability to transcend our self-interest in relating to others, even people we do not know personally.[40] A crucial source of that willingness is a moralistic culture that calls for good behavior even toward the stranger.

Trust, in this broad sense, never arose in most of the developing world, probably because moralism about civic values was lacking. In Latin America, for instance, a sense of failed legitimacy pervades politics, so that trust is low and institutions are left feeble.[41] Exploitative behavior toward people outside one's immediate circle is accepted, and this undercuts development, as culturalist critics say (see chapter 7).

The difference moralism makes was dramatized after Mennonite immigrants from Germany created a cooperative farm in Filadelfia, Paraguay, in the 1920s. Their great civility as well as hard work stood out compared to the Paraguayan norm. Their religious commitments mandated principled behavior toward others, including non-Mennonites. Over the years, that behavior generated trust in Filadelfia. Native Paraguayans flocked to work for the German immigrants. Decades later, together they had created, as one official said, "a Paraguay that works."[42]

Islam has at least as strong a sense of principled morals as Judaism or Christianity. But despite this, the Arab world never developed a moralistic culture comparable to the West's. Muslims have never incorporated public norms as deeply in their attitudes as Westerners have. In the Middle East, moral order continues to depend mostly on enforcement by the authorities, without the same trust in the individual conscience seen in Europe or America. Hence, a principled attitude toward other citizens and public institutions has never arisen—and this is what doomed the Arab Spring. In Egypt, for example, the recent rebellion against military rule was defeated, as much as anything, by the failure of the parties and institutions involved to trust one another. Politics was, in Huntington's phrase, "praetorian."[43]

There are, of course, variations in civility among and within rich countries. Northern and western European countries are more civic than southern and eastern ones. Southern Italy, for example, is noted for endemic distrust. Families in the region often feud with one another and hence cannot cooperate for common ends. Northern Italy, however, is much more civic.[44] Levels of civility and trust also vary within the United States, with northern, good-government states such as Minnesota and Wisconsin ranking higher than the big urban or Southern states.[45] But these differences do not obviate the general contrast in civic attitudes between the West and the non-West as a whole. In every Western country, praetorian politics is the exception, not the rule.

The incivility of government in poor countries is, perhaps, dramatized most by corruption—the widespread abuse of public office for private gain. Both officials who take bribes and the citizens who pay them gain something personally, but at the expense of the broader public. Corruption cannot be controlled unless that wider interest is somehow made more salient. Felipe Calderón, as president of Mexico from 2006 to 2012, launched a war against the drug cartels that controlled much of his country. He was defeated largely because the willingness to give and take bribes was so ingrained. Gang killings have since escalated to more than 20,000 a year.[46] "We need a stronger society," Calderón declared, "[one] that lives the principle of legality with conviction." He meant, Marc Lacey wrote, "that there has to be a line people will not cross, even for a suitcase full of cash."[47] That line, alas, is difficult to define or defend in a situational culture such as Mexico's, in which morals lack the rigidity to hold people to civic behavior.

Chapter 7 showed that cultural qualities of trust are strongly associated with economic wealth across countries. There is a similar association between trust and good government: the more that members of a society show trust and respect for others, even those outside their immediate circle, the higher is its governmental performance, in terms of rule of law and bureaucratic capability.[48]

As one might expect, individualist countries are the most likely to be democratic.[49] That may confirm the popular idea that democracy only means keeping government under control. Stable democracy, however, also requires that citizens in some ways avoid politics and display the virtues of the good citizen—obeying government's just demands.[50] Individualism, it turns out, promotes these attributes as well. Societies that emphasize people's autonomy rather than their embeddedness in the society, and that promote egalitarianism over hierarchy, tend to exhibit stronger rule of law, less corruption, and greater accountability, even controlling for many other factors. That association is particularly strong in countries with an Anglo and Protestant heritage.[51]

ASSERTIVENESS

Moralism promotes civic behavior not only by individuals, but also by government. That is because moralistic attitudes point outward as well as inward. Citizens expect others, especially those in government, to feel bound to observe the same principles that they themselves do. This motivates society at large to keep a watch on officeholders and prevent misbehavior.

In Western politics, that surveillance long predates formal democracy. It accounts for the strong emphasis on *justification* that pervaded European politics from the outset. Rulers constantly explained and rationalized their actions to a wider political class, even in early times when that class comprised only the aristocracy. Chinese emperors, by contrast, displayed far less need or inclination to explain themselves. They often behaved toward rivals with a ruthlessness unimaginable in the West.[52] That was not because they had no moral code—they claimed to follow a Confucian ethic—but because China's passive and deferential culture did not license criticism from outside the regime.

In Western politics, moralistic criticism of government has sometimes led to revolution, but most often it promotes restless reformism. Critics—in and out of office—constantly arraign the regime by critical standards. They point to shortcomings and demand improvements. During the nineteenth century, domestic opposition to corruption and inefficiency helped drive state-building in both Britain and America—even though these were already among the world's best-governed countries. In America, reformers fastened on corruption in cities populated with immigrants from less civic realms. The critics were often Protestants, reflecting the original moralism of the Puritans, but much of the political class shared a distaste for payoffs.[53]

High-performing societies tend to be self-critical, not complacent as one might expect. Only a confident country dares to expose itself to principled standards. Hence the paradox, noted in the introduction, that self-criticism is actually a sign of American primacy. By contrast, as the culturalists point out, self-criticism is rare in Latin America.[54] In the non-Western manner, Latin American societies typically assign responsibility for public problems more to the outside environment—including the West—than to themselves.

Western critics often blame weak opposition to misgovernment in other countries on the repressive policies of these regimes. Simply allow political freedoms, these critics say, and democracy will blossom. The trouble, however, is that, without a moralistic culture, there is often no middle between misrule and mayhem. Autocrats protest that they cannot allow open criticism, lest it snowball until the regime is overwhelmed. They have a point. That is what happened to the Soviet regime after Mikhail Gorbachev allowed "glasnost" in the waning days of Communism.[55] It happened again to the regimes overthrown in the Arab Spring. The rebels who toppled those autocrats had no capacity to restore order, to build a new regime.[56] This was because there was no tradition of anyone outside the old order assuming any responsibility to govern.

Political conflict in uncivil societies tends to be total and unending. That is because in non-Western cultures moral obligations extend mainly to people in one's immediate setting. Problems tend to be attributed mainly to distant people or politicians. The onus for conflict thus lies entirely with one's enemies. Lack of self-restraint is the great vice of Arab politics, the reason democracy cannot survive there.

One reason Western assertiveness can be civic is precisely that conflict in the West is almost never total. Politicians differ over the issues of the moment, yet they share a commitment to the "rules of the game." One must observe moral limits even toward one's opponents. Some think that, in the wake of Trump, these restraints are breaking down, but we are still far from the unbridgeable chasms seen in other countries.

RECONCILING FREEDOM AND ORDER

As mentioned earlier, individualist psychology permits a reconciliation of order and freedom that is unique to the West. Order is enforced mainly through internalized inhibitions, allowing public enforcement to be minimized. But in the non-West, heavier reliance on external authority forces societies far more to choose between freedom and order.

This difference explains why Western regimes progressively gave up controls over public opinion and yet stayed in power, as non-Western regimes usually cannot do. Hegel believed that human rights do not simply exist but rather emerge through the growth of individual self-discipline over time.[57] That is exactly what we observe in European history. As rulers saw their institutions take hold, they grew more confident that citizens would obey them despite divisions of opinion. So they gradually allowed more open criticism. By the eighteenth century, religious dissent was accepted in many countries, and by the nineteenth—following the French Revolution—free speech and a free press had spread over much of Europe.

When Tocqueville came to America in 1831, he confronted "a confused clamor" of conflicting opinion on all sides. There was "apparent disorder," even "a complete anarchy in society."[58] Still today, that is often how Western societies strike visitors from more controlled places. One such visitor was Sayyid Qutb (1906–1966), an Egyptian intellectual who came to America as a student. He was repelled at what seemed to him the moral squalor of American life. He returned to Egypt and became a leading theorist of Islamic *jihad* against the West.[59] As Tocqueville perceived, however, the superficial indulgences of American life are undergirded by a formidable institutional system. Freedom reigns, yet order is still secure. But this depends on individuals accepting the inner burdens of freedom (as I explain more fully in the next chapter).

That same fusion of freedom and order is essential to the constant innovations of the American economy. Inventors and entrepreneurs in America are free to develop new technologies, provided they assume the risks. They do this mostly on their own initiative, without approval or sponsorship from above. The Wright brothers, who invented the airplane, are the paradigm of innovators who come came out of nowhere to transform American life.[60] Entrepreneurship is possible only because strong public institutions hold the ring while the creators compete. Such innovation is discouraged in the non-West—in part because it would spawn too much change for the regime to tolerate.

ASIAN GOVERNMENT

In Asia, government is based far more on collective authority. Regimes are founded mostly on traditional notions of social hierarchy, and they lack any deep commitment to good government in the Western sense. China's Communist system, although first created by revolution, has more in common today with the immemorial rule of the emperors. It expresses the collectivist and nationalist idea that Chinese civilization is superior and everlasting, rather than the more individualist ideals of the West.[61] Although the regime today does operate through law and permits some local elections, these institutions lack the authority they have in the West. They may regularly be overridden by leaders for political reasons.[62]

The Chinese state—as the world's oldest nation—possesses a proven capacity to concentrate political power.[63] Because Chinese political culture is so strongly deferential, rulers have great freedom to act by their own lights, without explaining themselves to the society. But by the same token, society provides little support for their actions, and they do not always understand their people's needs. Several times in history, Chinese dynasties were overthrown by peasant revolts against misrule.

The system's apparent strength, and its actual weakness, are both rooted in the remarkable docility of Chinese culture. For millennia, Chinese peasants were taught that to assert themselves against superiors was "selfish and antisocial," so they deferred utterly to higher authority. "Individualism and liberalism in Chinese thinking were strictly limited parts of a larger collectivity," historians say. "The Chinese individual was subordinate to the group."[64] Despite democratic trappings, deference is still the system's leading norm. (That may be changing, as I note later, but mainly at an elite level.)

Japan achieved a far stronger government than China, even though its culture was no less collectivist. Here the regime has been just as confident, but it has governed far better and drawn far more support from its society. As discussed in chapter 2, that seems due to an exceptionally strong national identity coupled with far more openness to political contention than China ever allowed. Japanese government was already precocious before it led the nation's dramatic drive toward modernity and power in the late nineteenth century.[65] Tokyo also led the nation's equally dramatic emergence as a world economic power after World War II. As J. M. Roberts observed, "Post-war Japan could deploy intense pride and an unrivalled willingness for collective effort among its people; both sprang from the deep cohesiveness and capacity for subordinating the individual to collective purposes which had always marked Japanese society."[66]

The non-West's situational ethics does not generally provide strong support for effective government, because the social suasions to which people defer are too parochial. But in Japan the community of reference extends to the entire country, so a shame culture plays much the same role as moralistic guilt does in the West. The result is an unusually strong government for Asia. Japanese leaders feel seriously beholden to the nation, and those who fail will sometimes apologize publicly.

Japan, however, is a power in decline, mainly due to an aging population. Of Asian countries, China is the obvious giant, but its future is overshadowed by the fragility of its regime.

ENGLAND'S GIFT

As discussed, a moralistic culture appears to be the principal root of superior government in the West. But we must also explain the special excellence of the Anglo nations; as a group, they are the world's richest and best-governed countries, and those two attributes are closely linked. The Anglo edge appears due principally to the remarkable prowess that England and Britain showed, almost from the beginning, in all matters political.

The Germanic tribes that populated the British Isles in early medieval times appear no different from those that settled the rest of Europe. Yet mysteriously, England led all other countries at the central political tasks of forming a national community and achieving good government. Other nations in Europe were assembled painfully over centuries, mainly by kings conquering their own vassals, a process that left political scars.

In England, however, the West Saxon kings (Alfred the Great and his heirs) forged a unified kingdom in the ninth and tenth centuries with little sense of conquest. They created a coherent system of local government and courts covering the whole kingdom. Those institutions already expressed a national community. "Thus the groundwork of a nation state had been laid, perhaps more truly than in any Continental kingdom."[67]

Later kings established the rule of law and accepted government by consent with only limited political conflict. The English early came to see strong central authority as consistent with law and consent, rather than opposed. By late medieval times, these institutions made the English monarchy the strongest in Europe.[68] "The ability of English rulers to raise taxation and manpower was unequalled in Europe," but it required a "unique degree of involvement and consent by local communities, including even relatively humble subjects."[69] "By making the Common Law the permanent embodiment of a righteous king sitting in judgment," Arthur Bryant wrote, Henry II (reigned 1154–89) and later kings "established the English habit of obedience to law which has been the strongest of all the forces making for the nation's peaceful continuity and progress."[70]

The conflict between the Stuart kings and Parliament in the seventeenth century only confirmed this fusion of strong legal authority and consent. A.V. Dicey wrote that English leaders never opposed royal authority as such. Rather, "Their policy... was to leave the power of the King untouched, but to bind down the action of the Crown to recognized modes of procedure which, if observed, would secure first the supremacy of the law, and ultimately the sovereignty of the nation."[71] Popular moralism seized on these institutions until they "came to seem untouchable and immutable, as if in the nature of things, dating from time immemorial."[72] It was, as Arnold Toynbee remarked, "an astonishing tour de force" that defies easy explanation.[73] By the eighteenth century, British rule through an elected parliament became the template for democracy across Europe.

Britain's political gift, as much as its wealth, lifted the island kingdom to world primacy and also empowered it to found America, its even more formidable successor. Yet we should not exaggerate Britain's importance to Western politics.[74] The deepest root of good government in Europe remains the moralistic temperament of the West as a whole. The other major countries of Europe, which had more troubled histories than Britain, achieved unity and effective government much later. Yet in the twentieth century they finally closed the gap on the British with a rush. Since World War II, France, Germany, Spain, and finally the former Soviet satellites of Eastern Europe all gained the best constitutions in their history. Today, as figures 8.1 and 8.2 show, most European countries stand alongside Britain as exemplars of good government.

THE AMERICAN FOUNDING

In view of the epochal British achievement, America's own governmental prowess is less than we usually imagine. Some writers seem to suggest that the Americans created their country out of nothing, as if settlers to the New World had met in a forest clearing and forged a social contract in the manner suggested by Hobbes or Locke.[75] Supposedly, America was the first "new nation," just like the Third World countries that emerged from colonialism in the 1960s and had to decide their own identity and constitutions.[76]

But America was never a new nation in this sense. The British gave it the rule of law and government by consent on a plate. The Americans never had to develop these things on their own. Indeed, the colonialists governed themselves on a largely legal and elected basis even before the break with Britain. In 1776, many rebel leaders, such as Thomas Jefferson, were already experienced public officials.[77] After the Revolution, the rebels simply took over the same offices that British officials had held, including British legal precedents.

The Americans did have some important differences with the British. Aside from the specific grievances, such as taxation without consent, that triggered the Revolution, the colonists sought a less elitist, more democratic regime than prevailed in Britain; they also had more egalitarian social attitudes. They insisted on a written constitution based on federalism and separation of powers—features foreign to British government. The very violence of the break with London tended to accentuate these differences.[78]

But these were details or matters of degree, within the range of the Anglo tradition. In Fukuyama's terms, all were differences within history—among the individualist citizens of Western societies. After history—comparing West and non-West—what is more notable is America's *continuity* with Britain.

WHIG ILLUSIONS

The West's political achievements were decisive for Western and Anglo primacy, yet Anglo interpreters tend to misunderstand them. A Whig tradition among British historians misreads the British political story as one of setting limits on power rather than achieving it. In this view, the pivotal events were those in which royal pretensions were humbled—such as Magna Carta in 1215, when King John was forced to concede certain rights to his barons, or the revolutions of the 1640s and 1688, when Parliament overthrew the Stuart kings, who had attempted to rule without consent.[79] Some American scholars also see British and European government as having been unusually limited.[80]

The American political story, too, is often read in this way. Supposedly, the American Revolution was a revolt against excessive power. The Declaration of Independence is full of concrete complaints against British rule. The American founders also distrusted public power within America, so they set up a constitution that restrained government through federalism, the separation of powers, and the Bill of Rights. *The Federalist* justifies that structure as essential to restrain rapacious officeholders. Tocqueville accepted the idea that in America political power was unusually limited and dispersed, so that the people ruled. In the Whig view, all this distinguishes the United States—and the West as a whole—from the centralized autocracy that so often prevails in the non-West.

But this viewpoint reflects the struggles to improve Anglo government that prevailed within history. The view from *after* history is almost the opposite. Western—and especially Anglo—regimes are the strongest in the world. Compared to the non-West, what stands out most about the West—and especially the Anglos—is how relatively easily they achieved and maintained public authority, even amid political differences. During the English Civil War, the national legal system continued to function even while Royalist and Parliamentarian armies were killing each other.[81] The battle was entirely about who should rule and not about the legal nature of that rule. In America, the separation of authority from politics is not quite so clear. The populist, antigovernment streak in American culture does to some extent weaken the administrative side of the regime, as Trump's reign has recently shown.[82]

Both countries finally developed probably the strongest regimes in history. Only thus could they maintain efficient economies and ambitious programs at home while projecting military power to the ends of the earth. The specific checks on power stemming from earlier development were eased or cast aside as needed to get the job done. It was enough to maintain the central institutions of good government—legality and consent.

In the later eighteenth century, Britain defeated France for the leadership of Europe, in part because of its superior capacity to tax and borrow for war, as mentioned in chapter 2. In 1789, the Bourbon regime was forced to convene a parliament in an attempt to raise more revenue—and collapsed in the ensuing revolution. In much the same way, the United States challenged the Soviet Union to an arms race in the 1980s—forcing it too to elect a parliament, whereupon it too collapsed. The paradox was that the countries most dedicated to the state proved far worse governed than the Anglo constitutional regimes, and this was their undoing.[83]

Recently, some political economists have attempted to explain differences in world political development in a Whig manner. Their rational-choice methods—borrowed from economics—assume, much like *The Federalist*, that officeholders are entirely self-seeking, hence unwilling to serve any broader interest unless forced to do so by the political structure. According to Daron Acemoglu and James A. Robinson, countries achieve broad-based wealth and democracy only when they have "inclusive" institutions that provide opportunity to the general population, as in the West. Development fails when regimes are "extractive," serving only the governing elite, as in poor countries.[84] Similarly, Bruce Bueno de Mesquita and his coauthors argued that rulers in poor countries typically answer only to a small "selectorate" of the rich and well-connected, enabling them to persist in power despite ruining their societies. In the West, rulers face a democratic electorate, and so govern far better—yet stay in power far less.[85]

These theories account well for misrule in the non-West—but not the much better governance found in the West. They do not explain how an "inclusive" regime or a broad "selectorate" is ever established. Acemoglu and Robinson point to "critical junctures," such as Britain's Glorious Revolution in 1688, when a country turned decisively toward an inclusive style. In 1688 and other such moments, Barry Weingast contended, citizens agree on institutional triggers that will allow them to detect and defeat misrule, thus ensuring better government in future.[86] Adam Przeworski and Fernando Limongi found that, no matter in what way democracies are established, they are more likely to endure if they have relatively high per-capita income.[87]

All these theories turn too much on details.[88] Candid literature surveys admit that rational-choice approaches have failed to explain state development.[89] What is missing is culture—the willingness to trust and behave well in politics that the West derived from an individualist worldview. That attitude was established in Britain long before the events of 1688, which merely confirmed traditions of law and consent that were far older. Without those attitudes, the precedents set in the Glorious Revolution could never have endured. In America, similarly, the founders were far more civic-minded than their own cynicism could credit. *The Federalist* is often praised as a masterpiece of political science, but it entirely misses the true, civic basis of the American political achievement.

Political development outside the West has failed largely because moralism is typically lacking. The will to improve government within poor countries is remarkably tepid. The pressure to hold elections and reduce corruption often comes more from outside NGOs, external funders, or international organizations than it does from internal political forces. Without a more assertive culture, in which individuals accept more political responsibility, good government in these societies may simply be impossible.[90]

CONCLUSION

Oblivious to their own fortunate past, American observers continue to be surprised that democracy does not come as easily to many foreign lands as it has to the United States. They asked, when the Soviet Union collapsed, why its former Asian republics succumbed to strongmen rather than holding elections. Or why there have been some recent reverses of democracy.[91] When, in 2006, Morocco's transition to democracy faltered, *The Economist* wondered why the Moroccan king, Mohammed VI, should not become a constitutional monarch presiding over a democracy, as King Juan Carlos I had done in Spain, just across the Strait of Gibraltar.[92] The very notion reflects the sameness assumption—the belief of well-meaning Westerners that all nations and all people are fundamentally alike.

But the idea that Mohammed should do as Juan Carlos did is unimaginable. Morocco has different political traditions than Spain, and they are embedded in different popular psychologies. A traditional Islamic monarchy depends on public deference to outward public and religious authority. To replace that regime with "free" Western-style government would require replacing this outward structure with a whole set of inward commitments and inhibitions. Moroccans who now bear the outward burdens of necessity would have to internalize instead the very different burdens of freedom. Unless they did, to introduce elections would probably just repeat the tragedy of the Arab Spring. There can still be some positive change in Islamic countries, but it must be slow.[93]

Americans look outward from their citadel of civility to a world full of misrule. It can easily seem as though the only thing that oppressed peoples need is "freedom," American-style. But the Americans who journey out to help them seldom perceive the demanding structures they carry in their own heads, which make freedom possible. For the oppressed to become free would require that they assimilate these same burdens. The pressures they face could no longer just be external. For countless millions who struggle just to survive, that is a future they cannot imagine. In the near term, they must inevitably be ruled by others—or by chaos.

PART THREE

CHALLENGES
AT HOME

CHALLENGES AT HOME

So far, I have argued (in part 1) that an individualist culture chiefly explains Western and American world leadership and (in part 2) that other sources of power, including geography, economics, and government, are strongly shaped by that culture.

Cultural difference also matters within the United States. Chapter 9 shows, at several levels, how freedom fosters obligation and, in the end, is really a form of obligation. Life in America is much more demanding than we usually assume. Chapters 10 and 11 use that perspective to throw new light on the largest social problems in America—poverty and immigration. Many lower-income Americans struggle with the burdens of freedom. They are becoming less individualist, and that is the chief threat to continued American primacy.

If life in an individualist society is so demanding, some might ask, how is it any different from life in the non-West, where burdens typically are imposed from outside? The difference is that Westerners still pursue their *own* goals—and exactly that brings their heaviest burdens. To achieve their own ends, they must compete with others. To move forward is to create a headwind. Every force in one direction, as Isaac Newton said, generates an equal and opposite reaction.

CHAPTER NINE

FREEDOM AS OBLIGATION

A merican leaders say every day that the United States is a free country.[1] That is true in certain simple senses. In America, we enjoy the rule of law and civil liberties, government is elected, and the authorities will not arrest us in the middle of the night just for expressing our opinions. When we call other countries unfree, we typically mean that they lack these important protections. Conservative critics commonly say that government does not leave us free enough, and that, too, might be true in certain simple senses. The government does make us obey many laws and pay taxes, and some people regard those demands as oppressive.

This common view, however, presents freedom entirely in negative terms, as a lack of constraints. To be free is to be surrounded, so to speak, by empty space. We are thus "free" to move in any direction we wish. We say casually that "it's a free country," so you can "do anything you want" or "become anything you want." Such statements, however, ignore the many obligations that freedom brings. To understand America in a multicultural world, we have to stop thinking of freedom as the mere absence of limitation. Rather, we must think of it in positive terms, as a set of obligations that inevitably accompany a "free" society. Those burdens are inseparable from freedom. They are its very essence. Only by bearing them inwardly do Americans enjoy the outward freedom and wealth that they have.

As one sign of this, despite our rhetoric, most Americans do not experience life as free. Rather, it is a constant struggle to satisfy the many
demands upon them. Not freedom, but the burdens of freedom, are the
real center of American life. As discussed in chapter 7, a free market distributes the burdens of economizing more broadly than any collectivist
economy, and that is why it is more productive. The same can be said of
many other obligations—those stemming from society as well as from
personal goals. In most countries, much of the population avoids these
burdens. People shirk them or are exempted from them. But an individualist society disperses them to the entire population, thus generating an
output that few other societies can match.

Obligations impinge on freedom at many levels. First, to enjoy rights—
even in a free society—requires, as a practical matter, certain obligations.
As military veterans say, freedom isn't free. Even a free government must
expect its citizens to obey the law, pay taxes, serve on juries, and—if there
is a draft—serve in the military. Rights also directly imply obligation, in
that for anyone to claim them, others must respect them. My right to assert myself presumes your forbearance. Still further, a free society leaves
to private choice many contentious political and moral issues that in an
unfree country would be settled by the authorities. In an individualist
culture, those questions matter. They shape and reshape the moralistic
attitudes that chiefly structure Western societies. Above all, individuals
bear the burdens of their own goals. Whatever they seek, they must organize their lives to achieve it, often against the odds. That is the chief
impetus that drives them and the society onward.

THE ECONOMIC STRUGGLE

The struggles that Americans are most aware of are economic. Freedom,
American-style, was never carefree. Most people struggle every day simply
to get or keep a job, or to make ends meet. Few feel surrounded by empty
space—rather, they slog forward daily as if through a solid substance. And
this despite the fact that America is, by most measures, the richest country
in the world. Consider the adversities that this "free" country has recently
inflicted upon its citizens:

FALLING EMPLOYMENT. During the Great Recession (a decade ago), the
unemployment rate reached 10 percent. It has since fallen to 4 percent,

which many economists would regard as full employment. But almost 2 million people are still unemployed, most of them for more than half a year. And the share of the adult population that is working or looking for work has fallen below 63 percent, more than three points lower than before the recession.[2] *Why have so many Americans—especially middle-aged men—given up on work, even in good times?*

INEQUALITY. Historically, America boasted an affluent society that grew steadily richer. But for decades now, most Americans have seen little gain in their standard of living. Some of the least skilled have even lost ground. The country is still getting richer overall, but most of the recent gains have gone to people who were already affluent or rich—the "1 percent" derided by liberal commentators. *Why can't government spread the wealth more evenly?*

DEBT. Struggling to afford what they need, many Americans have gone deeply into debt to pay for home mortgages, health care, or their children's college education. Although the federal government subsidizes all these expenses, it is now heavily in debt itself. Despite some recent improvement, the national budget deficit is still well over $600 billion a year, and the national debt has soared to more than $20 trillion.[3] As the baby boomers retire, debt is certain to soar higher still. *Why can't a rich country pay its debts?*

As I argue below, declining individualism is a major cause of all these problems. But even without that, all these burdens would weigh down average Americans. How to tame the economic struggle is the main issue in national political campaigns, yet candidates propose only superficial solutions. In his presidential campaign, Donald Trump promised to revive the well-paying factory jobs that America has lost to Asia, but few think he can. So the strains of American life will go on. *Why is struggle unavoidable in a free country?*

THE SEARCH FOR OPPRESSION

American leaders typically blame our domestic struggles on some avoidable error or injustice at the hands of government. Conservatives say that taxes or regulations are too high or that government has mismanaged the economy, while liberals say that the rich enjoy unfair privileges. Both sides, that is, point to some *un*freedom that could be avoided. They search for oppression, and by ending it, they promise, they can make America still freer, and richer, than it is. For them, freedom is always something negative.

That is an illusion. The problems that each side cites may be real, but no reform is likely to put an end to them. Rather, they are deeply rooted in the nature of a free society. The struggle arises, in the first instance, simply from competition. If freedom in America were given just to one person, he or she might indeed be able to do or be anything. But the rule of law and broad opportunity open doors for a great many people. And many of them want the same things, so they compete to get them. They enter into America's major institutions, all of which become competitive arenas. Each institution has a smiling face, open to all. But to get anything from them, we must shoulder heavy burdens. Each institution transmutes freedom into obligation.

THE ECONOMY

Our free economy is open to all. Sellers eagerly solicit customers. Most Americans feel better served by capitalism, in fact, than they are by government.[4] But even in a free economy, what we want does not come without cost. We must pay what the market demands. To that end, Americans compete for jobs that pay well. Similarly, the market allows most producers to set their own prices. The left has always regarded that license as exploitative. But for the sellers, too, there is no "free lunch." As explained in chapter 7, a competitive market tends to minimize profits, so both buyers and sellers have to work hard.

Both conservatives and liberals tend to minimize the sheer labor that capitalism demands. Conservatives celebrate the "magic of the market," the fact that it outperforms more collectivist economies, producing more for the same effort. But that effort is still huge. Liberals, for their part, sometimes suggest that the "1 percent" have an easier life than the masses struggling to survive beneath them. In fact, their higher incomes come, at least in part, simply from working harder than most people. People who earn lower incomes typically work far less than those who earn more. In 2016, less than half of heads of households in the bottom fifth of the income distribution worked at all, while in the top fifth 71 percent worked full-time and full-year.[5] That is the reverse of the pattern during the Gilded Age, a century ago. In those days, New York City plutocrats relaxed at their vacation homes out in Newport, Rhode Island, while back in the city immigrant masses on the Lower East Side toiled long hours just to survive. If today's poor worked this hard today, they would seldom be poor at all, and incomes would be a lot more equal.

The American public is anxious about the economy, according to polls. Will economic growth continue, or will the economy topple into another recession? Commentators treat these worries as alarming and new. But the public is anxious about the economy pretty much all the time, and for good reason. Under capitalism, there is never any assurance that private employers will provide enough jobs for all workers, or wages sufficient for their families. Other insecurities come from trade and technology. Expanded exchange with Mexico and China, plus automation in the workplace, have clearly made America richer overall, yet there are now fewer well-paying jobs for low-skilled workers. Trump has decried these trends, but there is little he can do about them, as I explain below.

As discussed in chapter 7, collectivist policies once promised to shield Western publics from the worst insecurities of capitalism. But the cost of those policies proved excessive, so protections have been cut back. Most rich countries have increasingly trusted to the blind forces of supply and demand. The market is the tiger they have to ride, and they cannot get off.

THE SOCIETY

The society, like the economy, is apparently open to all. We may live where we want and how we want. Rights to pursue life, liberty, and happiness as we choose are written into America's founding documents. With the 2015 Supreme Court ruling in *Obergefell v. Hodges*—in favor of same-sex marriage—and, given the recent legalization of marijuana in many states, acceptance of diverse lifestyles has never been so great. But what is not accepted is a passive life.

As with the economy, competition restricts access to the things most people want. These include careers that are interesting and well-paying, as against low-paying, monotonous service jobs. Many people also aspire to live in affluent communities where good schools will give their children a head start in life. The economy can raise levels of affluence, at least for the society as a whole, but it cannot broaden rewards that involve one's standing *relative* to other people. In order for some to do well in status, others must do worse. That reality limits how productive even a free society can be.[6]

In today's America, the meritocracy—meaning competition for success in school—largely determines social status. Children who do well in the classroom, and thereby ascend to prestigious colleges, are the likeliest to get well-paying careers and nice houses in the suburbs—or in rich cities like New York and San Francisco. That largely explains why, for the middle class, competition for top colleges has become all-consuming. It is one reason why marriage has firmed up at the top of society in recent decades—parents know that their children need *two* parents behind them if they are to compete successfully for the Ivies.

The meritocracy is a great sorting machine that serves the needs of the economy ahead of private desires. While offering much choice, it ultimately steers individuals toward jobs that the economy needs and that they can best perform. (Such jobs may not be those they would prefer.) In the meritocracy, even more than in the economy, the rich get richer. The most talented have the confidence that goes with their gifts, and then they also win the best social positions. The less talented lose on both counts. Yet here, as in the market, it is socially optimal that competition reign.

Meritocratic competition is most heated among the young, who must weather early tests and selection for good schools in order to gain prominent careers. In Europe and Asia, workers often find that job security increases with age, and elderly workers are seldom fired. America offers people who do poorly in school more second chances to "make it" than many other countries. But that also means less security for adult workers, who may face competition or be "restructured" out of a job even in old age.

Some say that the playing field is far from level. The affluent can invest in their progeny to succeed in school and careers in ways others cannot. Although that is true, they seldom can bequeath their success to their children. Nepotism is frowned upon. Mostly, the heirs must succeed—or fail—on their own. And educational standards are much higher at the top of society than the bottom. Even among the "privileged," there are not enough top colleges and careers to go around. So even the most favored must work very hard to "make it."

Social competition seemed inclusive during most of the twentieth century, because the whole society moved up to higher levels of education and employment. A large majority of Americans gained at least a high school education and, along with it, white-collar employment and a home in the suburbs. It seemed as if everyone was "making it" together, although in terms of relative status many probably gained little. Only the poor, who usually lacked skills and regular employment, dropped off this upward escalator. But, in recent decades, "good" jobs have come to require at least some education beyond high school. That is more than perhaps most Americans can achieve. So now everyone is manifestly not "making it," and class divisions seem much sharper.

Schooling was not always the stern arbiter of success that it is today. Abraham Lincoln, perhaps our most gifted president, succeeded with hardly any formal education at all. Bill Gates and Steve Jobs dropped out of Harvard before founding their world-beating companies. Many people from obscure backgrounds still rise to the top of politics or business. But the chance to do so has a grip on the culture that it never had before. Of all freedom's burdens, this may be the heaviest, especially for the young.

GOVERNMENT

The most puzzling arena is government. Here, too, the institutions appear wide open, yet they do not do what people want. At all levels in America, governments are elected, so they are presumed to obey the people. Yet polls show that the voters are deeply alienated from government. Somehow it has not saved them from their struggles, especially the widespread fear that middle-class jobs are disappearing. No presidential candidate has a sufficient response. *Why doesn't government do more to help ordinary people*—for instance, by reducing income disparities, making jobs more secure, or shielding American producers from automation or foreign competition?

In part, government cannot do these things without denying the economy the freedom it needs to make America rich. As shown in chapter 7, there is a trade-off between security and productivity. With less struggle, many people would not work so hard, and affluence would decline. In part, as well, the voters are inconsistent. The will to distrust government is stronger than the will to use it to enact protections. Conservative politicians capitalize on that attitude to attack government. So public alienation has pushed public policy mostly to the right rather than the left.[7]

Popular economic grievances have not generated a coherent economic program. In recent years, we might have expected a New Deal-like movement from the left to do more to protect struggling workers. But what most Americans want from the economy is simply that good jobs be available; concern about inequality in any wider sense is tepid.[8] On the left, the Occupy Wall Street movement and 2016 presidential hopeful Bernie Sanders gained far more support from students than they did from workers. On the right, low-skilled white men powered the Trump campaign to victory in 2016, but how the White House could assuage their grievances remains quite unclear.

The real inhibitor is, again, competition. The political arena may be open to all, but to prevail in it one must organize support from others. Today's low-income Americans are little able to do that. They suffer from social problems (chapter 10) as well as the presence of many illegal aliens (chapter 11), who make it unclear who has rights in this country. Those confusions absorb much of the energy that the less advantaged once put into politics. Today they are mostly spoken for by better-off advocates, but that is a lot less effective than marching on Washington themselves. Since enacting the Affordable Care Act in 2010, Democrats have mostly been playing defense. Under Trump, Republicans have vowed to undo much that even Obama achieved.

THE LIMITATIONS OF REFORM

Thus, American institutions transmute freedom into obligation. They do not produce "justice" in the sense of some final deliverance from the public's trials. Some may say that the problem is really class: the system is formally open, but in the competition for rewards the rich enjoy huge advantages. The sharpest edge of Marxist rhetoric was always to contrast the formal fairness of a democratic regime with its actual biases toward the affluent. As Anatole France (1844–1924) sardonically remarked, "In its majestic equality, the law forbids *rich and poor* alike to *sleep under bridges*, beg in the streets and steal loaves of bread."

In response, again, advocates typically seek out some denial of opportunity or equity that explains the struggles. Reform it away, they promise, and freedoms will expand. The Progressives of a century ago persuaded most Americans, with some difficulty, that bigger government could serve individual freedom.[9] Even successful reforms, however, have not produced the hoped-for deliverance, because the rest of the competitive system remains unshaken. The labor movement did indeed expand opportunities for workers, as the civil rights movement did for blacks, the feminist movement did for women, and so on. But once liberated, those groups still had to compete fiercely to get anywhere in life. The playing field was now more level, but they still had to go out there and win the game.

And economic competition in America is closer to an arms race than a football game. In the struggle to get ahead, there are few limits on the efforts one can make. We can always put in more hours on the job. Some European countries limit the work week to thirty or thirty-five hours, to allow more leisure and family time, but in America such restrictions are unknown outside unionized workforces. Faced with rising competition, ambitious parents are putting more hours into their jobs as well as into raising their children. On average, mothers spend much more time working today than they did in the 1960s, and fathers only slightly less. And both parents spend more time on child care than formerly.[10] As this suggests, competition for careers and colleges now dominates middle-class life. Few lower-class people are so well organized, which is one reason that inequality has grown.

The rhetoric of reform sometimes suggests that the system cossets the rich and privileged, who are really less able than the recent insurgent groups. Only give workers, blacks, or women a fair chance, the promise goes, and they will speedily win places at the head table. Many individuals from disadvantaged backgrounds have indeed succeeded, or their children have. But in status and income, no group has yet equaled white men on average. America was always a highly competitive society, even before the social reforms of the last century, and it remains so today. The new groups can now get on the highway to success, but out there they find that the traffic is already moving fast. Getting up to speed is a lot tougher than getting onto the road.

A DEMOCRATIC SOCIETY

A second source of burdens in a free society is democratic mores. As explained in chapter 4, individualism has promoted a democratic society in the United States. America promotes stiff competition to get ahead, but it is also a community in which individuals seek the respect of others. Our competitors are also our peers. The point is not only to outdo them but also to impress them with our ability, effort, and character. In principle, that reward is not competitive. It is potentially available to all who give their best in the competitive struggle. Everyone may earn honor and self-respect—even the losers.

But, although winning is not required, one must at least be in the game, striving to get ahead. Americans still look for that effort today. What most of us find hardest to accept about poverty in America is not the cost of social programs but rather the faint effort that many impoverished adults seem to make on their own behalf. Few of them work regularly, still fewer if they are on welfare. As one participant in a focus group about welfare exclaimed, "Why don't these people fight for themselves?"[11] We would rather the poor were *more* assertive than they are, even if that made them *more* formidable as competitors—because then they would be our peers, of whom we could expect more than we do.

ESCAPING COMPETITION

American life could become less burdensome only if it became less free, or less competitive, or if protections against competition were given. Freedom might decline, for example, if the country elected a dictator to solve its current struggles—a new version of Franklin Roosevelt and his "hundred days." Our culture would also become less demanding if people cared less about getting ahead than they do. We see that happening now in Europe, where in recent decades the world's original individualist society has lost much of its vigor. It is aging faster than America, resigned to losing its former world leadership.

In the United States, there are just a few niches that shield workers from insecurities. One of these is affirmative action, or preferential hiring for the beneficiaries of the recent reform movements, especially minorities and women. Some of them thus get good jobs without having to compete as hard as they would otherwise. Probably more important is the security of government employment, protected as it usually is by civil service rules. Although unions have declined in the private sector, they remain strong in government. Another relatively secure niche is academia, in which many faculty members enjoy tenure and, effectively, cannot be fired.

All of these protections are under threat today, however, partly because they are costly but also because they offend populist mores. Most Americans struggle in the market, and they wonder why anybody should be protected from it. If some must struggle to get by, they reason, then everybody should. The majority still might favor more general protections, but not privileges for specific groups.

THE WELFARE STATE

More important than the advantages mentioned above is the welfare state, meaning public programs to support certain groups outside of employment. The recipients include people whom no one expects to work, such as children and the elderly, but also groups like the disabled and unemployed, whose inability to work is more judgmental. At its origin in Europe and America more than a century ago, the welfare state was seen as a "safety net," meant to catch those thrown out of work by impersonal forces, such as injury or mass unemployment. A generation or two ago, that system bid fair to make Western societies much less insecure.

But, as mentioned in chapter 7, the move toward collectivism has reversed. Some protective benefits have been cut, and others have been conditioned on employment. In the 1990s the United States drastically reformed family welfare, requiring most welfare mothers to work and driving most of them off the rolls into jobs. At the same time, it beefed up wage subsidies for the low-paid. Europe has followed suit, although it is still more generous than America.

Again, the motive behind these reforms is not only to save money on the poor. Welfare is cheap in the United States compared to larger middle-class programs such as Social Security and Medicare, which are financed largely by payroll taxes. Seventy-two percent of federal nondefense spending goes to various payments to individuals, most of them not poor or on welfare.[12] Many nonworkers are now seen as free-riding on the majority who struggle to work and get ahead—the effort that pays for government and generates income for everyone. So community is expressed precisely by insisting that more people work, not by excusing them from it.

CHOOSING GOALS

The burdens of freedom, then, include the just demands of government and the competitive demands of a free society, which are all-pervasive. All these might be seen as external forces. But more fundamental still are the goals that people in an individualist culture set for themselves and their families. Their goals may not be anything grand—merely to get a better job and afford a home in the suburbs, then to have their children do better. Those visions constitute the traditional "American dream." They are often presented as gifts bestowed by our free society. But we must organize our lives around those goals, and from this follows great demands.

The desire to "get ahead" in some manner is what drives people to compete for preferment in the first place and to risk all the insecurities that this implies. At middle-class parties, people edgily ask each other where they went to college and what they do for a living. The questions are feared, because the answers suggest how much one has achieved in life. Still more important, they suggest to what extent one has shown that brave individual effort that is most respected in a democratic society.

"Free" societies pride themselves on offering a "career open to talents." But freedom's ideologues seldom notice the huge insecurity that this implies for the less talented or the less motivated. Such people now face more exposure than they would in a less competitive society, even if it were less rich. Life is converted from something to get through, as it often is in poor countries, to a great gamble. The less able must commit their time and resources to goals that not everyone can reach. The problem is not primarily that the safety net is inadequate for those who fail, as liberals say, but rather that competition itself can be unforgiving. Even if one is allowed to withdraw from the fray and live on benefits, one has been found wanting. The resulting demoralization is probably one cause of the social problems discussed in the next chapter.

THE BURDENS OF AUTONOMY

A final burden follows from freedom itself, in the most elemental sense. In collectivist cultures, people orient to outward necessities and seek mainly just to get through life. They may wish that those barriers could be pushed back, and with rising wealth they may be. But however much life improves, to receive more leeway in this sense does not constitute freedom in the Western sense. Rather, freedom means to choose—to determine one's *own* direction; in this sense, to be autonomous. That inevitably means that we handle many barriers ourselves, rather than looking for others to do so. We *take on* the barriers and then decide how to respond. Our environment changes from an outward necessity to an inward challenge for which we assume responsibility.

From this perspective, freedom in the negative sense never exists at all. We are constrained in any event. The only question is whether we defer to outward necessities or internalize them as personal responsibilities. Freedom in the individualist sense is not liberation from necessity but an enterprising stance toward challenge. Freedom becomes not a condition but a project.

Hegel's philosophy captures well what this shift means and how it came about in Western culture. As described in chapter 5, Hegel perceived that over the course of history moral authority migrated from outside to inside the self. As cultural innovation moved westward in Eurasia, authorities that had been totally external, as in ancient China, increasingly became matters of individual conscience. Finally, in the modern West, people could be totally autonomous. This meant not that they became liberated in the sense of carefree, but rather that they could and had to decide for themselves what was right. That implied "challenging the external world to exhibit the same Reason" as the subject possessed. History's project was that this inner sense of right should finally correspond to the outward reality that society had achieved.[13]

In this moral progress, individuals became more and more responsible for their outward world. Freedom came to mean answering only to oneself and no longer deferring to any external force. Even to admit dependence on one's environment was to become unfree. Rather, individuals determined to take responsibility for their personal world, and it was this that made them free. As Hegel stated:

[T]he act whereby I take possession of my personality, of my substantive essence, and make myself a responsible being, capable of
possessing rights and with a moral and religious life, takes away
from these characteristics of mind just that externality which alone
made them capable of passing into the possession of someone
else.... This return of mine into myself, whereby I make myself exis-
tent as Idea, as a person with rights and moral principles, annuls the
previous position and the wrong done to my concept and my reason
by others and myself.[14]

This inner responsibility for one's own existence is what ultimately con-
stitutes Western freedom. The individual is defined utterly apart from the
society, answerable only to an inner Spirit.

The impulse to internalize one's world and assume responsibility for it
is perhaps the chief distinction of the West, the chief way it differs from
other civilizations. That reflex generates the urge to improve and reform
the outside world that made the West so uniquely dynamic, thus driving
it toward wealth and power. It generates that internal spirit that ambitious
individuals often claim for themselves. For the non-West, in contrast,
challenges remain largely outside the self, which adjusts to them; people
obey outward authority and necessity. That too is a burden, requiring the
virtue of endurance, but it differs from mastering adversity by seeking
change. To be responsible only to and for oneself is the ultimate burden
of freedom.

As described in chapter 8, an individualist culture empowers a society
to control its government as few collectivist cultures can do. Individualists
generate more resistance to governmental abuses than passive citizens
who accept direction from the society. The reason probably is that bearing the burdens of freedom gives people more authority and confidence
to confront officeholders. Collectivist publics can sometimes overwhelm
regimes in moments of protest, as the Arab Spring showed. But individualist publics do far better at the routine oversight of government. They
are much more able to sustain responsibility long-term.

The very idea of human rights—in relation to others or government—
depends upon an individualist psychology. It is only by shouldering inner
discipline that people show their mettle and thus can confront outward
injuries with any authority. That psychic force is finally what helped over-

throw every form of arbitrary governance in the West. Without such a capacity, rights become mere abstractions—something that society may award people, but not something they can truly claim. That is why human rights do not become realities in passive, non-Western cultures. To restrict government's power, citizens must first assert their own.

QUESTIONING FREEDOM

Freedom has been the supreme American value, but our current burdens are enough to make some question it. The problem is not fundamentally inequality or class. "Liberty to all," Lincoln said, is America's "apple of gold."[15] The worm in the apple is not capitalism, whose excesses can be tamed. Social reformers have achieved some success in this regard, as already mentioned. They have not, however, challenged the fundamental character of American society. They have not made it uncompetitive, and they have not stilled the democratic demand that citizens display effort that other citizens can respect. Thus the prophets of socialism, even Marx and Communism, were far less radical than they thought. Because even if the economy were totally collectivized, and even if the rich were totally expropriated, American life would remain competitive, strenuous, and insecure. The less favored would still have to show the effort needed to justify themselves.

True radicalism, rather, must question individualism itself, the very idea that one person's success can be separated from another's. The deepest critic of a free society was not Marx but Jean-Jacques Rousseau (1712–1778), the great Swiss antiliberal. Rousseau saw the competition of individuals to get ahead, which Americans prize, as the great flaw in modern society. As we each struggle for self-importance, we tear each other down and lose the harmonious life that we might have together. Only a communal society, in Rousseau's view, could really achieve freedom or democracy in any form worth having.

European social democracy went partway down that path, but Rousseau would have gone much further. His social ideal was not Athens but something like classical Sparta—a traditional, communitarian polity into which citizens sank their identities in order to become the greatest soldiers in Greece. They thus triumphed in war but gave up the matchless fruits of individual striving that empowered Athens—like America—to lead an entire civilization. Just as Athens was the "school of Hellas," so the United States has led the entire West toward the furthest reaches that individualism can achieve. To give up those sunlit heights for a more tranquil life is a bargain most Americans disdain. American freedom cannot be carefree. The thrill to compete and to excel is too essential to it.

Some recent communitarian philosophers also have criticized individualism, saying that people even in free America do not live isolated lives. They are at least partly "constituted," according to Michael Sandel, by the obligations they accept toward other people. American society, in this view, has recently become too individualist for its own good. Government has abetted that tendency by abandoning its attempts of the nineteenth and early twentieth centuries to cultivate civic virtue.[16] This criticism helps to justify the recent efforts to promote work and other civilities among the poor (see the next chapter).

But like Rousseau, communitarianism underplays the competitiveness that has made America rich and powerful. What generates community in America is not individuals' becoming less distinguishable from society, as in non-Western countries, but their manifesting the civility and the competence that draws the respect of others. The members of a soccer team, or an army platoon in combat, are bonded by their mutual excellence, the effort they show for each other, and not because they are submerged in the mass. Community in America is precious, but it is not a condition that people simply possess or receive—it is something that individualists achieve together.

SEEKING STRENGTH

The answer to America's domestic struggles, then, is not to give up individualism but to bear its burdens more easily than we do. That realization may be why education, broadly defined, has replaced redistribution of wealth as the central focus of American social policy. Despite the current upset over inequality, little fundamental change is likely on that front. Nor, following the Affordable Care Act, are there likely to be major expansions of the welfare state. More likely, we will pour further money and effort into improving education so that more young Americans gain the mastery to earn better wages in the current, demanding economy. We will also use the social programs already in place to promote employment rather than escape from it. Our chief goal will be not equality but competence.

This focus on individual skills disappoints many on the left. They view it as superficial, even a form of "blaming the victim." Why focus on individuals' shortcomings when we need changes in the basic institutions that, as shown earlier, weigh heavily on ordinary people? But society cannot just award status to people at one moment in time. To achieve belonging, it is far more important that citizens be in motion toward personal goals over time. That depends on their lifestyle and ultimately on their capacities. A free society always moves forward. Without capacities, the less favored will always be left behind, whatever resources are given to them.

From Aristotle (d. 322 BC) through John Rawls (d. 2002), political philosophers defined justice as giving everyone his or her due. That typically meant ensuring people equal or greater rights through some reform of basic institutions. But that vision took for granted an individualist society. Perhaps because individualism is now under challenge, some thinkers define justice in more personal terms. To Amartya Sen or Martha Nussbaum, the substance of development is not simply that society becomes richer and fairer overall, but that it generates the capabilities that people need to live well. Society may promote those attributes, yet they ultimately reside in the individual. Justice now connotes not equal claims but some common minimum of capacities.[17]

That idea suggests the actual substance of a free life today. It captures the shift we need in how we conceive freedom, from the negative to the positive. Freedom no longer means to be surrounded by empty space into which we may move. Nor does it entail receiving additional freedoms or rights from the society. Rather, freedom means to have the capacity to lead our lives well and thus share in a democratic society. The answer to struggle is not freedom but strength.

CONCLUSION

The conventional image of America as a "free" society is easygoing. In a free country, the suggestion is, Americans enjoy a milder life than in authoritarian regimes such as Putin's Russia or still-Communist China. But a candid appreciation of American life shows how demanding our society really is. The high expectations we hold for ordinary people still bear the stamp of the ambitious individualists who first formed the nation.

As already suggested in chapter 3, at the end of history, structural issues cease to dominate domestic politics, and questions of personality come to the fore. The chief question is no longer whether the market or government should organize the society but how competent regular citizens must be. Who must bear the burdens of freedom, and to what extent? Whom do we exempt from those obligations through social programs or other protections against competition? That question, as shown in the next chapter, has come to dominate social policy today.

CHAPTER TEN

SOCIAL PROBLEMS

If individualism is the deepest source of American primacy, then a loss of that temperament must be a threat to that leadership. Rising numbers of Americans are disengaged from producing the more material forms of power—wealth and military capacity—that the United States relies upon. Many are also abandoning marriage and succumbing to other social problems. By opting out of work and family, they weaken the great engine of individual effort that generates American wealth and power, including soft power. Because it means that the United States, although a beacon of freedom, has not produced the good life for all its citizens.

American social problems are severe only among those at low incomes. One might imagine that they pose little threat to the productivity of the rest of society. But they do, because a democracy resists any idea of a caste division. Most Americans yearn for a society where functioning standards are broadly the same. If social problems become severe among some, the temptation is to relax behavioral standards for everyone so as to minimize the division. To a degree that happened in urban America when crime and welfare was most rampant, in the 1970s and 1980s;[1] those problems have since declined. Society sensed that to accept disorder as normal would finally mean, not freedom, but simply chaos.

Experts traditionally have attributed adverse social trends to a decline in economic opportunity, especially the loss of well-paying factory jobs that even the low-skilled could do. But the evidence for this is weak. Recent changes in jobs and wages, although adverse for the less educated, are simply too small to account for the dissolution that we see in low-income society. More plausible is a change in culture, in which the moral imperatives of an industrious life no longer command authority.

The American social problem really reflects a decline in individualism. Many Americans are laying down the burdens of freedom and assuming instead those of necessity, the style more typical of the non-Western world. They are giving up the pursuit of personal goals in favor of simply surviving from day to day. This way of living—just getting through life—contributes far less to American wealth and power than the more ambitious individualist style. This shift reflects both a recent loss of individualism among low-skilled workers and long-standing poverty among minorities with origins in the non-Western world.

Recent adverse trends do not typically involve any question of values. The vast majority of Americans continue to profess belief in working for a living, obeying the law, having children within marriage, and so on—they simply obey these norms far less than they did a generation or two ago. To do that without good reason is to abandon a free life.

In causing social problems, low income and dependency in themselves matter less than a loss of the self-command that formerly empowered Americans to advance themselves. Traditionally, social policy has sought to expand opportunities for the poor, but to do that does not promote the assertive and responsible style that is really needed for American leadership. Recent more directive programs are more promising. The future of American primacy may well turn on whether they succeed.

INEQUALITY

In recent US election campaigns, the problem of rising economic inequality has received much attention. The upset is not primarily that incomes are highly unequal, which is nothing new, but that gains in income in recent decades have gone mainly to people who were already affluent. As figure 10.1 shows, since the 1970s the average American man has seen little gain in real income—that is, controlling for inflation—while the highest paid have realized large gains.

Inequality has recently been driven by the huge gains made by Wall

FIGURE 10.1 **Cumulative Changes in Real Hourly Wages of American Men, by Income Percentile, 1972–2012**

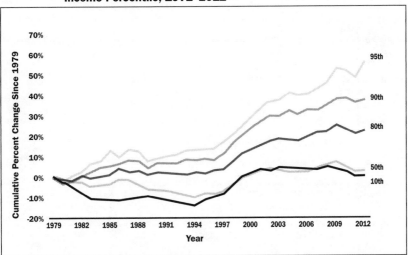

Source: Economic Policy Institute calculations from the Current Population Survey Outgoing Rotation Group, with inflation adjustment.

Street investors. To reverse that trend will require changes in tax and other economic policies.

Another important cause, however, has been falling work levels among the less affluent. Figure 10.2 shows changes in the share employed among various groups since 1980. The trend has recently been downward, driven in part by the 2007–2009 recession. As of 2013, 16 percent of prime-aged men (aged 25 to 54) no longer worked. This was more than three times the figure in the late 1960s.[2] The work rate for never-married mothers soared in the 1990s due to welfare reform, as I discuss further below. But recently they too have worked less. The work rate among young black men is especially low, posing serious difficulties for black society. With earnings falling toward the bottom of society, inequality is enhanced.

As figure 10.3 shows, the United States used to boast higher work levels than many other rich countries, but it has now fallen below them.

The share of the adult US population in the labor force (working or seeking work) was 66 percent or more from 1982 until the Great Recession. It then fell sharply—and kept on falling even after the recession ended. In mid-2018, it was less than 63 percent.[3]

The largest reason for the decline is the retirement of vast numbers of baby boomers. But in addition, many younger adults have given up

FIGURE 10.2 **Percentage of Americans Employed, by Social Group, 1980–2013**

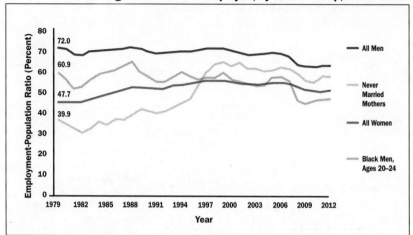

Source: Annual Social and Economic Supplement to the CPS. 1980–2013.

FIGURE 10.3 **Employment-Population Ratio in Select Countries, 1979–2009**

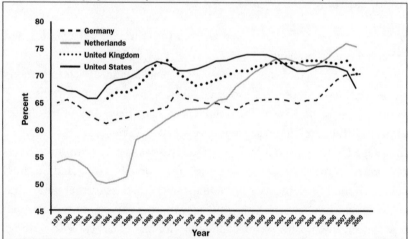

Source: Figures for population aged 15-64 from OECD Statistical Extracts.

looking for work. Rising numbers of people also claim to be incapacitated and have retired on disability benefits, even though health conditions in the population have not declined. Since disability coverage under Social Security began in 1957, that caseload has soared, coming to support 5 percent of all adults by 2012. By 2015, 9 million former workers were living on the program, up from 3 million in 1980.[4] Figure 10.4 also shows that labor-force participation is sharply lower among those with little education compared to college graduates.

FIGURE 10.4 **The Recent Decline in Labor-Force Participation**

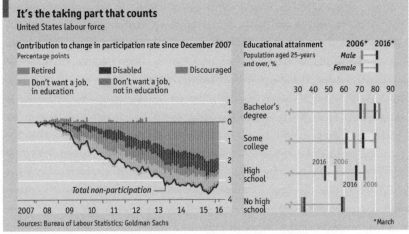

It's the taking part that counts
United States labour force

Sources: Bureau of Labour Statistics; Goldman Sachs   *March

Source: "The Force Awakens," *The Economist*, April 30, 2016, pp. 28–29.

The solution to inequality in America, therefore, must include measures to restore employment to its traditional levels, as I describe further below.

POVERTY AND WELFARE

The other major American social problem is poverty, yet poverty in the sense of unusually low income is less serious than it may appear. The federal government sets minimum incomes for various sizes of family, and the "poor" means those with income below these thresholds. By these standards, as figure 10.5 shows, overall poverty has declined substantially since 1959, when it was 22 percent, but in 2016 it was still 12.7 percent, with the rate among blacks and Hispanics well above that.[5]

That rate is overstated, however, because the official poverty definition counts only pre-tax cash income and thus misses some common income sources—in-kind benefits, such as food stamps (the Supplemental Nutrition Assistance Program, or SNAP), and wage subsidies, such as the Earned Income Tax Credit (EITC). Allowing for these and other factors, probably only 5 percent, rather than the official 14 percent, of the population was poor in 2013.[6] These measures gauge how many people are poor in a single year, but many people are poor only briefly. Of greater concern are the long-term poor—those who are poor for more than two years at a stretch—and they are my main focus here.

FIGURE 10.5 **Poverty Rates by Race or Ethnicity, 1959–2012**

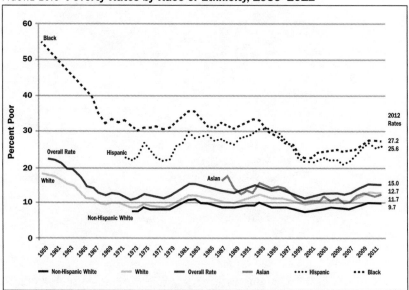

Source: U.S. Census Bureau, Historical Poverty Table 2; 2012 Census Report.
Note: Black poverty rate data from 1960 to 1965 is not available. The line shown connects the 1959 rate of 55.1 percent to the 1966 rate of 41.8 percent and is included to represent the trend but not to imply specific numerical data.

In truth, neither low nor high income has much to do with the nation's vitality. Consider that in 1914, by one estimate, 66 percent of Americans were poor by today's standard. That figure rose to 78 percent in 1932 (during the Depression) and fell to 24 percent by 1944.[7] Thus, in the nineteenth century or before, the vast majority of Americans had incomes *much* smaller than anyone could imagine living on today. Yet this did not stop them from building the world's richest and most powerful nation. Vitality is the chief source of wealth, not vice versa.

The flip side of poverty is dependency on government, but this too is less important than it seems. As mentioned, welfare reform radically reduced the rolls for cash aid for families, but SNAP, which was intended only to buy food, has exploded to more than 40 million people, with little decline even after the Great Recession. The Earned Income Tax Credit (EITC) has also grown to subsidize 27 million families with low earnings.[8] But these caseloads and costs are minor compared to those of the big middle-class health and retirement programs.

CAUSES OF POVERTY

More worrisome than poverty or dependency as such are the causes of those problems. Until recently, the roots of poverty were usually impersonal. Minorities suffered arbitrary exclusion from many jobs, while most other Americans struggled to make ends meet on low wages. The business cycle constantly threatened to deprive millions of work. The Great Recession of 2007 to 2009 was only the latest such episode.

Nonwork

Since the 1970s, the causes of poverty have become more personal. The most important is that the heads of poor families seldom work consistently, even when jobs are widely available. Although the general decline in work levels is recent, nonwork among the poor is long-standing. In 2016, less than a third of poor adults worked at all, compared to two-thirds of the general population. Yet less than 5 percent of nonworking poor adults blamed inability to find a job as their main reason for not working; they much more often cited illness, retirement, or the demands of family or school.[9]

Many observers have attributed this failure to work to social "barriers"—such as racial bias; lack of jobs, skills, or child care (needed for many parents to work); or the disincentives to work created by welfare, due to which recipients who take jobs lose most of their benefits. But though these factors influence how much people earn *if* they work, they have little to do with *whether* they work at all. Providing more benefits to help jobless poor people overcome barriers produces little change. The reason is not that the poor typically lack the desire to work. More likely, defeatism or a lack of organization keeps many poor people from working as they would like to.[10]

Nonmarriage

A cause of poverty second only to nonwork is female-headed families. When children are born outside marriage, the family typically has only the mother to support it, and among poor families neither the father nor the mother usually works consistently. As figure 10.6 shows, since 1970 the rate of unwed pregnancy has soared, particularly among the less educated. More than half of all births to women under thirty now occur outside marriage.[11]

FIGURE 10.6 **Percent of Births to Unmarried Women**

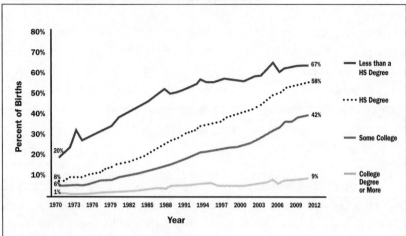

Source: Tabulations of data from Centers for Disease Control and Prevention National Center for Health Statistics Vital Stats.

Poverty is closely linked, as well, to social problems such as crime, drug addiction, and failing schools. As figure 10.7 shows, the rate of violent crime rose very steeply from the 1960s before declining in the 1990s, and it is still well above what it was in the 1960s. Not adverse social conditions but changes in attitudes best explain this upsurge.[12]

The trouble with all these patterns is that they violate the constructive lifestyles by which ordinary Americans traditionally advanced themselves and their families. Many people no longer bear the burdens of freedom. That is, they no longer exhibit that inward assumption of responsibility for life's challenges that is central to an individualist life. Instead, they are governed by outward forces and thus bear the burdens of necessity. Most will survive, but they no longer show the energy they once did in pursuing personal goals. They thus weaken the great social dynamism that generates wealth and power for the nation.

THE WORKING CLASS

Disarray due to work and family problems is long-standing among the poor, but recently scholars on both the right and the left found those same patterns spreading into the working class. In 2011, Charles Murray compared social trends among the top 20 percent and the bottom 30 percent of white Americans, defined largely in terms of education. The first group

FIGURE 10.7 **US Violent Crime Rate**

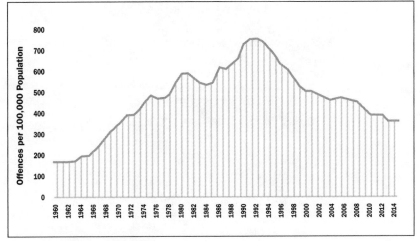

Source: FBI Uniform Crime Reports

had typically gone through college, while the second had completed high school or less. Murray found that, although traditional lifestyles (such as steady employment and stable marriage) had declined in general, they had fallen much more sharply at the bottom of society than the top.[13]

According to Murray, by 2008, among prime-aged males (aged 30 to 49), 12 percent of those who had not gone beyond high school were not in the labor force, compared to only 3 percent of college graduates.[14] Unemployment also ran much higher, and working hours lower, for the less educated. Figure 10.8 shows that as of 2017, white working men of limited education were doing far worse in unemployment, labor-force participation, and wages compared to the average, and these gaps had widened over time.

Family disarray is also apparent among working-class Americans. Although marriage declined in general after 1960, by 2010 only 48 percent of the less educated were married, compared to 83 percent of the more educated. The proportion of births out of wedlock soared among both groups, but much more so among the less educated (see figure 10.6). Murray found similar contrasts in law-abidingness and religious observance. If "lower class" chiefly means men unable to support a household or women raising children alone, then probably 20 percent of prime-aged whites now fall in this group, up from 8 percent in the 1960s.[15]

In a similar vein, Robert Putnam found that growing confusion in family life was the main reason why, in the 2010s, society no longer

FIGURE 10.8 **Employment-Related Trends
Among White Men, 1994–2016**

Source: "Forgotten Men," *The Economist*, February 18, 2017, p. 22.

provided young Americans the opportunities to grow up and get ahead that it did in the 1950s. Where Murray discusses mainly whites, Putnam finds the same trends among blacks and Hispanics.[16] Compared to generations ago, class today is defined more by family structure and less by economics. Youths from two-parent families have a much better chance to "make it" than those from single-parent families. Neighborhoods where intact families are the norm have much better schools, compared to those where single-parent families predominate and students are less ready to learn. Stronger families also support stronger community organizations. Turmoil in private life is now the principal force distracting lower-income America from the focused effort to advance that once drove social mobility in America.[17]

DECLINING CAPACITY

Due to these adverse trends, as well as to a growing proportion of minority students and rising immigration (see chapter 11), American schools are fighting a rearguard action against falling standards. Although more youths now graduate from high school and go on to college, compared to decades past, those gains have been offset by a dumbing down of standards at both levels. Partly to compensate, employers now demand higher credentials for many jobs. Unfortunately, American students and workers score poorly on international tests of skill.[18]

Although millions of workers have abandoned employment, millions of good jobs go begging for lack of qualified applicants. Employers need more carpenters, other skilled workers, medical technicians, and machine operators. These middle-skilled positions pay well but are undervalued by an education establishment addicted to "college for all." Even among students who do go to college, many shy away from the science, mathematics, and technology fields that the economy needs most and pays best.[19] After they leave school, the main thing that stops many low-skilled workers from upgrading their skills is, again, turbulent private lives.[20]

The decline of skill has weakened America's ability to profit from globalization rather than oppose it. As shown earlier, the United States has stemmed the Asian advance toward economic dominance by shifting toward highly specialized and technical goods and services, areas in which America is most competitive. But this requires a labor force of increasing sophistication. Many workers fear to move that way, and this has fed the backlash against globalization that helped hand Trump the presidency.[21]

A free country also imposes civic obligations, such as jury duty and military service. American society, however, no longer prepares youths for these burdens as seriously as it once did. In public schools, as early as 1983, civic education received less attention than accommodating handicapped students, who today have guaranteed rights, and the disadvantaged minority groups who now dominate the student body. And a volunteer military has, since 1973, freed youths from any obligation to serve in the armed forces.[22]

Up through the Vietnam War, the US military drafted a broad cross-section of youth, including both rich and poor, more educated and less educated. Since Vietnam, however, American youths have become less competent to serve. According to a study by military leaders, at the time of World War II, 40 percent of youths were ineligible to serve in the military due to poor nutrition, largely reflecting low incomes.

Today, however, 42 percent of Americans aged eighteen to twenty-four are overweight or obese. Another quarter of those aged seventeen to twenty-four cannot serve because they have not completed high school on time, and another 10 percent because they have criminal records. Overall, 75 percent of those aged seventeen to twenty-four cannot serve for one or more reasons. Even among active-duty service members, 12 percent are obese, a number that has risen 61 percent since 2002.[23] In other words, adverse lifestyles have replaced economic scarcity as the chief cause of incapacity to serve.

The "greatest generation"—the Americans who came of age in the 1930s and 1940s—won World War II, then went to school on the GI Bill and got on with their lives. Military service was only the beginning of their careers. For today's soldiers, however, it is too often the end. The share of veterans receiving disability payments for incapacity was only 15 percent after World War II, but it rose to 25 percent after Vietnam, then to nearly 50 percent after Iraq and Afghanistan. The cost of disability compensation for the military has tripled since 2000. Some of this increase reflects improved battlefield medicine, so that more of the wounded survive to live with impairments, but military leaders fear that they have promoted dependency. They ask who will fight future wars.[24]

The decline of the former working class also extends to health. From 1960 to 2010, the share of American adults who were obese nearly tripled, from about 13 percent to 36 percent, producing large increases in diabetes, and that trend was sharpest among minorities.[25] Among middle-aged white Americans, as figure 10.9 shows, death rates are soaring, even as they fall in other Western countries. The main reason is not the expected big killers like heart disease or diabetes but infirmities even more closely tied to lifestyle—alcoholism, substance abuse, drug addiction, and even suicide.[26] The opioid epidemic has ravaged the less privileged, especially low-income whites. Nearly 7 percent of US adults used these drugs in 2006, about double the rate in 1994.[27] Nothing else suggests so strongly that many Americans are simply giving up on living a purposeful life.

MINORITY POVERTY

Poverty and its causes are especially severe among minorities. In 2016, the poverty level among whites was 11 percent, among Asians 13 percent.

FIGURE 10.9 **Rates and Causes of Death among the Middle-aged, 1999–2013**

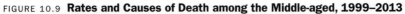

Deaths per 100,000 population, aged 45-54

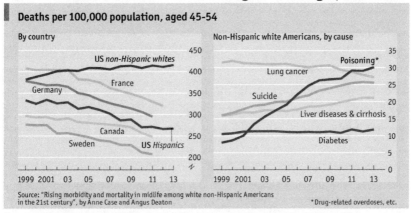

Source: "White America's Mid-life Crisis," *The Economist*, November 7, 2015, p. 24.

However, among blacks and Hispanics it was 22 percent and 19 percent, respectively.[28] Together, today blacks and Hispanics comprise 31 percent of the population but 50 percent of the poor and well over half of the long-term poor, who are my main focus here.[29] Since the Hispanic population is growing rapidly, the number of those in poverty is bound to increase. When the "war on poverty" began in the 1960s, policymakers assumed that poverty among minorities differed only in degree from that among whites, but we must now question that view.

The reason is not principally that minority poverty runs higher than average, but that the main *causes* of poverty among minorities run *very much* higher. While overall work levels do not differ greatly among whites, blacks, and Hispanics, rates of single-parent families and crime do. In 2015, 29 percent of non-Hispanic white births were outside marriage, but the figures were 53 percent for Hispanics (64 percent for Puerto Ricans) and 70 percent for blacks.[30] Thus, marriage is still usual among whites, but among minorities it is dying out.

As to crime, according to the latest figures (from 2009), the number of incarcerated men per 100,000 US residents was 1,398 overall, but it was only 708 for whites, compared to 1,822 for Hispanics and 4,749 for blacks. The figure for Hispanics is more than two and one-half times—and the figure for blacks more than six times—the figure for whites. Although female inmates are far fewer, their proportions are similar. Together, blacks and Hispanics comprise 31 percent of the population but a huge 61 percent of the men behind bars.[31] Such figures suggest a substantial breakdown of order in minority America, beyond anything seen among whites.

Still more significant is the sheer persistence of minority poverty over time. Blacks and Hispanics simply have more trouble moving up the social and economic ladder than do whites. While a black middle class has emerged since civil rights, most black Americans are still mired in low-income neighborhoods where schools are relatively poor and crime is much higher than in mainly white areas. Faced with adversity, black families on average have been much less able to advance themselves through education and careers than other ethnic groups, some of whom arrived as immigrants. Even in middle-class black areas, crime and gangs persist.[32] Somehow, most blacks seem never to gain the same control over their lives that immigrant Europeans did. That has forced sympathetic observers, such as Nathan Glazer, to abandon the idea that blacks are no different from other underprivileged groups.[33]

The difficulty that both blacks and Hispanics have with school in America is dramatized in figure 10.10. Despite some recent progress, both groups experience much more difficulty graduating from high school than do whites or Asians, and the gap at the college level is even greater. This despite the fact that blacks show their high esteem for education by the many schools and colleges they have founded and the many blacks who become teachers themselves. As with other aspects of poverty, divergent values are not a factor.

ECONOMIC CAUSES

The immediate causes of poverty among the working-aged are typically nonemployment and nonmarriage. But what accounts for these patterns? They are difficult to explain precisely because they arise initially from personal life, not from societal adversity. They also seem—at least to better-off observers—contrary to self-interest. Why do low-income adults *not* work when they obviously need money, and why do they become entangled in unwed pregnancy when it undermines private life? Traditionally, as mentioned above, poverty researchers have searched for outside "barriers" that might explain why few poor adults work or marry. Historically, the clearest cause of poverty was racial discrimination, which arbitrarily kept black Americans out of many jobs. But generations after the civil rights era, poor adults still seldom work regularly.

FIGURE 10.10 **US High School and College Graduation Rates, by Race and Ethnic Group**

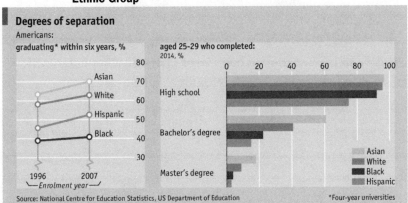

Source: "Class Divides," *The Economist*, November 21, 2015, p. 72.

Many scholars believe that since the 1960s the American economy has made regular employment much harder for low-skilled workers than it was before. Robert Putnam, for instance, described how globalization dealt a body blow to the wholesome, hardworking society that he remembered growing up in a small Midwestern town in the 1950s. In those days, according to Putnam, men with only a high school education could work in factories and support a family, while their children got educated and went on to middle-class careers. But when the factories closed or moved to Asia, the men could no longer provide. So marriages broke down, and both parents and children became involved in serial relationships, creating a slough of despond from which few progeny could rise. Without greater opportunity, the argument goes, it was no longer rational for the low-skilled to work hard or marry.[34]

As for the minority poor, in the 1980s and 1990s William Julius Wilson and his associates contended that unskilled black Americans, particularly men, could no longer find work in the inner city. The jobs once available in cities had moved to the suburbs or the South, where the poor could not follow them. And the jobs that remained in cities demanded more skills and education than the poor usually had. So, without work, women might have children with unskilled men but refused to marry them, thus producing weak families and the other ills of the inner city. There may be other social and psychological causes of poverty, according to Wilson, but all of them ultimately stem from this loss of economic opportunity.[35]

The evidence for these theories is too weak to support these claims. The truth is that well-paying factory jobs never were the norm for most unskilled workers. Work and family have collapsed among the poor even in cities that never had many factories. Jobs still appear to be available to the urban poor, including minorities. They themselves say this. It is shown by the success of poor single mothers in finding jobs during welfare reform in the 1990s and, even more, by the ready ability of low-skilled immigrants—many of them illegal—to find jobs in cities. Although wages for low-skilled work are stagnant, the combination of working in low-paying jobs and claiming benefits like the EITC and food stamps still allows families to escape poverty.[36] As Isabel Sawhill remarked, the role that lower male wages play in discouraging marriage is simply too small to account for the collapse of the family that we see.[37] Foregoing steady employment or a stable marriage is still an irrational way of life.

CULTURE

As an explanation for persistent poverty, cultural change is far more plausible. For obscure reasons, less-educated Americans are simply giving up the individualist commitments that previously structured their lives. Many whites are succumbing to what Murray called the "Europe Syndrome": In rich European countries, many people have abandoned stable ties to marriage, careers, local communities, and religion.[38] The responsibilities of a free life now seen onerous, so they are given up for the burdens of necessity—adjusting to conditions rather than pursuing personal goals. It is a life adrift, without larger purpose. In America, the chief result, as we have seen, is deep confusion in private life. What darkens the lives of troubled families is not the closing of the factories but the loss of trust in one's own relatives and neighbors.

The explanation for minority poverty is not so much cultural change as long-standing cultural difference. The great fact about both blacks and Hispanics is that—unlike most other Americans—*they did not come here from Europe*. Thus, they came here *not as individualists but with the more cautious and collectivist mind-set of the non-Western world*. This heritage best explains the two great impediments to minorities' progress in America—a relatively passive response to opportunity and an inability to maintain order in their own families and neighborhoods.

Living under slavery and Jim Crow, blacks' original instinct in America was to adjust to the demands made of them, as they had done in Africa, rather than to pursue personal goals. For many blacks, only after they moved from the South to Northern cities in the twentieth century did they seriously confront an individualist society. Then their progress depended on their becoming individualist themselves. In order to seize the opportunities of the big city, they had to abandon a life of necessity for a more organized life of achievement.

Most commentators attribute the relative passivity of blacks entirely to the mistreatment they have experienced in America. But if that were true, the group would be more withdrawn, less individualist than people in Africa. In fact, the opposite is true. When black Americans travel to Africa, they find they are far more individualist than the still largely traditional society their ancestors came from. Despite all the vicissitudes blacks have faced in America, they have become the richest black population in history. That is the achievement of an individualist society and of the blacks themselves who adjusted. They shouldered the burdens of freedom in order to reap the American dream.

Martin Luther King, Jr., a man of great insight, rebuked racism but embraced individualism: he called upon his followers to display the same "assertive selfhood" as other people in America.[39] For blacks, this was indeed the way forward. But the obstacle, as Shelby Steele wrote, was that they were "not a people formed in freedom."[40] That is, they had no history, as European Americans did, of accepting the inner and outer demands that went with a free society, as discussed in chapter 9. That included not only getting through school and pursuing success, but also braving competition and observing key civilities, such as the work ethic and law-abidingness.

Black Americans' other great challenge has been to maintain social order. If injustice was the real cause of their social problems, those problems should have been worst under Jim Crow, when blacks were denied formally equal rights in much of the country. In fact, the problems mushroomed chiefly *after* the civil rights reforms of the mid 1960s—rather than before. The reason probably was that blacks, like other non-Western groups, had depended heavily on external authority to keep social order. Jim Crow, however unjust, did provide that. But when poor Southern blacks moved to Northern cities, they lost that structure. Social order for them now depended mainly on the internalized norms that are assumed by an individualist culture. Lacking that mentality, they struggled to keep order. Many stopped working at low-paying jobs, and crime and unwed pregnancy soared.[41] The chief problem for low-income blacks was no longer oppression but freedom.

Many intellectuals and black leaders still assert that black Americans' problems are entirely due to white society. In a sense, that is true—but not in the way usually meant. The main white offense is no longer denying equal opportunity to blacks, meaning a fair chance to compete. Rather, it is to have created a competitive, individualist society for which blacks are ill-prepared—even when they do get a fair chance. *The whole American system presumes an individualist temperament.* Nobody, black or white, is to blame individually for the black predicament—it results simply from this clash of cultures.

The great fact is that Americans from non-Western backgrounds initially lack the individualist reflexes that Europeans had coming in. They have had to undergo a wholesale cultural change before they can become competitive. They have needed to stop thinking of life as survival and embrace the burdens of freedom. Middle-class blacks, roughly, are those who have done this, a huge achievement. The majority of black Americans, however, still display a passive and reactive temperament more typical of the non-Western world.

Hispanic Americans' story is much the same, even though they never were enslaved. They, like blacks, are a non-Western group that gained new opportunity from civil rights but has not always used it well. They were once known for strong families. In Mexico in 2013, only 18 percent of children lived in single-parent families; although most parents were unmarried, most stayed together. That reflected the conformist pressures of a traditional society. In the United States, however, 28 percent of Hispanic children lived in single-parent families, reflecting worse family decline in this far freer society.[42] For many Hispanics, as for many blacks, freedom has become a threat. As a result, although many achieve success, large numbers remain mired in poverty and unable to advance. Chapter 11 says more about this important group.

It was already clear in the 1960s that the best predictor of American children's success in school was their social background, not the school's resources. Students from middle-class families typically outpaced those from poor families, who were less attuned to education. But whether black children progressed in school depended most strongly on their attitudes—whether they believed they controlled their own destinies.[43] That faith, of course, is the essence of individualism—the capacity to take responsibility for one's constraints, to internalize them so that they become challenges to master rather than barriers.

In America, however, the poor tend to shrink from a challenge rather than embracing it. New opportunities provoke anxiety rather than confidence. The disadvantaged tend to remember past defeats, to play safe, to resist change. In this way, they can preserve what little security they have, rather than gambling it on some better future.[44] That cautious worldview, although shaped by America, is also a legacy of the non-Western world.

Culture must, ultimately, explain perhaps the innermost obstacle faced by poor minorities in America—withdrawal from personal responsibility. Whatever happens to them, even when it springs from their own actions, they often attribute to outside forces. They believe most deeply not in themselves but in their powerlessness. Advocates for poor minorities, as well as most researchers, also attribute responsibility entirely to American society. Government still imposes penalties on the poor for breaking the rules, but the political class is ambivalent about this precisely because the psychology of responsibility is so clearly lacking. The recent movement to reform criminal justice so that fewer members of minorities go to prison is well justified, but it partly reflects that feeling.[45]

The church is the chief institution in black society that traditionally did expect good behavior without apology. But even it has recently been powerless to stem the rise of black single parenthood and crime (although crime has recently fallen). How to establish, or reestablish, individual responsibility among the poor is the great question.[46]

ILLUSIONS OF FREEDOM

Ever since poverty became a national issue in the 1960s, observers both liberal and conservative have applied to it their standard prescriptions.[47] Liberals typically want government to do more for the poor, while conservatives seek less. That was the standard shape of Western politics before history ended. But neither approach succeeds unless the poor display a self-reliant personality willing to respond to opportunity. In the early days of the "war on poverty," they often did, and poverty fell, as figure 10.5

shows. In the 1960s, most poor adults still worked, so their wages rose in the good economy and poverty declined. The civil rights reforms also opened doors for the best-prepared blacks to get better jobs and ascend into the middle class. Higher Social Security benefits reduced poverty among the elderly and disabled.

After the early 1970s, however, progress halted, because now the remaining poor were largely not working, while unwed pregnancy, crime, and other social problems escalated. Now the passive temperament of the seriously poor, with its origins outside the West, became a lion in the path. While welfare rolls grew, a cascade of programs designed to improve education and skills among poor adults and their children showed scant effects. Conservatives called many of these efforts futile, even counterproductive, because they appeared to reward poverty rather than deter it, and so under Reagan some programs were cut back.[48] But to do or spend less also produced little progress.

Entrenched poverty was still seen as an economic condition, when it was really a defeated way of life. Whatever was done for poor adults, most of them continued to assign more power to their environment than to themselves. Doing either more or less for them only confirmed that stance. Liberals were frustrated that offers to help drew so little response. Conservatives blamed dependency on government, when the real problem was that the poor remained *dependent on their entire environment.* Merely to cut aid and demand self-reliance did not work either, producing only further withdrawal from challenge. The real solution to poverty was the will to internalize one's environment, to claim responsibility for it, which is the essence of individualism. No mere change in what government offers can produce that.

The trouble with liberal programming is its determinism. Endless ways can be imagined to help the poor overcome their disadvantages. Recent thinking has focused on the inner psychology of poverty and how to rescue children of impoverished parents from unhelpful ways of thinking.[49] But how can such solicitude, however skillful, ever motivate dependent people to turn around and claim responsibility for themselves? It tends, rather, to confirm their view that all power lies with outside forces. Equally, the conservative impulse to reduce aid fails to trigger self-reliance; it only confirms the stoic view of most poor Americans that life is hard whatever one does.

Very likely, a blend of conventional liberal and conservative responses could help overcome the withdrawal from work seen among the low-skilled working class. Most of this group at least have a work history, and most still accept some responsibility for themselves. They have not yet totally abandoned individualism. Improved training programs might help them adjust to the more high-skilled economy. In tandem, unemployment and disability programs might be tightened up, so that the employable cannot abuse these programs to escape work.[50] Then the incentives favoring work will be clearer. In Europe, measures like these have been the main basis of welfare reform to date.[51]

PATERNALISM

The harder problem is the long-term, usually minority poor, who have little history of individualism. Experience has shown that no mere benefit, or denial of benefits, is likely to increase the number of poor adults who work regularly. The EITC, which supplements low wages by as much as 45 percent, does make low-paid workers better off *if* they work, yet it does not cause more of them *to go to* work.[52] To suppose that it would is already to assume exactly the economizing personality that is usually lacking.

More promising than incentives to work are directive programs known as paternalism.[53] Orthodox thinking, whether conservative or liberal, treats *freedom* in some form as the answer to poverty. Free the poor from the toils of either the economy or government, the conventional view goes, and more of them will go to work and "get ahead." Paternalists, in contrast, say that the answer to poverty is *constraint*. The poor suffer from having too many choices, not too few. They are all too free to choose ways of life harmful to themselves, especially failure to work and obey the law. Social programs must tell them explicitly what to do, rather than just expand their choices. Requiring good behavior of welfare recipients, such as working, forces them to take at least *some* responsibility for themselves, which merely raising or cutting benefits does not do. Recipients of aid now must *do* things to work or comply with other requirements, and in so doing they will gain some control over their lives. Over time, their sense of agency should rise. Tying practical aid to the poor to specific functioning requirements—linking "help and hassle"—offers society's best hope of turning around the psychology of powerlessness that blocks progress out of poverty.

The leading success of paternalism came with welfare reform in the 1990s. The public had long urged that welfare mothers be expected to work as a condition of aid. From the 1980s, work programs in which welfare recipients had to participate showed positive impacts on their employment and earnings. After Republicans took control of Congress in 1994, work requirements were greatly raised. Then the same recipients who had resisted work incentives and other voluntary suasions left welfare in droves and mostly took jobs. Although a good economy and the EITC helped, the crucial change was that work was now clearly commanded as it was not before. While the implementation of reform has caused some hardship, it is still government's leading success against poverty among the working-aged.[54]

Meanwhile, other mandatory or directive programs aimed at students, youths who are not in school, and ex-offenders have shown better results than the more voluntary or nondirective programs that preceded them. All these programs maintain order while communicating clear standards about the behavior expected. That leaves their clients with no doubt about what getting ahead requires, so they are more likely to comply.[55] The most successful of these programs are highly structured charter schools where academic standards are clear, struggling students get extra help, and order is strictly maintained, so that more effort goes toward learning.[56]

Following welfare reform, our best hope for raising work levels further is probably what might be called welfare reform for men. Many poor men father welfare families, but welfare reform largely ignored them. However, many of them owe child support to support the families, or they are ex-offenders on parole from prison. Both groups are obligated to work. Many local child support and criminal justice agencies have already developed mandatory work programs to which such men can be referred if they fail to work. Early evaluations of these programs suggest promise, although further development is needed.[57]

Some critics object to paternalism because it seems contrary to freedom, always America's supreme value. It is true that, in part, the programs seem to succeed because they restore some of the outward authority that disadvantaged groups with non-Western origins seem to need to live more constructive lives. That reflects the largely external authority structure they or their forebears knew in their countries of origin. But ultimately the goal still is freedom. As argued in chapter 9, self-discipline is essential to living a free life. The aim is to restore or strengthen individualism at the bottom of American society, and from that will flow greater capacity for freedom.[58]

CONCLUSION

Despite current inequality, there is more opportunity for ordinary people to get ahead in the United States than anywhere else in the world. To seize that opportunity, however, does assume an individualist personality. That condition is more important than any economic barrier that today's poor are likely to face. And that demand is not small. To conceive of a goal, and then to organize one's life around it, requires considerable self-command. No one achieves that all the time. Yet the great majority of citizens are capable of achieving some progress.

Another condition for progress, however, is that society be able to set standards for itself. It must dare to say to the mainstream workers who are dropping out of the economy, and to the long-term poor, that they must work harder and meet other behavioral expectations. The most successful Americans usually do meet those standards, but they do not, as Charles Murray says, often "preach what they practice." That reluctance is one reason why disorder still reigns at the bottom of American society, despite recent progress.[59]

For American leaders, in and out of government, the instinct is to impose responsibility on oneself, not others, whereas for the less successful it is to shift responsibility to their environment. Each finds in this reflex the basis for its standing in the society, so change is feared. Leaders know that their position depends on their mastery, so they tend to hoard their obligations. But progress requires change on both sides. The fortunate must lay down some of their responsibilities for the less fortunate, who must pick them up. Only then can a more equal citizenship emerge.[60]

CHAPTER ELEVEN

IMMIGRATION

The United States is facing challenges from the non-Western world—both externally, in the form of Asian rivals, and internally, in the form of social problems.[1] Immigration is a test that involves both the foreign and the domestic realms.

Most immigrants around the globe today are non-Western peoples seeking to move to the West for a better life. That is a sign of the world dominance of the West, but it creates problems within Western countries. That is why it has become central to politics in both Europe and America. President Trump has made reducing immigration his signature goal, but the issue long precedes him.

Contrary to Trump's rhetoric, the threat posed to America is not principally that immigrants will commit terrorism or crime or go on welfare. Rather, it is cultural, stemming from the attitudes about life and government that immigrants bring with them. *In today's numbers*, migrants might weaken the individualist culture that has made America and the West affluent, well-governed, and strong. That danger is sensitive, but it must be discussed precisely to preserve a multicultural America.

Traditionally, most Americans have looked back on past immigration as successful. Intake from many nations vastly enriched the society. *But at current rates*, immigration is turning America into a mainly Asian and Latin American society. That goes too far. Asian and Latin American cultures have many strengths, but they do not exhibit the same individualist spirit that made America a beacon of affluence and good government. Immigration and multiculturalism should continue, but to promote assimilation we must set firmer limits.

RECENT IMMIGRATION

Arnold Toynbee wrote that dominant civilizations must contend with opposing cultures not once but twice: First they defeat them as military or economic rivals. But then migrants from those same societies seek to enter the dominant civilization to reap its greater affluence and opportunity. "The social price that a successfully aggressive civilization has to pay is a seepage" of these different cultures into its own "life stream." Thus, less fortunate peoples are "re-emerging in our midst."[2]

With the end of history, the West has defeated alternatives to democracy and capitalism. But although many countries have sought to implement those institutions, most remain far poorer and worse-governed than the West, as discussed earlier. So millions around the globe are abandoning their homelands and seeking refuge in Europe or America.

In 1965, Congress changed immigration law in ways that allowed much greater numbers of Asians and Latin Americans to immigrate to America than formerly. In the ensuing half century, nearly 59 million people moved to the United States, vastly more than to any other nation. Before 1965, the flow was mostly from Europe. Since then, more than half of all immigrants to the United States have come from Latin America—28 percent from Mexico alone, the most from any one country—and a quarter have come from Asia.[3]

That has sharply shifted the nation's makeup, as table 11.1 shows: Between 1965 and 2015, the Hispanic and Asian populations increased from low levels to nearly a quarter of the population. And by 2065, *if current trends continue*, minorities will compose more than half of all Americans.[4] Blacks have seen little immigration, so their proportion has changed little. Meanwhile, whites, who dominated the population in 1965, are already less than two-thirds of it and by 2065 are projected to be less than half.

As figure 11.1 shows, the majority of public school students in the United States are already Hispanic or black, with the big growth coming from Hispanics, due both to recent immigration and to relatively high

TABLE 11.1 **Percentage of US Population, by Social Group**

	1965	**2015**	**2065**
Hispanics	4	18	24
Asians	<1	6	14
Blacks	12	12	13
Whites	84	62	46

Source: "Modern Immigration Wave Brings 59 Million to US, Driving Population Growth and Change through 2065" (Washington, DC: Pew Research Center, September 28, 2015).

birth rates. Just as global warming causes the seas to rise, so immigration is a demographic tide that is slowly encroaching on Western societies, just as Toynbee said.

The potential for further immigration remains large, especially from Mexico and Central America, where endemic drug violence reigns. A tenth of Mexico's 116 million citizens already live in the United States, half of them illegally, and 40 percent of adults still in Mexico—another 30 million—would move here if they could.[5] The potential for immigration from more distant countries is even greater. According to a 2009 Gallup poll, "700 million people would permanently leave their countries if they could, with the United States as the top choice of 165 million of them."[6] Even more recently, Paul Collier judged that 40 percent of poor populations everywhere would emigrate to the West if they could.[7]

GAINS AND DANGERS

Immigration was long a boon to the United States. Since its founding chiefly by British Protestants, America has become a multinational nation, largely due to immigration—and that was an improvement. Peoples from many traditions have come to America and vastly enriched its way of life. One thinks immediately of the deepening of American religious experience by Catholics, Jews, and Muslims and, above all, of the prodigious contributions by black Americans to many aspects of American culture. The black impact on the arts, and especially on music, has been transformative. Without spirituals, jazz, gospel, and many other forms invented or developed by blacks, America simply would not be the paragon it is. Blacks also figure prominently in US politics, the media, the military, and

FIGURE 11.1 **Share of Enrollment in US Public Elementary and Secondary Schools, by Social Group, 1997–2022 (projected)**

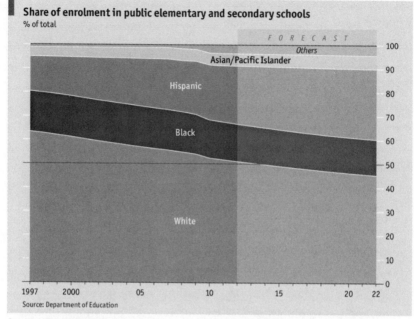

Source: Department of Education

Source: "The New White Minority," *The Economist*, August 23, 2014, p. 22.

college and professional sports. Because of the visibility of these fields, blacks are "on stage" all the time, dramatizing what is best—and sometimes worst—about American life.[8]

As mentioned in chapter 4, Western culture is a huge force for wealth and power, but it is relatively weak in aesthetic and communal dimensions. The black presence and later immigration, however, have helped American culture, while retaining its original civic and economic strengths, to become stronger in these other realms. The combination of the original assets with these later, more creative elements generated a popular culture of extraordinary force. Hollywood, the media, and the internet have propelled it around the world.

That is the multicultural mix that today's immigrants—including Hispanics—could further enrich.[9] Historically, Mexico has had different goals than America. F. S. C. Northrop wrote of its "highly developed appreciation of the aesthetic and its religion of the emotions," much in contrast to America's "excessively pragmatic, economically centered culture."[10] That worldview has value—provided that the United States can also remain a Western nation.

A multicultural society makes for a challenging life. In America, members of any one social group constantly encounter others with different worldviews. We learn who we really are through encounters with others who differ from us. To face those differences becomes one of the burdens of freedom. At its best, the result is growth for everyone. The non-Western elements come from traditions that are more collective-minded than the West, but in America they become fused with the older, European elements to produce a richer individualism. That is the alchemy that made US immigration a boon for so long.

Multiculturalism also accounts for much of America's soft power. Diversity within our society advertises to the world that the American way of life is not limited to particular races, religions, or traditions. Rather, it is potentially available to everyone willing to bear the burdens of freedom. This disarms opponents, such as Islamic radicals, who cannot claim the same openness. That image of America, however, depends on assimilation. Immigrants must become individualist, taking on the burdens of freedom, just as the rest of the society adjusts to them.

The original Anglo foundation remains indispensable to America's achievements. That culture first made America rich and powerful and continues to do so. Without economic dynamism, there would have been no job opportunities to draw non-Western groups here. Without civility, enforced by a moralistic culture, the very tolerance needed for a multicultural society could not endure. Third World countries that are ethnically divided but lack Western mores, such as Iraq, Malaysia, Rwanda, and Sri Lanka, are simply conflicted. A strong civic identity must complement ethnic differences to make a multiethnic community sustainable. That is what America's original Anglo foundation provided. Even J. Hector St. John de Crèvecoeur (1735–1813), an early celebrator of American diversity, asserted that the early English settlers "brought along with them their national genius, to which they principally owe what liberty they enjoy, and what substance they possess."[11]

The danger is that *at current levels*, immigration will weaken those institutional foundations. Before the immigration rules changed in 1965, migration to the United States was either large-scale from Europe or small-scale from other regions, such as China. Only since 1965 has it been both large-scale and chiefly non-Western. If unchecked, the intake could steadily turn America into a non-Western nation, reducing traditional America to a European rump. What can prevent that is improved assimilation so that more entrants from the non-West become individualist themselves, thus supporting America's traditional civic and economic project. Better assimilation, in turn, requires that the current intake be slowed.

THE IMMIGRATION ISSUE

The American public is uneasy about globalization, including immigration. It would like much less immigration than we have.[12] However, the politics of immigration have been dominated by interests that favor more intake rather than less. Recent immigrants seek to bring in their family members from abroad, while businesses and farmers seek cheap labor; and advocate groups defend migrants seeking asylum.[13] These specific policies draw more public support than decreasing the overall immigration level, so they have been hard to resist.[14]

But if public opposition is somewhat irresolute, it is still strong enough to block elite proposals for a major immigration reform in which undocumented migrants would be granted legal status. Besides fear of market competition from new entrants, there is a broad anxiety, especially about Hispanic immigrants.[15] This probably reflects the concerns about cultural difference that I spotlight here. People feel as though migration is changing the nation fundamentally while our leaders evade the problem. Immigration has become a highly contentious issue, yet the debate fails to address the overall scale and nature of immigration, which is the big question.[16]

Controversy focuses obsessively on illegal immigration and not on the rules for legal entry, which produce many more migrants. It focuses, furthermore, mostly on the concrete costs and benefits of immigration, such as effects on the labor market or on government budgets, which are minor. From an economic viewpoint, the gains from immigration appear dominant, since migrants gain vastly higher wages by coming here, at little measurable cost. That is one reason why many academics favor open borders. The only non-economic issue has been bilingualism—the increasing willingness of business and even government to operate in Spanish as well as English.

Almost nobody addresses how immigration affects the overall character of the society. Trump was the first leading politician to give voice to that concern. Even government reports and virtually all other studies of immigration ignore the tensions between America's still strongly individualist way of life and the mostly non-Western peoples now coming here.[17] Culture has become the elephant in the room. Some European leaders have spoken more candidly of the threats to the culture, religion, or heritage of their countries. The will to limit intake has been far stronger and more effective there than in the United States.[18] Some countries have also begun to demand that immigrants assimilate more seriously.[19]

WHY DIFFERENCE IS DENIED

Among American elites, there is a belief that any open discussion of culture is racist.[20] Anyone who portrays immigrants' ways of life as different in any way is assumed to imply that they are inferior. In fact, as discussed in chapter 4, the culture of immigrants has no necessary connection to race or ethnicity at all. To focus the immigration debate on race is a red herring, a way to block discussion of cultural difference. Our leaders also feel the moral injunction to succor the less fortunate, which is stressed in all our religious traditions. Many migrants to Western countries are people simply fleeing poverty, oppression, or war. What Peter Brimelow has called a "sea of pain" in the developing world drives millions to seek refuge in the West—above all, in America, which admits more immigrants than any other nation.[21]

If they are discussed at all, cultural differences between immigrants and mainstream American society are treated as nonexistent, minor, or transient. Any differences between newcomers and native-born individualists are assumed to vanish as soon as they enter the country. Supposedly, anyone can come here, become a new person, and begin a new life. In 1912, Woodrow Wilson asserted that "America lives in the heart of every man everywhere who wishes to...be free to work out his destiny as he chooses."[22] A print advertisement for Citicorp in 1989 proclaimed that "The instant you become an American, whether by birth or by choice,.... [y]ou are guaranteed the freedom to succeed. You are free to dream your own dream of success, to study, to work, to create and discover and build, for yourself and your children, the success you want." The ad depicts new Americans of several races taking their oath of citizenship, their eyes uplifted.[23] Such is the romance of immigration.

This attractive image often was historically valid. Before 1965, the fact that immigrants came mostly from Europe eased their assimilation. On arrival, migrants had to learn English and the details of American life, but most of them were already individualist in outlook, so most hit the ground running. Most of today's immigrants, however, are not individualists coming in. For them, assimilation entails a lot more than learning English or about American politics. They must also take on a new and demanding psychology, where they accept far more responsibility for their lives. So their assimilation has been much more troubled, as discussed below.

The notion that immigrants are just like other Americans is belied by comparisons of home countries. That the European immigrants of a century ago assimilated easily is understandable, given that nearly all European countries have become rich and powerful by world standards, right alongside America. The Asian and Latin American homelands of most of today's newcomers, however, remain very different from the West and typically much less developed. Immigrants from these largely passive and deferential societies are bound to show that temperament. The adjustment they face here is thus much greater than that faced by the "huddled masses" that Emma Lazarus celebrated. For them to resemble the Europeans would be surprising.

If cultural differences are admitted, the orthodox view is to attribute them entirely to differences in opportunity. That is, if immigrants to America do not display the confident and responsible style of the native-born, this is only because they have not been given the same chances to get ahead, either in their home countries or in America. Structure, in other words, determines culture. However, on this view, Western cultural features should have emerged as a result of Western development. But as noted earlier, even centuries ago, the West was already more individualist and civic than the non-West. It was these qualities that chiefly generated the prosperous, dynamic, and well-governed Western world we see today.[24] In short, culture generated structure and is independently important.

A related view is that the only thing today's immigrants need to "make it" in America is more "human capital." Give them more education, and they will speedily start getting ahead like the native-born. Adherents of this view include culturalists like Lawrence Harrison and David Landes (mentioned in chapter 7), as well as Thomas Sowell.[25] But "making it" in

America requires more than schoolbook skills. It requires an inwardly driven, self-reliant personality. That temperament was what propelled Europe and the Anglo countries toward primacy—long before most of their citizens had the education levels that are common today. That mind-set is what most of today's immigrants lack. Most of them come here to escape adversity and enjoy a better life, not to choose freedom and its burdens. When they arrive, many are overwhelmed by the demands of a free society.

None of this denies that immigrants become more individualist over time, as discussed further below. But that process is lengthy and not automatic. It requires that immigration numbers be limited enough so that assimilation can occur and that society take other steps to promote it.

CULTURAL DIFFERENCE

Once we dare to look closely at today's immigrants, most will appear very different from mainstream society, in either the United States or Europe, at least on average. By comparison, the largely European migrants that we remember fondly from a century ago hardly seem like immigrants at all.

Hispanics

Morris Janowitz wrote in 1983 that "Mexicans, together with other Spanish-speaking populations, are creating a bifurcation in the social-political structure of the United States.... Latinos are the most pronounced exception to the absorptive capacity of the American social structure."[26] That division is far more apparent today. While Hispanics as a group are less collectivist-minded than blacks, their contrast with mainstream American culture is still great.

The chief reason is that most Hispanics originate in Native America south of the border, not Europe.[27] They typically display the passive and tentative style characteristic of the non-West, very distant from the confident individualists who formed America. Hispanic writers themselves describe their group in such terms.[28] Hispanics are, in Lionel Sosa's words, "an oppressed underclass" with a "collective psyche... rooted in passivity and underachievement." Their stance toward life is typically one of silent forbearance, not the activism more typical of the West. Their watchword is *aguantar*, meaning "to bear, to endure, to stand, to tolerate, to put up with." That fatalism might partly reflect the hard times some have faced in America, but authors agree that its roots extend back to the authoritarian rule of the Spanish and, before them, Aztec and other Native American cultures. Until they arrive in the United States, most Hispanic immigrants have never known a free society.[29]

Admittedly, Anglo behavior toward Hispanics has often been unconscionable. In their headlong expansion across North America in the nineteenth century, European settlers simply appropriated Mexicans' lands and businesses, reducing them to peons. But in explaining immigrant problems, the Mexicans' relatively passive response is just as important. Mostly, they have silently accepted a lowly place rather than using the opportunities America provided to fight back and advance, either individually or as a group. Compared to them, even the most disadvantaged European immigrants—the Irish and Italians—were much more assertive, both economically and politically. Some Hispanics have recently protested efforts to deport illegal aliens, but that is still far from characteristic of the group.

Asians

The other major non-Western immigrant group is Asians, who might appear very different from Hispanics. Consider, for example, the many Indian students and professors at American business schools or the software engineers who helped create Silicon Valley. Asians are often perceived as a "model minority" that assimilates with little effort. On average, Chinese and other East Asian immigrants do much better in school and careers than Hispanic immigrants, indeed better even than native-born whites. Some policy experts think they should receive even more preferment at leading American universities than they already do.[30] That positive perception is partly due to the strong selection that decides which Asians come to America. Few Asians today, unlike Hispanics, can enter the United States illegally. In addition, many come to study at American colleges and universities, which requires that they possess academic credentials and at least some English ability.

Nonetheless, contrary to such images, Asian immigrants to America are far from uniformly successful. Many in fact remain poor. A visit to Chinatown in any American city shows this. Like blacks and Hispanics, the group has bifurcated between the upwardly mobile, who have risen into the middle class or beyond, and a more traditional group that resists assimilation and still lives a non-Western life of adjustment to circumstance.[31]

Even successful Asian immigrants, like Hispanics, are less individualistic than the American norm. Like non-Westerners generally, they tend to adjust to the expectations around them. Their families expect them to succeed, and so they do. They succeed, however, within a pre-existing structure. In school and then college, they expect to be rewarded for repeating what teachers tell them. That is because rote learning is largely what education means in Asia.

But from the time they go to college, American students are expected to think for themselves. The highest honors go to students who dare to make personal arguments—who even challenge their teachers. This Asian students typically find more difficult than students with origins in Europe.[32] Asian applicants to Harvard have impressive grades and test scores, yet many are rejected for lack of more personal and individual qualities that are also needed to succeed in America.[33]

Asians in America typically do better in school than they do afterward. Many of them fear to step free of family and act or think for themselves, as mainstream American culture expects. Even second-generation Asian Americans tend to show these traits, because their parents still think in Asian terms.[34] In an individualistic society, leaders are expected to ask questions, not just answer them. They must assert themselves, deal with unstructured problems, and take more risks than most Asians are comfortable doing. In other words, Asians tend to bear the burdens of necessity, not those of freedom. Some Asian observers recognize that *this* is the group's main problem—not some "bamboo ceiling" imposed by others.[35]

Islam

The United States has relatively few Islamic immigrants, and those who do come to America are usually highly selected to accept our culture of freedom, with its inner demands. In Europe, the impact of Islamic migration has been much larger and more negative, due to sizable intake from Turkey, South Asia, and North Africa. In 2015 and 2016, the surge of refugees from war-torn Syria and Iraq exacerbated the immigration issue, producing crises within the European Union. The EU struggled first to resettle and then to resist the legions fleeing from Middle Eastern conflicts.

Islamic migrants have reacted to the free culture of Europe like oil to water. Accustomed to Islam's rigid social strictures, especially in Arab countries, many are offended and disoriented by what seems to them the West's permissive society. Some protest criticism of Islam in the media. A few turn to violence. The radicals who committed the 9/11 attacks in America and more recent attacks in Europe were largely recruited within Europe rather than the Arab world. Social problems also run high among Islamic families in Europe, but, as in America, elite taboos prevent discussing these openly.[36]

The background cause of these upsets is that Islam, despite its severity, has not generated a moralistic culture capable of reconciling freedom and order in the Western manner. In Arab countries, the moral structure depends far more on external enforcement and far less on the conscience of the public than in the West. In addition, the political class does not enforce good behavior on itself, as in the West. Whereas Western regimes are tolerant but strong and civic, Islamic governments are repressive but weak and corrupt. Unable to control their own regimes, Islamic radicals project their problems onto the West, where commentators are far more willing to accept blame. Arab leaders and those they represent have failed to assume civic responsibilities toward each other, and that ultimately reflects the external and conformist character of non-Western culture.[37]

In Europe, as in America, candid discussion of immigration tends to be suppressed lest it violate strong Western strictures that oppose racism and favor compassion toward the unfortunate. The recent immigrant wave from the Middle East, however, forced public alarm out into the open. Figure 11.2 shows a poster used by the UK Independence Party in the 2016 British referendum on withdrawal from the European Union. (The figure standing in front is UKIP leader Nigel Farage.) The poster suggests how, to many Europeans, immigration has come to seem both threatening and unlimited.

Africans

The other major group of immigrants to Europe are those fleeing war and poverty in Africa. Historically, Africa has seen the weakest political development of any world region.[38] In recent decades, governments there have been particularly prone to breakdown (see chapters 8 and 13). Meanwhile, moderate gains in income, plus improved transportation,

FIGURE 11.2 **UK Independence Party poster used in Brexit Referendum, 2016**

have enabled many Africans—especially young men—to flee to Europe in hope of a better life.

The usual assessments of immigration, in Europe as in America, are narrowly economic. In those terms, immigrants gain, and there seems to be little downside. But as Paul Collier has written, African migration poses serious dangers to European society. The more immigration there is, the more it tends to snowball, as existing immigrants help others to follow them. And heavy concentrations of immigrants tend to undermine the civic and cooperative culture that rich countries have evolved over centuries. Lacking the same civic background, Africans do not bring with them constructive "social models." Their entry brings higher crime, lower school performance, nonwork, and dependency on benefits. By leaving, immigrants may also undermine progress in their countries of origin. To avoid these costs, firmer limits on immigration are essential.[39]

Figure 11.3 dramatizes the cultural contrast between African migrants and the West. It captures Africans climbing over a fence from Morocco to Melilla, a small Spanish enclave on the North African coast. If they succeed, they will be safe in Europe and able to claim the protections that only the West provides. The Africans bear the burdens of necessity in an extreme form. Many of them are quite literally fleeing for their lives. Waiting to receive them, however, is an official of the Spanish Red Cross. He bears the burdens of freedom, not necessity. He works within the institutional order of Europe, far stronger than any in Africa. He must be

FIGURE 11.3 **African migrants climbing into Melilla (Spain) from Morocco**

Source: Suzanne Daley, "Africans, Battered and Broke, Surge to Europe's Door," *New York Times*, February 28, 2014, pp. A4, A10.

true to the *inner* obligations of his job and to the civic values of the West, which demand that migrants be received humanely. For the migrants, the demands are all external; for him, internal.

Like many in the non-West, these Africans show impressive fortitude in the face of hardship. The orthodox view is that, if they behave badly in the non-West, it is due only to the adversities they have faced. All they need is freedom. But, contrary to the romance of immigration, coming to the West means more than escape from necessity. It also means shouldering the burdens of freedom, which are in some ways more demanding. The African migrants' struggle with Europe is perhaps today's sharpest conflict between Western and non-Western ways of life.

DIVERSITY AMONG IMMIGRANTS

A further reason many commentators resist admitting cultural differences is variation among immigrants. Every group is diverse, even if averages differ. American meritocracy rewards individualism, so the leaders of all social groups tend to be inner-driven achievers. Those who represent immigrants or minorities inevitably assume that the less successful members of their groups are like them, or would be if they had better opportunities. So they advocate the traditional American solution to any social problem—greater freedom in some form. But *those solutions take an individualist personality for granted*. They do not promote it.

The way US immigration appears publicly disguises the problems. The media are careful to appear multicultural. News anchors, journalists, and others who appear on television are always confident and articulate, while they are also chosen to represent all groups and genders. So, to viewers, American society appears to be already integrated. What problem, then, could immigration pose? To limit immigration would be to exclude these talented people from America. But the minority exemplars we see are, unfortunately, not typical of their groups, which are usually far less capable, confident, and integrated.

Some immigrants who come here have been selected in advance to be consistent with an individualist ethos. These include many of the Asians who attend American colleges and graduate schools and go on to successful careers.[40] These immigrants are certainly an asset to America, not a threat. But they do not imply that the immigrant threat is a chimera. The overachievers are not at all typical of immigrants in general, let alone of the traditional, non-Western societies from which they come.

The majority of immigrants come here without much selection at all. Modern air travel has made coming to the West far easier than it was a century ago. Higher incomes—even in the Third World—mean more people can afford to come here, either legally or illegally.[41] Even very unskilled people can now come to America in large numbers. Today, it is more likely than ever in history that people will flock here simply to escape the "sea of pain," not because they otherwise choose to become American. Lenient family reunification rules also allow many family members to join those already here, and most of whom are low-skilled. Still less selected are the illegal immigrants, who constitute about a quarter of the inflow.[42] These are the groups that most clearly challenge America's individualist way of life.

A plurality of immigrants are Hispanics (who may be of any race). To some, that label suggests formation by Spain, a Western country, which colonized most of Latin America. But among immigrants, Western influence was strong only for Cubans. They are the most individualist of Hispanics and thus have done well in the United States. Their assertive and ambitious temperament is highly compatible with the still-dominant individualism of America.[43] Cubans have even earned praise as "the Jews of the Caribbean."[44] But they are far outnumbered by people from Mexico and Central America, who are much more tentative and, on average, much less successful.

Like Asians, recent black immigrants, often from Haiti or elsewhere in the Caribbean, are also highly selected and hence do relatively well in America. That does not mean, however, that other blacks do not pose a significant challenge for American society. Most black Americans descend from Africa, a strongly collectivist culture, and they came here, like most Hispanics, without any selection. Blacks have contributed greatly to American life, as noted, but they still lag in social and economic status. Their prospects hinge on more blacks learning to be individualists, a slow and ongoing process.

All these non-Western groups have enriched America. But those that are fast-growing—Asians and Hispanics—have also made our society less individualist. There is thus a danger that America could come to resemble Mexico or Brazil, in which non-Western peoples greatly outnumber those from a European formation. Like those nations, the United States would still be an important country, with a significant culture, but it would no longer display the strong dynamic and civic qualities that once empowered it to lead the world. It could still show those strengths only if the non-Western intake were slowed enough so that more of the newcomers could become individualist themselves. The key to successful multiculturalism is assimilation.

DAMAGE TO DYNAMISM

What concretely is the damage done by today's immigration? America's traditional dynamism depended on a population that was well enough organized to pursue personal advancement and innovation. Individual striving was the great engine that drove the nation forward. But immigration has deepened social problems that undercut that capacity. Among newcomers, families often falter when they come to this freer, less traditional society, as shown in the last chapter. Most Hispanic children are today born outside marriage, a serious handicap to their getting ahead. There is a similar breakdown of order in

Europe, where the influx of Islamic migrants has increased crime and mistreatment of women. To maintain order, Europe will have to reproduce, through public authority, some of the external order found in Islamic societies.[45] It will be a version of the paternalism that has developed in America.

In America, heavy Hispanic immigration raises poverty rates above the norm. In California, in 2016 the poverty rate was 16 percent, above average for the country; it was 23 percent among Hispanics, who were 40 percent of the state's population and growing rapidly.[46] Nationwide, even in the 1990s, when most Americans rode a booming economy to higher incomes, Hispanics' household income slid downward due to low education, low-paying jobs, and social problems.[47] The persistence of poverty even during that prosperous decade was heavily due to growing immigration from the south. "From 1990 to 2004, the number of Hispanics in poverty rose by 52 percent, accounting for 92 percent of the increase in poor people [in that period]."[48] Some immigrants returned home, having found life here too demanding, as many migrants did in earlier eras.[49]

As noted in chapter 10, Hispanics in America have unusual difficulty getting through school. In 2000, only 34 percent of foreign-born Mexican Americans were high school graduates, compared to 87 percent of the native-born. Very few Mexican Americans go on to college, and only a minority attain professional credentials. Most do no better than unskilled work. Even fourth-generation Mexican Americans fall well short of the national average in terms of education, career status, and home ownership.[50] The problem here is a lot more than a lack of "human capital." There is a fear to take leave of family, choose one's own direction in life, and compete for success. Even Hispanic students who reach college often feel "profoundly lonely" there due to "separation from family, from home." A "wall" that is "made of culture," Earl Shorris wrote, shuts Hispanics off from the routine advancement in school and careers that all the European immigrant groups enjoyed.[51]

American schools, above all, are the frontier where the battle to integrate the new immigrants must be fought and won. Figure 11.4 shows the percentage of students in the public schools with incomes low enough to qualify for subsidized lunches. The minority presence is strongest in the South and Southwest, where blacks and Hispanic immigrants predomi-

FIGURE 11.4 **Percent of Low-Income Students in US Public Schools, 2013**

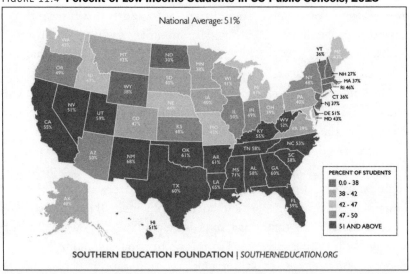

National Average: 51%

PERCENT OF STUDENTS
- 0.0 - 38
- 38 - 42
- 42 - 47
- 47 - 50
- 51 AND ABOVE

SOUTHERN EDUCATION FOUNDATION | *SOUTHERNEDUCATION.ORG*

Source: US Department of Education, National Center for Education Statistics, Common Core of Data.

nate. As those groups migrate farther north, Northern states face similar tensions and challenges.

Ever since the 1960s, the nation has struggled to uplift the academic performance of poor black students. Now the Hispanic wave has redoubled that burden. In many big cities, blacks and Hispanics together dominate the public schools. In New York City public schools, already 41 percent of students are Hispanic, while 27 percent are black and 16 percent Asian; only 15 percent are white. In Dallas, 93 percent of students are Hispanic or black. And most nonwhite students are low performers.[52] Even school districts that embrace diversity, such as in Morristown, New Jersey, must devote increasing resources to a disadvantaged Hispanic population that grows steadily. Said one superintendent, just "staying ahead of the tidal wave of poverty" was a constant struggle.[53]

As the enrollment numbers show, urban white students have mostly fled public education for private schools. That is a loss to educational quality as well as integration, because more integrated schools would probably perform better overall. But keeping their children in largely nonwhite schools is a hard sell to white parents who are concerned about standards and order. So the schools come to mirror the division between the more and less skilled that now characterizes the whole society.

After school, the gap in skills and thus in earnings between immigrants and the native-born has widened greatly, due chiefly to the Hispanic influx. In the late nineteenth and early twentieth centuries, newcomers to America typically arrived with capabilities not far below those of the native-born, one reason why most of them assimilated successfully. Today, however, the gap is much greater, largely due to the shift in the main source of immigrants from Europe to Latin America and Asia. That increases the economic incentives to migrate, since the gain in wages from coming to America is even larger than formerly. But the benefits of immigration to the American economy are far less clear.[54]

Among Hispanics, crime and poverty levels run unusually high, as they also do among blacks. In the first generation, immigrants typically work hard and have lower crime and family problems than the native-born, as their advocates point out. But in later generations Hispanic children often work less hard, and social problems among them climb toward national averages.[55] Hispanics, like blacks, tend to bifurcate, with part of the group progressing toward the middle class but another part becoming long-term poor. Much of Hispanic America is becoming a second underclass, alongside the long-term black poor.[56] While many immigrants succeed splendidly, overall they are markedly less successful than the mostly European newcomers of a century ago. Immigration experts liken Hispanics to this earlier immigrant wave, but poverty experts, more realistically, class them along with blacks as facing special disadvantages.

The culture of poverty is an extreme version of the worldview that pervades much of the non-West. The essence of both is an absence of moralism. Social values such as marriage, the work ethic, and law-abidingness are affirmed in principle but are observed in practice much less often than among the middle class. People orient to outward constraints, not inward principles and purposes. Such attitudes undercut the ability to advance oneself that an individualist culture assumes. Paternalist social programs are an attempt to restore the structure that low-income Americans need in order to live constructive lives.

Integration traditionally occurs in America through school or the workplace, where people of different backgrounds converge around common tasks. They compete and also cooperate to meet these challenges. That is in the nature of a democratic society. People assert themselves not only as individuals, but also to vindicate the group from which they come—defined by class, ethnic group, race, gender, and so on. Each person seeks to show what people of *his or her* sort can do. While only some will get ahead in competitive senses, all can win the respect earned by giving a good account of themselves. And that respect breaks down distrust between groups over time. For this to occur, however, members of all groups must be in the game. By failing to compete seriously in school or careers, many of today's immigrants remain outsiders.

DAMAGE TO CIVILITY

Immigration also weakens America's civic culture. Hispanic crime levels run much above white, as shown earlier. For illegal immigrants, having a visa or work permit is a matter only of "papers," a detail. This attitude is found even among well-off and well-educated Mexicans.[57] American regions with heavy immigration—such as Eastern and Midwestern cities and the Southwest—are relatively low in governmental quality. Corruption is low by world standards but high by American standards.[58]

These features mirror attitudes that many immigrants bring with them from south of the border. Mexicans have what appears to be a democratic and law-governed polity, similar to America. But in practice, the system is dominated by elites, with little public input. The rule of law is violated by leaders and led alike. Mexican political culture is "aspirational." The Mexican Revolution of 1910 established democratic norms, but they are perceived as distant goals, not binding in the present.[59] It is the same separation of norm and fact found in the culture of poverty. Recently, Mexico has become more democratic, less dominated by a single party, but politics remains elitist and administration weak and corrupt.

In American politics, Hispanics and Asians are typically more passive than the native-born and less likely to vote. Hispanic leaders portray their group as victims of white injustice, like black Americans, but rank-and-file Mexicans are usually uninvolved in political activism, neither empowering their leaders nor holding them accountable. Due to mutual distrust, Hispanics have trouble organizing on their own behalf. The activist organizations that speak for them—such as La Raza—are largely funded by outside foundations. Immigrant neighborhoods today manifest "the almost total absence of organized political life."[60] This incapacity contrasts starkly with the ability of America's original settlers to form associations for all manner of common purposes, at which Tocqueville marveled.[61]

American politics presumes that citizens will obey the law while holding officeholders accountable. Those who oppose current policies comply with them while agitating for change. In contrast, Hispanics tend to be evasive about the law yet politically passive. They sidestep rules that they find inconvenient, but they seldom protest against them. That passivity undercuts government's capacity to achieve any common purpose. It is one thing for Hispanics to obtain political rights in America, as they have since civil rights. It is quite another, Shorris remarks, to "make Englishmen in the barrios."[62] Those patterns mirror Mexico and Latin America generally, where lack of a moralistic culture has made drug gangs in some countries more powerful than the government.

Research by Robert Putnam found that rising ethnic pluralism, chiefly due to immigration, undercuts American social capital—the capacity to collaborate with strangers for common purposes. Native-born whites are becoming more distrustful of strangers—even other whites. Blacks and Hispanics are especially distrustful.[63] Again, this is more than a transitional problem.

America's founders imagined a society of equal citizens, where people might differ in wealth but not in identity. All were "created equal" and actively pursued "life, liberty, and happiness." Tocqueville in 1835 described a society that had substantially achieved that vision. But, like all Western political thinkers, he took for granted an individualist culture. Since the 1960s, immigration has brought to America the much more passive and cynical attitudes typical of the non-West. Unless that tide is slowed, the Founders' vision will die.

ASSIMILATION

A cultural reading of immigration accepts that culture can change over time. Attitudes are determined largely by upbringing, not by national, ethnic, or racial background. People in any country mostly live out the culture in which they were raised. Assimilation, over time, can fuse cultural traditions that were originally distinct. That has happened in America, where assimilation of past immigrants has produced today's multicultural society.

The long-running success of assimilation has proved that a nation created chiefly by British Protestants could accept much diversity without losing its essence. Experience has shown that every element of the population need not embody the original American ethos to the same extent. It is enough that a clear majority of the public do so. Newcomers who initially differed could be absorbed, provided that their numbers were limited, they moved toward an individualist ethos over time, and their leaders accepted this. Meanwhile, they could contribute their distinctive gifts to a common society.

It is more doubtful that current assimilation will succeed, simply because the cultural difference between immigrants and the receiving society is now much greater. Defenders of immigration point out that absorption of the largely European immigrants of a century ago proved easier than alarmists of the time predicted. But the countries those migrants came from differed far less from America than do the homelands of immigrants today. As Toynbee wrote, the ability of immigrants to "become Westernized" depends on "their capacity for entering into the middle-class Western way of life,"[64] and that is very much in doubt. Also, racial sensitivities make society less insistent on assimilation than it was a century ago.

Even those earlier immigrants had a tougher time adjusting to America than is often remembered. That is one reason why many immigrant groups have retained a separate identity as "hyphenated Americans."[65] Contrary to the romance of immigration, newcomers did not immediately adopt American mores. Rather, they continued to display the political attitudes of their countries of origin—as their descendants still did *even generations later*.[66] Our sense that past migrants assimilated easily arises mostly because they caused little change in the culture already established. More recent immigrants show a similar persistence but are also much more distinct from the West. On past evidence, their struggle to assimilate must be even more protracted.

Advocates of immigration point out that, by most measurable indicators, assimilation of the recent intake looks strong. Recent immigrants and their descendants are gaining ground on average Americans in terms of education, income, occupation, home ownership, English ability, and intermarriage with other groups. But immigrant children do less well when compared to the native-born of their own generation rather than to their parents. Wage gaps between immigrant heirs and the native-born persist, even across generations. Indications are the worst for Mexicans, the largest immigrant group, a sign of the difficulty they have getting through school, mentioned earlier.[67]

And none of this directly addresses culture. Jacob Vigdor developed an index that measures how dissimilar immigrants are from native-born Americans. It shows that economic assimilation (several indicators of employment, income, and wealth) is indeed high, but assimilation in terms of culture (language, intermarriage, marital status, etc.) and civics (naturalization, military service, etc.) is low. Overall, assimilation is much lower than it was a century ago. Today, Mexicans are less assimilated than any other immigrant group. Although assimilation does improve over time, gains are unusually slow for cultural assimilation and for Mexicans and Central Americans.[68] Government studies of assimilation and the effects of immigration entirely ignore this dimension.

The feel-good part of immigration is allowing desperate people to come here and enjoy more security and opportunity than they ever had before. The far harder part is schooling newcomers in the distinctive burdens of a free society, which are considerable—obeying the law, working for a living, getting through school, competing for advancement, and so on. By neglecting assimilation, the nation has stored up a vast cultural debt, akin to the huge financial debt we have incurred by running large government budget deficits for decades.

In 1957, the Broadway musical *West Side Story* portrayed two rival gangs, one Italian and the other Puerto Rican. The two ethnic groups were then similar in status. That is exactly how the usual immigration discourse portrays today's newcomers—disadvantaged only in status. But since then, most Italian Americans have risen into the middle class and ceased to be a visible minority, except on Columbus Day. Puerto Ricans, meanwhile, have succumbed to the wave of unwed pregnancy mentioned earlier, becoming the poorest of all Hispanic groups. The Italians affirmed their identity as Western individualists. They have asserted control of themselves and their families, and thus progressed in a free society. The Puerto Ricans have not. That is the difference that culture makes.

WHAT TO DO?

To preserve a multicultural America, we need not halt immigration, let alone restore a lily-white America, which no one should wish. The key, rather, is simply to *reduce the rate* of immigration closer to what assimilation can absorb, as well as to legalize it. Although most current immigration is legal, much is not, and the illegal migrants put the most strain on American institutions and culture. Public alarm about recent immigration is driven partly by the scale of it and also by a sense—quite accurate—that it is out of control. Intake has recently exceeded 1 million a year. That rate must be at least halved, to around 500,000, counting both legal and illegal immigrants. That is the recommendation also made by other immigration critics.[69] But they do not make the cultural case I make for it here.

Advocates often suggest that immigration at current rates is unstoppable, simply because America is so much richer than most migrants' countries of origin. In fact, just a few legal changes would cut the flow substantially.

ILLEGAL ALIENS. The presence of more than 11 million illegal migrants in the country, chiefly from Latin America, is deeply contentious. Sending these people home may sound harsh, but it is essential to limiting and legalizing the flow. Recently we have somewhat toughened our border with Mexico, one reason the undocumented population has not grown still larger. But more important is enforcement within the United States.

Advocates contend that the nation never could deport the 11 million illegal aliens. But there is no need to do this. It is enough to expand the E-Verify system, which determines whether applicants for employment have valid Social Security numbers. The system need only be mandated for all hires, as it is not now. That would prevent the undocumented from getting legal jobs and thus press most of them to leave the country—without deportation. The main resistance to this solution comes from businesses seeking low-skilled labor, for whom easy hiring of illegal aliens remains highly convenient.[70]

FAMILY REUNIFICATION. Under current policy, about two-thirds of legal immigration is for purposes of family reunification. Legal residents may bring in many relatives beyond their immediate families, including parents and adult siblings. These family members can then bring in further relatives, producing "chain migration." Instead, reunification should be limited to spouses and minor children, as recommended by the Jordon Commission in the 1990s.

BIRTHRIGHT CITIZENSHIP. Current policy accords citizenship to all children born in the United States, even if their parents are here illegally. Canada is the only other Western country to allow this. Several other rich countries have recently revoked or limited birthright citizenship, because it makes controlling immigration too difficult. It is very difficult to deport an illegal alien whose child is a citizen by birth, which, in turn, encourages more illegal entry. President Obama sought to give legal status to these families under Delayed Action for Parents of Americans, or DAPA, which would have made enforcing immigration limits even harder, but he was thwarted by the courts.

Many people believe that birthright citizenship is mandated by the 14th Amendment to the Constitution. The amendment stipulates that citizenship be granted to all those born or naturalized in the United States "and subject to the jurisdiction thereof." Legal experts say that whether this applies to the children of illegal aliens is unclear and has never been resolved by the courts. However, the drafters of the amendment meant it to ensure citizenship to former slaves, not to reward illegal immigration. Congress could probably end or limit the birthright rule by ordinary legislation, and it should.[71]

ASYLUM. Under current rules, any migrant can enter the United States without a visa and request asylum, meaning protection from dangers in his or her country of origin. In theory, those claims are adjudicated, and only a minority of claimants are given legal status. But in practice the great majority are released into American society pending this review and can remain, legally or illegally, whether or not their claims are approved. The realization that asylum was an open door prompted asylum claims to explode by 1,700 percent in the last ten years. The Trump administration has struggled to limit that wave.[72] Asylum should be ended and only legal refugees admitted, since their claims to hardship have to be approved before they enter the country.

AMNESTY. The one legal change to avoid is awarding legal status to current illegal residents. Some Americans think that amnesty would put an end to the immigration travail. However, we must remember that the Immigration Reform and Control Act of 1986 legalized many illegal residents of that time, and the main result was simply even more illegal migration.

The undocumented tide is highly sensitive to expectations, as the recent asylum crisis shows. Control is impossible unless it is clear that illegal aliens must go home, asylum and amnesty are off the table, and there is no way into the country except by meeting the rules for legal entry.[73]

These legal changes may sound radical, but all they do is reverse the unfortunate policies and practices that in recent decades have permitted open-ended immigration, which most Americans oppose. The goal is not to prevent all entry but to promote assimilation among immigrants who have come legally. Many observers believe that the sharp limits that Congress set on immigration in the 1920s promoted assimilation of the large intake during the Progressive era. Similarly, today, entry must be limited in order to consolidate the new, multicultural America.

ASSIMILATION. We need new efforts specifically to assimilate immigrants. A cultural perspective should shift the focus from raising "human capital" and incomes to promoting America's individualist and inner-directed style. Simply to reduce the inflow and the number of illegal immigrants would serve this end, as it would slow the growth of insulated immigrant communities and promote interaction with nonimmigrant society. To do that, in turn, would reduce further immigration, both legal and illegal.[74]

For assimilation, schools and religious organizations are crucial. Both played key roles in teaching the ways and burdens of freedom to the immigrants of a century ago. They must do so again, more forcefully than they recently have. In school, Hispanic children should learn English quickly, with or without bilingual instruction. Conversely, ESL programs should be expanded so that more immigrant parents also learn English.

The nation's long struggle to raise educational standards for black students must be extended to Hispanic students as well. The latter, due to language and other problems, typically approach school with even less optimism than blacks. The best hope to overcome that outlook is the paternalist schools described in chapter 10. But to expand them will be costly.[75]

In that earlier era, churches also strongly promoted a responsible individualism among immigrants and their children. Although first seen as a threat to a Protestant America, the Catholic church that came to the country with Irish and Italian immigrants proved to be a strong force for their integration.[76] Catholic churches admonished the Irish to reduce the significant familial problems that they harbored in the nineteenth century, in some ways comparable to those of minorities today, thus empowering them to achieve the middle class.

But like black churches, most of which are Protestant, the Catholic church has not seriously opposed family collapse and other problems in minority communities. It has far less impact on Mexicans today than it did on the Irish and Poles before them.[77] That has to change. The clergy of all denominations must more firmly preach middle-class norms if their flocks are to advance.

CONCLUSION

Successful immigration requires more than liberation—more than just offering opportunity to desperate peoples, as advocates demand. Rather, it requires mutual learning between newcomers and the established society, and lately the society has borne too much of that burden. At the same time, the American vision of citizenship remains general and optimistic, detached from any precondition about race or ethnicity. As Gunnar Myrdal wrote in 1944, to solve the race problem, the United States did not need to change its values, only be true to those it already had.[78] The same is true for immigration. Until the recent era, it was always assumed that immigrants should embrace the burdens of freedom. We must return to that tradition.

The United States still should welcome anyone who "plays by the rules" and aspires to a democratic life. Just as Athens was the "school of Hellas" in ancient times, so America is a school of individualism today. But that creed is not a natural or universal one. Human beings do not always espouse it once they are free, as our rhetoric imagines. Rather, it is exceptional and must be learned. And for successful learning, there have recently been too many students in the classroom.

Our leaders, moralistic to a fault, sometimes suggest that we must atone for our affluence and past racism by throwing our borders open to the world. But to do that would undo the society that attracts immigrants in the first place. It would not achieve but threaten a multicultural society. It would absorb our national life entirely in immediate personal concerns, in survival. That is the life of the non-West, from which today's migrants come. Such an America would lack the energy, focus, and daring, the political and economic enterprise, that Tocqueville discovered here. We would, in his words, "not corrupt, but enervate, the soul and noiselessly unbend its springs of action."[79]

PART FOUR

FUTURE CHALLENGES

FUTURE CHALLENGES

In these last two chapters, I draw final conclusions about American primacy: will it continue, and what should American policymakers do to sustain it? Appraising the United States and its rivals from a cultural viewpoint yields a different reckoning than the usual one focused on specific kinds of power. The United States will probably remain the leading nation, primarily because it has the strongest institutions of any large country.

As to policy, my conclusions tend toward caution abroad but more demanding policies at home. If, as I argue, the United States is not a universal nation, but an exceptional one, then we cannot presume that unfree countries overseas seek principally to be liberated and assume our way of life. To become free, they must shoulder their own burdens of freedom—America cannot do it for them. Failed states, however, will continue to demand costly responses. At home, our chief need is to strengthen individualism through measures to uphold work and family. A society in which ordinary people still achieve their own advancement is the innermost basis of American power.

CHAPTER TWELVE

THE FUTURE OF PRIMACY

The usual appraisal of world leadership focuses first on nations' economic wealth, then on military strength and sometimes soft power, or reputation abroad. Nothing is said directly about culture, but in fact the contest for primacy is substantially between opposing ways of life. In the usual reckoning, the United States does quite well, as noted in chapter 1. Yet its distinctive strengths ultimately arise from an individualist culture in which citizens bear the burdens of freedom.

Despite the rise of Asia, America still possesses a huge economy and is easily the richest nation in per-capita terms. As figure 12.1 shows, the share of world GDP accounted for by the United States has held up at around a quarter since 1970. It has declined only slightly in recent years—far less than the European share—despite the sharp growth of Asia.[1] That wealth supports America's unparalleled military machine and its enduring appeal as a model for modernity.[2]

A deeper reason to expect continued American primacy, however, is that nations around the world now vary in institutional capacity even more than they do in wealth. Paul Kennedy famously argued that world power depends centrally on economic strength, since the wealthiest countries can afford the most advanced armaments. But this proved true chiefly within history, where for several centuries the strongest countries tended to be the richest.[3] And this was also because power was fragment-

FIGURE 12.1 **Share of World GDP, 1970–2030 (projected)**

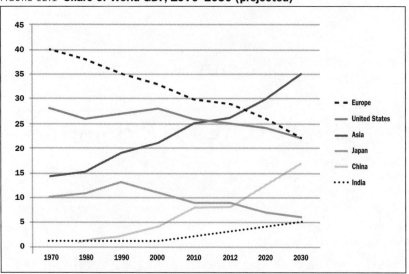

Source: Economic Research Service, US Department of Agriculture, https://www.ers.usda.gov.

ed among several leading countries. All of them possessed states strong enough to make modern war, so their varying economies were their main difference. But today—after history—a "democratic peace" deters conflict within the West. The United States towers above its (mostly non-Western) rivals, above all in its capacity to project force, resting on the strength of its far stronger regime. Economic differences are no longer so central to power, great though they still are.[4]

The primacy contest now turns far more on general cultural differences than on specific forms of power. The question is which country or region's *way of life* provides the strongest basis for future power of any kind. Which country generates the effort and the excellence from its citizens that is needed to impact and impress the rest of the world? A dominant nation exerts influence in many forms, and that energy comes from a characteristic view of life. In practice, that implies a focus on institutions. A country's values are expressed, above all, in how it organizes for economic and political effort. Among institutions, at the end of history we normally assume that the market economy and democratic governance are superior, but there are other alternatives.

Although American primacy will likely endure, that verdict is hostage to cultural change both at home and abroad. The United States has become less individualist than it once was, while Asia has become more so. Which society can recover its original coherence, or find another? The primacy contest will probably turn on the answer. The current contenders for world leadership—Europe, radical Islam, China, India, other Asian countries, and America—differ radically, which is itself a sign of the end of history.

EUROPE

Of global power centers, Europe is culturally the most like America. Here was the original individualist society that came to dominate the world and, thus, to found the United States. Today, however, its energy has ebbed. Although it is larger than America and almost as wealthy, its economy is less dynamic and its military capacity far smaller. It hesitates to compete all-out in the global economy or to send troops to war. European life today is dominated not by daring new enterprises at home or abroad, but by consumerism and a generous welfare state that cushions the populace against the insecurities of capitalism.[5]

Britain and France are partial exceptions. Since the 1980s, Margaret Thatcher's economic reforms made Britain once again the most dynamic large country in Europe, generating a greater will and capacity to project power abroad. Britain was America's firmest ally in its wars in Afghanistan and Iraq, although these efforts were controversial within Britain. Lately, France led the European campaign to oust Muammar Gaddafi in Libya, and both countries have defended former colonies in Africa against insurgencies. Together, Britain and France account for nearly half of Europe's total defense spending.[6]

Before history ended, international relations featured arm's-length competition for power among Western countries and Japan, all of which had strong, independent states. Now, however, the Europeans increasingly depend on America. They must sue simply to be heard in Washington on security concerns.[7] President Trump's demand that they spend more on their own militaries rather than rely so heavily on the United States has only exacerbated those tensions. Perhaps the Libyan campaign and the current weakening of the European Union, due to the British decision to leave, may revive European assertiveness. But any European challenge to American leadership is remote.

RADICAL ISLAM

Islam presents a complete contrast to Europe. This civilization—at least in its Arab form—appears assertive, even aggressive. Radical Islam aspires to take over the world. It is a throwback to Islam's early centuries, when it conquered a vast empire and became a leader in medieval science. But Islam soon lost that dynamism, because it could not tolerate, as Europe did, the questioning that ongoing progress required. And Islam never developed strong institutions. That is why its claims to power remain largely imaginary. Its economies never grew as strong as the West's, because rulers over-controlled them to bolster their own positions. Down to the present, that is the main reason Arab countries cannot offer their young people satisfying economic opportunities, which in turn foments protest against the regimes and the West.[8]

Arab governments serve the rulers far more than their societies. The Ottoman Empire, which succeeded the early caliphates, became a machine for extracting revenue from subject peoples. Officials purchased their offices and despoiled both state and society. Still today, Arab governors seek mainly just to hold on to power over passive and resigned societies.[9] The problem, it is often said, is that Islam allows no separation between church and state. But Muslim clerics have seldom ruled directly (Iran is an exception). The real problem is that Islamic government has little authority of its own. The mosque overshadows the state. Rulers lack the independent authority to govern that they always possessed in the West. This was why, during the Arab Spring, protesters could overthrow rulers but had little idea how to replace them.[10]

The fundamental problem is psychological. Arab Islam never developed the West's capacity for individual discipline *or* Asia's collective solidarity. Western moralism generated a civic culture in which leaders and led accepted moral commitments to each other. These internalized norms allowed public institutions to evolve, independent of religion. That empowered the West to reconcile questioning with order, thus to become rich, and then to project power around the world. The Arab world has never shown the same capacity. In the West, leaders must accept feedback regarding their failures, whereas Arab leaders tend to shift blame for all problems in the region to Israel.[11]

The strongest Islamic states today are Iran and Turkey, neither of

which is Arab. Both draw on unique national identities and civic traditions that predate Islam. It is possible that a more individualistic Islam is
developing in Arab cities, where some preachers appeal to a middle-class
clientele in a personal manner that recalls the Reformation in Europe.[12]
Out of that style might evolve greater moralism and thus a stronger civic
culture. In the meantime, however, the great fact about Islam is its institutional poverty. Without strong government, it cannot threaten the West
as the Communist world once did. Its challenge consists, indeed, largely
of stateless terrorists. That is a principal reason why history has ended.

CHINA

America's major Asian rival, China, is again a complete contrast. It is
neither individualist like Europe nor institutionally bereft like Islam. It appears to have a formidable institutional presence, but one based chiefly on
a collectivist psychology quite different from the West's. But that culture
ultimately limits how far China can really challenge American primacy.

China has become a huge economic power, with a growing military
and an expanding world influence. It is already, as Zakaria said, "the
second most important country in the world."[13] A Communist country
that originally boasted a statist economy, China introduced elements
of market competition and openness to trade starting in 1978, leading
to huge increases in foreign investment, trade, and economic growth.
That river of wealth has raised incomes and reduced poverty on a scale
never before seen. It has financed huge investments in infrastructure and
military forces. But the Communist regime has kept its monopoly on
political power, repressing all serious questioning. Its leaders boast that
this statist capitalism is superior to the West's reliance on the free market
and democracy, and some Western commentators credit that model with
growing influence.[14]

Some authors warn that China may take over American primacy and
threaten Western freedoms. It could become the Big Brother that the
Soviet Union once threatened to be.[15] This prediction, however, greatly
overestimates the confidence of the regime. China, after all, has little history of projecting power abroad, let alone of trying to lead the world. A
collectivist culture imposes important limits on what China can achieve,
and this is apparent in each major area of Chinese life.[16]

The Economy

China has become wealthier chiefly by opening its economy to the market, yet it still harbors a large state-owned sector of inefficient firms, maintained largely to provide employment. Currently, that sector is strengthening.[17] Much economic investment controlled by local party leaders and officials is wasteful. Chinese cities are festooned with empty apartment buildings built on speculation, without regard to demand. In addition, China (like Japan and other Asian countries before it) has relied largely on foreign direct investment, low-skilled labor, and the production of low-quality or low-tech goods for export. Recently, China's breakneck growth has slowed. Its labor force is aging, wages are rising, and some manufacturing is being lost to lower-wage employers in Vietnam and other parts of Asia. To maintain growth, China will have to reduce its state sector and produce more rarified products and services, thus facing more direct competition with the West—especially America.[18]

Yet state industries resist cutbacks, and it is difficult to develop higher-value products in China because of reliance on pirated goods and technology, weak patent protection, and a general lack of legal enforcement there.[19] There is also fear of shifting the economy toward consumption, as outside studies advise, because this would only strengthen demands by the middle class for greater political involvement, as discussed below. An increasingly free economy ultimately does imply a more open political order, and that is something the Chinese regime must resist.[20]

In part due to Chinese competition, the American economy has shifted toward high-end, sophisticated products and services where it is most competitive. To rival the United States, China must ultimately show greater innovation at this level, and this is precisely where its cultural inhibitions are greatest. It is difficult to imagine how a society so conformist, and strictly controlled by the regime, could ever give rise to anything like Silicon Valley. Currently, China is investing heavily in tech industries, such as artificial intelligence, but is still well behind the United States. In any technological arms race, it risks having all this effort made obsolete by some new American breakthrough.[21]

Education

China has invested heavily in education, knowing that this sector is crucial for economic innovation, but so far it has produced quantity more than quality. Chinese students score very well on international tests, but schools emphasize rote learning over problem-solving and the independent thinking needed to lead in the knowledge economy.[22] At the post-secondary level, China appears to be producing huge numbers of graduates with technical skills, but an independent study found that only 10 percent of them were employable by the standards of Western firms. This was because in Chinese schools the emphasis, again, is on set skills rather than analysis and problem-solving. Despite huge numbers, China is in fact producing far fewer leaders than it needs to compete in the global economy.[23]

Western firms are looking for creativity. As noted earlier, the will and ability to *take on* external problems is central to an individualist culture. The outward challenge becomes the inward mission. Individuals must conceive some new solution to a problem and then achieve this in the outside world. Often that requires redefining the problem in some way so that it can be solved. The essence of leadership in the West is less to solve problems directly than to decide what the problems are. The Asian style, however, presumes that the task is already defined by some higher authority, and one's duty is only to apply some specific technique to it. The element of *personal* responsibility and creativity is missing.

China is building up its universities, even hiring away leading Chinese-born academics from America. But funding is uncertain, and there is strong cultural resistance to the questioning and rigor that goes with Western-style academic life.[24] The quality of Chinese universities is undermined by rampant cheating among students and fraud and plagiarism among faculty (although of course these abuses are not unknown in the United States). American universities encounter the same problems when they open branches in China.[25] These features dramatize the contextual nature of Asian morals, in which social pressures largely define what people regard as right and wrong: students and professors are expected to get ahead, and so they do what that requires. The Western belief that morals have a principled and independent basis, that fraud and dishonesty are simply wrong, is largely lacking.

Some 3 million Chinese students have abandoned their own system to study abroad. More than a quarter of them come to the United States, usually paying full tuition to do so, because American universities are among the world's most prestigious. Of Chinese PhD graduates in America, 85 percent do not return to their home country.[26] But those who come to the

West bring their cultural proclivities with them. Zinch China, an educational consulting firm, estimates that 90 percent of Chinese applicants to American universities submit false recommendations, 70 percent do not write their own personal essays, 50 percent have forged high school transcripts, and 10 percent claim academic awards and other honors that they did not receive.[27]

American faculty who teach Chinese students often find them less impressive in person—and far less fluent in English—than they appeared on their applications. The students often expect to get credit simply by repeating what teachers say on their tests and papers, rather than making personal arguments. Usually quiet and submissive, they may appear "learning disabled" compared to more voluble and assertive American students. They also have trouble with the theoretical nature of Western thinking, which focuses on analysis and background causes rather than the Asian sense of context. For the West, mind is an independent force that creates truth and seeks power over the world, whereas for Asians it is largely the passive mirror of experience.[28]

The Military

In the West, growing wealth led directly to growing military power and a capacity to project power overseas. Early modern Europeans explored the world. Britain—and, later, America—built vast navies and forged ties to foreign countries on the basis of either empire or alliances. Observers of China's rapid economic growth have assumed that China will do the same, but that is doubtful.

For a huge country that has overshadowed the rest of East Asia for centuries, China has remarkably little history of extending power abroad. It has used its military chiefly domestically, to expand its own borders and uphold the regime within. It is now rapidly building up its forces. It has developed a few naval bases elsewhere in Asia, and it seeks to dominate the South China Sea by claiming islands there, provoking alarm among its neighbors. However, its only clear territorial objective is to recover Taiwan, which it never officially recognized as a separate nation after the Chinese Civil War. China is not likely to become an aggressive and expansionist power similar to European countries, the United States, the Soviet Union, or Japan.

One explanation is that Chinese culture is profoundly self-centered.

China sees little need to reach out to the world, because it believes it *is* the world. As mentioned in chapter 2, for a brief period in its history, China sought to explore distant countries, but the Ming dynasty halted these ventures. For the better part of its existence, China expected foreign countries to come and pay homage to it, believing it had little or nothing to learn from them. The Chinese even assert their racial superiority to other peoples, a belief that alienates potential allies.[29] During World War II, China allied with the United States and Britain in order to fight Japan, but since Communist China broke with the Soviet Union in the 1950s it has once again stood largely aloof and alone.

Western powers never identified themselves so completely with their civilization. Rather, they viewed Christianity and modernity as a heritage that they should represent worldwide. That helped spur their aggression, even their imperialism. However, it also finally held them accountable to their own democratic principles, leading eventually to the dissolution of their empires. Throughout history, the West showed an interest in learning from the outside world—an interest that is largely absent in the non-West. Japan was a notable exception, which is one reason it so rapidly became a world power in the late nineteenth century.[30] Since World War II, the West and especially America have constructed international institutions, such as the United Nations and the World Trade Organization, intended to help govern the world while minimizing distinctions among nations. China has acceded to that system only reluctantly.

Military forces seldom generate power by themselves. They must support the ends for which a nation stands. The ability to serve a larger purpose—if only to restrain aggressors—is the main reason past exertions of British and American power have generally drawn wide support. China can claim no such cause. Very likely its military power will continue to be used mainly close to home.

Government

China's regime is simultaneously its greatest apparent strength and a critical weakness. An authoritarian system such as China's does give rulers freedom to decide many issues without opposition. The current Chinese system artfully coopts intellectual and economic elites, rewarding them provided they conform, while avoiding the generalized repression seen in the Mao era. Controls are aimed mostly against protests or other forms of organization that directly challenge the system, and the media, including the internet, are closely controlled.[31] Any popular threat to the regime seems distant. Under the current Chinese president, Xi Jinping, the regime's determination to block all challenge has even intensified.

China does have a capacity to mobilize unparalleled millions of citizens for great causes when the nation is threatened, as it did during the wars of the last century and under Mao. Leaders in China face less need to explain and justify their actions than do leaders in Western polities, where demands for consent are far more pressing. Yet without clear accountability, Mao's heirs are prone to err in matters of routine policy and fail to gain the support of the society.

The Chinese regime is continually embarrassed by revelations of its own corruption. Without popular mandates or the rule of law, rulers cannot easily prevent local party and government leaders from making illicit gains, often through involvement in local development projects. President Xi has cracked down on some flagrant cases, seeking at least to make rent seeking less conspicuous, but there is strong resistance among party cadres.[32] As one official confided, "Not fighting corruption would destroy the country; fighting it would destroy the party."[33]

At the local level, there is growing protest against misrule, including corruption but also land requisition for development, environmental pollution, and arbitrary decisions by local officials. In 2010, there were 180,000 such protests. Because unrest like this helped topple imperial dynasties in the past, Beijing takes it seriously, but it can do little as long as routine channels for public feedback are lacking.[34]

Since the repression of the pro-democracy demonstration in Tiananmen Square in 1989, the regime has believed that it can continue to rule without consent only if it continues to deliver rising incomes to the populace. But that very growth has also made the society more complicated and loosened control from the top.[35] A growing market economy necessarily permits less detailed control than a planned one. It also has created a growing middle class that seeks to be heard and accommodated. A turning of economic policy toward more domestic consumption would only accelerate that process.[36]

Some observers believe that the system must soon collapse: China will have to choose between control and consent. That is, it must accept more detailed repression, at the expense of economic growth, as under President Xi; or it must accept far more explicit accountability to the society, perhaps by subjecting more government and party officials to election. (Only some limited local elections are allowed now.) The Arab Spring generated official fear that such protest could spread to China, which prompted Chinese security forces to repress even the smallest sign of discontent.[37]

One sign of fading confidence is that many rich Chinese are shifting their families and assets overseas—preferably to America or Canada. By 2012, more than 16 percent of China's rich had already emigrated or handed in immigration papers, while 44 percent intended to do so soon. More than 85 percent were planning to send their children abroad for their education, and one-third owned assets overseas. Some Chinese even send their children to high school in America, the better to get into a leading American college later. Professionals are also leaving China, not only for better opportunities but because they are fearful of regime change. In 2010, for example, more than half a million Chinese left for OECD countries (45 percent more than did in 2000), although some expatriates return when their new lives disappoint.[38]

As this suggests, China generates little soft power. It does not represent ideals that inspire other countries or even its own people. Some Americans travel to China on business, some to study, but very few to live permanently, unlike the legions who clamor to come to America.[39] Westerners say that China is unfree, but as argued above, the West is not free in any simple sense either. The real difference is in where discipline resides. In China, it is mainly external, in the many social forces that tell people how to behave. In America, it is mostly internal, in the civic values that individuals learn to observe. That allows for the potent fusion of freedom and order that only individualism can achieve. And to the extent the world moves in that direction, as it is slowly doing in Asia, Chinese holism becomes less sustainable.

The underlying problem is that China has never forged any basic concordat between government and society. From ancient times, none seemed necessary so long as individuals did not differentiate themselves from the mass. Since the unification of the country in 221 BC, the state has asserted an authority to rule. Most of the time, this claim has been passively accepted by the people. But the regime never gained the active consent that would give it a deeper legitimacy, as was achieved finally by all the Western powers and Japan. China cannot postpone that reckoning indefinitely.

INDIA

India presents another sharp contrast. Similar to China, it is a vast Asian country with a huge population and a basically non-Western way of life. It also has seen accelerating economic growth due to greater acceptance of the market in economic policy, although growth has been less dramatic than in China.

The regime, however, is fundamentally different from China's. In Indian history, rulers governed largely to serve themselves, as in other early empires. Except for the Mughals, an Islamic dynasty, none of them unified much of the country. India was a religious civilization long before it was a nation. In two centuries of colonial rule, however, the British succeeded in implanting some Western institutions. This means that India today has embraced the burdens of freedom, at least in its public life, in a way that China never has. Its economy is far more market-based, political freedoms are allowed, and the government is elected and legal, even if it is far less honest and efficient than most Western regimes.

By reckoning thus with freedom, India may have earned a better prospect than China, although still a distant one. It already shows some of that ability to combine freedom and order seen in the West. The regime is unafraid of growth and social change. Tolerance for the market has nurtured a high-tech economic sector that is the envy of Asia. Indian software and internet firms already compete with Western counterparts at the top end of the world economy. The resulting wealth has powered a modest military buildup and strengthened Indian influence in the wider world. Well trained and fluent in English, Indian elites—leaders, entrepreneurs, academics, and students—have made a deep and favorable impression on many Western countries, including the United States.

But it is too easy to treat India as "a kind of giant Silicon Valley with worse roads and spicier food."[40] The progressive side of India is still only a thin veneer atop a huge and traditional society that has only begun to modernize. The entire high-tech and export sectors account for only 2 percent of all Indian employment.[41] The country faces enormous internal problems, stemming from its scant development over the centuries before British rule.[42] It cries out for massive investments in transportation, power generation, and schools. High-tech firms often have to provide infrastructure for themselves, because government cannot. And the rest of the economy is not notably efficient or competitive. These internal challenges must long limit the influence India can wield in the world, even though its sway is growing.[43]

Education in India dramatizes this tension between promise and tradition. At all levels, both the quantity and the quality of instruction are mediocre at best. The country has impressive high-tech institutes, but because entry to them is famously competitive, many students must instead seek education in the West, leading to the wave of Indian students seen on American campuses.[44] Much like China, India generates legions of graduates in technical subjects, but their capabilities are limited. Of 500,000 engineering graduates a year, only 4 to 18 percent would qualify to work for Western firms.[45]

Because it is elected, government in India can claim far deeper legitimacy than in China, but it is also corrupt, inefficient, and indecisive. In the past, it overregulated the economy, stifling growth. Even today, when enterprise is freer, it has responded to infrastructural problems only fitfully. Many Indian politicians accept payoffs, and politics at the federal and state levels is dominated not by problem-solving but by serving certain castes, religious groups, and other interests. A weak state drags India down.[46] The most hopeful sign may be that popular movements have recently arisen to oppose corruption, showing that the political culture is slowly becoming more moralistic.[47]

Up to now, China has achieved faster development than India, because its centralized regime allows it to impose change. India's democratic regime is far less resolute. At the top, India has shouldered the burdens of freedom, with impressive effect. But a more collectivist and cautious way of life still dominates most of the society. Until more Indians take on an individualist and moralistic way of life, change will remain slow and government disappointing. Although America has come to see India as a partner in helping it run the world,[48] the day when it could lead on its own is distant.

OTHER ASIAN COUNTRIES

Some other Asian countries—South Korea, Taiwan, Hong Kong, and Singapore—have developed even more successfully than either China or India, but none is large enough to contest American leadership. All these countries have combined essentially democratic and capitalist institutions with collectivist societies. All did so under American pressure or example after World War II. All have thus avoided China's autocratic but insecure regime, but they have achieved much greater wealth than democratic but poorly governed India. Yet limitations set by culture are still apparent.

An important model for all of these countries was Japan. The Japanese first showed how a collectivist society, if strongly led, could achieve Western levels of wealth and power. But today Japan faces limits, due not only to recent economic problems and a declining population, but also cultural reasons. As the nation grew rich, the manufacturing economy on which it had relied mostly shifted to cheaper countries. To maintain growth, it now must compete in high-end technical products and sophisticated services where the United States is far more formidable. And to do this it must become more innovative, which is difficult for a collectivist culture.[49] Japan generates more patents than America, but far fewer Nobel prizes.[50]

The "Asian tigers" that followed Japan face similar dilemmas. South Korea must transition from a largely manufacturing economy to a more advanced services economy in which its firms, which are mostly small and family-based, will be less competitive. Larger firms could achieve more but depend on government sponsorship because the country lacks the strong trust that has let such firms arise privately in Japan.[51] As in China, the Korean educational system places severe competitive pressures on students but stresses rote learning rather than innovation and problem-solving. This alienates many Korean students, who then choose to study abroad, undermining the traditional system.[52] Like China, the "tigers" face growing pressures for individualism at the top, producing internal tensions.

And success stories like these are far from universal in Asia. Other countries—Indonesia, Malaysia, Myanmar, the Philippines, and Thailand—have seen some growth, but not on the same level as Japan, the "tigers," or China. All these are collectivist, traditional societies that strongly resist change. They have been unable to parlay that mind-set into a basis for strong government and rising wealth as the richer countries have done.

Their regimes remain weak and corrupt by the standards of the West, or Japan.[53] Thus, for them, greater wealth and power on a collectivist basis must be difficult. Any prospect for growth on an individualist basis, as in the West, is even more distant. These countries belie the illusion, entertained by many development experts, that with the right policies any country can get rich. Culture remains the lion in the path.

AMERICA

The conventional view, as mentioned in chapter 1, is that American primacy will endure because the United States remains superior in specific kinds of power. From a cultural viewpoint, however, what stands out about the United States is the simplicity and strength of its basic structure. America is democratic and capitalist, like Japan and India, but it is also an individualist society. It thus distributes the burdens of freedom much more widely and bears them at a much deeper level than any of its rivals. Initiative and responsibility are borne far more broadly in America than anywhere in Asia.

Always self-critical, many Americans think that the United States has been outclassed in the global economy by Asia or by certain European countries. In this they generalize too much from the decline of the factories. In fact, viewed from any distance, America remains a formidable competitor, as figure 12.1 suggests. Its economic assets go right back to the nation's founding—an individualist culture coupled with strong institutions spread across an entire continent. In the centuries since, the United States has built the world's most open domestic market, the world's best universities, the most efficient capital markets, and a skilled and flexible labor force, and all this overseen by a strong and stable regime.[54] No other country can boast such assets.

America need not catch up with anyone. Born modern, it never had to compromise with traditional cultures as everywhere in the non-West has had to do. Rather, it is the exemplar toward which many less developed nations aspire.[55] Although America built its wealth in part through exporting to Europe, it is far less dependent on trade today than its Asian competitors. The domestic market is fully developed and dominates the economy. Nor does it lack basic infrastructure or educational institutions, as in much of the non-West. America of course must improve its infrastructure and education, and it must address the social and financial problems mentioned above. But as David Brooks remarked, "Americans would be crazy to trade their problems for those of any other large nation."[56]

These features all depend on an individualist culture. In America, the burdens of freedom are inescapable. The free market is more pervasive in America than in any large Asian country.[57] It spreads responsibility for economizing across the entire society, and only relatively small groups are shielded from it. The American educational system rewards the same imaginative, problem-solving talents that are demanded by the economy, rather than rote learning as in Asia.[58] A high proportion of the labor force not only does a job but is strongly encouraged to improve efficiency or productivity in some way. So the economic machine steadily improves. In an individualist culture, all this occurs spontaneously, with limited direction from the top.

At the same time, as mentioned earlier, individualism generates the "market morality" that allows producers and consumers to interact without the moral fears that confine exchange to personal acquaintances, as in most of Asia except Japan. That is particularly important in today's "flat world" economy, in which much business is transacted among total strangers on the internet. As one entrepreneur told Thomas Friedman, this "hard floor" of trust is what empowers firms to innovate without worrying that they will be taken advantage of by others or by government.[59] American culture is also more tolerant of the flat organizations and rapid changes characteristic of e-commerce, whereas Asia demands more hierarchy and stability.[60]

The same broad responsibility is seen in American government and politics. Again, self-criticism is misleading. Commentators deplore the partisan polarization that has impeded action in Washington and, even more, the confusions of the Trump administration. But they overlook the trust and efficiency that characterizes most routine government in America, at least relative to most of the world. Here again, problem-solving is widespread. Officials accept feedback from citizens and cooperate with them, and with civic groups, to make government work better.

The individualist lifestyle, at its best, combines personal initiative with an ability to collaborate with others for common ends.

The greatest wealth of countries like the United States and Great Britain is not their mineral deposits or their agricultural land. It is not the money that they have in the bank. It is the mentality and habits of the nation at large. These are people accustomed to governing themselves, accustomed to promoting enterprise, ready to join in spontaneous and private activities of all kinds—but also accustomed to an ordered liberty whose roots now are many centuries old. This human and social capital is by far the most valuable to have—and by far the hardest to get.

In much of the world today, powerful states represent attempts to overcome the absence of this dynamism and order.[61]

Much of the secret to American primacy is the ability to combine a decentralized economy with a strong state that can mobilize wealth for the projection of power. Vast tax revenues empower the American military machine, as well as the financial aid that Washington uses to support and reward its foreign clients. America trumpets freedom yet also asserts power, including soft power. That potent combination, in the end, goes back to the fusion of assertiveness and moral principle in individualist psychology.

CULTURAL CHANGE

But will that psychology endure? America's whole nature is bound up with individualism, and so is its future. The same goes for Asia's more collectivist culture. Each side has generated wealth and power in a distinctive way, but can it continue to do so? On both sides, the chief threat to power is not international rivalry but domestic cultural change.

In research on world cultures, as noted above, individualism is closely linked to affluence. Richer cultures are more inner-driven than poor ones, and urban populations more than rural.[62] In chapter 5, I argued that, to a long view over history, an individualist culture did more to create affluence than the reverse. Ronald Inglehart and his associates, however, have argued that affluence drives individualism, and the World Values Surveys provide some support for this in recent times. The clearest changes, toward "post-materialist" values, have been in Europe, but one may also attribute the growing restiveness among Asian elites, especially in China, to growing individualist tendencies driven by economic growth.[63]

Protest against misrule, of course, has a long tradition in China, but previously it lacked much political content. Local people demanded that incompetent or corrupt officials be ousted, but they did not demand any general change in the regime. So revolt did not mean revolution, and misrule recurred. Today, however, criticism and protests in China evidence "a growing sense of individual entitlement and rights," perhaps reflecting Western influence. Many Chinese have now studied in the West, or have family members or associates who have, and the internet publicizes freer conditions in other countries. Some intellectuals have demanded that the regime live up to its own constitution by allowing press freedoms and an independent judiciary, if not opposition parties.[64]

The social basis for these pressures is a growing Chinese middle class that has begun to think for itself and expects more response from officials than in the past. The problem is not only that a more advanced economy is increasingly difficult for Chinese authorities to control, but also that affluence itself generates greater restiveness. More autonomy and self-expression lead, in turn, to greater demands for consent and response by elites.[65] These same trends are apparent in other successful Asian countries, but their governments are more open and representative and hence less at risk.

However, this restive minority is not about to remake China or Asia. There is no cause yet to resurrect the sameness ideology, the idea that everyone is really alike. Asian cultural change appears to be confined to the most affluent.[66] There is of course a Chinese business class that is entrepreneurial, but it is largely based outside China, in other Asian countries. The great majority of Chinese citizens have far less sense of choice and make fewer demands. They continue, mainly, to obey what their leaders say or to react to market pressures. Japan, meanwhile, has become far richer than China but has remained strongly collectivist. Overall, Asians continue to bear the burdens of necessity much more than the burdens of freedom.

In America, as explained already, the changes are largely in the other direction—away from freedom and its burdens and toward a life of necessity. And the shifts are mostly at the bottom of society, while at the top individualism has intensified. It is chiefly among lower-income and less educated Americans, especially low-skilled whites, minorities, and immigrants, that we see resistance to an enterprising life. Rather, many now accept a more limited existence of adjustment to their environment. It is a silent protest against the demands of mainstream American society, which remain great.

Of course, America's regime is not in danger, unlike China's. The alienated believe they have been neglected, but they are not calling for a different kind of government. Their protest is driven not by overt injustices but by defeats they have suffered in the economy's competitive scramble. Their style is much more defeated than defiant. The fires of competition and achievement continue to burn brightly at the center of American life, but around its edges rising numbers have retired from the game. That is the growing problem that Trump's victory has dramatized.

The danger is not disruption from below but withdrawal. The more poverty remains entrenched and immigration too great to assimilate, the less commitment there is to the individual striving that traditionally generated American wealth and power. More of our society is working, if at all, only to live, rather than working to achieve.

There is also preoccupation at the top. Government must now struggle to respond to the new working-class problem, alongside the struggles with poverty and immigration that are long-standing. The costs of redress will also increase America's budget problems. And social change is bound to weaken America's soft power, because a way of life that defeats many of our own citizens is no longer so attractive to the outside world.

To reorder American society is essential to maintaining American primacy, and the reverse is also true. Should the United States cede world leadership to China, the case for maintaining an individualist society at home would weaken. One of the reasons Britain lost much of its social discipline after World War II was that its leaders came to believe that British power was in decline worldwide, so they actually promoted the liberated social attitudes of the 1960s and 1970s. For Margaret Thatcher to restore Britain's economic leadership, as she did in the 1980s, she first had to restore a more traditional and individualist society.[67] America today needs a similar renewal.

CONCLUSION

A cultural assessment thus confirms the usual verdict that American primacy will likely persist despite the advance of Asia. But here that conclusion rests not so much on predictions about economic or military resources as on the nature of two disparate regimes. China's achievements, though impressive, will ultimately be limited by the character of its society.

A collectivist culture seconded by free-market policies has helped China and other Asian countries grow rapidly. That ethos supports strong leaders who can dictate change, but it confines problem-solving mostly to the top. The bulk of the society benefits from rising wealth but is not fully engaged in producing it. That limits Asian economic potential.

Politically also, the Chinese regime concentrates initiative at the top and thus forfeits the benefits of robust feedback from the populace—other than the inchoate force of local protests. The regime's legitimacy is increasingly in question. Yet no easy transition to a more representative regime is imaginable. China has no tradition of open politics, and what elections there are currently play only a small role in government. Any outbreak of open dissent at the center, as in Tiananmen Square in 1989, would likely produce not democracy but breakdown and reversion to even more autocratic rule, as has happened before. The other East Asian countries also find innovation difficult, and only Japan seems fully comfortable with democracy. India has an open regime but is far less developed in other senses.

In America, by contrast, an individualist culture permits tremendous innovation while still supporting strong government and a capacity to project power. The very moralism of American policy, while sometimes grating to our Asian clients, promotes trust. Most foreigners do not believe that the United States serves only itself. China, however, is distrusted by its neighbors because it views itself as the rightful leader of Asia. It denigrates the achievements of the other advanced Asian countries, who in developmental terms have achieved more. Partly for this reason, South Korea, Taiwan, and Vietnam, as well as Japan, continue to base their national security on ties with the distant United States rather than with nearby China. Without changing that attitude, Beijing cannot hope to eclipse American leadership in Asia, let alone in the rest of the world, as even some Chinese recognize.[68]

Ultimately, the contest for primacy is a contest between cultures. In Asia, authoritarianism has had good uses, but is finally limited in its capacity to create wealth and power. In Asia, the masses obey, but only a few take responsibility for change. America, however, is unreservedly committed to individualism. The main threat our nation faces is not the rising power of unfree countries but the demands of its own free society. The major question is whether it can reconcile the less privileged to those demands. A society fully equal to the burdens of freedom must sweep all before it.

CHAPTER THIRTEEN

POLICY DIRECTIONS

W hat does a cultural view of American power imply for policy? The implications flow from the global division between Western and non-Western cultures. American policymakers can no longer assume that the most serious challenges they face, either at home or abroad, involve people much like themselves. Rather, they as individualists must engage nations and peoples who have a far more cautious and collectivist disposition.

Past chapters have already suggested that the United States should be less ambitious overseas than it recently has been. America should no longer seek to remake the world in its own image. In domestic policy, conversely, it must be more demanding. Programs for low-income Americans must promote the autonomy and the self-reliance that historically has generated American wealth and power. As Samuel Huntington wrote, we must accept cultural diversity in the world while maintaining a dominantly Western society at home.[1]

Our overall goal should be to come to terms with the non-West, learning from it and conceding it much influence but also preserving an individualist society. Abroad, that means managing the demands of many foreign countries, a few of whom are rivals, but most of whom seek support or sustenance from the West. At home, it means accepting multiculturalism but also doing more to make it work through limiting immigration and investing in assimilation.

The two tasks are connected. Success overseas is essential to maintaining individualism at home. Only if an individualist nation can still lead a largely collectivist world, including China, will many Americans think it worth continuing to bear the burdens of freedom. And more practically, managing foreign demands is essential to limiting the migration flows that have become the principal challenge to an integrated society at home.

In neither arena is greater freedom the answer, as Americans usually imagine. Many developing countries, even those that appear unfree, actually require *greater* order than they currently have. Nor, as decades of experience have shown, is liberation the chief answer to entrenched poverty and inequality at home. A restoration of order among the less privileged is actually essential to achieving a free society as Americans have understood it. Inward discipline is a precondition for the outward pursuit of opportunity.

American policies both at home and abroad are already moving in these directions. That shows that a cultural analysis is realistic. But few policymakers yet admit what they are doing, even to themselves. The myth of sameness endures. There is inevitably criticism from advocates who have long demanded a more vigorous pursuit of human rights abroad or an expansion of social rights at home. They insist that nothing has changed from decades ago. But it has.

DIFFERENCE OVER SAMENESS

The idea that the United States should regard other countries as different from itself offends many traditional attitudes in foreign policymaking. Realist experts project their own calculating mentality onto other countries. They easily imagine foreign leaders reasoning how to respond to American predominance in the world, just as Western countries maneuvered against each other up through the twentieth century. Today, foreigners supposedly still calculate how to achieve their own ends, differing from America only in their resources.[2] Rational-choice scholars imagine a similar mentality.[3] But the fact is that few countries outside the West are likely to calculate in this inner-driven way. Mostly, they adjust to outside pressures. That is what cautious, non-Western cultures advise, and it is all their very limited governments are able to do.

A traditional issue in American foreign policy is how assertive to be. Some favor a confident policy with ambitious goals; others a more cautious one, even isolationism. A similar issue is how far to assert ourselves unilaterally, imposing solutions through American power alone, as against collaborating with other nations or international bodies. On both these issues, the George W. Bush administration favored the first alternatives and the Obama administration the second.[4] Trump has reverted to unilateralism. But all these positions, again, assume that other countries are basically like us.

The sameness assumption implies that America can retire from the world if it chooses. But that assumes that other countries can maintain the international order without us. American isolationism after World War I, which helped precipitate World War II, disproved this idea—and that was in a world where America interacted mainly with other strong states in Europe and Japan. Today an American abdication might trigger a worse breakdown. Some of Trump's recent policies seem to risk that. We now must deal chiefly with weak states outside the West, many of which struggle even to govern. American leadership is no less indispensable to world order today than it was a hundred years ago.

DEPENDENCY OVER CONFLICT

The United States does face a few genuine adversaries where realist assumptions still apply. In confronting Iran or North Korea over nuclear weapons or Russian aggression in the Ukraine, only "hard" forms of power will suffice. America must rally its allies and prepare, if necessary, for armed conflict. That may also be the outcome if China becomes a thoroughgoing adversary and confronts the United States over Taiwan.

Hard-headed conflict may also occur over trade. Trump has repeated long-standing complaints about China's unfair trade practices, such as depressing the value of its currency and forcing transfers of American technology, thus imposing huge trade deficits on America. The 2016 presidential campaign also raised suspicion of foreign trade deals that seem to destroy high-paying manufacturing jobs in America. President

Trump has imposed some tariffs on China, a reversal of America's recent commitment to expanding free trade.[5]

But in general, overt conflict among self-respecting competitors is no longer the *leitmotif* of foreign affairs, one sign that history has ended. Most non-Western countries, rather, seek some degree of dependency on the West, especially the United States. Poor countries petition for favorable trade terms and various forms of military or economic aid. Some also rely on Western banks and global financial institutions for bailouts after financial crises.

The situation resembles that of low-income Americans who rely on government income programs. Just as Western governments have imposed work tests on some aid programs, so financial bodies sometimes condition bailouts of poor countries on reforms in their economic policies. Some countries also send migrants to the West, where they can receive much higher wages and remit their earnings to families back home. They find in our society the open and vibrant labor market that they cannot create in their own.

Of course, due to its deficits in trade and government spending, the United States is dependent on other countries—particularly China—to finance its own borrowing. But the United States has, so far, been able to carry its debt and still maintain international confidence, because of its enormous wealth and productivity. Even in poorer countries, government, business, and the affluent are often prepared to invest more in America than they are in their own economies.

Too much is at stake for ourselves and others around the world for America to retire from global leadership. The real issue is no longer how involved to be but rather how much to demand from dependent countries *in return* for support. It is the same issue, in essence, that dominates domestic social policy—not how generous to be but reciprocity. To motivate change, we must deploy not only economic incentives but also authority.

PROMOTING DEMOCRACY

Another clear implication of cultural difference is that the United States should abandon the direct promotion of democracy abroad (aka nation-building). America has been an exemplar of popular government since before its founding. From the start, many American leaders have seen their mission as exporting democracy to less fortunate lands. For Ronald Reagan, democracy was a weapon against the "evil empire" of the Soviet Union, for George W. Bush a means to defeat Islamic radicalism.

But these crusades typically took no account of the cultural preconditions of good government, stressed in chapter 8. No attention was paid to the lack of a moralistic, civic culture able to maintain elected institutions after America had installed them. The United States has (after the World Wars and the end of Communism) successfully fostered democracy in Germany, Japan, and Eastern Europe, but these were all countries that already possessed many civic qualities and a prior history of elected government. It has conspicuously failed to achieve stable democracy where it has recently intervened—in far less civic Somalia, Haiti, and Bosnia, and above all in Afghanistan and Iraq.[6] The recent Arab Spring also saw repeated defeats of democracy.

Americans too readily assume that political rights and accountable government are compatible with order, as they almost always have been in our own history (and in British history before that). They seldom reckon with the exceptional, individualist psychology that reconciles freedom with order. In the rest of the world, claims to individual rights simply undercut the more collective authority that most countries depend on for basic government. The United States might once have been a "status quo" power compared to international Communism. But in current times its character is that of the world's most "revolutionary nation."[7] To help govern today's world, we must restrain ourselves.

Human-rights advocates typically assume that people living under autocrats want democracy, as the advocates themselves do. But what most people in these places mostly seek is not a freer life, with all the burdens that implies, but a quiet and predictable life, which autocratic regimes can often provide. To subject undemocratic authority to elections will likely produce only turmoil and rule by different autocrats than before, as the Arab case shows. As Samuel Huntington remarked, "Western intervention in the affairs of other civilizations is probably the single most dangerous source of instability and potential global conflict in a multicivilizational world."[8]

It is facile to liken the Arab Spring to past rebellions against autocratic rule in the West, such as the short-lived revolutions in Europe in 1848.[9] Western revolutions drew on far deeper precedents of political and legal rights, which in turn rested on an individualist culture able to internalize norms of good citizenship. That civility enabled the West to scale back external forms of authority or subject them to consent without succumbing to chaos. But in the more collective-minded non-West, there is little such capacity. There is no clear way to "get to Denmark"—the stable, high-quality government typical of the West.[10] Progress is still possible, but it cannot assume sameness, and it must be slow.

As Robert Putnam and his associates showed in Italy, successful democratic politics is deeply path-dependent, relying on civic attitudes and trust among citizens which took centuries to build. Regions that are superficially similar but lack the same attitudes will be much worse governed. Other factors, such as economic development, are secondary.[11] There seems to be no easy way for a society that never had positive political attitudes to acquire them in the present. Unfortunate regions, such as the Balkans, typically suffer from deep ethnic and religious divisions that time has not healed, and this makes them virtually ungovernable.[12]

The will to improve non-Western government has often been stronger in the West or in international agencies than in misgoverned countries themselves.[13] Real change can come only when the desire for freedom, and its burdens, strengthens within undemocratic societies. There must be demands for political rights that arise internally, without external support from the West.

THE MARITIME SYSTEM

The best general approach to American policy toward a diverse world may be what Walter Russell Mead has called the maritime system. He refers to the way that the British maintained world primacy for a century after 1815 with very little overt conflict. They achieved this even though several other countries were or became economically or militarily stronger.[14]

The British succeeded partly because they had the world's dominant navy, allowing them to punish offenders with little fear of defeat or reprisal. But they also had dominant soft power. They were widely trusted as honest brokers in conflicts among and even within other countries. They also embodied, as much as any country, the most progressive values of their time. This combination allowed Britain to sustain a dominant position at affordable expense for decades. During a long string of European crises, they discouraged conflict among several European powers, abolished the slave trade, and secured the independence of Belgium and Greece.[15]

The maritime system stood for self-determination among nations, international peace, and open trade. It also favored regimes that observed progressive principles, although they did not have to be democratic. The main expectations were international—that all nations should join in a world economy without conflict or serious trade barriers. This was the system that the United States took over when it inherited world primacy from Britain after World War I. Indeed, the principles of the system were best stated by Woodrow Wilson in his Fourteen Points of 1918 and in the Atlantic Charter issued by Franklin Roosevelt and Winston Churchill in 1941. This is the structure that the United Nations and world economic agencies, under US sponsorship, still defend today.

The maritime system has served Anglo and world interests by putting autocratic rivals on the defensive without having to confront them openly. An international economy in which protection or autarky is discouraged tends to favor the most open and modernized economies, which historically have been Western and especially Anglo. That forces all countries to worry about their competitiveness, which puts pressure on governments to be effective internally, which in turn favors the rule of law and accountability. All these suasions work against the instinct of authoritarian countries simply to clamp down and resist outside criticism.

President Trump may seem to be disrupting that system with his "America first" demands on Chinese trade policies and NATO, but ostensibly he is only demanding reciprocity—expecting more from countries that have taken our generosity too much for granted. By enforcing this system, the United States might find a "happy medium" between tolerating oppressive regimes and toppling them to no purpose, because despots return. The United States might well demand more of its few overt adversaries while condoning offenses by more cooperative countries.

China may not accept Wilsonian principles, but it fears their appeal, even to its own people.[16] It easily turns aside demands for political rights as assaults on Chinese sovereignty when they are voiced by American leaders or advocate groups. But demands from the UN or the World Trade Organization are harder to resist. The Chinese must belong to such bodies for practical reasons and hence cannot avoid deferring to their principles. Over time, that compromises the authority of their unelected regime.

FAILED STATES

While the United States should not promote democracy, it must accept some responsibility for extreme situations of misrule, where a government is killing its own people or collapses due to internal rebellion. In 2017, some fourteen countries, mostly in Africa, were classified as having failed states by the Fund for Peace.[17] In the most extreme cases, such as Somalia, society has virtually returned to a state of nature.[18] This has forced the United Nations to undertake numerous peacekeeping missions to restore or maintain order in these places. While such missions have occurred in every non-Western region, the largest number have been in Africa. In these territories, the UN military is in command and NGOs have replaced the government, in what is effectively a return to colonialism.[19]

Chaos like this has been almost unknown in the West since medieval times. Strong Western states long ago achieved a monopoly of armed force in their own territories and today control them without question. Many weak regimes, however, do not achieve this. That was one reason why European powers were able to take over many African and Asian countries in the nineteenth century with little resistance. Ultimately, such empires could not be justified in terms of Western values, so they were dissolved. Liberation assumed that the successor states would become strong and democratic, in the mold of their colonizers. Most often, however, they have been autocratic, and chaos has returned.

Thus, local leaders' claims to take back these countries in the name of democracy is less credible today than it was when the empires folded. Many such leaders have been educated in the West, yet they usually retain the uncivic attitudes of their home societies. Thus, once in office, they are likely largely to serve themselves. The populace may prefer to remain under foreign rule. Consider the example of Haiti: following the earthquake in 2010 that prostrated the government, many people continued to live in refugee camps run by NGOs rather than trust to their own authorities.[20]

UN peacekeeping troops may come from many countries. The United States has been involved directly in only a few of these operations. But it has supported the missions, and it seems fated to play a larger role in state rescue in future. Perhaps America must often take over from Britain, not only general primacy, but become the governor of some failed states. There may truly be no alternative.[21]

As a nation born of rebellion against British rule, the United States will never be comfortable as an explicit imperialist. Far more likely is a piecemeal empire in which NGOs based in America send personnel abroad to provide what is effectively government in collapsed societies. Already, many young Americans find their calling in this work. It is a continuation of the huge outreach to foreign countries that, as described in chapter 6, began with missionary work in the nineteenth century and broadened into many other purposes over the twentieth century. One way or another, many Americans are still engaged in saving the world. To chaotic countries they must bring governance as well as compassion, and both those goals arise from the Western mentality.

DOMESTIC CHALLENGES

At home, American policymakers must above all restore an individualist way of life at the bottom of society, where it was always weakest and has deteriorated in recent decades. The immediate reason is the need to improve America's economic competitiveness, especially against Asia. Efforts are already underway. Starting in the 1970s, in response to foreign competition, America progressively abandoned much of its manufacturing in order to concentrate on higher-value products and services. In the 1980s, reforms made the economy more efficient—by reducing regulation, taxes, and antitrust enforcement, and by weakening trade unions. The payoff to all these changes was the superlative economy of the 1990s, when the country achieved splendid growth and the broadest wage gains since the 1960s while also rebuffing the Asian challenge. All this was the price of continuing to lead the world.[22]

But the changes made many workers less secure. Trade competition works socially only if workers in the abandoned sectors can transition to equally well-paying jobs in the growing sectors. Trade in fact has been only a minor cause of job loss; the relentless drive for efficiency within the domestic economy (often driven by automation) is much more important. The hard fact is that "many—perhaps most—of our country's workers appear unable to compete internationally at the level required to maintain anything like their current standard of living."[23] To support a middle-class life now usually requires education or training above the secondary level. To attain that may be beyond the ability of many Americans.

The globalizing economy has paid the highest incomes to the college-educated, but college in the traditional sense—a four-year liberal arts degree—is unattainable by most young Americans today. What many non-academic youth can do is skilled work in traditional craft trades such as electrical or mechanical work, although updated to deal with computerized production. The economy already lacks enough skilled workers even though it pays well for them. For many students, high schools should reorient toward career and technical education (CTE) and apprenticeships. These middle-skilled jobs offer the best hope to preserve middle-class incomes for average Americans.[24] America must also invest far more in training programs and community colleges, which traditionally have dominated CTE. To accept this change has become one of the necessities of a free society.[25]

SOCIAL PROBLEMS

As problematic as low skills are the more long-standing social problems surveyed in chapter 10. Today's youth may lack specific capabilities, but above all many lack the traditional individualist self-discipline to seek skills and get ahead as best they can. Much of the skills deficit is due to confusions in the private life of lower-income America, which have escalated due to marriage decline, irregular employment, and substance abuse. These struggles sap the energy that people could otherwise put into doing well in school, learning useful skills, and building a job history. When much of the workforce consists of single mothers and men without a stable job history, it is rare to find the focused effort needed to succeed at either school or work.[26]

The problems of men without regular jobs are too easy to blame on the economy. It is facile to imagine that work levels would rise if skills and wages improved. The truth is that to acquire skills and better jobs, the unskilled first have to show the discipline to do less demanding, lower-paid work. But society can make low-skilled, low-paying jobs more attractive by subsidizing wages and providing more benefits outside employment.[27] The message must be that an individualist society expects everyone to work who can. But it also respects all steady workers at any level.

Equally essential is a vigorous response to immigration, as detailed in chapter 11. Recent, low-skilled immigrants—especially Hispanics— are the likeliest to drop out of an individualist society or never to join it. The first step to minimizing this problem is simply to halve the migrant flow. Drastically reducing intake is essential to ensuring that those who enter our individualist society adapt to it, instead of changing it to resemble the more collective-minded society they have left. Only then will they face the need to lay aside the burdens of necessity and take up the very different burdens of freedom.

The second essential step is to intensify assimilation. Here education is paramount. The struggles of Hispanic immigrants and their children in school lead them toward marginal employment on the edge of mainstream society—too much like the life they or their parents lived in the old country. Schools must better engage disadvantaged newcomers than they usually do today. Foreign youths afraid of freedom and competition must face challenges and see the rewards early in life. Only then will freedom beckon as a new life.

Americans cannot simply give non-Westerners the freedom and opportunity that they have. The great condition is that newcomers first take on the inner responsibilities of a free life. They must appropriate as their own many new burdens that at the outset seem entirely external.

To restore self-command to our government, we must rein in huge fiscal deficits and make larger investments in infrastructure and the military.[28] Both individually and collectively, to become more free we must first expect more, not less, of ourselves. Wealth and world leadership do not ease these burdens, but increase them.

OVERLOAD

I have emphasized that freedom American-style rests on obligation. It entails bearing burdens for ourselves and others that are inherent in a free society. These burdens are growing. They include the extra effort, just mentioned, that American workers have had to make in order to meet the Asian challenge. They also include mounting obligations to care for the less fortunate not only at home but around the world.[29]

Several authors have said that the United States must assume the leading onus for maintaining the international order simply because no other country can do so. They mean that America not only is the richest and most powerful country, and hence has the greatest ability to lead, but also is the most willing to lead. Other rich countries that might do more—such as Europe or Japan—often free ride on the United States.[30] The advent of China as a major power will not likely change this. Nor will President Trump.

American responsibility reflects the fact that most of the world is simply unable to maintain order on its own. President Obama tried to conduct a more collaborative foreign policy than George W. Bush, but he found it difficult to "lead from behind." This was because, as Secretary of State Hillary Clinton declared, "The world is counting on us."[31] Other countries could not pacify Bosnia or fight Muammar Gaddafi in Libya without American involvement.

As argued in chapter 6, first Britain and then America felt drawn to lead the world because of a sense of moral obligation at least as much as out of self-interest. Although Obama's foreign policy was cautious, he stocked his administration with zealous appointees who imagined new moral missions for America. The US must advance human rights around the globe or promote a world legal or political order.[32] Such is the natural bent of American and Western elites. President Trump has rejected any such notion, but he cannot undo the very real foreign dependence on America.

This sense of obligation to the unfortunate extends beyond any notion of legal onus or justice. The United States does not "owe" anything, strictly speaking, to most of the legions who look for its sustenance or seek its shores. Any notion that it is responsible for the poverty or oppression of people outside the West is speculative at best. No such notion can settle how to respond, for example, to Haitian refugees fleeing their disaster-stricken island, seen in figure 13.1. They are escaping their home, devastated by an earthquake, which is only one of many recent disasters there. The sheer fortitude of the migrants impresses. In the distance awaits a US Navy ship, exemplifying the technical mastery of its far more

FIGURE 13.1 **Haitian Refugee Boat and USS *Carter Hall***

Source: Liz Hazelton and David Williams, "Shattered Haiti Hit by Second Earthquake Measuring 6.1," *Daily Mail*, January 20, 2010.

fortunate nation. Should we rescue the Haitians, knowing that endless more of them might follow?

Much of the world looks to America for attention amid misfortunes, because Western media and governments are more likely to respond than their own regimes.[33] It is the natural reflex of non-Western societies that assign power chiefly to their environment. They thus expect change to come mainly from outside themselves.

THE MORAL DILEMMA

Westerners respond to these appeals to the extent they do because of the strong injunction to care for the unfortunate in all our religious traditions—Jewish, Christian, Mormon, and Muslim. Those burdens have become, in some ways, more extreme today than ever imagined in scripture. In the Bible, the command to succor the outcast occurs within a community in which rich and poor alike accept the same rules of good behavior. So, in principle, there could be reciprocity, in which the rich man who gives to the poor man today might be helped himself by the poor man tomorrow. The poor, or the prophets who voiced their cause, never imagined that they were outside the moral law entirely. At least some community linked rich and poor. High and low were linked by shared notions of mutual obligation to the other.

Today, however, due to cultural difference, calls to "do the right thing" bear much more heavily on the affluent than on those who appeal to them.[34] The former are mostly Western individualists, while the latter come from non-Western backgrounds where the moral structure is not so general or forcing. The American poor, in particular, are regarded by many as too disadvantaged to be held responsible for anything. That they should ever be givers rather than receivers becomes unimaginable. So the command to support them becomes entirely one-sided. Beyond rhetoric, there is no longer any community uniting rich and poor.

A second major difference is that, in the Bible, the poor are always a minority who might be aided without much effect on the surrounding society. Today, however, they are much more numerous. In the United States alone, they comprise 41 million people, or 13 percent of the population, by the official estimation. Perhaps half of these are poor long-term. And, as mentioned in chapter 11, outside the United States there are hundreds of millions more poor who yearn to migrate to the West. Such numbers could not be welcomed or aided without destroying the giving society, however rich it was.

The specter of giving that is unilateral and unlimited may be why demands for humanitarian response have lately drawn diminishing returns in the West. Well-off Americans and Europeans, faced with too many needy at home and abroad, suffer from "compassion fatigue." We may respond well to isolated victims, but the huge numbers arising from war or other disasters far away are overwhelming.[35] There seems to be no end to the humanitarian demands. We face a life of material privilege but also of deep moral inequality.

THE FUTURE OF INDIVIDUALISM

Individualist Americans who seek to preserve their way of life face a tough road ahead. They are far outnumbered by collective-minded people around the globe and even a growing number at home. They cannot claim that Western culture is superior to non-Western culture in any general sense. And the burdens of freedom are heavy, even in a peaceful and affluent country. Can individualism survive?

Much will hinge on the relative attractions of the two opposing life-styles. Individualism's chief attraction, perhaps, is its ambition. Its symbol is Prometheus, the god who stole fire from heaven. Individualism proclaims the infinite possibilities of even ordinary lives. To realize those possibilities, many people even in strongly collectivist countries have become willing to shoulder the burdens of freedom.

One sign of this is the growing demand for freedom in Asia, at least among elites. Another sign is the growing appeal of Pentecostal religion in many countries, particularly in Latin America and Africa. By connecting directly to the Spirit outside of any authority structure, believers begin to assert themselves in unaccustomed ways.[36] These brave explorers have begun the long trek that Europe undertook centuries before. It is what Walter Russell Mead has called "traveling westward"—away from received authorities and toward the pursuit of the individual's own vision and values, even at the risk of meaninglessness.[37] The result could eventually be greater dynamism, moralism, and civility for these societies.

The United States remains the supreme exemplar of a spiritually free society. It continues to broadcast the appeal of openness and democracy, in ways stretching beyond any specific form of power.[38] Toynbee wrote that "So long as a civilization is growing, its cultural influence radiates into and permeates its...neighbours to an indefinite distance."[39] That is the effect that American popular culture still has around the world. This appeal may still inspire people in unfree countries to find their own voices, and thus begin to hold their rulers more accountable.

But caution is called for. Cultural difference remains deeply rooted. In none of the countries where elites have recently looked Westward has the bulk of the population given up non-Western ways. For societies that prize stability, those mores have advantages. Nor do modernizing groups in any of these countries have enough power to drive the more ambivalent among them toward their own ambitious goals, as they did in Europe. The likely result will be increased conflict within these countries, between elements favoring and those opposing modernizing change. That conflict is already visible in China and is the major threat to that huge country's ambitions.

In addition, the United States cannot sell values abroad that its own people no longer seem to believe in. The rising tide of cautious collectivism in America threatens our ability to effect world cultural change.

Toynbee warned that if "a civilization has broken down," its "charm ceases to act." He judged that the "divine spark of creative power" was still alive in the West, but that was in the 1950s. At that time, the West was not yet challenged by Asia, and its current social problems, with their strong tie to non-Western groups, had not yet become pressing.[40]

That is why our current struggles to help our own poor and to assimilate immigrants are so vital to maintaining American primacy. The greatest barrier to doing that may be the very self-critical moralism of American culture, the belief of many leaders that we must no longer demand individualism of our own people.[41] That is, we can no longer expect of the less favored the same self-command we do of ourselves.

But for those leaders, the burdens of freedom are still growing. American society has never produced elites so well-trained and competent as it does today. They truly are a natural aristocracy—recruited by the meritocracy from every background, certified by the world's leading universities, and dedicated to ambitious lives of achievement. But for the foreseeable future, such masterful individuals will be less free to pursue their own interests and enrichment than they once were. Pressures to devote their lives to uplifting or governing the less masterful, both at home and overseas, are already strong, and bound to increase.

The ultimate question is whether America is "rich enough to play the role of Atlas," the Greek god who was condemned to hold up the sky for all eternity (figure 13.2).[42] The irony is that America should have acquired such burdens in spite of an ethos that initially pursued only "life, liberty, and happiness" for its own citizens. Its success in that venture brought it a world leadership it had not initially sought. Responsibility for the world has become the ultimate burden of freedom.

The ultimate mystery, perhaps, is why such a mind-set became general only in Europe, so that America could become its exemplar. Why have more societies not sought out freedom and its burdens? The lack of individualist competitors outside the West is astonishing. It is ultimately why the world's burdens descend uniquely on the United States. That is simply the way it is. If we resent that destiny, our quarrel is with God.

FIGURE 13.2 **Atlas Bearing the World**

NOTES

CHAPTER ONE — INTRODUCTION

1   Deepak Lal, in *Unintended Consequences: The Impact of Factor Endowments, Culture, and Politics on Long-Run Economic Performance* (Cambridge, MA: MIT Press, 1998), makes an argument similar to mine. He, too, attributes American ascendency to an individualist culture, but he attributes the latter too narrowly to certain doctrines of the medieval church. He also says that American individualism has become excessive, whereas I think it is in decline.

2   David Goodhart, *The Road to Somewhere: The Popular Revolt and the Future of Politics* (London: Hurst and Co., 2017).

3   John J. Mearsheimer, *The Tragedy of Great Power Politics* (New York: Norton, 2001).

4   G. John Ikenberry, *Liberal Leviathan: The Origins, Crisis, and Transformation of the American World Order* (Princeton, NJ: Princeton University Press, 2012).

5   By "primacy," I mean a condition where a country is stronger than any one other country, although not necessarily all of them together. This is similar to the "hegemon" as defined in Mearsheimer, *Tragedy of Great Power Politics*, chap. 1.

6   Charles A. Kupchan, *No One's World: The West, the Rising Rest, and the Coming Global Turn* (New York: Oxford University Press, 2012); Fareed Zakaria, *The Post-American World*, Release 2.0 (New York: Norton, 2012).

7   Christopher Layne, "Impotent Power? Re-examining the Nature of America's Hegemonic Power," *The National Interest*, no. 85 (September/October 2006): 41–47; idem, "The Global Power Shift from West to East," *The National Interest*, no. 119 (May/June 2012): 21–31; Robert A. Pape, "Empire Falls," *The National Interest*, no. 99 (January/February 2009): 21–34; Arvind Subramanian, "The Inevitable Superpower: Why China's Dominance Is a Sure Thing," *Foreign Affairs* 90, no. 5 (September/October 2011): 66–78.

8   Zakaria, *Post-American World*; Robert J. Lieber, *Power and Willpower in the American Future: Why the United States Is Not Destined to Decline* (New York: Cambridge University Press, 2012); Joseph S. Nye, Jr., *The Future of Power* (New York: Public Affairs, 2011); idem, *Is the American Century Over?* (Cambridge, UK: Polity Press, 2015).

9   CIA World Factbook, downloaded July 9, 2018.

10 Stockholm International Peace Research Institute, downloaded July 9, 2018; "The Piecemaker," *The Economist*, November 12, 2016, pp. 19–21.

11 Joseph S. Nye, Jr., *Bound to Lead: The Changing Nature of American Power* (New York: Basic Books, 1990); idem, *Future of Power*.

12 "The Soft Power 30: A Global Ranking of Soft Power 2017" (London: Portland, 2017); "Time to Cheer Up," *The Economist*, November 23, 2013, p. 13.

13 According to John Lee, in "An Exceptional Obsession," *The American Interest* 5, no. 5 (May/June 2010): 35–43, the Chinese themselves see America as a many-sided power with great resources, especially soft power. However, *Burdens of Freedom* is not an argument for "American exceptionalism" in the sense usually meant in American studies. By that term, scholars typically mean something unusual about America compared to other advanced countries, such as its Madisonian constitutional system or its relatively limited welfare state. Much more, I argue for the exceptionalism of the West as a whole, due to its uniquely individualist culture. To use Fukuyama's idea, America is exceptional mostly within history, but the West is exceptional mostly after history.

14 Lawrence M. Mead, "The Primacy Contest: Why Culture Matters," *Society* 52, no. 6 (November/December 2015): 527–32.

15 According to *Webster's New Collegiate Dictionary*, racism means "a belief that race is the primary determinant of human traits and capacities and that racial differences produce an inherent superiority of a particular race" (Springfield, MA: Merriam-Webster, 1979, p. 943).

16 Lal, *Unintended Consequences*; Samuel P. Huntington, *The Clash of Civilizations and the Remaking of World Order* (New York: Simon and Schuster, 1996); Adda B. Bozeman, *Politics and Culture in International History: From the Ancient Near East to the Opening of the Modern Age*, 2nd ed. (New Brunswick, NJ: Transaction, 1994).

17 Robert W. Tucker and David C. Hendrickson, "The Sources of American Legitimacy," *Foreign Affairs* 83, no. 6 (November/December 2004): 18–32; Stephen M. Walt, "Taming American Power," *Foreign Affairs* 84, no. 5 (September/October 2005): 105–20; idem, "The End of the American Era," *The National Interest*, no. 116 (November/December 2011): 6–16.

18 Evan Osnos, "Making China Great Again," *New Yorker*, January 8, 2018, pp. 36–45.

19 Kupchan, *No One's World*, is the only treatment of American primacy I have read that provides a serious account of how Western primacy arose. But Kupchan attributes European dynamism to the "political weakness" of European regimes. That might be true within history, but not after it. More likely, Western primacy arose due to those governments' unusual strength and willingness to serve their societies.

20 I use the word "modern" to connote a society in which norms of science and meritocracy prevail and in which the dominant goal is to manipulate the natural world to produce material gains such as wealth. "Premodern" connotes a society more dedicated to preserving tradition or nonmaterial goals, including religion.

21 I credit Kirt Mead with this powerful formulation. Of course, North America was already occupied by Native Americans. But they were too few in number and lacking in technology to resist the European invasion.

22 Robert Kagan, *Dangerous Nation* (New York: Knopf, 2006), chaps. 1–6.

23 "Anglo" nations connotes Britain and the daughter nations that it founded chiefly through emigration of its own people to territories overseas— Australia, Canada, and New Zealand, as well as the United States. It excludes other countries that Britain or America ruled as colonies, such as India and South Africa, where the bulk of the population never was Anglo, even though the British ruled or settled there and imposed their own institutions and language.

24 Fukuyama, "The End of History?" *The National Interest*, no. 16 (Summer 1989): 3–18; idem, *The End of History and the Last Man* (New York: Free Press, 1992).

25 A good definition of First World might be "countries in which the municipal water supply is safe to drink." Potable water is common in the West but rare outside of it.

26 The following is based on several authors, particularly Geert Hofstede, *Culture's Consequences: International Differences in Work-Related Values* (Newbury Park, CA: Sage, 1980), Richard E. Nisbett, *The Geography of Thought: How Asians and Westerners Think Differently... and Why* (New York: Free Press, 2003), and F. S. C. Northrop, *The Meeting of East and West: An Inquiry concerning World Understanding* (New York: Macmillan, 1946). See further in chapter 4.

27 Here and throughout, I usually mean "collective" or "collectivist" to connote the typical culture of the non-West rather than a big-government governing philosophy, the meaning more common in the West.

28 Kai Hammerich and Richard D. Lewis, *Fish Can't See Water: How National Culture Can Make or Break Your Corporate Strategy* (Chichester, UK: Wiley, 2013).

29 David Brooks, "Harmony and the Dream" (opinion), *New York Times*, August 12, 2008, p. A21.

30 Jared Diamond, *Guns, Germs, and Steel: The Fates of Human Societies* (New York: Norton, 1999); Ian Morris, *Why the West Rules—For Now: The Patterns of History, and What They Reveal about the Future* (New York: Farrar, Straus, and Giroux, 2010).

31 Derek Bok, *The State of the Nation: Government and the Quest for a Better Society* (Cambridge, MA: Harvard University Press, 1996), pp. 33–36, 89–91, 367–72.

32 Francis Fukuyama, *State-Building: Governance and World Order in the 21st Century* (Ithaca, NY: Cornell University Press, 2004), chap. 1; idem, *The Origins of Political Order: From Prehuman Times to the French Revolution* (New York: Farrar, Straus, and Giroux, 2011).

33 Lawrence M. Mead, "Why Anglos Lead," *The National Interest*, no. 82 (Winter 2005/2006): 124–31.

34 Lawrence M. Mead, *Beyond Entitlement: The Social Obligations of Citizenship* (New York: Free Press, 1986), pp. 241–46.

35 "Declinism Resurgent," *The Economist*, May 12, 2012, p. 40.

36 Joel Kotkin, "Down for the Count, Again," *The American Interest* 2, no. 2 (November/December 2006): 21–30; Edward Luttwak, "The Declinists, Wrong Again: The Atlantic Future of the 21st Century," *The American Interest* 4, no. 2 (November/December 2013): 6–13.

37 Josef Joffe, "The Default Power: The False Prophecy of America's Decline," *Foreign Affairs* 88, no. 5 (September/October 2009): 21–25.

38 Alfred Lord Tennyson, "Ulysses."

CHAPTER TWO — HISTORY

1 William H. McNeill, *The Rise of the West: A History of the Human Community, with a Retrospective Essay* (Chicago: University of Chicago Press, 1991), pp. xv–xxx; J. M. Roberts, *The New History of the World* (Oxford: Oxford University Press, 2003).

2 McNeill, *Rise of the West*, p. 804; Roberts, *New History*, pp. 37, 199.

3 Roberts, *New History*, pp. 283–84.

4 *The Benedictine Handbook* (Collegeville, MN: Liturgical Press, 2003), p. 11.

5 Ricardo Duchesne, *The Uniqueness of Western Civilization* (Leiden: Brill, 2011), p. 183.

6 Of course, it was only Europeans who needed to discover America. Native Americans were already there. Alas, they would be crushed as European settlers rushed to occupy and exploit the new territory.

7 Eric Jones, *The European Miracle: Environments, Economics and Geopolitics in the History of Europe and Asia*, 3rd ed. (Cambridge, UK: Cambridge University Press, 2003), p. 251.

8 Jones, *European Miracle*, chap. 3; David S. Landes, *The Wealth and Poverty of Nations: Why Some Are So Rich and Some So Poor* (New York: Norton, 1998), chap. 3.

9 Roberts, *New History*, pp. 535, 561; McNeill, *Rise of the West*, pp. 547–58, 566; John M. Headley, *The Europeanization of the World: On the Origins of Human Rights and Democracy* (Princeton, NJ: Princeton University Press, 2008), p. 30.

10 Here and throughout the book I use "development" to connote the evolution of increasingly productive economic and political systems, able to generate more and more wealth and power. A close synonym is "modernization."

11 Ian Morris, *Why The West Rules—For Now: The Patterns of History, and What They Reveal about the Future* (New York: Farrar, Straus, and Giroux, 2010); Kenneth Pomeranz, *The Great Divergence: Europe, China, and the Making of the Modern World Economy* (Princeton, NJ: Princeton University Press, 2000).

12 Philip C. C. Huang, "Development or Involution in Eighteenth-Century Britain and China? A Review of Kenneth Pomeranz's *The Great Divergence: China, Europe, and the Making of the Modern World Economy*," *Journal of Asian Studies* 61, no. 2 (May 2002): 501–38.

13 Edwin Williamson, *The Penguin History of Latin America*, rev. ed. (London: Penguin, 2009); Howard J. Wiarda, *The Soul of Latin America: The Cultural and Political Tradition* (New Haven, CT: Yale University Press, 2001).

14 David S. Landes, "Why Europe and the West? Why Not China?" *Journal of Economic Perspectives* 20, no. 2 (Spring 2006): 3–22.

15 Dr. Martin Luther King, Jr. (31 March 1968), "Remaining Awake through a Great Revolution," sermon delivered at the national Cathedral. The Martin Luther King, Jr., Research and Education Institute, Stanford University.

16 Adda B. Bozeman, *Politics and Culture in International History: From the Ancient Near East to the Opening of the Modern Age*, 2nd ed. (New Brunswick, NJ: Transaction, 1994), chap. 9.

17 Roberts, *New History*, pp. 339, 342.

18 Bozeman, *Politics and Culture*, p. 414; McNeill, *Rise of the West*, pp. 495–505.

19 Roberts, *New History*, chap. 6.

20 Francis Fukuyama, *The Origins of Political Order: From Prehuman Times to the French Revolution* (New York: Farrar, Straus, and Giroux, 2011), chaps. 5–9.

21 Jones, *European Miracle*, chap. 11; Morris, *Why the West Rules*, chaps. 7–8.

22 Francis Fukuyama, *Political Order and Political Decay: From the Industrial Revolution to the Globalization of Democracy* (New York: Farrar, Straus, and Giroux, 2014), chap. 26.

23 Jones, *European Miracle*, pp. 157–59; Landes, *Wealth and Poverty*, p. 368.

24 Landes, *Wealth and Poverty*, chap. 22; Karl A. Wittfogel, *Oriental Despotism: A Comparative Study of Total Power* (Hew Haven, CT: Yale University Press, 1957), pp. 197–200.

25 See chapter 8.

26 Jones, *European Miracle*, p. 186; Roberts, *New History*, pp. 609–11.

27 Here and below I draw on Wittfogel, *Oriental Despotism*, and Ernest Gellner, *Plough, Sword and Book: The Structure of Human History* (Chicago: University of Chicago Press, 1988). For a parallel argument, see Daron Acemoglu and James A. Robinson, *Why Nations Fail: The Origins of Power, Prosperity, and Poverty* (New York: Crown, 2012).

28 John King Fairbank and Merle Goldman, *China: A New History*, 2nd enlarged ed. (Cambridge, MA: Harvard University Press, 2006), pp. 107, 126–27, 160.

29 I say this on the basis of several trips to China since 2002 and a lecture I gave in Singapore in 2007.

30 Acemoglu and Robinson, *Why Nations Fail*, chap. 5; Deepak Lal, *Unintended Consequences: The Impact of Factor Endowments, Culture, and Politics on Long-Run Economic Performance* (Cambridge, MA: MIT Press, 1998), chaps. 2–4.

31 Jones, *European Miracle*, pp. 233–34.

32 Gellner, *Plough, Sword and Book*, pp. 99, 204.

33 Nathan Rosenberg and L. E. Birdzell, Jr., *How the West Grew Rich: The Economic Transformation of the Industrial World* (New York: Basic Books, 1986).

34 Gellner, *Plough, Sword and Book*, p. 121.

35 Hilary Mantel, *Wolf Hall: A Novel* (New York: Henry Holt, 2009), p. 484.

36 Niall Ferguson, *Empire: The Rise and Demise of the British World Order and the Lessons for Global Power* (New York: Basic Books, 2002), p. xii.

37 Here and below I speak of "England" when discussing events up through Tudor times, then of "Britain" following England's union with Scotland in 1603.

38 Landes, *Wealth and Poverty*, pp. 220–21.

39 Rodney Stark, *The Victory of Reason: How Christianity Led to Freedom, Capitalism, and Western Success* (New York: Random House, 2005), chaps. 5–7.

40 Landes, *Wealth and Poverty*, p. 219. Emphasis in the original.

41 Paul M. Kennedy, *The Rise and Fall of the Great Powers: Economic Change and Military Conflict from 1500 to 2000* (New York: Random House, 1987), p. 80; Thomas Ertman, *Birth of the Leviathan: Building States and Regimes in Medieval and Early Modern Europe* (Cambridge, UK: Cambridge University Press, 1997), pp. 220–21.

42 Roberts, *New History*, pp. 708–9; Morris, *Why the West Rules*, p. 497.

43 Roberts, *New History*, p. 712; Michael W. Doyle, *Empires* (Ithaca, NY: Cornell University Press, 1986), p. 241.

44 Ferguson, *Empire*, p. 240.

45 Walter Russell Mead, *God and Gold: Britain, America, and the Making of the Modern World* (New York: Knopf, 2007), p. 351.

46 George Louis Beer, *The English-Speaking Peoples, Their Future Relations and Joint International Obligations* (New York: Macmillan, 1917), p. 186.

47 Arthur Herman, *To Rule the Waves: How the British Navy Shaped the Modern World* (New York: HarperCollins, 2004), p. 155.

48 David McCullough, *1776: America and Britain at War* (London: Penguin, 2005), p. 158.

49 Stephen Budiansky, *Perilous Fight: America's Intrepid War with Britain on the High Seas, 1812–1815* (New York: Knopf, 2010), pp. xv, 358; Robert Kagan, *Dangerous Nation* (New York: Knopf, 2006), p. 154.

50 Kagan, *Dangerous Nation*, pp. 47, 127; Niall Ferguson, *Colossus: The Rise and Fall of the American Empire* (New York: Penguin, 2005), frontispiece; Alexis de Tocqueville, *Democracy in America*, ed. J. P. Mayer, trans. George Lawrence (Garden City, NY: Anchor Books, 1969 [1835]), p. 407.

51 Kagan, *Dangerous Nation*, p. 156.

52 Kennedy, *Rise and Fall of the Great Powers*, pp. 179, 242–44; Fareed Zakaria, *From Wealth to Power: The Unusual Origins of America's World Role* (Princeton, NJ: Princeton University Press, 1997), chap. 3.

53 James T. Patterson, *Grand Expectations: The United States, 1945–1974* (New York: Oxford University Press, 1996), p. 61.

54 Kagan, *Dangerous Nation*, p. 308.

55 Roberts, *New History*, pp. 778–79; Kagan, *Dangerous Nation*, chap. 10. National commitment to equal rights for blacks was, however, still partial, not to advance further until the civil rights era a century later.

56 Zakaria, *From Wealth to Power*, chap. 4; Stephen Skowronek, *Building a New American State: The Expansion of National Administrative Capacities, 1877–1920* (Cambridge, UK: Cambridge University Press, 1982); Fukuyama, *Political Order and Political Decay*, chaps. 9–11.

57 Kennedy, *Rise and Fall of the Great Powers*, pp. 356–57.

58 In chapter 4, I will provide more rigorous, statistical evidence of this connection.

59 Acemoglu and Robinson, *Why Nations Fail*, chap. 4; Chris Stewart and Ted Stewart, *The Miracle of Freedom: 7 Tipping Points That Saved the World* (Salt Lake City, UT: Shadow Mountain, 2011).

60 W. R. Mead, *God and Gold*; Daniel Hannan, *Inventing Freedom: How the English-Speaking Peoples Made the Modern World* (New York: HarperCollins, 2013).

61 Headley, *Europeanization of the World*.

CHAPTER THREE — THE END OF HISTORY

1 The following summarizes Francis Fukuyama, "The End of History?" *The National Interest*, no. 16 (Summer 1989): 3–18, and idem, *The End of History and the Last Man* (New York: Free Press, 1992).

2 Georg Wilhelm Friedrich Hegel, *The Philosophy of History*, trans. J. Sibree, preface by C. J. Friedrich (New York: Dover, 1956), p. 19.

3 "The Long Life of Homo Sovieticus," *The Economist*, December 10, 2011, p. 30.

4 I refer here to Arab Islam, not the more peaceable and less radical Islam of Southeast Asia.

5 Samuel P. Huntington, "The Clash of Civilizations?" *Foreign Affairs* 72, no. 3 (Summer 1993): 22–49; idem, *The Clash of Civilizations and the Remaking of World Order* (New York: Simon and Schuster, 1996).

6 Because cultural conflict is not historical in Fukuyama's sense, Fukuyama and Huntington, his teacher, need not be in disagreement, as some suppose. Wars between civilizations have no clear bearing on the ideological divisions that drive history in Hegel's sense.

7 Huntington, *Clash of Civilizations*, chap. 12; Adda B. Bozeman, *Politics and Culture in International History: From the Ancient Near East to the Opening of the Modern Age*, 2nd ed. (New Brunswick, NJ: Transaction, 1994), introduction.

8 The rest of this chapter is based largely on Lawrence M. Mead, *Beyond Entitlement: The Social Obligations of Citizenship* (New York: Free Press, 1986), and idem, *The New Politics of Poverty: The Nonworking Poor in America* (New York: Basic Books, 1992). *New Politics*, published the same year as Fukuyama's *End of History*, has a similar theme but applies it to domestic politics rather than international relations.

9 Paul Pierson, *Dismantling the Welfare State? Reagan, Thatcher, and the Politics of Retrenchment* (Cambridge, UK: Cambridge University Press, 1994).

10 Mark Lilla, "The End of Identity Liberalism" (opinion), *New York Times*, November 20, 2016, pp. SR1, SR6; idem, *The Once and Future Liberal: After Identity Politics* (New York: HarperCollins, 2017).

11 "Then and Now," *The Economist*, August 8, 1992, p. 81.

12 Michael Kazin, "Whatever Happened to the American Left?" (opinion), *New York Times*, September 25, 2011, p. SR4; Theodore R. Marmor and Jerry L. Mashaw, "How Do You Say 'Economic Security'?" (opinion), *New York Times*, September 24, 2011, p. A21; Catherine Rampell, "Somehow, the Unemployed Became Invisible," *New York Times*, July 10, 2011, pp. BU1, BU6.

13 Leslie McCall, *The Undeserving Rich: American Beliefs about Inequality, Opportunity, and Redistribution* (New York: Cambridge University Press, 2013). However, most voters remain more concerned about opportunity than inequality.

14 Alexis de Tocqueville, *Democracy in America*, ed. J. P. Mayer, trans. George Lawrence (Garden City, NY: Anchor Books, 1969 [1835]), pp. 241–45.

15 Nathan Glazer and Daniel P. Moynihan, *Beyond the Melting Pot: The Negroes, Puerto Ricans, Jews, Italians, and Irish of New York City*, 2nd ed. (Cambridge, MA: MIT Press, 1970), pp. 137–80, 217–87.

16 Nicholas Lemann, *The Promised Land: The Great Black Migration and How It Changed America* (New York: Knopf, 1991), pp. 6–7, 149, 200; idem, "The Other Underclass," *Atlantic Monthly*, December 1991, pp. 96–110.

17 Mead, *New Politics of Poverty*, chaps. 10–11.

18 Lawrence M. Mead, "Trump's Impact: The End of Sameness," *Society* 54, no. 1 (January/February 2017): 14–17.

19 Matthew Arnold, "Dover Beach," 1867.

CHAPTER FOUR — CULTURAL DIFFERENCE

1 Generally, I use "individualism" to refer to Western culture as a whole, but in this chapter I sometimes use it more narrowly to refer to a culture that emphasizes individual autonomy. That may be distinguished from the other key Western attributes—moralism and theoretical thinking. Note also that I do not simply identify the West with an individualist culture. Rather, "West" is initially defined geographically, as Western Europe and its offshoots (e.g., America). Whether its culture is individualist is then an empirical question. Research clearly shows that it is individualist. Only then may we plausibly say that this culture explains Western dominance.

2 For the contrasts of Western and non-Western culture that follow, my principal sources include Geert Hofstede, *Culture's Consequences: International Differences in Work-Related Values* (Newbury Park, CA: Sage, 1980); Richard E. Nisbett, *The Geography of Thought: How Asians and Westerners Think Differently… and Why* (New York: Free Press, 2003); Ronald Inglehart and Christian Welzel, *Modernization, Cultural Change, and Democracy: The Human Development Sequence* (New York: Cambridge University Press, 2005); F.S.C. Northrop, *The Meeting of East and West: An Inquiry concerning World Understanding* (New York: Macmillan, 1946); David C. McClelland, *The Achieving Society* (New York: Free Press, 1967); and Harry C. Triandis, *Individualism and Collectivism* (Boulder, CO: Westview Press, 1995). Harry C. Triandis, "The Many Dimensions of Culture," *The Academy of Management Executive* 18, no. 1 (February 2004): 88–93, emphasizes that scholars mostly confirm Hofstede and agree about the basic contrasts.

3 Nisbett, *Geography of Thought*, p. 158.

4 Nisbett, *Geography of Thought*, p. 97.

5 Nisbett, *Geography of Thought*. Nisbett's findings have special authority, because they are based on recent and rigorous studies. They are, however, much like those from older, less systematic studies that I also cite here.

6 Ruth Benedict, *The Chrysanthemum and the Sword: Patterns of Japanese Culture* (New York: World Publishing, 1972 [1946]); Alasdair MacIntyre, "Individual and Social Morality in Japan and the United States: Rival Conceptions of the Self," *Philosophy East and West* 40, no. 4 (October 1990): 489–97.

7 Georg Wilhelm Friedrich Hegel, *Hegel's Philosophy of Right*, trans. T. M. Knox (Oxford: Clarendon Press, 1964), pp. 22–29, 35.

8 Hofstede, *Culture's Consequences*, chap. 5.

9 Hofstede, *Culture's Consequences*, chaps. 3–4, 6–7, 9.

10 Ronald Inglehart and Wayne E. Baker, "Modernization, Cultural Change, and the Persistence of Traditional Values," *American Sociological Review* 65, no. 1 (February 2000): 19–51; Ronald Inglehart, "Mapping Global Values," *Comparative Sociology* 5, nos. 2–3 (May 2006): 115–36. According to the World Values Surveys web site, there has been modest change in the position

of the various world cultures over the years of the surveys (1981–2015), with Latin America becoming somewhat more individualist since 2000. Figure 4.3 shows the cultures as of 2010-14. I address cultural change further in chapters 5 and 12.

11 Olwen Bedford and Kwang-Kuo Hwang, "Guilt and Shame in Chinese Culture: A Cross-Cultural Framework from the Perspective of Morality and Identity," *Journal for the Theory of Social Behavior* 33, no. 2 (June 2003): 127–44.

12 Geert Hofstede and Michael Harris Bond, "The Confucius Connection: From Cultural Roots to Economic Roots," *Organizational Dynamics* 16, no. 4 (1988): 5–21; Martin Jacques, *When China Rules the World: The End of the Western World and the Birth of a New Global Order* (New York: Penguin, 2009), pp. 398–99.

13 Conrad, *The End of the Tether*, in *The Nigger of the Narcissus and The End of the Tether* (New York: Dell, 1964), pp. 223–24.

14 Joseph Conrad, *Lord Jim* (London: J. M. Dent and Sons, 1958), p. 38.

15 Northrop, *Meeting of East and West*, pp. 381–93, 425.

16 Fareed Zakaria, *The Post-American World*, Release 2.0 (New York: Norton, 2012), chaps. 4–5.

17 The following relies on Jonathan Haidt, *The Righteous Mind: Why Good People Are Divided by Politics and Religion* (New York: Pantheon, 2012).

18 The following section relies mainly on Nisbett, *Geography of Thought*, and Northrop, *Meeting of East and West*.

19 Charles Murray, *Human Accomplishment: The Pursuit of Excellence in the Arts and Sciences, 800 B.C. to 1950* (New York: HarperCollins, 2003).

20 Northrop, *Meeting of East and West*, p. 299.

21 Leigh Kathryn Jenco, "'What Does Heaven Ever Say?' A Methods-Centered Approach to Cross-Cultural Engagement," *American Political Science Review* 101, no. 4 (November 2007): 741–55.

22 Immanuel Kant, *Groundwork of the Metaphysics of Morals*, trans. H. J. Paten (New York: Harper and Row, 1964).

23 Nisbett, *Geography of Thought*, pp. 69–70.

24 Richard Nisbett, personal communication, July 19, 2015; Harry C. Triandis, "The Self and Social Behavior in Differing Cultural Contexts," *Psychological Review* 96, no. 3 (1989): 510.

25 Kai Hammerich and Richard D. Lewis, *Fish Can't See Water: How National Culture Can Make or Break Your Corporate Strategy* (Chichester, UK: Wiley, 2013); David C. McClelland, *The Achieving Society* (New York: Free Press, 1967), pp. 287–89. For parallel results, see Erin Meyer, *The Culture Map: Breaking through the Invisible Boundaries of Global Business* (New York: Public Affairs, 2014). Hofstede, Hammerich and Lewis, and Meyer show that business scholars have been more open to world cultural differences than have international relations scholars.

26 Richard Nisbett, personal communication, July 19, 2015.

27 Such as the Sikhs and Gujaratis of India. See "Going Global," *The Economist*, December 19, 2015, pp. 105–7.

28 Nisbett, *Geography of Thought*, p. 71. Asians, of course, are one non-Western group that is conspicuously successful in America. These Asians who come

here, however, are highly selected to be compatible with our society and
are not typical of the far more traditional societies from which they come.
Nevertheless, as I show in chapter 11, many Asians still have trouble with the
demands of America's individualist culture, and Asian poverty is a significant
problem.

29 Triandis, "The Self and Social Behavior," p. 510.

30 Edward C. Banfield, *The Moral Basis of a Backward Society* (Glencoe, IL: Free
    Press, 1958); Herbert J. Gans, *The Urban Villagers: Group and Class in the
    Life of Italian Americans* (New York: Free Press, 1962). This characterization
    of Italians applies best to the chiefly southern Italians who came to America.
    Northern Italy is more civic and presumably more classically Western; see
    Robert D. Putnam, with Robert Leonardi and Raffaella Y. Nanetti, *Making
    Democracy Work: Civic Traditions in Modern Italy* (Princeton, NJ: Princeton
    University Press, 1993).

31 McClelland, *Achieving Society*, chap. 9.

32 Nisbett, *Geography of Thought*, p. 41.

33 Aristotle, *Politics*, trans. Ernest Barker (New York: Oxford University Press,
    1962), book 7, chap. 7, p. 296. I credit Paul Moreno for pointing out this
    precedent.

34 J. M. Roberts, *The New History of the World* (Oxford: Oxford University Press,
    2003), pp. 633, 688–89, 893, 1026, 1177–78.

35 McClelland, *Achieving Society*.

36 Francis Fukuyama, *The End of History and the Last Man* (New York: Free
    Press, 1992), chap. 15.

37 McClelland, *Achieving Society*, pp. 427–30.

38 Thucydides, *The Complete Writings of Thucydides: The Peloponnesian War*,
    trans. Richard Crawley, intro. John H. Finley, Jr. (New York: Modern Library,
    1951), pp. 40, 237–38, 411.

39 Thucydides, *Peloponnesian War*, chap. 6, books 7–8.

40 Simon Schama, *A History of Britain: Vol. 2—The Wars of the British, 1603–
    1776* (New York: Hyperion, 2001), chap. 3.

41 Robert Kagan, *Dangerous Nation* (New York: Knopf, 2006), p. 38.

42 Alexis de Tocqueville, *Democracy in America*, ed. J. P. Mayer, trans. George
    Lawrence (Garden City, NY: Anchor Books, 1969 [1835]), pp. 242, 244, 284.

43 Walter McDougall, *Freedom Just around the Corner: A New American
    History, 1585–1828* (New York: HarperCollins, 2005); idem, *Throes
    of Democracy: The American Civil War Era, 1829–1877* (New York:
    HarperCollins, 2008); Richard M. Huber, *The American Idea of Success* (New
    York: McGraw-Hill, 1971).

44 McClelland, *Achieving Society*, pp. 309–13, 418–19.

45 Sebastian Junger, *Tribe: On Homecoming and Belonging* (New York: Twelve,
    2016); Triandis, *Individualism and Collectivism*, chap. 7.

46 Earl Shorris, *Latinos: A Biography of the People* (New York: Norton, 1992), p.
    105.

47 Ross Douthat, "The Misery Filter" (opinion), *New York Times*, October 29,
    2017, p. SR9.

48 David Remnick, "Blood at the Root: In the Aftermath of the Emanuel Nine,"
    New Yorker, September 28, 2015, pp. 26–34.

49 Ian Morris, *Why the West Rules—For Now: The Patterns of History, and What They Reveal about the Future* (New York: Farrar, Straus, and Giroux, 2010), p. 29; Francis Fukuyama, *The Origins of Political Order: From Prehuman Times to the French Revolution* (New York: Farrar, Straus, and Giroux, 2011), chap. 2.

50 Howard Shuman, Charlotte Steeh, and Lawrence Bobo, *Racial Attitudes in America: Trends and Interpretation* (Cambridge, MA: Harvard University Press, 1985).

51 When Representative Paul Ryan (R-WI) recently spoke of poverty as rooted in culture, some took him to be racist. See Paul Krugman, "That Old-Time Whistle" (opinion), *New York Times*, March 16, 2014, p. A23; Charles M. Blow, "Paul Ryan, Culture and Poverty" (opinion), *New York Times*, March 22, 2014, p. A21.

52 Richard J. Herrnstein and Charles Murray, *The Bell Curve: Intelligence and Class Structure in American Life* (New York: Free Press, 1994). My review of this book appeared as Lawrence M. Mead, "Despite Some Cracks, Truth Rings Out in 'Bell Curve,'" *Washington Times*, November 6, 1994, pp. B7, B9.

53 Moise Velasquez-Manoff, "Should Doctors Ignore Race?" (opinion), *New York Times*, December 10, 2017, pp. SR1, SR4; David Reich, "'Race' in the Age of Modern Genetics" (opinion), *New York Times*, March 25, 2018, pp. WR1, WR4–WR5. Yuriy Gorodnichenko and Gerard Roland, in "Culture, Institutions and the Wealth of Nations," *Review of Economics and Statistics* 99, no. 3 (July 2017): 402–16, do find that certain genes correlate with a tendency toward collectivist views, but this does not establish causation; it means only that the genes may be used as instruments for collectivism in statistical analyses.

54 McClelland, *Achieving Society*, pp. 337–40; Lawrence E. Harrison, "The End of Multiculturalism," *The National Interest*, no. 93 (January/February 2008): 91.

55 Karl A. Lamb, *The Guardians: Leadership Values and the American Tradition* (New York: Norton, 1982).

56 Edward W. Said, *Orientalism* (New York: Vintage, 2003). My own students urged that I address Said's perspective, as I do here.

57 Michel Foucault, *Discipline and Punish: The Birth of the Prison*, trans. Alan Sheridan (New York: Vintage, 1977). For a similar application of these ideas to the Middle East, see Timothy Mitchell, *Colonizing Egypt* (Cambridge, UK: Cambridge University Press, 1988).

58 Quoted in Ricardo Duchesne, *The Uniqueness of Western Civilization* (Leiden: Brill, 2011), p. 285.

59 Said, *Orientalism*, pp. 8, 158.

60 Michael W. Doyle, *Empires* (Ithaca, NY: Cornell University Press, 1986), chaps. 8–9.

CHAPTER FIVE — THE ORIGINS OF DIFFERENCE

1 David S. Landes, *The Wealth and Poverty of Nations: Why Some Are So Rich and Some So Poor* (New York: Norton, 1998), p. 177.

2 Daron Acemoglu and James A. Robinson, *Why Nations Fail: The Origins of Power, Prosperity, and Poverty* (New York: Crown, 2012), chaps. 2–3.

3 David C. McClelland, *The Achieving Society* (New York: Free Press, 1967), pp. 376, 421–23, 425–27.

4 Georg Wilhelm Friedrich Hegel, *The Philosophy of History*, trans. J. Sibree, preface by C. J. Friedrich (New York: Dover, 1956), p. 18.

5 Hegel, *Philosophy of History*, part 1.

6 Hegel, *Philosophy of History*, parts 2–3 (quotations pp. 253, 329).

7 Hegel, *Philosophy of History*, part 4.

8 Nathan Rosenberg and L. E. Birdzell, Jr., *How the West Grew Rich: The Economic Transformation of the Industrial World* (New York: Basic Books, 1986), pp. 128–34.

9 J. M. Roberts, *The New History of the World* (Oxford: Oxford University Press, 2003), pp. 693–95; Walter Russell Mead, *God and Gold: Britain, America, and the Making of the Modern World* (New York: Knopf, 2007), pp. 191–99.

10 Richard E. Nisbett, *The Geography of Thought: How Asians and Westerners Think Differently... and Why* (New York: Free Press, 2003), chap. 2.

11 Karl A. Wittfogel, *Oriental Despotism: A Comparative Study of Total Power* (New Haven, CT: Yale University Press, 1957).

12 "You Are What You Eat," *The Economist*, May 10, 2014, p. 78; T. M. Luhrmann, "Wheat People vs. Rice People" (opinion), *New York Times*, December 4, 2014, p. A31.

13 Ronald Inglehart and Christian Welzel, *Modernization, Cultural Change, and Democracy: The Human Development Sequence* (New York: Cambridge University Press, 2005); Christian Welzel, *Freedom Rising: Human Empowerment and the Quest for Emancipation* (New York: Cambridge University Press, 2013). Harry C. Triandis, "The Self and Social Behavior in Differing Cultural Contexts," *Psychological Review* 96, no. 3 (1989), p. 510, notes a general association of greater individualism with "cultural complexity and affluence."

14 Welzel, Freedom Rising, chaps. 3. 11, makes this case. Other authors also say that material conditions in Europe favored development, but they do not argue that such conditions generated individualism. See Landes, *Wealth and Poverty of Nations*, chap. 2; Eric Jones, *The European Miracle: Environments, Economics, and Geopolitics in the History of Europe and Asia*, 3rd ed. (Cambridge, UK: Cambridge University Press, 2003), chaps. 1–2.

15 Ricardo Duchesne, *The Uniqueness of Western Civilization* (Leiden: Brill, 2011).

16 William H. McNeill, *The Rise of the West: A History of the Human Community, with a Retrospective Essay* (Chicago: University of Chicago Press, 1991), pp. 103–4, 539.

17 Duchesne, *Uniqueness of Western Civilization*, p. 481.

18 Leon Kass has stressed this point to me.

19 Duchesne, *Uniqueness of Western Civilization*, p. 347.

20 Jones, *European Miracle*, chap. 1.

21 Jones, *European Miracle*, chaps. 4, 8, passim. Kenneth Pomeranz, in *The Great Divergence: Europe, China, and the Making of the Modern World Economy* (Princeton, NJ: Princeton University Press, 2000), argues that there were also population pressures in Europe, but they were less severe.

22 Thomas Robert Malthus, *On Population*, ed. Gertrude Himmelfarb (New York: Modern Library, 1960 [1798]).

23 McNeill, *Rise of the West*, pp. 188–217, 203–4.

24 Roberts, *New History*, p. 170.
25 Hannah Arendt, *The Human Condition* (Chicago: University of Chicago Press, 1958), chap. 5.
26 Duchesne, *Uniqueness of Western Civilization*, p. 300.
27 Adda B. Bozeman, *Politics and Culture in International History: From the Ancient Near East to the Opening of the Modern Age*, 2nd ed. (New Brunswick, NJ: Transaction, 1994), chap. 5.
28 McNeill, *Rise of the West*, p. 294.
29 Roberts, *New History*, pp. 260, 490–91.
30 Duchesne, *Uniqueness of Western Civilization*, p. 258.
31 Roberts, *New History*, p. 543.
32 Rosenberg and Birdzell, *How the West Grew Rich*, p. 261.
33 The Galatians translation is from the New English Bible; the others are from the Revised Standard Version.
34 Martin Luther, *Martin Luther: Selections from His Writings*, ed. and intro. John Dillenberger (Garden City, NY: Doubleday, 1961), p. 24.
35 Francis Fukuyama, *Trust: The Social Virtues and the Creation of Prosperity* (New York: Free Press, 1995), p. 286.
36 Macfarlane, *The Origins of English Individualism: The Family, Property and Social Transition* (Oxford: Basil Blackwell, 1978), p. 163.
37 The natural manner in which England became Protestant is suggested by its ancient cathedrals. They seem Anglican as they are today, quite different from the Catholic cathedrals of the Continent—far less encrusted with votive candles and the statues and chapels of saints. And yet they were built before the schism with Rome. So even Catholicism probably was more individualist in England than elsewhere.
38 McClelland, *Achieving Society*, pp. 139–40.
39 Roberts, *New History*, p. 296; Arthur Herman, *To Rule the Waves: How the British Navy Shaped the Modern World* (New York: HarperCollins, 2004), pp. 46–47; Lawrence James, *Warrior Race: A History of the British at War* (New York: St. Martin's Griffin, 2004).
40 Walzer, *The Revolution of the Saints: A Study of the Origins of Radical Politics* (New York: Atheneum, 1968), p. 149.
41 G. M. Trevelyan, *Illustrated History of England* (London: Longmans, Green and Co., 1956), p. 272.
42 William Shakespeare, *Twelfth Night*, act 2, scene 3.
43 I went to school and university in Britain on three occasions in the 1960s and early 1970s. Coming from a Puritan family in America, I was surprised to find how relaxed the English had become. I saw my future as involving wide competition, choice, and challenge, but most of my schoolmates sought mainly to find a niche in the existing class system, which remained strong. In the 1980s, however, Margaret Thatcher revived Britain's individualism somewhat, and the class system is today weaker than it was earlier. But on average, today's British remain less enterprising than their own forebears or their American heirs.
44 Other candidates would include the early disciples of the Christian church and the Bolshevik revolutionaries who founded Communism in Russia and made it an international force.

45 David Hackett Fischer, *Albion's Seed: Four British Folkways in America* (New York: Oxford University Press, 1989). One founding group not emphasized by Fischer is the Catholics who settled Maryland. For a similar formulation that has influenced political science, see Daniel J. Elazar, *American Federalism: A View from the States*, 3rd ed. (New York: Harper and Row, 1984), chap. 5.

46 Samuel P. Huntington, *Who Are We? The Challenges to America's National Identity* (New York: Simon and Schuster, 2004), chap. 4.

47 Fischer, *Albion's Seed*, p. 85.

48 Matthew Hutson, "Still Puritan after All These Years" (opinion), *New York Times*, August 5, 2012, p. SR4.

49 Alexis de Tocqueville, *Democracy in America*, ed. J. P. Mayer, trans. George Lawrence (Garden City, NY: Anchor Books, 1969 [1835]), vol. 1, part 1, chap. 2.

50 *Democracy in America*, vol. 1, part 1, chap. 2.

51 David Hackett Fischer, *Paul Revere's Ride* (New York: Oxford University Press, 1994).

CHAPTER SIX — GEOGRAPHY

1 David S. Landes, *The Wealth and Poverty of Nations: Why Some Are So Rich and Some So Poor* (New York: Norton, 1998), chap. 2.

2 Landes, *Wealth and Poverty*, chap. 1; David C. McClelland, *The Achieving Society* (New York: Free Press, 1967), pp. 383–87.

3 Roberts, *The New History of the World* (Oxford: Oxford University Press, 2003), p. 478.

4 Diamond, *Guns, Germs, and Steel: The Fates of Human Societies* (New York: Norton, 1999).

5 *Guns, Germs, and Steel*, chap. 18.

6 Jones, *The European Miracle: Environments, Economics, and Geopolitics in the History of Europe and Asia*, 3rd ed. (Cambridge, UK: Cambridge University Press, 2003), chap. 4; Jacques, *When China Rules the World: The End of the Western World and the Birth of a New Global Order* (New York: Penguin, 2009), pp. 23–29; Pomeranz, *The Great Divergence: Europe, China, and the Making of the Modern World Economy* (Princeton, NJ: Princeton University Press, 2000), pp. 10–14, 17–25, 113.

7 Philip C. C. Huang, "Development or Involution in Eighteenth-Century Britain and China? A Review of Kenneth Pomeranz's *The Great Divergence: China, Europe, and the Making of the Modern World Economy*," *Journal of Asian Studies* 61, no. 2 (May 2002): 501–38.

8 Morris, *Why the West Rules—For Now: The Patterns of History, and What They Reveal about the Future* (New York: Farrar, Straus, and Giroux, 2010), chaps. 9–10.

9 Jones, *European Miracle*, pp. xxxiv, 250–51.

10 Edwin Williamson, *The Penguin History of Latin America*, rev. ed. (London: Penguin, 2009), part 1.

11 Jones, *European Miracle*, pp. 227–29.

12 Francis Fukuyama, *Political Order and Political Decay: From the Industrial Revolution to the Globalization of Democracy* (New York: Farrar, Straus, and Giroux, 2014), pp. 236–40.

13 Jones, *European Miracle*, chap. 6.

14 John J. Mearsheimer, *The Tragedy of Great Power Politics* (New York: Norton, 2001); Paul M. Kennedy, *The Rise and Fall of the Great Powers: Economic Change and Military Conflict from 1500 to 2000* (New York: Random House, 1987).

15 Trevelyan, *Illustrated History of England* (London: Longmans, Green and Co., 1956), p. 357.

16 Jones, *European Miracle*, pp. 157–59.

17 Mahan, *The Influence of Sea Power upon History, 1660–1783*, 15th ed. (Boston: Little, Brown, 1898 [1890]).

18 Mackinder, *Democratic Ideals and Reality: A Study of the Politics of Reconstruction* (New York: Henry Holt, 1942); Spykman, *America's Strategy in World Politics: The United States and the Balance of Power* (New York: Harcourt, Brace and Company, 1942).

19 Kennedy, *Rise and Fall of the Great Powers*, p. 364; Michael Warner, "A New Strategy for the New Geopolitics," *The Public Interest*, no. 153 (Fall 2003): 94–95.

20 James T. Patterson, *Grand Expectations: The United States, 1945–1974* (New York: Oxford University Press, 1996), chap. 4.

21 Luce, "The American Century," *Life*, February 17, 1941, pp. 61–65.

22 Arnold J. Toynbee, *A Study of History*, abridgement of volumes 7–10 by D. C. Somervell (New York: Oxford University Press, 1957), p. 152.

23 This is the main theme of the classic history by Francis Parkman, *France and England in North America*, 2 vols. (New York: Library of America, 1983).

24 Walter Russell Mead, *Special Providence: American Foreign Policy and How It Changed the World* (New York: Knopf, 2001).

25 Niall Ferguson, *Empire: The Rise and Demise of the British World Order and the Lessons for Global Power* (New York: Basic Books, 2002), chap. 3.

26 Mead, *Special Providence*, chap. 5.

27 David Brooks, "The Organization Kids," *Atlantic Monthly*, April 2001, pp. 40–54. My grandfather, the first Lawrence M. Mead, was a Princeton graduate of that era who heard that call. He had planned to enter the family business—McKim, Mead, and White, the famed architectural firm of the Gilded Age—but he instead became a missionary in Beijing, where he spent his career teaching English to Chinese students.

28 Robert D. Woodberry, "The Missionary Roots of Liberal Democracy," *American Political Science Review* 106, no. 2 (May 2012): 244–74.

29 Alexis de Tocqueville, *Democracy in America*, ed. J. P. Mayer, trans. George Lawrence (Garden City, NY: Anchor Books, 1969 [1835]), pp. 189–95, 513–17.

30 Arthur C. Brooks, "Philanthropy and the Non-Profit Sector," in *Understanding America: The Anatomy of an Exceptional Nation*, ed. Peter H. Schuck and James Q. Wilson (New York: Public Affairs, 2008), chap. 18.

31 See, for example, Joel Brinkley, *Cambodia's Curse: The Modern History of a Troubled Land* (New York: Public Affairs, 2011).

32 Nicholas Kristof, "The D.I.Y. Foreign-Aid Revolution," *New York Times Magazine*, October 24, 2010, pp. 49–53; Rebecca Solnit, "Medical Mountaineers," *New Yorker*, December 21 and 28, 2015, pp. 78–87.

33 Elizabeth Gudrais, "Reclaiming Childhood," *Harvard Magazine* 115, no. 2 (November/December 2012): 32–38, 78–79.

34 Lawrence Wright, "Five Hostages," *New Yorker*, July 6 and 13, 2015, pp. 48–73.

35 Kissinger was one of my teachers in graduate school at Harvard. At my oral examinations, he asked me, "What is the American national interest?" It was by far the toughest question I faced. Later, when he was secretary of state, I briefly wrote speeches for him, and I witnessed his own struggles with the same issue.

36 Robert Kagan, "Why the World Needs America," *Wall Street Journal*, February 11–12, 2011, pp. C1–C2.

37 National Security Council, *The National Security Strategy of the United States of America* (Washington, DC: National Security Council, September 2002); Joseph S. Nye, Jr., *The Future of Power* (New York: Public Affairs, 2011), chap. 5.

38 Warner, "New Strategy for the New Geopolitics," pp. 97–99.

CHAPTER SEVEN — THE MARKET

1   Fareed Zakaria, *The Post-American World* (New York: Norton, 2009), chap. 1.

2   Walter Russell Mead, *God and Gold: Britain, America, and the Making of the Modern World* (New York: Knopf, 2007), p. 185.

3   The following relies on Nathan Rosenberg and L. E. Birdzell, Jr., *How the West Grew Rich: The Economic Transformation of the Industrial World* (New York: Basic Books, 1986).

4   Max Weber, *The Protestant Ethic and the Spirit of Capitalism*, trans. Talcott Parsons, foreword by R. H. Tawney (New York: Scribner's, 1958), pp. 66–69.

5   E.g., E. P. Thompson, *The Making of the English Working Class* (New York: Vintage, 1963).

6   H. Mark Roelofs, *Ideology and Myth in American Politics: A Critique of a National Political Mind* (Boston: Little, Brown, 1976), pp. 60–67.

7   Adam Smith, *An Inquiry into the Nature and Causes of the Wealth of Nations*, ed. Edwin Cannan (New York: Modern Library, n.d.), pp. 3–16, 423.

8   William H. McNeill, *The Rise of the West: A History of the Human Community, with a Retrospective Essay* (Chicago: University of Chicago Press, 1991), p. 456.

9   Binyamin Appelbaum, "Long-Simmering Anger about Trade Is Boiling Over for Voters," *New York Times*, March 30, 2016, pp. A1, B2; "Land Ahoy," *The Economist*, April 9, 2016, p. 58; David Goodhart, *The Road to Somewhere: The Popular Revolt and the Future of Politics* (London: Hurst and Co., 2017).

10 Douglass C. North and Robert Paul Thomas, *The Rise of the Western World: A New Economic History* (New York: Cambridge University Press, 1973).

11 This is the case that Friedrich Hayek famously made against collectivist economies in *The Road to Serfdom* (Chicago: University of Chicago Press, 1944).

12 Rosenberg and Birdzell, *How the West Grew Rich*, pp. 261, 328, 332–33.

13 Eric Jones, *The European Miracle: Environments, Economics and Geopolitics in the History of Europe and Asia*, 3rd ed. (Cambridge, UK: Cambridge University Press, 2003), chap. 5.

14 J. M. Roberts, *The New History of the World* (Oxford: Oxford University Press, 2003), p. 563.

15 W. R. Mead, *God and Gold*, pp. 297–315.

16 "Transatlantic Model Wars," *The Economist*, September 27, 2008, p. 68.

17 Francis Fukuyama, *The Origins of Political Order: From Prehuman Times to the French Revolution* (New York: Farrar, Straus, and Giroux, 2011), pp. 315–16.

18 McNeill, *Rise of the West*, pp. 776–81.

19 Alan Macfarlane, *The Origins of English Individualism: The Family, Property and Social Transition* (Oxford: Basil Blackwell, 1978), pp. 201–2.

20 Geert Hofstede, *Culture's Consequences: International Differences in Work-Related Values* (Newbury Park, CA: Sage, 1980), chap. 5.

21 Yuriy Gorodnichenko and Gerard Roland, "Culture, Institutions and the Wealth of Nations," *Review of Economics and Statistics* 99, no. 3 (July 2017): 402–16. Alberto Alesina and Paola Giuliano, in "Culture and Institutions," *Journal of Economic Literature* 53, no. 4 (December 2015): 898–944, argue that culture and institutions may be interactive, with each shaping the other, but they admit that, in Gorodnichenko and Roland's study, the effect of culture on structure is by far the stronger.

22 Lawrence E. Harrison, *Who Prospers? How Cultural Values Shape Economic and Political Success* (New York: Basic Books, 1992), chaps. 3–4; Geert Hofstede and Michael Harris Bond, "The Confucius Connection: From Cultural Roots to Economic Roots," *Organizational Dynamics* 16, no. 4 (1988): 5–21.

23 Lucian W. Pye, "'Asian Values': From Dynamos to Dominoes?" in *Culture Matters: How Values Shape Human Progress*, ed. Lawrence E. Harrison and Samuel P. Huntington (New York: Basic Books, 2000), chap. 18.

24 A good example would be Indonesia as portrayed in Clifford Geertz's *Interpretation of Cultures: Selected Essays* (New York: Basic Books, 1973).

25 "Of Cars and Carts," *The Economist*, September 19, 2015, pp. 21–24.

26 "Open for Business?" *The Economist*, June 25, 2011, p. 16–18.

27 "The 50-Year Snooze," *The Economist*, April 19, pp. 31–32.

28 Peter S. Goodman, "Failure Offers Lessons Japan Would Rather Forget," *New York Times*, September 6, 2009, p. WK3.

29 "The Next Wave," *The Economist*, September 23, 2017, pp. 20–22; "The Golden Rice-Bowl," *The Economist*, November 24, 2012, p. 49.

30 "The Wealth of Nations," *The Economist*, September 8, 2012, p. 59.

31 "The World Bank Hires a Famous Contrarian," *The Economist*, July 18, 2016.

32 David Segal, "Is Italy Too Italian?" *New York Times*, August 1, 2010, pp. B1, B6; "Special Report: Italy," *The Economist*, June 9, 2011, pp. 8–9; Suzanne Daley, "Push to Remove Barriers to Jobs Rattles Greece," *New York Times*, October 15, 2010, pp. A1, A3.

33 Robert A. Packenham, *The Dependency Movement: Scholarship and Politics in Development Studies* (Cambridge, MA: Harvard University Press, 1992).

34 Helen V. Milner, "Globalization, Development, and International Institutions: Normative and Positive Perspectives," *Perspectives on Politics* 3, no. 4 (December 2005): 833–54.

35 "More a Marathon than a Sprint," *The Economist*, November 7, 2015, pp. 41–42.

36 "Left Behind," *The Economist*, September 17, 2016, pp. 45–46.

37   Nancy Birdsall, Dani Rodrik, and Arvind Subramanian, "How to Help Poor Countries," *Foreign Affairs* 84, no. 4 (July/August 2005).

38   Daphne Eviatar, "Spend $150 Billion per Year to Cure World Poverty," *New York Times Magazine*, November 7, 2004, pp. 44–49.

39   Birdsall et al., "How to Help Poor Countries"; Easterly, *The White Man's Burden: Why the West's Efforts to Aid the Rest Have Done So Much Ill and So Little Good* (New York: Penguin, 2006).

40   Kenneth L. Sokoloff and Stanley L. Engerman, "History Lessons: Institutions, Factor Endowments, and Paths of Development in the New World," *Journal of Economic Perspectives* 14, no. 3 (Summer 2000): 217–32.

41   Peter S. Goodman, "An Economic Apartheid Bedevils South Africa," *New York Times*, October 24, 2017, pp. A1, A10–11.

42   "Sense, not Sensenbrenner," *The Economist*, April 1, 2006, p. 11.

43   David C. McClelland, *The Achieving Society* (New York: Free Press, 1967), p. 256.

44   Adam Gopnik, "Market Man," *New Yorker*, October 18, 2010, pp. 82–87; David Leonhardt, "Theory and Morality in the New Economy," *New York Times Magazine*, August 23, 2009, p. 23; Yuval Levin, "Recovering the Case for Capitalism," *National Affairs*, no. 3 (Spring 2010): 121–36.

45   McClelland, *Achieving Society*, pp. 195–96, 399; Rosenberg and Birdzell, *How the West Grew Rich*, pp. 128–34.

46   Francis Fukuyama, *Trust: The Social Virtues and the Creation of Prosperity* (New York: Free Press, 1995).

47   Luigi Guiso, Paola Sapienza, and Luigi Zingales, "Does Culture Affect Economic Outcomes?" *Journal of Economic Perspectives* 20, no. 2 (Spring 2006): 23–48; Søren Serritzlew, Kim Mannemar Sønderskov, and Gert Tinggaard Svendsen, "Do Corruption and Social Trust Affect Economic Growth? A Review," *Journal of Comparative Policy Analysis: Research and Practice* 16, no. 2 (2012): 121–39; Guido Tabellini, "Institutions and Culture" (Milan: Bocconi University, Institute for Economic Research, September 2007).

48   Richard M. Titmuss, *The Gift Relationship: From Human Blood to Social Policy* (New York: Random House, 1972).

49   Harrison, *Who Prospers*; idem, *Underdevelopment Is a State of Mind: The Latin American Case* (Lanham, MD: Harvard University, Center for International Affairs, and University Press of America, 1985); idem, *The Central Liberal Truth: How Politics Can Change a Culture and Save It from Itself* (New York: Oxford University Press, 2006). A good short summary of this thinking appears in Lawrence E. Harrison, "Culture Matters," *The National Interest*, no. 60 (Summer 2000): 55–65.

50   David S. Landes, *The Wealth and Poverty of Nations: Why Some Are So Rich and Some So Poor* (New York: Norton, 1998), pp. 516–17.

51   Oscar Arias, "Culture Matters: The Real Obstacles to Latin American Development," *Foreign Affairs* 90, no. 1 (January/February 2011): 2–6.

52   David B. H. Denoon, ed., *The New International Economic Order: A US Response* (New York: New York University Press, 1979).

53   Landes, *Wealth and Poverty of Nations*, pp. 523–24.

54   On the debate between culturalists and their critics, see Harrison and Huntington, eds., *Culture Matters*.

55 Roberts, *The New History of the World* (Oxford: Oxford University Press, 2003), p. 793.

56 Macfarlane, *Origins of English Individualism*, p. 202.

57 Weber, *Protestant Ethic*, pp. 157n10, 172.

58 Robert H. Nelson, in "Is Max Weber Newly Relevant? The Protestant-Catholic Divide in Europe Today," *Finnish Journal of Theology* (University of Helsinki) 5 (2012): 420–45, finds that these differences are better explained by religion than by geography.

59 McClelland, *Achieving Society* pp. 132–49, 391–438.

60 Michael Walzer, *The Revolution of the Saints: A Study of the Origins of Radical Politics* (New York: Atheneum, 1968).

61 Rodney Stark, *The Victory of Reason: How Christianity Led to Freedom, Capitalism, and Western Success* (New York: Random House, 2005).

62 R. H. Tawney, *Religion and the Rise of Capitalism: A Historical Study* (New York: Mentor, n.d.).

63 This roughly is the conclusion of Robert W. Green, ed., *Protestantism, Capitalism, and Social Science: The Weber Thesis Controversy*, 2nd ed. (Lexington, MA: D.C. Heath, 1973), which reviews many of the main arguments for and against the Weber thesis.

64 Harvey Leibenstein, "Allocative Efficiency vs. 'X-Efficiency,'" *American Economic Review* 56, no. 3 (June 1966): 392–415.

65 Weber, *Protestant Ethic*, pp. 13–17.

66 "The United States of Entrepreneurs: America Still Leads the World," *The Economist*, March 12, 2009.

67 W. R. Mead, *God and Gold*, pp. 234–47.

68 Karl Polanyi, *The Great Transformation* (Boston: Beacon Press, 1957).

69 For a powerful statement of that appeal, see Edward Bellamy, *Looking Backward* (New York: Dover, 1996 [1888]).

70 T. H. Marshall, "Citizenship and Social Class," in *Class, Citizenship, and Social Development: Essays by T. H. Marshall*, intro. Seymour Martin Lipset (Garden City, NY: Doubleday, 1964), chap. 4.

71 Lawrence M. Mead, *Beyond Entitlement: The Social Obligations of Citizenship* (New York: Free Press, 1986); Pierre Rosanvallon, *The New Social Question: Rethinking the Welfare State*, trans. Barbara Harshaw (Princeton, NJ: Princeton University Press, 2000).

72 Tony Judt, "What Is Living and What Is Dead in Social Democracy?" *New York Review of Books*, December 17, 2009, pp. 86–96; Joel F. Handler, *Social Citizenship and Workfare in the United States and Europe: The Paradox of Inclusion* (Cambridge, UK: Cambridge University Press, 2004).

73 Ivar Lødemel and Heather Trickey, eds., *"An Offer You Can't Refuse": Workfare in International Perspective* (Bristol, UK: Policy Press, 2001); Ivar Lodemel and Amilcar Moreira, eds., *Activation or Workfare? Governance and the Neo-Liberal Convergence* (New York: Oxford University Press, 2014). For a comparison of welfare reform in Europe and America, see Lawrence M. Mead and Ron Haskins, "Activation in Welfare: Europe vs. America," in *Labor Activation in a Time of High Unemployment: Encouraging Work while Preserving the Social Safety-Net*, ed. Douglas Besharov and Douglas Call (New York: Oxford University Press, forthcoming), chap. 5.

74 Landes, *Wealth and Poverty of Nations*, pp. 516–17.

75 Lawrence E. Harrison, "The Culture Club: Exploring the Central Liberal Truth," *The National Interest*, no. 83 (Spring 2006): 100.

76 McClelland, *Achieving Society*, p. 429.

CHAPTER EIGHT — GOOD GOVERNMENT

1 "Time to Cheer Up," *The Economist*, November 23, 2013, p. 5.

2 Samuel P. Huntington, *Political Order in Changing Societies* (New Haven, CT: Yale University Press, 1968), pp. 24–32.

3 "Living in Truth," *The Economist*, December 31, 2011.

4 Taiwan and South Korea score nearly as well as Japan on these indicators but are too small to count as major nations.

5 "Order in the Jungle," *The Economist*, March 15, 2008, pp. 83–85.

6 Adam Smith, *An Inquiry into the Nature and Causes of the Wealth of Nations*, ed. Edwin Cannan (New York: Modern Library, n.d.), pp. 508–9.

7 "The Earthbound Bite Back," *The Economist*, November 24, 2012, pp. 39–40.

8 Friedman, *The World Is Flat: A Brief History of the Twenty-First Century*, updated and expanded ed. (New York: Farrar, Straus, and Giroux, 2006), pp. 461–62.

9 William H. McNeill, *The Rise of the West: A History of the Human Community, with a Retrospective Essay* (Chicago: University of Chicago Press, 1991), p. 355.

10 Adda B. Bozeman, *Politics and Culture in International History: From the Ancient Near East to the Opening of the Modern Age*, 2nd ed. (New Brunswick, NJ: Transaction, 1994), chap. 8.

11 Thomas Ertman, *Birth of the Leviathan: Building States and Regimes in Medieval and Early Modern Europe* (Cambridge, UK: Cambridge University Press, 1997).

12 Francis Fukuyama, *The Origins of Political Order: From Prehuman Times to the French Revolution* (New York: Farrar, Straus, and Giroux, 2011), chap. 22.

13 Stephen Skowronek, *Building a New American State: The Expansion of National Administrative Capacities, 1877–1920* (Cambridge, UK: Cambridge University Press, 1982); Fareed Zakaria, *From Wealth to Power: The Unusual Origins of America's World Role* (Princeton, NJ: Princeton University Press, 1997); Francis Fukuyama, *Political Order and Political Decay: From the Industrial Revolution to the Globalization of Democracy* (New York: Farrar, Straus, and Giroux, 2014), chaps. 9–11.

14 Bozeman, *Politics and Culture*; Ernest Gellner, *Plough, Sword and Book: The Structure of Human History* (Chicago: University of Chicago Press, 1988); Michael W. Doyle, *Empires* (Ithaca, NY: Cornell University Press, 1986).

15 Sen, "Democracy Isn't 'Western,'" *Wall Street Journal*, March 24, 2006, p. A10.

16 William Finnegan, "The Kingpins," *New Yorker*, July 2, 2012, pp. 40–53; Ioan Grillo, "Mexico's New Blood Politics" (opinion), *New York Times*, January 17, 2016, pp. SR1, SR6; "How to Handle a Drug Gang," *The Economist*, November 21, 2015, pp. 35–36; "Way, José," *The Economist*, May 28, 2016, p. 32.

17 J. H. Pole, *The Pursuit of Equality in American History* (Berkeley: University of California Press, 1978).

18 Robert F. Worth, "'We Will Have to Go through Hell to Reach Our Future. There Is No Other Way.' On the Ground in Yemen," *New York Times Magazine*, July 24, 2011, pp. 24–31, 46–47.

19 "Bismarck's Tropical Misadventures," *The Economist*, February 17, 2018, p. 32.

20 Georg Wilhelm Friedrich Hegel, *The Philosophy of History*, trans. J. Sibree, preface by C. J. Friedrich (New York: Dover, 1956), pp. 105–6; Eric Jones, *The European Miracle: Environments, Economics, and Geopolitics in the History of Europe and Asia*, 3rd ed. (Cambridge, UK: Cambridge University Press, 2003), p. 167.

21 Fukuyama, *Political Order and Political Decay*, chap. 36.

22 The following is based heavily on works by Huntington and Fukuyama cited earlier and on Samuel P. Huntington's "Political Development and Political Decay," *World Politics* 17 (April 1965): 405–17.

23 Alberto Alesina, William Easterly, and Janina Matuszeski, "Artificial States," *Journal of the European Economic Association* 9, no. 2 (April 2011): 246–77; Raymond Hinnebusch, *The International Politics of the Middle East* (Manchester, UK: Manchester University Press, 2003).

24 Daron Acemoglu, Simon Johnson, and James A. Robinson, "The Colonial Origins of Comparative Development: An Empirical Investigation," *American Economic Review* 91, no. 5 (December 2001): 1369–1401; idem, "Reversal of Fortune: Geography and Institutions in the Making of the Modern World Income Distribution," *Quarterly Journal of Economics* 117 (November 2002): 1231–94; idem, "Institutions as a Fundamental Cause of Long-Run Growth," in *Handbook of Economic Growth*, vol. 1A, ed. Philippe Aghion and Steven N. Durlauf (Boston: Elsevier, 2005), chap. 6; Robert E. Hall and Charles I. Jones, "Why Do Some Countries Produce So Much More Output per Worker than Others?" *Quarterly Journal of Economics* 114, no. 1 (February 1999): 83–116.

25 J. M. Roberts, *The New History of the World* (Oxford: Oxford University Press, 2003), p. 443; Fareed Zakaria, *The Post-American World* (New York: Norton, 2009), pp. 140–46.

26 Niall Ferguson, *Empire: The Rise and Demise of the British World Order and the Lessons for Global Power* (New York: Basic Books, 2002).

27 Bozeman, *Politics and Culture*, pp. xv–xliii, 3–14.

28 "The Road Less Travelled," *The Economist*, November 28, 2015, pp. 55–56.

29 Fareed Zakaria, "The Rise of Illiberal Democracy," *Foreign Affairs* 76, no. 6 (November/December 1997): 22–43; Steven Erlanger, "Are Western Values Losing Their Sway?" *New York Times*, September 13, 2015, p. SR4.

30 Thomas Carothers, "The End of the Transition Paradigm," *Journal of Democracy* 13, no. 1 (January 2002): 5–21; idem, "The Rule of Law Revival," *Foreign Affairs* 77, no. 2 (March/April 1998): 95–106.

31 Seymour Martin Lipset, "Some Social Requisites for Democracy: Economic Development and Political Development," *American Political Science Review* 53, no. 1 (March 1959): 69–105; idem, *Political Man: The Social Bases of Politics* (Garden City, NY: Anchor Books, 1963).

32 Quoted in Friedman, *The World Is Flat*, p. 465.

33 Huntington, "Political Development and Political Decay"; Fukuyama, *Origins of Government*, chap. 30.

34 Fukuyama, *Political Order and Political Decay*, chap. 36.

35 Hannah Arendt, *On Revolution* (New York: Viking, 1965).

36 Fukuyama, *Origins of Political Order*, part 2.

37 Northrop, *The Meeting of East and West: An Inquiry concerning World Understanding* (New York: Macmillan, 1946), pp. 381–93, 425.

38 Jones, *European Miracle*, chap. 7.

39 Failure to address cultural difference is the main limitation of Fukuyama's *Origins of Political Order* and his *Political Development and Political Decay*, impressive though these works are.

40 Francis Fukuyama, *Trust: The Social Virtues and the Creation of Prosperity* (New York: Free Press, 1995), pp. 350–51.

41 Edwin Williamson, *The Penguin History of Latin America*, revised ed. (London: Penguin, 2009).

42 Tony Smith, "Paraguay Mennonites Find Success a Mixed Blessing," *New York Times*, August 10, 2003, p. 4.

43 Peter Hessler, "Revolution on Trial," *New Yorker*, March 10, 2014, pp. 26–32.

44 Edward C. Banfield, *The Moral Basis of a Backward Society* (Glencoe, IL: Free Press, 1958); Robert D. Putnam, with Robert Leonardi and Raffaella Y. Nanetti, *Making Democracy Work: Civic Traditions in Modern Italy* (Princeton, NJ: Princeton University Press, 1993).

45 Daniel J. Elazar, *American Federalism: A View from the States*, 3rd ed. (New York: Harper and Row, 1984), chap. 5.

46 Max Fisher and Amanda Taub, "Mexico's Record Violence Is a Crisis 20 Years in the Making," *New York Times*, October 29, 2017, p. A16; "A Tropical Crime Wave," *The Economist*, May 5, 2018, pp. 34–36.

47 Lacey, "In Mexico, Sorting Out Good Guys from Bad," *New York Times*, November 2, 2008, p. A6.

48 Guido Tabellini, *Institutions and Culture* (Milan: Bocconi University, Institute for Economic Research, September 2007).

49 Yuriy Gorodnichenko and Gerard Roland, "Culture, Institutions and Democratization," mimeo (Berkeley: University of California, Department of Economics, 2013).

50 Gabriel A. Almond and Sidney Verba, *The Civic Culture: Political Attitudes and Democracy in Five Nations* (Princeton, NJ: Princeton University Press, 1963).

51 Amir N. Licht, Chanan Goldschmidt, and Shalom H. Schwartz, "Culture Rules: The Foundations of the Rule of Law and Other Norms of Governance," *Journal of Comparative Economics* 35, no. 4 (December 2007): 659–88.

52 Fukuyama, *Political Order and Political Decay*, pp. 330–32.

53 Fukuyama, *Political Order and Political Decay*, pp. 206–7, 539.

54 Lawrence E. Harrison, *Underdevelopment Is a State of Mind: The Latin American Case* (Lanham, MD: Harvard University, Center for International Affairs, and University Press of America, 1985), pp. 159–62.

55 Philip Taubman, "When the Kremlin Tried a Little Openness," *New York Times*, May 18, 2008, pp. WK1, WK5.

56 Ben Hubbard and Rick Gladstone, "Arab Spring Countries Find Peace Is Harder than Revolution," *New York Times*, August 15, 2013, p. A11.

57 Ricardo Duchesne, *The Uniqueness of Western Civilization* (Leiden: Brill, 2011), p. 326.

58 Alexis de Tocqueville, *Democracy in America*, ed. J. P. Mayer, trans. George Lawrence (Garden City, NY: Anchor Books, 1969), pp. 90, 242.

59 Omar Sacirbey, "The Muslim Brotherhood's 'Intellectual Godfather,'" *Washington Post*, February 12, 2011.

60 David McCullough, *The Wright Brothers* (New York: Simon and Schuster, 2015).

61 Martin Jacques, *When China Rules the World: The End of the Western World and the Birth of a New Global Order* (New York: Penguin, 2009), pp. 133–36, 233–71, 421–22, 432.

62 Jacques, *When China Rules the World*, pp. 424–25; Fukuyama, *Origins of Political Order*, chap. 21; Dwight H. Perkins, "Law, Family Ties, and the East Asian Way of Business," in *Culture Matters: How Values Shape Human Progress*, ed. Lawrence E. Harrison and Samuel P. Huntington (New York: Basic Books, 2000), chap. 17.

63 Fukuyama, *Origins of Political Order*, pp. 147–50.

64 John King Fairbank and Merle Goldman, *China: A New History*, 2nd enlarged ed. (Cambridge, MA: Harvard University Press, 2006), p. 258.

65 Fukuyama, *Political Order and Political Decay*, pp. 335–53. The parallels with Britain are remarkable, as I explain just below.

66 Roberts, *New History*, p. 1115.

67 J. E. A. Jolliffe, *The Constitutional History of Medieval England: From the English Settlement to 1485*, 4th ed. (London: Adam and Charles Black, 1961), pp. 100, 117.

68 Ertman, *Birth of the Leviathan*.

69 Robert Tombs, *The English and Their History* (New York: Knopf, 2014), p. 37.

70 Bryant, *The Fire and the Rose* (London: Collins, 1966), p. 16.

71 Dicey, *Introduction to the Study of the Law of the Constitution* (Indianapolis: Liberty Classics, 1982), p. 313n12.

72 Tombs, *The English*, p. 83.

73 Toynbee, *A Study of History*, abridgement of volumes 1–6 by D. C. Somervell (New York: Oxford University Press, 1946), pp. 236–38.

74 Walter Russell Mead, in *God and Gold: Britain, America, and the Making of the Modern World* (New York: Knopf, 2007), tends to do this, although his analysis is insightful.

75 The nearest thing to an American social contract, perhaps, was the Mayflower Compact that the Pilgrims of 1620 signed aboard ship before landing on Cape Cod.

76 Seymour Martin Lipset, *The First New Nation: The United States in Historical and Comparative Perspective* (New York: Basic Books, 1963), chaps. 1–2. Lipset does admit that the recent former colonies faced more serious divisions and problems than the United States (pp. 24–25, 91–98).

77 John Meacham, *Thomas Jefferson: The Art of Power* (New York: Random House, 2012).

78 Francis Fukuyama, *State-Building: Governance and World Order in the 21st Century* (Ithaca, NY: Cornell University Press, 2004), pp. 109–11; Gordon S. Wood, *The American Revolution: A History* (New York: Modern Library, 2003); Samuel H. Beer, *To Make a Nation: The Rediscovery of American Federalism* (Cambridge, MA: Harvard University Press, 1993).

79 A recent example is Daniel Hannan, *Inventing Freedom: How the English-Speaking Peoples Made the Modern World* (New York: HarperCollins, 2013). Hannan does, however, appreciate how unusually strong British government is.

80 W. R. Mead, *God and Gold*, chap. 9; Charles A. Kupchan, *No One's World: The West, the Rising Rest, and the Coming Global Turn* (New York: Oxford University Press, 2012), chap. 2.

81 Hannan, *Inventing Freedom*, p. 163.

82 Almond and Verba, *The Civic Culture*, pp. 215–25.

83 Lawrence M. Mead, "Why Anglos Lead," *National Interest*, no. 82 (Winter 2005/2006): 124–31.

84 Acemoglu and Robinson, *Why Nations Fail: The Origins of Power, Prosperity, and Poverty* (New York: Crown, 2012).

85 Bruce Bueno de Mesquita and Hilton L. Root, "The Political Roots of Poverty: The Economic Logic of Autocracy," *National Interest*, no. 68 (Summer 2002): 27–37; Bruce Bueno de Mesquita, Alastair Smith, Randolph M. Siverson, and James D. Morrow, *The Logic of Political Survival* (Cambridge, MA: MIT Press, 2004).

86 Weingast, "The Political Foundations of Democracy and the Rule of Law," *American Political Science Review* 91, no. 2 (June 1997): 245–63.

87 Przeworski and Limongi, "Modernization: Theories and Facts," *World Politics* 49, no. 2 (January 1997): 155–83.

88 Fukuyama, *State-Building*, pp. 32–35.

89 Barbara Geddes, "What Do We Know about Democratization after Twenty Years?" *Annual Review of Political Science* 2 (1999): 115–44; John R. Heilbrunn, "Paying the Price of Failure: Reconstructing Failed and Collapsed States in Africa and Central Asia," *Perspectives on Politics* 4, no. 1 (March 2006): 135–50; Margaret Levi, "Why We Need a New Theory of Government," *Perspectives on Politics* 4, no. 1 (March 2006): 5–19.

90 Fukuyama, *State-Building*, p. 42; idem, *Political Order and Political Decay*, pp. 545–48.

91 Clifford J. Levy, "The Lands Autocracy Won't Quit," *New York Times*, February 27, 2011, p. wk1; Larry Diamond, "The Democratic Rollback: The Resurgence of the Predatory State," *Foreign Affairs* 87, no. 2 (March/April 2008): 36–48.

92 "In His Father's Shadow," *The Economist*, April 8, 2006, pp. 45–46.

93 "A Climate of Change," *The Economist*, July 13, 2013.

CHAPTER NINE — FREEDOM AS OBLIGATION

1 This chapter expands on Lawrence M. Mead, "Burdens of Freedom," *National Affairs*, no. 29 (Fall 2016), pp. 167–78.

2 Data from the US Bureau of Labor Statistics for June 2018.

3 Historical Tables (Washington, DC: Office of Management and Budget, 2018), tables 1.1 and 7.1, for fiscal 2017.

4 Robert E. Lane, *The Market Experience* (Cambridge, UK: Cambridge University Press, 1991).

5 US Census Bureau, Annual Social and Economic Supplement, 2016, table FINC-06.

6 Fred Hirsch, *Social Limits to Growth* (Cambridge, MA: Harvard University Press, 1976).

7 Katherine J. Cramer, *The Politics of Resentment: Rural Consciousness in Wisconsin and the Rise of Scott Walker* (Chicago: University of Chicago Press, 2016).

8   Leslie McCall, *The Undeserving Rich: American Beliefs about Inequality, Opportunity, and Redistribution* (New York: Cambridge University Press, 2013).

9   Herbert Croly, *The Promise of American Life*, ed. Arthur M. Schlesinger, Jr. (Cambridge, MA: Harvard University Press, 1965).

10 "Choose Your Parents Wisely," *The Economist*, July 26, 2014.

11 John Doble and Keith Melville, *Options for Social Welfare Policy: The Public's Views* (New York: Public Agenda Foundation, 1986), p. 23.

12 Historical Tables (Washington, DC: Office of Management and Budget, 2018), table 6.1.

13 Georg Wilhelm Friedrich Hegel, *The Philosophy of History*, trans. J. Sibree, preface by C. J. Friedrich (New York: Dover, 1956), p. 439.

14 Georg Wilhelm Friedrich Hegel, *Hegel's Philosophy of Right*, trans. T. M. Knox (Oxford: Clarendon Press, 1964), p. 53.

15 *The Collected Works of Abraham Lincoln*, ed. Roy P. Basler (New Brunswick, NJ: Rutgers University Press, 1953), 4:168–69.

16 Michael J. Sandel, *Liberalism and the Limits of Justice* (Cambridge, UK: Cambridge University Press, 1982); idem, *Democracy's Discontent: America in Search of a Public Philosophy* (Cambridge, MA: Harvard University Press, 1996).

17 Sen, *Development as Freedom* (New York: Oxford University Press, 1999); Nussbaum, *Women and Human Development: The Capabilities Approach* (Cambridge, UK: Cambridge University Press, 2000).

CHAPTER TEN — SOCIAL PROBLEMS

1   Daniel Patrick Moynihan, "Defining Deviancy Down," *The American Scholar* 62, no. 1 (Winter 1993): 17–30.

2   Binyamin Appelbaum, "The Vanishing Male Worker, Waiting It Out," *New York Times*, December 12, 2014, pp. A1, B10.

3   James Pethokoukis, "Why Is the US Labor Force Participation Rate So Low— Even Lower than Germany, Japan, and UK?" (Washington, DC: American Enterprise Institute, 2015); labor market data from US Bureau of Labor Statistics, June 2018.

4   "Not Working," *The Economist*, January 24, 2015, p. 26; Scott Winship, "How to Fix Disability Insurance," *National Affairs*, no. 23 (Spring 2015): 3–6.

5   US Bureau of the Census, Current Population Survey, March 2017 Annual Social and Economic Supplement, table 1.

6   Christopher Jenks, "The War on Poverty: Was It Lost?" *New York Review of Books*, April 2, 2015; Bruce D. Meyer and James X. Sullivan, "Winning the War: Poverty from the Great Society to the Great Recession" (Cambridge, MA: National Bureau of Economic Research, January 2013). The government has recently developed a Supplemental Poverty Measure (SPM) that assesses income more accurately and makes other adjustments.

7   Estimates by Robert D. Plotnick and coauthors, cited in Daniel R. Meyer and Geoffrey L. Wallace, "Poverty Levels and Trends in Comparative Perspective," in *Changing Poverty, Changing Policies*, ed. Maria Cancian and Sheldon Danziger (New York: Russell Sage Foundation, 2009), p. 44.

8   SNAP and EITC figures from the US Department of Agriculture and US Internal Revenue Service websites, June 19, 2017.

9   US Bureau of the Census, Current Population Survey, March 2017 Annual Social and Economic Supplement, tables 22, 24.

10   Lawrence M. Mead, *The New Politics of Poverty: The Nonworking Poor in America* (New York: Basic Books, 1992), chaps. 4–7.

11   Jason DeParle and Sabrina Tavernise, "Unwed Mothers Now a Majority before Age 30," *New York Times*, February 18, 2012, pp. A1, A16.

12   Barry Latzer, *The Rise and Fall of Violent Crime in America* (New York: Encounter, 2016).

13   Murray, *Coming Apart: The State of White America, 1960–2010* (New York: Crown Forum, 2012), chaps. 1–13.

14   Murray, *Coming Apart*, p. 174.

15   Murray, *Coming Apart*, chap. 13.

16   Putnam, *Our Kids: The American Dream in Crisis* (New York: Simon & Schuster, 2015), chaps. 1–5. Murray, in *Coming Apart*, chap. 16, also found similarity between whites and other groups but did not analyze the latter in the same depth.

17   Putnam, *Our Kids*. For a similar description, see Nicholas Eberstadt, *Men without Work: America's Invisible Crisis* (Conshohocken, PA: Templeton Press, 2016). Vance, in *Hillbilly Elegy: A Memoir of a Family and Culture in Crisis* (New York: Harper, 2016), found similar patterns among less-educated Appalachian whites, but here there is less sense of deterioration over time.

18   "Pisa Envy," *The Economist*, January 19, 2013, p. 61; "What Can You Do?" *The Economist*, October 12, 2013, p. 10.

19   Steven Greenhouse, "Paycheck 101," *New York Times*, March 1, 2012, pp. F1, F6; "Here, There and Everywhere," *The Economist*, January 19, 2013; "No Degree Required," *The Economist*, May 31, 2014, p. 25; Charles Duhigg and Keith Bradsher, "How US Lost Out on iPhone Work," *New York Times*, January 22, 2012, pp. 1, 20–21; Christopher Drew, "Why Science Majors Change Their Mind," *New York Times Education Life*, November 6, 2011, pp. 16–19.

20   Adam Davidson, "Making It in America," *The Atlantic*, January/February 2012, pp. 58–70; David Brooks, "Free-Market Socialism" (opinion), *New York Times*, January 24, 2012, p. A27.

21   Kenneth F. Scheve and Matthew J. Slaughter, "A New Deal for Globalization," *Foreign Affairs* 86, no. 4 (July/August 2007): 34–47.

22   Morris Janowitz, *The Reconstruction of Patriotism: Education for Civic Consciousness* (Chicago: University of Chicago Press, 1983).

23   "Too Fat to Fight: Retired Military Leaders Want Junk Food out of America's Schools" (Washington, DC: Mission: Readiness, 2010); Ron Nixon, "Poor Fitness in Military Poses Peril, Report Says," *New York Times*, September 18, 2014, p. A20.

24   "The Waiting Wounded," *The Economist*, March 23, 2013, p. 33; "What Next?" *The Economist*, December 6, 2014, p. 30; Dave Phillips, "Veteran's Campaign Would Rein In Disability Pay," *New York Times*, January 8, 2015, pp. A1, A11; Ken Harbaugh, "The Risk of Over-Thanking Veterans" (opinion), *New York Times*, June 1, 2015, p. A19; "Who Will Fight the Next War?" *The Economist*, October 24, 2015, pp. 25–28.

25   Data from the National Institutes of Health; Anahad O'Connor, "Threat

Grows from Liver Illness Tied to Obesity," *New York Times*, June 14, 2014, pp. A1, A3.

26 Gina Kolata, "Rise in Deaths For US Whites in Middle Age," *New York Times*, November 3, 2015, pp. A1, A19; "The Great American Relapse," *The Economist*, November 22, 2014, pp. 25–26.

27 "The Problem of Pain," *The Economist*, May 28, 2016, pp. 53–55.

28 US Bureau of the Census, Current Population Survey, March 2017 Annual Social and Economic Supplement, table 1. I omit Native Americans, who are few in number but have the highest poverty rate of all.

29 No recent study directly shows that minorities dominate the long-term poor, which roughly means those who are poor for more than two years at a stretch. One older study that does show this is Greg J. Duncan et al., *Years of Poverty, Years of Plenty: The Changing Economic Fortunes of American Workers and Families* (Ann Arbor: University of Michigan, Institute for Social Research, 1984), tables 2.2 and 3.2. But experts routinely assume that most of the seriously poor are black or Hispanic.

30 National Center for Health Statistics, *Health, United States, 2016* (Washington, DC: US Government Printing Office, 2015), p. 94. All these rates have declined slightly in the last few years, suggesting that they may have peaked.

31 Heather C. West, "Prison Inmates at Midyear 2009—Statistical Tables" (Washington, DC: US Department of Justice, Bureau of Justice Statistics, June 2010), tables 16, 18.

32 Jason DeParle, *American Dream: Three Women, Ten Kids, and the Nation's Drive to End Welfare* (New York: Viking, 2004), pp. 45–46.

33 Glazer was more optimistic about black advancement in the first edition of Nathan Glazer and Daniel P. Moynihan, *Beyond the Melting Pot: The Negroes, Puerto Ricans, Jews, Italians, and Irish of New York City*, in 1963, than he was in the second, in 1970. In Nathan Glazer, "Black and White after Thirty Years," *The Public Interest*, no. 121 (Fall 1995): 61–79, he was more pessimistic still.

34 Putnam, *Our Kids*, pp. 72–75; idem, "Crumbling American Dreams" (opinion), *New York Times*, August 4, 2013, p. SR9; Andrew Cherlin and W. Bradford Wilcox, "The Generation That Can't Move on Up," *Wall Street Journal*, September 3, 2010, p. 17.

35 Wilson, *The Truly Disadvantaged: The Inner City, the Underclass, and Public Policy* (Chicago: University of Chicago Press, 1987); idem, *When Work Disappears: The World of the New Urban Poor* (New York: Knopf, 1996).

36 L. M. Mead, *New Politics of Poverty*, chap. 5.

37 Sawhill, *Generation Unbound: Drifting into Sex and Parenthood without Marriage* (Washington, DC: Brookings Institution Press, 2014), pp. 31, 81. On the Wilson theory and other structural approaches to poverty, see L. M. Mead, *New Politics of Poverty*, chaps. 4–6.

38 Charles Murray, *In Our Hands: A Plan to Replace the Welfare State* (Washington, DC: AEI Press, 2006), pp. 83–87.

39 Quoted in Anthony Lewis, "A New National Scripture," *New York Times Magazine*, January 18, 2009, p. 10.

40 Shelby Steele, *The Content of Our Character: A New Vision of Race in America* (New York: St. Martin's Press, 1990), p. 54.

41 That might be why recent black migrants from the South do better in Northern cities than blacks who are born there. See David Whitman, "Great Sharecropper Success Story," *The Public Interest*, no. 104 (Summer 1991): 3–19.

42 OECD Family Database, downloaded June 20, 2016; Sara McLanahan and Christopher Jencks, "Was Moynihan Right?" *EducationNext* 15, no. 2 (Spring 2015), figure 1.

43 James S. Coleman, "Equal Schools or Equal Students?" *The Public Interest*, no. 4 (Summer 1966): 70–75.

44 Harry Eckstein, "Civic Inclusion and Its Discontents," *Daedalus* 113, no. 4 (Fall 1984): 107–45; Lee Rainwater, "The Problem of Lower-Class Culture and Poverty-War Strategy," in *On Understanding Poverty: Perspectives from the Social Sciences*, ed. Daniel P. Moynihan (New York: Basic Books, 1969), p. 238.

45 Jeremy Travis, Bruce Western, and Steve Redburn, eds., *The Growth of Incarceration in the United States: Exploring Causes and Consequences* (Washington, DC: National Academies Press, 2014). I was a member of the committee that produced this report.

46 Orlando Patterson, "The Moral Crisis of the Black American," *The Public Interest*, no. 32 (Summer 1973): 43–69; Glenn C. Loury, "The Moral Quandary of the Black Community," *The Public Interest*, no. 79 (Spring 1985): 9–22.

47 The following is based largely on L. M. Mead, *New Politics of Poverty* and idem, *Beyond Entitlement: The Social Obligations of Citizenship* (New York: Free Press, 1986).

48 Charles Murray, *Losing Ground: American Social Policy, 1950–1980* (New York: Basic Books, 1984).

49 Paul Tough, "The Poverty Clinic," *New Yorker*, March 21, 2011, pp. 25–32; Nicholas Kristoff and Sheryl WuDunn, "The Way to Beat Poverty" (opinion), *New York Times*, September 14, 2014, pp. WR1, WR6; Cara Feinberg, "The Science of Scarcity," *Harvard* Magazine 117, no. 5 (May/June 2015): 38–43.

50 For apt proposals to do this, see Scott Winship, "How to Fix Disability Insurance."

51 Lawrence M. Mead and Ron Haskins, "Activation in Welfare: Europe vs. America," in *Labor Activation in a Time of High Unemployment: Encouraging Work while Preserving the Social Safety-Net*, ed. Douglas Besharov and Douglas Call (New York: Oxford University Press, forthcoming).

52 Some statistical studies find that the EITC raises work levels, but other, more direct evidence, such as evaluations, refutes this. See Lawrence M. Mead, "Overselling the Earned Income Tax Credit," *National Affairs*, no. 21 (Fall 2014): 20–33; idem, "Can Benefits and Incentives Promote Work?" *Journal of Policy Analysis and Management* 37, no. 4 (Fall 2018): 897–903.

53 The following relies on Lawrence M. Mead, ed., *The New Paternalism: Supervisory Approaches to Poverty* (Washington, DC: Brookings, 1997).

54 Ron Haskins, "TANF at Age 20: Work Still Works," *Journal of Policy Analysis and Management* 35, no. 1 (Winter 2016): 224–31.

55 Peter Z. Schochet, John Burghardt, and Sheena McConnell, "Does Job Corps Work? Impact Findings from the National Job Corps Study," *American Economic Review* 98, no. 5 (December 2008): 1864–86; Megan Millenky, Dan Bloom, Sara Muller-Ravett, and Joseph Broadus, *Staying on Course:*

Three-Year Results of the National Guard Youth ChalleNGe Evaluation (New York: MDRC, June 2011); Cindy Redcross, Megan Millenky, Timothy Rudd, and Valerie Levshin, *More Than a Job: Final Results from the Evaluation of the Center for Employment Opportunities (CEO) Transitional Jobs Program* (Washington, DC: US Administration for Children and Families, 2012).

56 David Leonhardt, "Schools That Work" (opinion), *New York Times*, November 6, 2016, p. SR2; David Whitman, *Sweating the Small Stuff: Inner-City Schools and the New Paternalism* (Washington, DC: Thomas B. Fordham Institute, 2008).

57 Lawrence M. Mead, *Expanding Work Programs for Poor Men* (Washington, DC: AEI Press, 2011).

58 For recent reports from both liberal and conservative experts on how to reduce poverty and inequality that include paternalistic proposals, see AEI/ Brookings Working Group on Poverty and Opportunity, *Opportunity, Responsibility, and Security: A Consensus Plan for Reducing Poverty and Restoring the American Dream* (Washington, DC: American Enterprise Institute and Brookings Institution, 2015); and Working Class Study Group, *Work, Skills, Community: Restoring Opportunity for the Working Class* (Washington, DC: Opportunity America, American Enterprise Institute, and Brookings Institution, 2018). I was a member of both these working groups.

59 Murray, *Coming Apart*, pp. 287–91, 294.

60 L. M. Mead, *Beyond Entitlement*.

CHAPTER ELEVEN — IMMIGRATION

1 This chapter expands Lawrence M. Mead, "Immigration: The Cultural Dimension," *Society* 53, no. 2 (March/April 2016): 116–22.

2 Toynbee, *A Study of History*, abridgement of volumes 1–6 by D. C. Somervell (New York: Oxford University Press, 1946), p. 419; idem, *A Study of History*, abridgement of volumes 7–10 by D. C. Somervell (New York: Oxford University Press, 1957), p. 221.

3 "Modern Immigration Wave Brings 59 Million to US, Driving Population Growth and Change through 2065" (Washington, DC: Pew Research Center, September 28, 2015).

4 Some say that these census figures overstate the decline of the white population because many Hispanics identify as white. See Herbert J. Gans, "The Census and Right-Wing Hysteria" (opinion), *New York Times*, May 14, 2017, p. SR2. But in my analysis, the Hispanic surge is worrisome because it is non-Western, not because it is nonwhite.

5 Lizette Alvarez, "A Growing Stream of Illegal Immigrants Choose to Remain Despite the Risks," *New York Times*, December 20, 2006, p. 26; Roberto Suro, "Attitudes toward Immigrants and Immigration Policy: Surveys among Latinos in the US and in Mexico" (Washington, DC: Pew Hispanic Center, August 16, 2005), pp. 13–15.

6 Mark Krikorian, "The Real Immigration Debate: Whom to Let In and Why," *Wall Street Journal*, March 24, 2017.

7 Collier, *Exodus: How Migration Is Changing Our World* (New York: Oxford University Press, 2013), pp. 166–68.

8 Of course, most blacks came to America initially as slaves, not immigrants.

However, they resemble most of today's immigrants in coming from the non-West, and much of their huge and favorable cultural impact seems to derive from this.

9   One impressive expression of the Hispanic ethos is the new Catholic Cathedral of Our Lady of the Angels, in Los Angeles.

10 Geoffrey Fox, *Hispanic Nation: Culture, Politics, and the Constructing of Identity* (Secaucus, NJ: Carol Publishing Group, 1996), pp. 73–74; Northrop, *The Meeting of East and West: An Inquiry concerning World Understanding* (New York: Macmillan, 1946), pp. 15–65, 436.

11 Crèvecoeur, *Letters from an American Farmer* (London: J. M. Dent, n.d.), p. 39.

12 John S. Lapinski, Pia Peltola, Greg Shaw, and Alan Yang, "Trends: Immigrants and Immigration," *Public Opinion Quarterly* 61, no. 2 (Summer 1997): 356–83; Kenneth F. Scheve and Matthew J. Slaughter, *Globalization and the Perceptions of American Workers* (Washington, DC: Institute of International Economics, 2001); Roy Beck and Steven A. Camarota, "Elite vs. Public Opinion: An Examination of Divergent Views on Immigration" (Washington, DC: Center for Immigration Studies, 2002).

13 Kenneth K. Lee, *Huddled Masses, Muddled Laws: Why Contemporary Immigration Policy Fails to Reflect Public Opinion* (Westport, CT: Praeger, 1998); Peter H. Schuck, "The Disconnect between Public Attitudes and Policy Outcomes in Immigration," in *Debating Immigration*, ed. Carol M. Swain (New York: Cambridge University Press, 2007), chap. 2.

14 Morris Levy, Matthew Wright, and Jack Citrin, "Mass Opinion and Immigration Policy in the United States: Re-assessing Clientelist and Elitist Perspectives," *Perspectives on Politics* 14, no. 3 (September 2016): 660–80.

15 Ted Brader, Nicholas A. Valentino, and Elizabeth Suhay, "What Triggers Public Opposition to Immigration? Anxiety, Group Cues, and Immigration Threat," *American Journal of Political Science* 52, no. 4 (October 2008): 959–78.

16 Peter Skerry and Devin Fernandes, "Citizen Pain: Fixing the Immigration Debate," *New Republic*, May 8, 2006, pp. 14–16.

17 Three major National Academy of Sciences studies of immigration give virtually no attention to cultural difference in the sense I mean here: James P. Smith and Barry Edmonston, eds., *The New Americans: Economic, Demographic, and Fiscal Effects of Immigration* (Washington, DC: National Academy Press, 1997), Mary C. Waters and Marisa Gerstein Pineau, eds., *The Integration of Immigrants into American Society* (Washington, DC: National Academies Press, 2015); and Francine D. Blau and Christopher Mackie, eds., *The Economic and Fiscal Consequences of Immigration* (Washington, DC: National Academies Press, 2017). This is true also of the Brookings-Duke Immigration Policy Roundtable, *Breaking the Immigration Stalemate: From Deep Disagreements to Constructive Proposals* (Washington, DC: Brookings Institution Press; Durham, NC: Duke University, Kenan Institute for Ethics, 2009).

18 Martin A. Schain, *The Politics of Immigration in France, Britain, and the United States: A Comparative Study*, 2nd ed. (New York: Palgrave Macmillan, 2012).

19 Ellen Barry and Martin Selsoe Sorensen, "Danish State Demands: Give Us Your Children," *New York Times*, July 1, 2018, p. A1.

20 The few authors who have raised cultural concerns about immigration, as I do here, include Collier, *Exodus*; Peter Brimelow, *Alien Nation: Common Sense about America's Immigration Disaster* (New York: Random House, 1995); and Samuel P. Huntington, *Who Are We? The Challenges to America's National Identity* (New York: Simon and Schuster, 2004). Mainstream discussions of immigration seldom cite these authors or respond to their arguments.

21 Brimelow, *Alien Nation*, p. 248.

22 Quoted in Peter D. Salins, *Assimilation, American Style* (New York: Basic Books, 1997), p. 105.

23 *Time*, January 2, 1989, pp. 106–7.

24 David S. Landes, *The Wealth and Poverty of Nations: Why Some Are So Rich and Some So Poor* (New York: Norton, 1998), chaps. 3–4; Ernest Gellner, *Plough, Sword and Book: The Structure of Human History* (Chicago: University of Chicago Press, 1988).

25 Thomas Sowell, *Race and Culture: A World View* (New York: Basic Books, 1994); idem, *Wealth, Poverty, and Politics: An International Perspective* (New York: Basic Books, 2015). Sowell does not draw any general contrast between Western and non-Western culture as I do here.

26 Janowitz, *The Reconstruction of Patriotism: Education for Civic Consciousness* (Chicago: University of Chicago Press, 1983), chap. 5; Brimelow, *Alien Nation*; Huntington, *Who Are We?*

27 Of course, some Hispanics are not immigrants by origin but Mexican settlers in Western America who became Americans without choice when the United States conquered Mexico's territories north of the current border.

28 My sources for Hispanic culture include the references in chapter 4 and these first-hand accounts: Fox, *Hispanic Nation*; Peter Skerry, *Mexican Americans: The Ambivalent Minority* (New York: Free Press, 1993); Earl Shorris, *Latinos: A Biography of the People* (New York: Norton, 1992); and Lionel Sosa, *The Americano Dream: How Latinos Can Achieve Success in Business and in Life* (New York: Dutton, 1998). Shorris and Sosa are Hispanic themselves, while Fox married into Puerto Rican culture and Skerry is a sympathetic observer. Sosa is especially useful, as he contrasts Latino and Anglo culture explicitly, framing the differences much as I do.

29 Sosa, *Americano Dream*, p. 2; Shorris, *Latinos*, chap. 7; Howard J. Wiarda, *The Soul of Latin America: The Cultural and Political Tradition* (New Haven, CT: Yale University Press, 2001).

30 "The Model Minority Is Losing Patience," *The Economist*, October 3, 2015, pp. 23–25.

31 Adeel Hassan and Audrey Carlsen, "How 'Crazy Rich' Asians Have Led to the Largest Income Gap in the US," *New York Times*, August 17, 2018. https://www.nytimes.com/interactive/2018/08/17/us/asian-income-inequality.html

32 That is my experience of teaching a multicultural student body, including many Asians, at New York University since 1979. Other college teachers have told me the same.

33 "Affirmative Dissatisfaction," *The Economist*, June 23, 2018, p. 26; Anemona Hartocollis, Amy Harmon, and Mitch Smith, "Z-Lists, and Other Secrets of Harvard Admission," *New York Times*, July 30, 2018, pp. A1, A10.

34 Kyle Spencer, "It Takes a Suburb," *New York Times Education Life*, April 9, 2017, pp. 14–17.

35 Sandra Tsing Loh, "My Chinese-American Problem—and Ours," *The Atlantic*, April 2011, pp. 83–91; Wesley Yang, "Paper Tigers," *New York Magazine*, May 16, 2011.

36 Christopher Caldwell, *Reflections on the Revolution in Europe: Immigration, Islam, and the West* (New York: Doubleday, 2009); idem, "Islam on the Outskirts of the Welfare State," *New York Times Magazine*, February 5, 2006, pp. 54–59.

37 Landes, *Wealth and Poverty*, chaps. 24, 28; Bernard Lewis, *What Went Wrong? The Clash between Islam and Modernity in the Middle East* (New York: Harper Perennial, 2003).

38 Francis Fukuyama, *Political Order and Political Decay: From the Industrial Revolution to the Globalization of Democracy* (New York: Farrar, Straus, and Giroux, 2014), chap. 26.

39 Collier, *Exodus*.

40 "A Model Minority," *The Economist*, November 26, 2016, p. 77.

41 Timothy J. Hatton and Jeffrey G. Williamson, *Global Migration and the World Economy: Two Centuries of Policy and Performance* (Cambridge, MA: MIT Press, 2005), pp. 211–15. Illegal immigrants pay substantially to be smuggled into the United States, so they are not always poor.

42 Waters and Pineau, *Integration of Immigrants*, p. Sum-7. However, the share of immigrants with college degrees has recently increased, according to "Six Degrees of Separation," *The Economist*, June 10, 2017, p. 27–28.

43 Shorris, *Latinos*, p. 66.

44 I credit this phrase to a Puerto Rican student of mine. One such Cuban was my great-grandfather, José Machado, a pugnacious overachiever who did very well in business.

45 Collier, *Exodus*, chap. 12.

46 Adam Nagourney and Jennifer Medina, "At 78 Percent Latino, Santa Ana Presents the Face of a New California," *New York Times*, October 12, 2016, pp. A12, A17.

47 Carey Goldberg, "Hispanic Households Struggle amid Broad Decline in Income," *New York Times*, January 30, 1997, pp. A1, A16; James M. Lindsay and Audrey Singer, "Changing Faces: Immigrants and Diversity in the Twenty-First Century," in *Agenda for the Nation*, ed. Henry J. Aaron, James M. Lindsay, and Pietro S. Nivola (Washington, DC: Brookings Institution Press, 2003) pp. 241–44.

48 Robert Samuelson, ""Discovering Poverty (Again)," *Washington Post*, September 21, 2005, p. A23; Heather Mac Donald, "Seeing Today's Immigrants Straight," *City Journal* 16, no. 3 (Summer 2006): 34.

49 Tara Zahra, "America, the Not So Promised Land" (opinion), *New York Times*, November 15, 2015, p. SR4.

50 Huntington, *Who Are We?* chap. 9.

51 Dale Russakoff, "'The Only Way We Can Fight Back Is to Excel," *New York Times Magazine*, January 29, 2017, p. 43; Shorris, *Latinos*, chap. 14.

52 Nikole Hannah-Jones, "Worlds Apart," *New York Times Magazine*, June 12, 2016, pp. 34–39, 50–53, 55; Dana Goldstein, "In Dallas, Opening Up Long-Divided Schools," *New York Times*, June 20, 2017, pp. A1, A13.

53 Kyle Spencer, "A School District That Works Hard at Making Integration Work," *New York Times*, December 13, 2016, pp. A25–A26.

54 George J. Borjas, *Heaven's Door: Immigration Policy and the American Economy* (Princeton, NJ: Princeton University Press, 1999); Hatton and Williamson, *Global Migration and the World Economy*; David Card, John DiNardo, and Eugena Estes, "The More Things Change: Immigrants and the Children of Immigrants in the 1940s, the 1970s, and the 1990s," in *Issues in the Economics of Immigrants*, ed. George J. Borjas (Chicago: University of Chicago Press, 2000), chap. 6 (pp. 227–70).

55 Waters and Pineau, *Integration of Immigrants*, p. Sum-6.

56 William Finnegan, "The New Americans," *New Yorker*, March 25, 1996, pp. 52–71; Jason DeParle, "Struggling to Rise in Suburbs Where Failing Means Fitting In," *New York Times*, April 19, 2009, pp. A1, A22–A23; Ann Coulter, *Adios, America! The Left's Plan to Turn Our Country into a Third World Hellhole* (Washington, DC: Regnery, 2015); Lawrence E. Harrison, "The End of Multiculturalism," *The National Interest*, no. 93 (January/February 2008): 93–96; Jonathan Blitzer, "Trapped," *New Yorker*, January 1, 2018, pp. 20–26.

57 Roberto Suro, "Attitudes toward Immigrants and Immigration Policy: Surveys among Latinos in the US and in Mexico" (Washington, DC: Pew Hispanic Center, August 16, 2005), pp. 13–15.

58 Skerry, *Mexican Americans*, chap. 2.

59 Gabriel A. Almond and Sidney Verba, *The Civic Culture: Political Attitudes and Democracy in Five Nations* (Princeton, NJ: Princeton University Press, 1963), chaps. 8–9. Ann L. Craig and Wayne E. Cornelius, "Political Culture in Mexico: Continuities and Revisionist Interpretations," in *The Civic Culture Revisited*, ed. Gabriel A. Almond and Sidney Verba (Boston: Little, Brown, 1980), chap. 9, criticize this interpretation on various grounds but do not, in my opinion, invalidate the broad contrast of American and Mexican political culture that I draw here.

60 Skerry, *Mexican Americans*; idem, "'This Was Our Riot, Too': The Political Assimilation of Today's Immigrants," in *Reinventing the Melting Pot: The New Immigrants and What It Means to Be an American*, ed. Tamar Jacoby (New York: Basic Books, 2004), chap. 17.

61 Alexis de Tocqueville, *Democracy in America*, trans. Henry Reeve (New York: Knopf, 1980), 1:191–98; 2:106–10.

62 Shorris, *Latinos*, p. 408.

63 Robert D. Putnam, "*E Pluribus Unum*: Diversity and Community in the Twenty-First Century: The 2006 Johan Skytte Prize Lecture," *Scandinavian Political Studies* 30, no. 2 (June 2007): 137–74.

64 Toynbee, *Study of History*, vols. 7–10, p. 185.

65 Oscar Handlin, *The Uprooted: The Epic Story of the Great Migrations That Made the American People* (New York: Grosset and Dunlap, 1951); Nathan Glazer and Daniel P. Moynihan, *Beyond the Melting Pot: The Negroes, Puerto Ricans, Jews, Italians, and Irish of New York City*, 2nd ed. (Cambridge, MA: MIT Press, 1970).

66 Tom W. Rice and Jan L. Feldman, "Civic Culture and Democracy from Europe to America," *Journal of Politics* 59, no. 4 (November 1997): 1143–72; Eric M. Uslaner, "Where You Stand Depends upon Where Your Grandparents Sat: The Inheritability of Generalized Trust," *Public Opinion Quarterly* 72, no.

4 (Winter 2008): 725–40; Erzo F. P. Luttmer and Monica Singhal, "Culture, Context, and the Taste for Redistribution," *American Economic Journal: Economic Policy* 3, no. 1 (February 2011): 157–79; Guido Tabellini, "Institutions and Culture" (Milan: Bocconi University, Institute for Economic Research, September 2007).

67 Borjas, *Heaven's Door*, chap. 7; Waters and Pineau, *Integration of Immigrants*.

68 Jacob L. Vigdor, *Measuring Immigrant Assimilation in the United States*, 2nd ed. (New York: Manhattan Institute, 2009). Cultural assimilation would be still lower if education were included in cultural rather than in economic assimilation.

69 Borjas, *Heaven's Door*, pp. 200–203; Krikorian, "Real Immigration Debate"; idem, *The New Case against Immigration: Both Legal and Illegal* (New York: Sentinel, 2008), chap. 7; and the US Commission on Immigration Reform (Jordon Commission) in 1995.

70 Agriculture does need some farm workers to tend and harvest crops. In the past, such workers have often been illegal. How to legalize them and ensure that they return to their countries of origin when their jobs end is an unresolved problem.

71 Peter H. Schuck, "Birthright of a Nation," *New York Times*, August 13, 2010; Peter H. Schuck and Rogers M. Smith, "The Question of Birthright Citizenship," *National Affairs*, no. 36 (Summer 2018): 50–67; John Feere, "Birthright Citizenship in the United States: A Global Comparison" (Washington, DC: Center for Immigration Studies, August 2010).

72 Michael D. Shear and Eileen Sullivan, "Trump Suspends Asylum Rights for Everyone Entering the U.S. Illegally," *New York Times*, November 10, 2018, p. A12. U.S. Department of Homeland Security, June 18, 2018.

73 Compromises can be imagined. One is to give current illegal residents legal status, allowing them to work, but deny them citizenship and the right to bring in further relatives; see Peter Skerry, "Splitting the Difference on Illegal Immigration," *National Affairs*, no. 14 (Winter 2013): 3–26. Another half measure is "touchback"—requiring that illegal residents leave the country but then giving them some preference toward reentering legally later. This avoids flouting the rule of law by legalizing illegal aliens within the country.

74 Collier, *Exodus*, chap. 12.

75 David Whitman, *Sweating the Small Stuff: Inner-City Schools and the New Paternalism* (Washington, DC: Thomas B. Fordham Institute, 2008), describes several highly effective, mostly charter schools, some of which serve immigrant or Hispanic populations.

76 Glazer and Moynihan, *Beyond the Melting Pot*, pp. 217–87.

77 Skerry, *Mexican Americans*, pp. 187–89.

78 Myrdal, *An American Dilemma: The Negro Problem and Modern Democracy* (New York: Harper and Row, 1944).

79 Alexis de Tocqueville, *Democracy in America*, trans. Henry Reeve (New York: Knopf, 1980), 2:133.

CHAPTER TWELVE — THE FUTURE OF PRIMACY

1 Jim Manzi, "Keeping America's Edge," *National Affairs*, no. 2 (Winter 2010): 8–9.

2 My conclusions resemble those of Fareed Zakaria, *The Post-American World* (New York: Norton, 2009), but he makes much less of cultural differences than I do.

3 Paul M. Kennedy, *The Rise and Fall of the Great Powers: Economic Change and Military Conflict from 1500 to 2000* (New York: Random House, 1987).

4 Kennedy himself partially concedes this argument. See Paul Kennedy, "Empire without 'Overstretch,'" *Wilson Quarterly* 26, no. 3 (Summer 2002): 62–63.

5 Arthur C. Brooks, "An Aging Europe in Decline" (opinion), *New York Times*, January 7, 2015; Carl Schramm and Robert E. Litan, "Can Europe Compete?" *Commentary*, September 2007, pp. 33–37; Robert Shapiro, "The Next Globalization," *Democracy*, no. 10 (Fall 2008): 41–52; Ivan Krastev, "A Retired Power," *American Interest* 5, no. 6 (July/August 2010): 17–19.

6 "A Retreat but Not a Rout," *The Economist*, October 23, 2010, p. 69; "A Force for Good," *The Economist*, March 26, 2011, p. 64.

7 Robert Kagan, *Of Paradise and Power: America and Europe in the New World Order* (New York: Vintage, 2004).

8 Michael Slackman, "Dreams Stifled, Egypt's Young Turn to Islamic Fervor," *New York Times*, February 17, 2008, pp. 1, 16; "Look forward in Anger," *The Economist*, August 6, 2016, pp. 16–18.

9 Eric Jones, *The European Miracle: Environments, Economics and Geopolitics in the History of Europe and Asia*, 3rd ed. (Cambridge, UK: Cambridge University Press, 2003), pp. 175–79; Anthony Shadid, "In Peril: The Arab Status Quo," *New York Times*, January 16, 2011, pp. wk1–wk3.

10 Roger Scruton, "The Political Problem of Islam," *Intercollegiate Review* 38, no. 1 (Fall 2002): 3–15; Wendell Steavenson, "Radicals Rising," *New Yorker*, April 30, 2012, pp. 27–28.

11 David Brooks, "A War of Narratives" (opinion), *New York Times*, April 8, 2007, p. wk10.

12 Samantha M. Shapiro, "Ministering to the Upwardly Mobile Muslim," *New York Times Magazine*, April 30, 2006, pp. 46–53, 68, 76–77; "Holy Smoke," *The Economist*, October 29, 2011, p. 72.

13 Zakaria, *Post-American World*, pp. 92–93.

14 Edward Wong, "Booming, China Faults US Policy on the Economy," *New York Times*, June 17, 2008, pp. A1, A8; Ian Bremmer, *The End of the Free Market: Who Wins the War between States and Corporations* (New York: Penguin, 2010); Stefan Halper, *The Beijing Consensus: How China's Authoritarian Model Will Dominate the Twenty-First Century* (New York: Basic Books, 2010).

15 Eamonn Fingleton, *In the Jaws of the Dragon: America's Fate in the Coming Era of Chinese Hegemony* (New York: St. Martin's Press, 2008); Martin Jacques, *When China Rules the World: The End of the Western World and the Birth of a New Global Order* (London: Penguin Press, 2009).

16 On China, my conclusions here and below resemble those of David Shambaugh, *China Goes Global: The Partial Power* (Oxford, UK: Oxford University Press, 2013); idem, "The Illusion of Chinese Power," *The National Interest*, no. 132 (July/August 2014): 39–48.

17 "Reinstatement," *The Economist*, July 22, 2017, pp. 55–57.

18 "Capitalism Confined," *The Economist*, September 3, 2011, pp. 67–70; "The End of Cheap China," *The Economist*, March 10, 2012, pp. 75–76; Ruchir Sharma, "How China Fell Off the Miracle Path" (opinion), *New York Times*, June 5, 2016, pp. SR4–SR5.

19 "The Xi Manifesto," *The Economist*, November 23, 2013, pp. 47–48; "Stamping It Out," *The Economist*, April 23, 2016, pp. 51–52; "Time to Change the Act," *The Economist*, February 21, 2009, pp. 69–71.

20 Michael Wines, "Chinese Juggernaut Treads Path That Isn't Free of Pitfalls (Just Ask Japan)," *New York Times*, May 26, 2010, p. A12; David Barboza, "Report Says China Puts Growth at Risk Unless It Eases Grip on Economy," *New York Times*, February 28, 2012, pp. A4, A7.

21 "Chinese Tech v. American Tech," *The Economist*, February 17, 2018, p. 61; David P. Goldman, "Must We Fight?" review of *Destined for War: Can America and China Escape Thucydides's Trap?* by Graham Allison, *Claremont Review of Books*, Fall 2017, pp. 83–89.

22 David Barboza, "Shanghai Schools' Approach Pushes Students to Top of Tests," *New York Times*, December 30, 2010, p. A4. This reported emphasis on rote learning is difficult to square with a recent study finding that Chinese students learn stronger critical skills at the secondary level than Americans; Americans, however, improve more than Chinese in college; see Javier C. Hernández, "Chinese Students Better in Thinking, till College," *New York Times*, July 31, 2016, p. A9.

23 Diana Farrell and Andrew Grant, *Addressing China's Looming Talent Shortage* (San Francisco: McKinsey Global Institute, 2005); "The Battle for Brainpower," *The Economist*, October 7, 2006, pp. 14–16.

24 Richard C. Levin, "Top of the Class: The Rise of Asia's Universities," *Foreign Affairs* 89, no. 3 (May/June 2010): 63–75; "Schrodinger's Panda," *The Economist*, June 4, 2016, pp. 75–76.

25 "Replicating Success," *The Economist*, July 24, 2010, p. 43; Andrew Jacobs, "Rampant Fraud Threatens China's Brisk Ascent," *New York Times*, October 7, 2010, pp. A1, A16; "Scientists Behaving Badly," *The Economist*, October 9, 2010, pp. 115–16; "Campus Collaboration," *The Economist*, January 5, 2013, p. 33; "Looks Good on Paper," *The Economist*, September 28, 2013, pp. 39–40; Amy Qin, "China Tarnished by Science Fraud," *New York Times*, October 14, 2017, pp. A1, A8.

26 Tamar Lewin, "Taking More Seats on Campus, Foreigners Also Pay the Freight," *New York Times*, February 5, 2012, pp. 1, 23; "A Matter of Honors," *The Economist*, November 22, 2014, pp. 39–40.

27 Tom Bartlett and Karin Fischer, "Culture Shock," *New York Times Education Life*, November 6, 2011, pp. 24–27.

28 Richard E. Nisbett, *The Geography of Thought: How Asians and Westerners Think Differently…and Why* (New York: Free Press, 2003), pp. 195–96, 210–12.

29 Jacques, *When China Rules the World*, pp. 269, 388–94, 432.

30 David S. Landes, *The Wealth and Poverty of Nations: Why Some Are So Rich and Some So Poor* (New York: Norton, 1998).

31 Minxin Pei, "How China Is Ruled," *American Interest* 3, no. 4 (March/April 2008): 44–51.

32 "Life and Death Struggle," *The Economist*, December 8, 2012, pp. 47–48; Andrew Jacobs, "Chinese Officials Find Misbehavior Now Carries Cost," *New York Times*, December 26, 2012, pp. A1, A3; Andrew Jacobs, "Elite in China Face Austerity under Xi's Rule," *New York Times*, March 28, 2013, pp. A1, A12.

33 Gordon G. Chang, "The End of the Chinese Miracle?" *Commentary*, March 2008, p. 34.

34 Francis Fukuyama, *Political Order and Political Decay: From the Industrial Revolution to the Globalization of Democracy* (New York: Farrar, Straus, and Giroux, 2014), pp. 381, 383–84; Rodney MacFarquhar, "In China, Fear at the Top" (opinion), *New York Times*, May 21, 2012, p. A23; "Out Brothers, Out!" *The Economist*, January 31, 2015, pp. 37–38.

35 Halper, *Beijing Consensus*, pp. 138, 215; John King Fairbank and Merle Goldman, *China: A New History*, 2nd enlarged ed. (Cambridge, MA: Harvard University Press, 2006), chap. 21; Pei, "How China Is Ruled."

36 "Rising Power, Anxious State," *The Economist*, June 25, 2011, p. 14; "The New Class War," *The Economist*, July 9, 2016, pp. 1–2; David M. Lampton, "How China Is Ruled," *Foreign Affairs* 93, no. 1 (January/February 2014): 74–84.

37 Andrew Jacobs and Jonathan Ansfield, "Well-Oiled Security Apparatus in China Stifles Calls for Change," *New York Times*, March 1, 2011, pp. A1, A11.

38 "BoP until You Drop," *The Economist*, August 4, 2012, p. 40; Ian Johnson, "Wary of Future, Professionals Leave China in Record Numbers," *New York Times*, November 1, 2012, pp. A1, A3; Brook Larmer, "The New Kids," *New York Times Magazine*, February 5, 2017, pp. 40–45.

39 James Fallows, "How America Can Rise Again," *The Atlantic*, January/ February 2010, pp. 44–46.

40 "Adventures in Capitalism: Business in India," *The Economist*, October 22, 2011, p. 4.

41 Thomas L. Friedman, *The World Is Flat: A Brief History of the Twenty-First Century*, updated and expanded ed. (New York: Farrar, Straus, and Giroux, 2006), p. 470.

42 Pankaj Mishra, "The Myth of the New India" (opinion), *New York Times*, July 6, 2006, p. A21.

43 "Adventures in Capitalism: Business in India," *The Economist*, October 22, 2011, p. 4; Jim Yardley, "For India's Ruling Party, Biggest Challenge Remains Governing," *New York Times*, April 29, 2010, p. A10; "Hard Questions," *The Economist*, June 11, 2011, p. 85.

44 Jim Yardley, "Indian Students Wield Tests and Tutorials for Plum College Spots," *New York Times*, March 24, 2010, p. A4.

45 "The Engineering Gap," *The Economist*, January 30, 2010, p. 76; "Aim Higher: Special Report on India," *The Economist*, September 29, 2012, p. 12.

46 Jim Yardley and Vikas Bajaj, "India's Economy Slows, with Global Implications," *New York Times*, May 30, 2012, pp. A1, A3; "A Million Rupees Now," *The Economist*, March 12, 2011, p. 47; Devesh Kapur, "India's Promise," *Harvard Magazine*, August 2005, pp. 36–39.

47 "The Fast and the Furious," *The Economist*, April 16, 2011, p. 45.

48 "A Suitable Boy?" *The Economist*, April 16, 2016, pp. 30–31.

49 Martin Fackler, "Amid Decline, Japan Weighs a Reinvention," *New York Times*, pp. A1, A3.

50 The Economist, *Pocket World in Figures, 2015 edition*, pp. 63, 98.

51 Francis Fukuyama, *Trust: The Social Virtues and the Creation of Prosperity* (New York: Free Press, 1995), chaps. 6, 12.

52 "What Do You Do When You Reach the Top?" *The Economist*, November 12, 2011, pp. 79–81; Se-Woong Ku, "How South Korea Enslaves Its Students" (opinion), *New York Times*, August 3, 2014, p. SR4; "The One-Shot Society," *The Economist*, December 17, 2011, pp. 77–80.

53 "Power to the People! No, Wait…," *The Economist*, March 19, 2011, p. 52.

54 Friedman, *The World Is Flat*, chap. 7.

55 "A Game of Catch-Up," *The Economist*, September 24, 2011, pp. 1–3.

56 David Brooks, "An Innovation Agenda" (opinion), *New York Times*, December 8, 2009, p. A37; idem, "Is US as Great as US Athletes Are?" (opinion), *New York Times*, August 19, 2016, p. A23.

57 Of Asian countries in 2017, only Hong Kong, Singapore, and Taiwan ranked higher than the United States in economic freedom, according to a Heritage Foundation index.

58 Zakaria, *Post-American World*, pp. 193–95.

59 Friedman, *The World Is Flat*, p. 320.

60 Geert Hofstede, *Culture's Consequences: International Differences in Work-Related Values* (Newbury Park, CA: Sage, 1980), chaps. 3–4.

61 Walter Russell Mead, *God and Gold: Britain, America, and the Making of the Modern World* (New York: Knopf, 2007), p. 329.

62 Harry C. Triandis, "The Self and Social Behavior in Differing Cultural Contexts," *Psychological Review* 96, no. 3 (1989): 510.

63 Ronald Inglehart, "The Renaissance of Political Culture," *American Political Science Review* 82, no. 4 (December 1988), pp. 1203–30; idem, "Changing Values among Western Publics from 1970 to 2006," *West European Politics* 31, nos. 1–2 (January/March 2008): 130–46; Ronald Inglehart and Wayne E. Baker, "Modernization, Cultural Change, and the Persistence of Traditional Values," *American Sociological Review* 65, no. 1 (February 2000): 19–51; Ronald Inglehart and Christian Welzel, "How Development Leads to Democracy: What We Know about Modernization," *Foreign Affairs* 88, no. 2 (March/April 2009): 33–48; Hofstede, *Culture's Consequences*, chap. 8, finds some evidence for change toward greater individualism in forty countries from 1968 to 1972.

64 Fairbank and Goldman, *China*, pp. 438–39; "Defining Boundaries," *The Economist*, January 5, 2013, pp. 32–33; Edward Wong and Jonathan Ansfield, "Reformers Aim to Get China to Live Up to Own Constitution," *New York Times*, February 4, 2013, p. A5.

65 Ronald Inglehart and Christian Welzel, *Modernization, Cultural Change, and Democracy: The Human Development Sequence* (New York: Cambridge University Press, 2005), chaps. 7–8.

66 According to McKinsey, the Chinese middle class numbers perhaps 225 million, out of a total population of 1.4 billion; see "New Class War," *The Economist*, p. 4.

67 Robert Tombs, *The English and Their History* (New York: Knopf, 2015), chaps. 19–20.

68 "We're Back," *The Economist*, November 19, 2011, p. 43; Yan Xuetong, "How China Can Defeat America" (opinion), *New York Times*, November 21, 2011, p. A29.

CHAPTER THIRTEEN — POLICY DIRECTIONS

1 Huntington, *The Clash of Civilizations and the Remaking of World Order* (New York: Simon & Schuster, 1996), chap. 12.

2 Stephen G. Brooks and William C. Wohlforth, "American Primacy in Perspective," *Foreign Affairs* 81, no. 4 (July/August 2002): 20–33.

3 Bruce Bueno de Mesquita, *The Predictioneer's Game* (New York: Random House, 2009).

4 Douglas Feith and Seth Cropsey, "The Obama Doctrine Defined," *Commentary*, July/August 2011, pp. 12–18.

5 David B. H. Denoon, *Real Reciprocity: Rebalancing US Economic and Security Policies in the Pacific Basin* (New York: Council on Foreign Relations, 1993).

6 Michael Mandelbaum, *Mission Failure: America and the World in the Post–Cold War Era* (New York: Oxford University Press, 2016); Walter A. McDougall, *The Tragedy of US Foreign Policy: How America's Civil Religion Betrayed the National Interest* (New Haven, CT: Yale University Press, 2016).

7 Robert Kagan, *Dangerous Nation* (New York: Knopf, 2006).

8 Huntington, *Clash of Civilizations*, p. 312.

9 That parallel is suggested in Francis Fukuyama, *Political Order and Political Decay: From the Industrial Revolution to the Globalization of Democracy* (New York: Farrar, Straus, and Giroux, 2014), chaps. 27–30.

10 Francis Fukuyama, *State-Building: Governance and World Order in the 21st Century* (Ithaca, NY: Cornell University Press, 2004), p. 22.

11 Robert D. Putnam, with Robert Leonardi and Raffaella Y. Nanetti, *Making Democracy Work: Civic Traditions in Modern Italy* (Princeton, NJ: Princeton University Press, 1993).

12 Robert D. Kaplan, *Balkan Ghosts: A Journey through History* (New York: Vintage, 1994); Rebecca West, *Black Lamb and Grey Falcon: A Journey through Yugoslavia* (London: Penguin, 1940).

13 Fukuyama, *State-Building*, pp. 32–42.

14 Walter Russell Mead, *God and Gold: Britain, America, and the Making of the Modern World* (New York: Knopf, 2007), chaps. 20–23.

15 Robert Tombs, *The English and Their History* (New York: Knopf, 2015), pp. 543–46.

16 Walter Russell Mead, *Special Providence: American Foreign Policy and How It Changed the World* (New York: Knopf, 2001), pp. 166–73; Stefan Halper, *The Beijing Consensus: How China's Authoritarian Model Will Dominate the Twenty-First Century* (New York: Basic Books, 2010), chap. 7.

17 "Conquering Chaos," *The Economist*, January 7, 2017, p. 47.

18 Robert F. Worth, "'We Will Have to Go through Hell to Reach Our Future. There Is No Other Way.' On the Ground in Yemen," *New York Times Magazine*, July 24, 2011, pp. 24–31, 46–47.

19 "Helping to Calm a Continent," *The Economist*, June 9, 2012, pp. 54–55; Paul Johnson, "Colonialism's Back—and Not a Moment Too Soon," *New York Times Magazine*, April 18, 1993, p. 22.

20 "The Long, Hard Haul," *The Economist*, March 19, 2011, p. 46.

21 Niall Ferguson, *Colossus: The Rise and Fall of the American Empire* (New York: Penguin, 2005), chaps. 5, conclusion. For a sophisticated vision of what a modern neocolonialism might mean, see Paul Collier, *The Bottom Billion: Why the Poorest Countries Are Failing and What Can Be Done about It* (New York: Oxford University Press, 2008), chap. 11.

22 Jim Manzi, "Keeping America's Edge," *National Affairs*, no. 2 (Winter 2010): 8-9.

23 Manzi, "Keeping America's Edge," pp. 14–15.

24 Robert I. Lerman, "Helping Out-of-School Youth Attain Labor Market Success: What We Know and How to Learn More" (Washington, DC: Urban Institute, 2005).

25 AEI/Brookings Working Group on Poverty and Opportunity, *Opportunity, Responsibility, and Security: A Consensus Plan for Reducing Poverty and Restoring the American Dream* (Washington, DC: American Enterprise Institute and Brookings Institution, 2015), chap. 4; Working Class Study Group, *Work, Skills, Community: Restoring Opportunity for the Working Class* (Washington, DC: Opportunity America, American Enterprise Institute, and Brookings Institution, 2018), chaps. 3–4.

26 This is one reason why all tested programs to achieve employment retention or advancement for former welfare mothers have so far shown only small or no impacts. See Richard Hendra, Keri-Nicole Dillman, Gayle Hamilton, Erika Lundquist, Karin Martinson (Urban Institute), and Melissa Wavelet, with Aaron Hill and Sonya Williams, *How Effective Are Different Approaches Aiming to Increase Employment Retention and Advancement? Final Impacts for Twelve Models* (New York: MDRC, April 2010).

27 Michael Lind, "Good Lives without Good Jobs" (opinion), *New York Times*, September 18, 2016, pp. SR1, SR6.

28 Thomas L. Friedman and Michael Mandelbaum, *That Used to Be Us: How America Fell behind in the World It Invented and How We Can Come Back* (New York: Farrar, Straus, and Giroux, 2011); Richard N. Haass, *Foreign Policy Begins at Home: The Case for Putting America's House in Order* (New York: Basic Books, 2013).

29 The following is based on Lawrence M. Mead, "Moral Overload," *American Affairs*, January 18, 2018.

30 Samuel P. Huntington, "Why International Primacy Matters," *International Security* 17, no. 4 (Spring 1993): 82–83; Robert Kagan, "Why the World Needs America," *Wall Street Journal*, February 11–12, 2011, pp. C1–C2; Josef Joffe, "The Default Power: The False Prophecy of America's Decline," *Foreign Affairs* 88, no. 5 (September/October 2009): 21–35; Bradley Thayer, "In Defense of Primacy," *The National Interest*, no. 86 (November/December 2006): 32–37.

31 Mark Landler, "In a Speech on Policy, Clinton Revives a Theme of American Power," *New York Times*, September 9, 2010, p. A8.

32 Samantha Power, "Force Full," *New Republic*, March 3, 2003, pp. 28–31; Anne-Marie Slaughter, "Good Reasons to Be Humble," *Commonweal*, February 15, 2008, pp. 10–11; idem, *A New World Order* (Princeton, NJ: Princeton University Press, 2004); Harold Hongju Koh, "Why Transnational Law Matters," *Pennsylvania State International Law Review* 24, no. 4 (Spring 2006): 745–53. Under Obama, Power, a noted human-rights activist, became ambassador to the United Nations, Slaughter became head of the State Department planning staff, and Koh became legal advisor to the State Department.

33 For example, some in the Islamic world are aggrieved that America does not suffer over their losses to terrorism as much as it does its own. See Anne

Barnard, "Muslims Stung by Indifference to Their Losses," *New York Times*, July 6, 2016, pp. A1, A7.

34 Mead, "Moral Overload."

35 Benedict Carey, "Becoming Compassionately Numb," *New York Times*, October 2, 2011, p. SR5.

36 "Ecstasy and Exodus," *The Economist*, January 23, 2016, pp. 53–54.

37 Mead, *God and Gold*, chaps. 10–13.

38 Joseph S. Nye, Jr., *The Future of Power* (New York: Public Affairs, 2011), pp. 87–90.

39 Arnold J. Toynbee, *A Study of History*, abridgement of volumes 7–10 by D. C. Somervell (New York: Oxford University Press, 1957), p. 372.

40 Arnold J. Toynbee, *A Study of History*, abridgement of volumes 1–6 by D. C. Somervell (New York: Oxford University Press, 1946), p. 254; idem, *A Study of History*, abridgement of volumes 7–10, p. 372.

41 James Kurth, "The Late American Nation," *The National Interest*, no. 77 (Fall 2004): 117–26.

42 Ferguson, *Colossus*, p. 17.

INDEX

Page numbers in *italics* indicate images.

abstract thought, 78–80
aesthetics, culture and, 87–88
affluence. *See* wealth
Affordable Care Act, 57, 188, 196
Afghanistan, 8, 210, 257, 281
Africa: climate and, 119; colonial rule and, 161; economic growth and, 140, 141; failed states and, 284; government and, 93, 161; history of, overview, 30; immigrants in US, 234–36; multi-active style, 81–82; US involvement in, 15
African Americans. *See also* race: as collectivist, 82, 215; education and, 212–13; individualism and, 92, 219; as percentage of US population, 225; poverty and, 203–4, 211; social order and, 215–16; tragedy, coping with, 88–89
African migrants climbing into Melilla (Spain) from Morocco, *236*
agriculture, 29, 30, 39, 44, 98, 119, 132
aguante (stoic endurance), 88
"American Century," the, 124–25
American Creed, the, 110
American dream, the, 192, 215
American Enterprise Institute, xi
American exceptionalism, 296n13
American policies, about, 277–78
American primacy. *See* primacy
Anglo government. *See* United States
anti-market policies, 139
antipoverty programs, 59, 64
Arab countries: economic protections and, 138; moralistic culture and, 166
Arab Spring, 162, 194, 265, 281
Arias, Oscar, 143
Aristotle, 83, 197

Arnold, Matthew, 66–67
art, culture and, 87–88
Asia: better government and, 154; capitalism in, 151; as challenge to American primacy, 3; climate and, 119; as collectivist, 70–74; Communism and, 50; cultural differences, variations in, 81; demand for freedom in, 291; as economic competition, 53; economic system and, 12; European governments and, 93; GDP of, 256; global responsibility and, 76–77; government of, 170–72; history of, overview, 28; immigrants in US, 232–33, 304n28; innovation and, 31, 33, 36, 260, 268, 274; moral direction and, 75–76; Open Door policy and, 45; primacy of, 7, 268–69; revolutions in, 32; wealth and power of, 5, 10, 93; World Values Survey and, 73–74
Asians, as percentage of US population, 225
assimilation of immigrants. *See* immigration
Ataturk, Kemal, 143
autocratic governments, 35–36
autonomy. *See* individualism

Biblical religion, 102–3
birthright citizenship, 247
black Americans. *See* African Americans
Brazil, 138, 143, 160
Britain. *See* Great Britain
Bush, George W., 279, 281, 288
business, 63, 81–82, 146, 187, 270, 280. *See also* market economy
Byzantium, 32